W9-DHX-830

CORALS

A Quick Reference Guide

by Julian Sprung

Book Design by Daniel N. Ramirez

Published by Ricordea Publishing
Coconut Grove, Florida 33133 USA

Oceanographic Series™
Corals: A Quick Reference Guide

First Printing September 1999
10 9 8 7 6 5

Published by Ricordea Publishing
Miami, Florida, USA

Distributed by Two Little Fishies, Inc.
4016 El Prado Blvd., Coconut Grove
Florida, 33133 USA

Printed and bound by Arnoldo Mondadori
Design and production by Daniel N. Ramirez
Photographs by Julian Sprung
Back cover photo: Leon Corry

ISBN 1-883693-09-8

This book is dedicated to the late Michael Hedges,
composer of "Muzak for nuclear attack submarines"
and an amazing performer.

Anyone who experiences the magic of viewing a coral reef for the first time feels overwhelmed by what seems like an endless variety of unfamiliar and outrageously shaped or coloured creatures. It approaches the sensation one might have visiting another planet inhabited by alien life forms. Coral reefs are "other worlds" we can see here on earth.

Reef building stony corals and soft corals that live on and around coral reefs draw attention because they are among the most important contributors to the reef structure, they are readily observed, and often exquisitely formed or coloured. Sorting the myriad forms by type (branchy, brain-like, leafy, lettuce-like, etc.) the first-time observer begins to distinguish gross external features. One might also notice the shapes of the polyps, number of tentacles, or special skeletal features, if one is inclined to look closely.

Another distinguishing feature by which to categorize different corals is the typical habitat. A single coral reef can be composed of numerous connected and quite different habitats with respect to depth, light availability, water motion, water quality, and temperature. The assemblages of adjacent creatures adapted to the abovementioned physical parameters also create a habitat distinction that is itself a physically limiting constraint for other creatures, including corals. Some corals occur in most types of habitats while others are limited to only one or a few. Furthermore, the growth form of the same species of coral may look completely different from one type of habitat to the next. This feature is sometimes observable on the scale of even a single colony. Certain stony coral species have column shaped or branchy growth on their tops, which receive the most light, and laminar plates or folded whirls on the sides where the light is less direct. There is similar variability in the soft corals, and examples exist of "ecomorphs" which have developed the ability to retain the distinguishing growth form despite changes in their environment.

Such variation presents a bewildering problem for someone trying to identify corals. Because of corals' long life, their ability to hybridize, reproduce vegetatively, self fertilize, and their partnership with zooxanthellae which affects their growth and coloration, corals are especially elusive with respect to positive identification. Attempts to separate them by their physical appearance are also foiled by the existence of different species, sometimes genera, that share the same skeleton or polyps. That fact is widely known for some stony corals and suspected for some soft corals. It is an elegantly ugly fact. An excellent reference which offers insightful perspectives on the concept of species, the evolution of corals and problems in their taxonomy is *Corals in Space and Time*, by J.E.N. Veron.

Veron's (1986) *Corals of Australia and the Indo Pacific* lists with each entry similar corals and the distinguishing characteristics. That is helpful to the reader/coral watcher, and I have borrowed the idea here. What I wanted to do with this book additionally is to present photographically some cases for which the casual observer (or even the experienced one) is likely to confuse the coral identification. In some examples there appears to be something quite like mimicry taking place.

Taking this idea further, based on similarities in the living polyps, skeletons, and coral *behavior*, I propose in this book some taxonomic relationships that have not been scientifically established. Based also on the skeletons and living polyps I propose that some accepted taxonomic relationships are in error. In these instances I am careful to point out where this is my opinion only, not the conventional scientific view. These questions are presently being sorted out by specialists studying the DNA of corals to establish relative relatedness of the different genera.

The stony corals presented in this book are species from the Caribbean, Brazil, Mediterranean, Red Sea, Indonesia, Solomon Islands, Fiji, and Australia. Many of the Indo-Pacific forms have widespread distributions, and so the book truly covers most of the types (genera) of stony corals of the world. I have not attempted to make this guide a definitive corals of the world compendium that features every species of stony coral associated with coral reefs. That monumental task is being undertaken by J.E.N. Veron and Mary Stafford-Smith, and the work will fill three volumes! The title is *Corals of the World*, and it will be released in the year 2000. It is sure to be the definitive work on stony corals.

While the stony corals are mostly well known to the level of genus, with few new discoveries being made, the soft corals are nowhere near as well known, with many new species being discovered, and new genera being erected as well. Nevertheless the majority of soft corals encountered by a diver or aquarist are known to the level of genus at least, and many to species, though identification of the species is only sometimes possible at a glance. In most cases positive identification requires examination of the minute sand-like skeletal elements known as sclerites.

This book covers the common genera of soft corals associated with coral reefs of the world. Compared to the coverage of stony corals, the coverage of soft coral genera here is by far less complete. A much needed, much more complete guide to soft corals of the Indo-Pacific region is being prepared by

Phil Alderslade and Katharina Fabricius as a joint AIMS and MAGNT production, with Alderslade as the taxonomist and Fabricius as the ecologist and main photographer.

I have attempted with my book to include all of the genera that enter the aquarium trade, including species from the Caribbean, Brazil, Mediterranean, Red Sea and Indo-Pacific.

By including genera from reefs around the world while at the same time limiting the scope and size of this book I intended to make it useful as an international guide, and easy to translate to many different languages. In this way I hope to make this guide accessible and useful to divers, coral reef researchers, and reef aquarium keepers all over the world.

Including corals from different oceans in one volume presented a choice regarding whether to segregate them by region or relation. I opted for the latter, with the intention of showing relatedness among corals from the different regions. As I've already mentioned, some of the "positions" I've placed corals in do not fit the existing taxonomic divisions of them by family. I have not included family names in this text, but have grouped corals that are closely related, or at least seem to be so, in my opinion.

I have borrowed from Veron, (1986), the feature of phonetically demonstrating the correct pronunciation of the Latin for the genera of the corals. As Veron explained, while these phonetic examples demonstrate pronunciation according to modern Latin usage, people in different countrys nevertheless use quite different versions of these pronunciations. Therefore the phonetic examples here serve as a guide only for those who don't know how to say the names, not a suggestion to change the way people say the names. In addition, in some instances I have included in parentheses some commonly used (though not necessarily correct) alternative pronunciations.

The common names included in this book are based on names I have seen listed on aquatic life importers' availability lists, aquatic dealers price lists and heard in conversations with aquarists or divers. These names are subject to changes and additions. I include the common names here because many people are intimidated by the Latin ones and prefer to have a "user friendly" descriptive name.

On the subject of "user friendliness," I have admired the simplicity of presentation utilized in Bornemann and Putterbaugh's (1996) *A Practical Guide To Corals* and Tepoot and Tepoot's (1997) *Marine Aquarium Companion.* These popular books have been well received because of the use of simple diagrams that give practical information, something that seems to be appreciated more nowadays as reading comprehension becomes passe, reading too time consuming (said with a degree of sarcasm). Many aquarium hobbyists have pointed out to me that the aforementioned books have been really handy for them when making purchasing decisions because they can quickly refer to a coral or fish and, at a glance, determine whether or not it is hardy and suitable for their aquarium.

In the series I co-authored with Charles Delbeek, *The Reef Aquarium* Volumes One and Two, we offer more detailed descriptions with each coral. If you are among the rare folks who like to read and want to get more detailed information about these corals, their biology, and the biology and husbandry of other reef creatures, I refer you to these books and the not-yet-released Volume Three of the series.

Some other books of related interest include Paul Humann's *Reef Corals*; Wilkens' two volume Set *Marine Invertebrates*; Fosså and Nilsen's *Modern Coral Reef Aquarium* series; Behrens, Gosliner, and Williams *Coral Reef Animals of the Indo Pacific*; Allen and Steene's *Indo-Pacific Coral Reef Field Guide*; and Colin and Arneson's *Tropical Pacific Invertebrates*. In the bibliography section I include additional suggested readings.

The reader having the opportunity to look at all of the abovementioned books, compared to this one, will note many instances where a pictured coral is identified by more than one Latin name. Errors of identification are to be expected due to various factors: mislabelled photos, differences of opinion among consulted experts, recent changes of the names, and consulting of old texts with incorrect identifications, to name a few. This book represents many years of consultation with experts in coral taxonomy. I have also spent a great deal of time researching coral taxonomy in library collections of journals and reference texts, in particular at the University of Miami's Rosenstiel School of Marine and Atmospheric Sciences. I have done my best to insure that the photos in this book are correctly identified, and I am responsible for any errors here. I am aware of the differences between the names I've used and those used in other texts, and have chosen to use these names based on the latest taxonomic information, and my own opinion.

The information provided in quick-reference charts regarding the care requirements of the corals is based on my personal experience with them in my own aquaria and reports from fellow aquarists or observation of the corals in their aquaria. For some corals the information is based just on observation of the corals in their natural habitat and having experience maintaining their closest relatives in aquaria. I explain how to use the charts in the following pages.

The reader may wonder why I include husbandry information for restricted Caribbean species not available to the aquarium trade. At the time of publication it is legal to collect and sell Caribbean corals growing on rocks placed on leased sea bottom as part of an aquaculture project. This law opens the door to farm-raised Caribbean corals of all kinds.

As with my other books, this one represents a collaborative effort with Daniel Ramirez who designed the format and composed the physical realization of the ideas and images I wanted to communicate. As always I am really happy with and proud of the result.

Julian Sprung, August, 1999

So many people have literally made this book. To start, J.E.N. Veron provided a "road map" with his references on coral taxonomy. He has also, through our correspondence, taught me a great deal about what's what in stony corals and inspired me to put what I've seen and learned in this book. Regarding the soft corals, I have also learned so much the past several years from Phil Alderslade. Phil has has spent a tremendous amount of time examining specimens I've sent him, offering his very detailed opinions with enthusiasm and wit. While I am deeply appreciative of the help I've received from these and other coral reef researchers, any errors of identification in this book are my sole responsibility, as I did not send the manuscript for review. I wish to thank Gary Williams, Stephen Cairns, and Fred Bayer who have also helped me with coral identifications. Also, Dr. Bruce Carlson who has effectively brought recognition to the importance of the research that can be done with living corals and reef ecosystems in aquariums. Over the years he has offered me sound advice, helped shape the directions I have taken in my career, and shown me some special dive sites in Hawaii, Fiji, and the Solomons. Thanks to Ann Fielding who organized the two trips to the Solomons on board the Spirit of Solomons. As a result I had a very comfortable opportunity to document the corals there. Thanks to Paul and Vicki, Jim and Kaye and the crew. Thanks to Crystal and Dwayne at Island Ventures for taking me to the Pillar Coral reef and the crew at Quiescence, who also took very good care of me in Key Largo.

Thanks to Peter Wilkens for inspiring me and a whole generation of reef aquarists with his original work, and for arranging a marvelous trip to Israel and the Sinai, which had a great impression on me. Thanks to Robert and Yael Brons who took good care of us in Eilat, to David Fridman, who really created something spectacular at Coral World, and to "Cheeripaha."

Thanks to Charles Delbeek who, as my friend and co-author of *The Reef Aquarium* series has taught me a great deal about coral biology and aquarium keeping, and challenged me by sharing his insightful viewpoints.

Thanks to Millie, Edwin, Ted, Jean, Mabel, Nene, et. al at All Seas who have always supported my work, treated me to good food, and notified me about unusual corals they've received.

Thank you to Kathleen Berg, Ken Erickson, George at Gables Aquarium, Peter Glynn for the live *Diaseris,* Henry Feddern, Klaus and Rosalia Grube for the *Pinnigorgia,* Daniel Knop, Rolf Hebbinghaus at the Löbbecke Museum., Alf Nilsen and Svein Fosså, Dr. Jean Jaubert and Dr. Nadia Ounais at the Musee de Oceanographique, Monaco, Sandy Trautwein and Ken Yates at Long Beach Aquarium, Rudi and Johannes at Vivarium Karlsruhe, Uwe Richter at Hagenbecks Tierpark, John Jackson, Odyssey publishing, Dave Palmer, Melissa Phipps at Riverbanks Zoo and Aquarium, Bob Mankin, Salty Dave and Sea Dwelling Creatures, Jean Claude and Marti Ringwald in France, Broggi Paolo, Gianluca Ventura, Dario, Elos, Reef International, and Mondo Sommerso in Milan, Ricardo Miozzo and Alexandre Talarico in Brazil, Mike and Jan Living Seas in Chicago, Marc, John and Lottie at A-Pet, Alain Bertschy and Jean Jacques Eckert of Aquarium Systems France, Dave Keeley and Des Ong of Underworld in England, and of course David Saxby. Thanks to the many other aquarists and public aquarium curators who have allowed me to photograph their corals. I know that I have not noted all of your names, but wish to express my sincere thanks. Any omissions aren't intentional.

For their help with my sometimes successful attempts at underwater photography, I thank Rob and Robin Burr, Burt Jones and Maurine Shimlock, Woody Mayhew, Richard Harker, and Laura and Larry Jackson who loaned me a very essential piece of equipment. Thanks also to Tropicolor and Thompson photo Imaging.

A big thank you to my brother Elliot Sprung, who once again did wonders in photoshop with my images. Thanks again to Danny Ramirez, and his wife Carmen, for the numerous dinners and breakfasts I was treated to in the endless last days of completing this book. Thanks also to Alexis, Daisy and Ruby at Two Little Fishies for handling the extra work load so well while Danny and I were preoccupied with completing this book. And thanks of course to Mom and Dad for being so supportive of me and my endeavors.

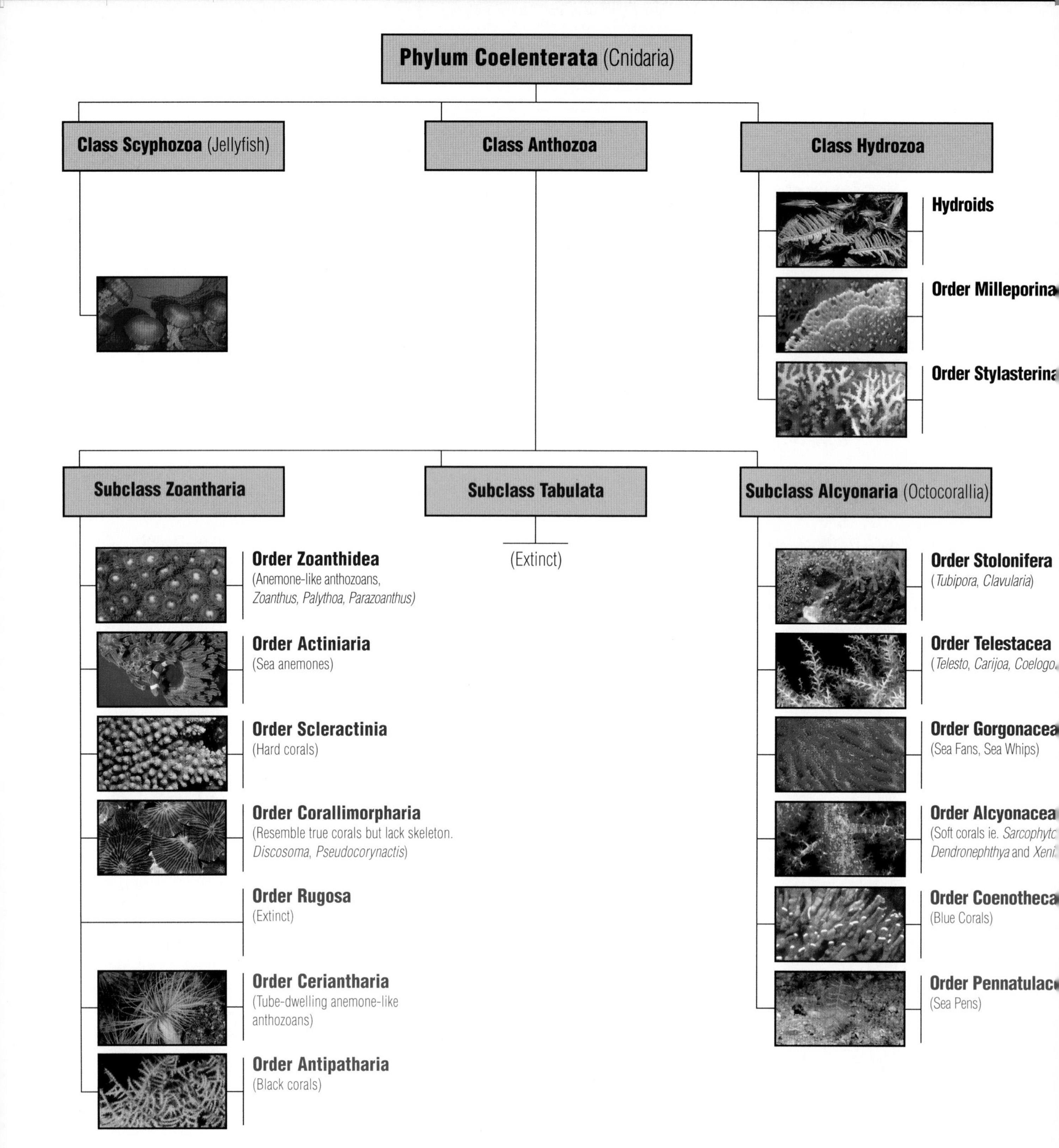
Phylum Coelenterata (Cnidaria)
Class Scyphozoa (Jellyfish)
Class Anthozoa
Class Hydrozoa
Hydroids
Order Milleporina
Order Stylasterina
Subclass Zoantharia
Subclass Tabulata
Subclass Alcyonaria (Octocorallia)
(Extinct)
Order Zoanthidea
(Anemone-like anthozoans,
Zoanthus, Palythoa, Parazoanthus)
Order Actiniaria
(Sea anemones)
Order Scleractinia
(Hard corals)
Order Corallimorpharia
(Resemble true corals but lack skeleton.
Discosoma, Pseudocorynactis)
Order Rugosa
(Extinct)
Order Ceriantharia
(Tube-dwelling anemone-like
anthozoans)
Order Antipatharia
(Black corals)
Order Stolonifera
(Tubipora, Clavularia)
Order Telestacea
(Telesto, Carijoa, Coelogo
Order Gorgonacea
(Sea Fans, Sea Whips)
Order Alcyonacea
(Soft corals ie. Sarcophyt
Dendronephthya and Xeni
Order Coenotheca
(Blue Corals)
Order Pennatulac
(Sea Pens)

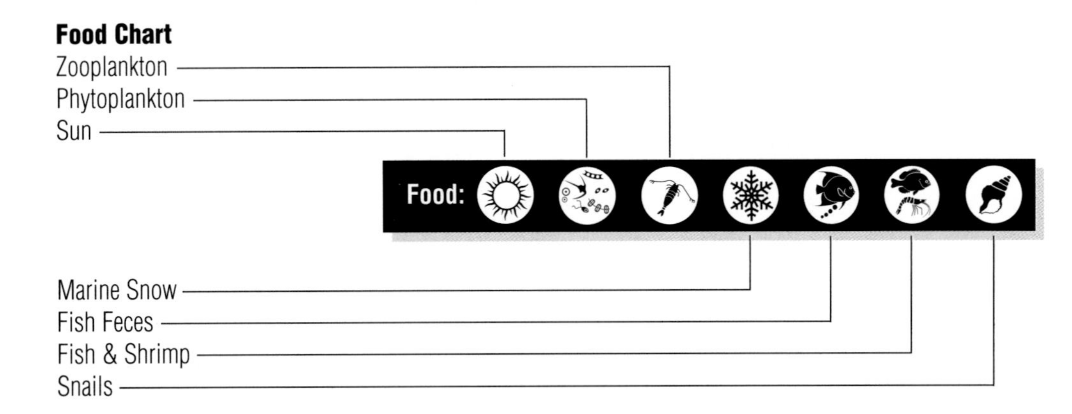

Food Chart - These symbols represent the various sources corals utilize for their nutrition. The *sun* symbol indicates that the coral needs light to obtain food produced through photosynthesis by its symbiotic zooxanthellae. The *phytoplankton* and *zooplankton* symbols indicate that the coral feeds on minute plants and animals from the water column. The *marine snow* symbol indicates that the coral feeds on particulate and dissolved organic matter. The *fish feces* symbol points out the nutrition corals receive by being shelter for fishes. The *fish and shrimp* symbol refers to prey larger than microscopic plankton, such as small shrimps, fish, and worms. The *snail* symbol refers to snails or other mollusks that bottom-dwelling large-polyped corals often consume.

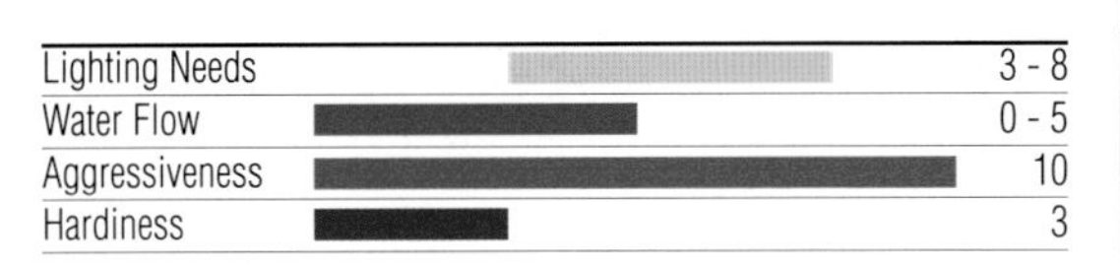

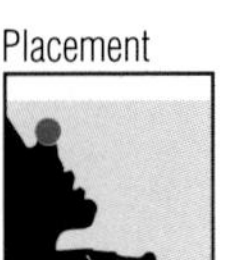

Bar Chart - This chart indicates the range of the coral's physical parameter requirements, the coral's hardiness, and the strength of the coral's aggressive attacks on other creatures in its immediate vicinity. In the ranges given for *lighting* and *water flow*, 0 represents lowest, 10 represents highest strength. A color bar highlights the range of the parameters the coral requires. *Aggressiveness* is expressed as a single value: 0 indicating lowest aggression and 10 highest. The rank is based on how many out of 10 different sessile creatures placed next to the coral would be harmed by it. The *hardiness* rank is based on how many aquarists out of ten would be likely to succeed in growing the coral.

Placement Chart - This side view of an aquarium shows with colored dots the proper positions for the coral, assuming overhead lighting. Note: some corals that don't require light may tolerate strong illumination.

Hard Corals

Hard or "stony" corals, scleractinia, are among the most important contributors to the structure and framework of the ecosystems known as coral reefs, but they are not the only corals that build a hard skeleton. The red precious coral from the Mediterranean is an octocoral, as is the organ-pipe coral, *Tubipora*, and the blue coral, *Heliopora*. Soft octocorals such as *Sinularia* sometimes form solid reef structures with the dense fused sand-like skeletal elements in their bases. Fire corals, more closely related to hydroids, also contribute to the reef structure with their fast growing hard skeletons. Shells of mollusks, calcareous algae, foraminiferans, sponges, tube worms, and other calcifying creatures help to build and bind the reef together as well. Nevertheless, when one hears the description "coral reef," the myriad forms of scleractinia is what comes to mind.

The majority of stony corals covered in this book are species that have a symbiotic relationship with the photosynthetic dinoflagellates known as zooxanthellae. Reef building corals are often referred to as "hermatypic," which literally means that they build reefs. In common usage, however, the term segregates those corals that contain zooxanthellae from those that do not. This is misleading since many corals that don't contain zooxanthellae, the so-called ahermatypes, build reefs and/or contribute significantly to reef structure while many small free-living corals containing zooxanthellae contribute little to the solid reef, forming only sand and gravel. Furthermore some corals, *Oculina* and *Madracis* for example, have reef building species that live with or without zooxanthellae.

This book concentrates on the more obvious (though sometimes rare or cryptic) hermatypic corals that a diver is likely to encounter. I have neglected a significant number of ahermatypes that occur in very deep water or in the darker recesses of coral reefs. I have missed a few important hermatypic coral genera too, but I have also included some new species and ones never before illustrated in a book. They are featured in this chapter and in chapter four.

Stylocoeniella

Pronunciation: STY-lo-SEE-nee-EL-la

Common Name: Thorn Coral

Region: Red Sea, Indo-Pacific to south central Pacific

Description: Colonies typically inconspicuous small encrustations, but sometimes massive or columnar, particularly in temperate localities. Small polyps like *Porites* or *Madracis*, but with very distinctive projecting skeletal spines (styles) in between the polyps.

Similar Corals: Similar to *Porites*, *Palauastrea*, and especially *Madracis*. Note the characteristic large pointed spinules projecting from the coenosteum (area around polyps) in *Stylocoeniella*. The corallites have a style-like columella.

Lighting Needs	3 - 8
Water Flow	2 - 9
Aggressiveness	1
Hardiness	9

Placement

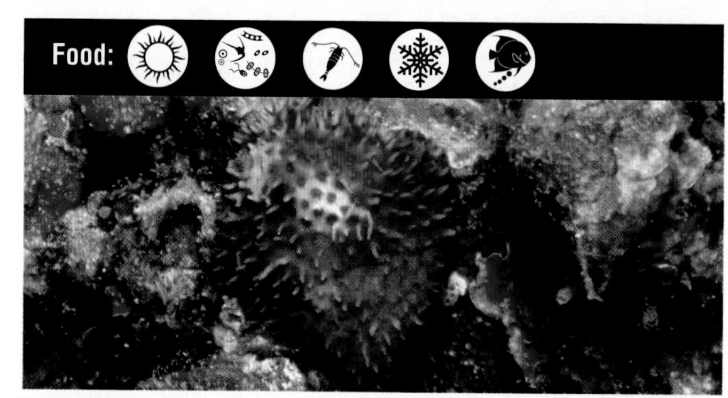

Note the projecting spines in this small *Stylocoeniella* cf. *armata*. Solomon Islands

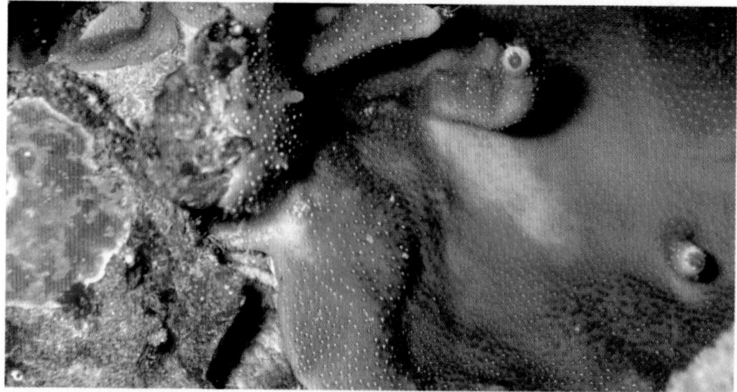

Stylocoeniella cf *guentheri* growing with commensal vermetid snails in the aquarium of Terry Siegel.

Stylocoeniella cf *guentheri*, Solomon Islands. Compare this colony with *Madracis decactis*.

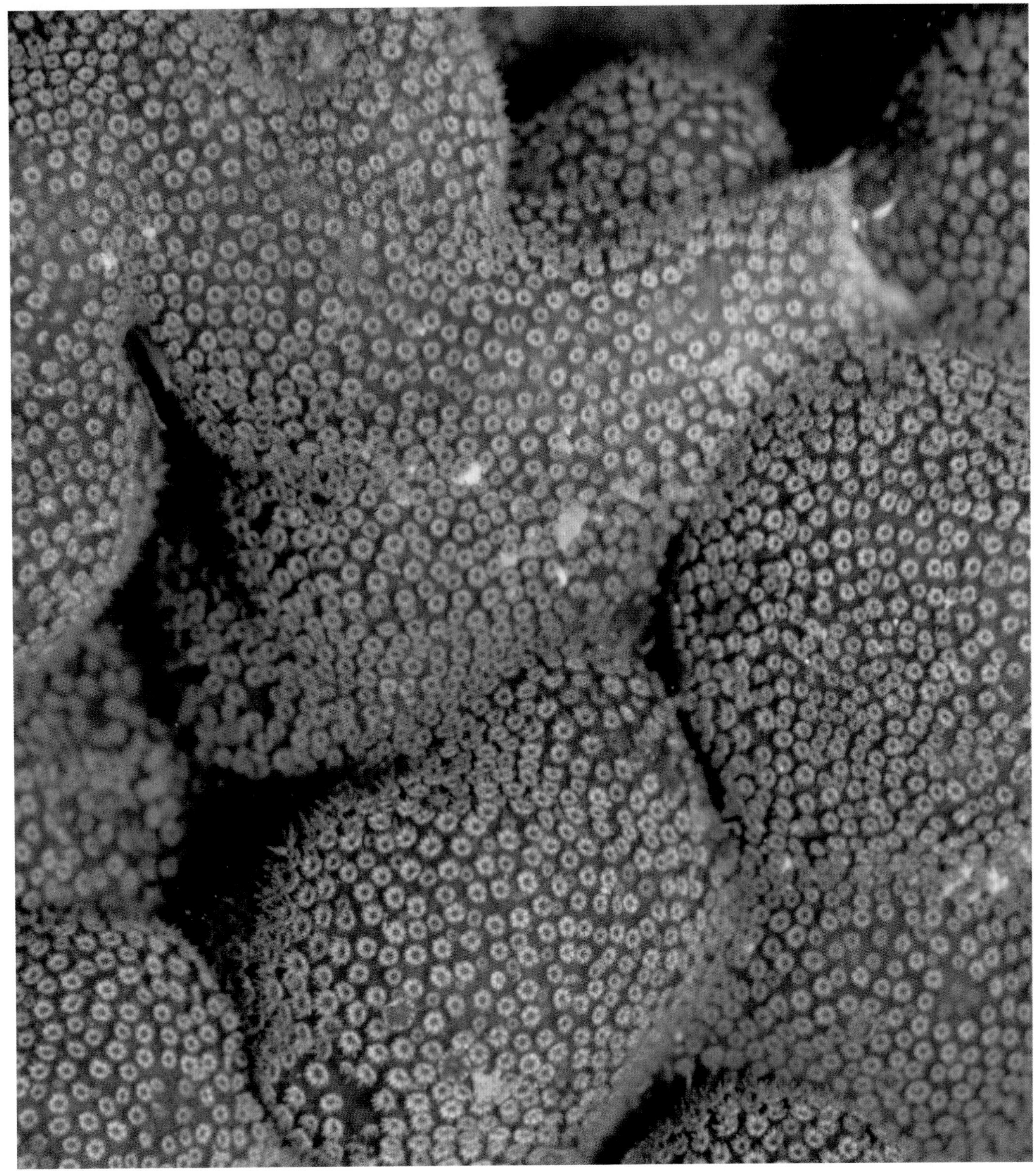

Stylocoeniella cf *guentheri*. Solomon Islands.

Madracis

Pronunciation: mad-RAY-sis

Common Name: Finger Coral

Region: Caribbean, Atlantic, Mediterranean, & Western Pacific

Description: Encrusting, massive, columnar, or branchy colonies with small circular slightly projecting corallites.

Similar Corals: In the western pacific *Madracis* could be confused with *Stylocoeniella*, but has larger corallites and lacks the spines projecting from the coenosteum. In the Caribbean, *Madracis* can be confused with small *Stephanocoenia*, the latter forming domed colonies when mature. The Caribbean branchy yellow finger coral, *Madracis mirabilis*, is remarkably similar to *Palauastrea* from the western Pacific. *Palauastrea* has thicker branches.

Lighting Needs	2 - 8
Water Flow	2 - 8
Aggressiveness	1
Hardiness	9

Placement

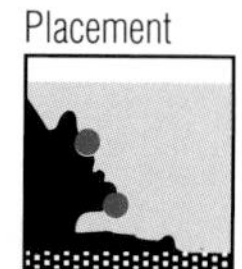

Food:

Madracis decactis. Key Largo, Florida.

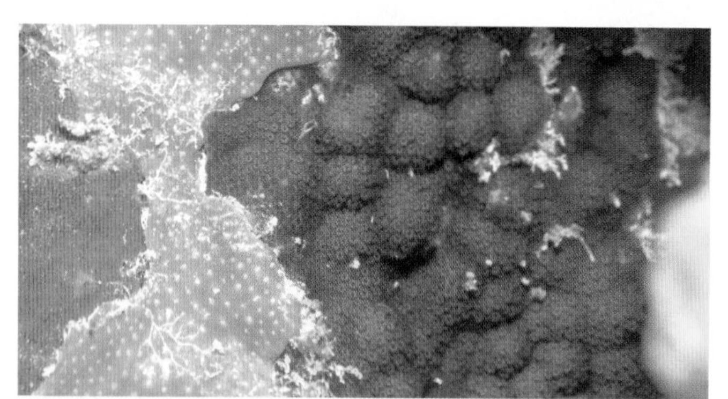

Madracis decactis. Key Largo, Florida.

Madracis decactis. Key Largo, Florida.

Madracis mirabilis. Bahamas.

Stephanocoenia
Pronunciation: STEF-an-oh-SEE-nee-uh

Common Name: Blushing Star coral, Star coral

Region: Caribbean.

Description: Brown mounds with small circular polyps. May be encrusting or form large heads. Usually occurs as small dome shaped colonies attached to hard bottom. Colonies "blush" pale when the polyps contract.

Similar Corals: Polyps are very much like *Madracis*, but the colony forms are distinct, except compared to small encrusting *Madracis*. At a distant glance small pale brown mound-like colonies may be confused with *Solenastrea bournoni* or *Siderastrea* spp.

Lighting Needs	3 - 8
Water Flow	3 - 8
Aggressiveness	1
Hardiness	9

Placement

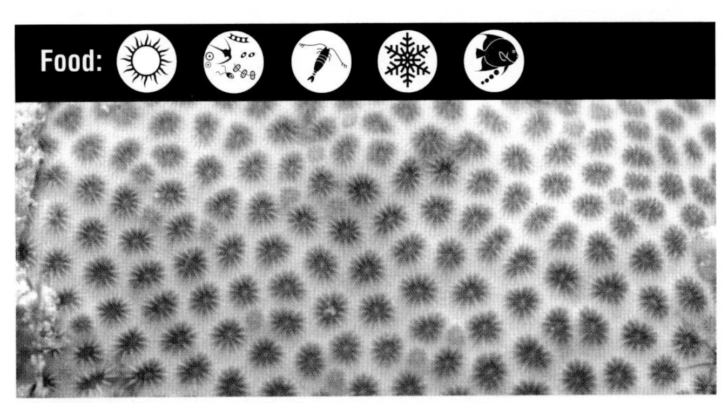

Stephanocoenia michellini, Florida. This colony "blushed" white as the polyps contracted.

Stephanocoenia michellini, Florida.

Palauastrea
Pronunciation: PAL-oh-ASS-tree-uh

Common Name: Finger coral

Region: Indonesia, Phillipines, Southeast Asia, New Guinea, Solomon Is., Australia

Description: Colonies composed of slightly tapering slender, cylindrical pale yellow branches with blunt ends.

Similar Corals: Similar to *Porites cylindrica*, which occurs in the same region. The latter is common on reef slopes and flats while *Palauastrea* is found in shallow turbid water over sandy or muddy bottoms. Porites have more densely packed polyps and the branches tend to be more tapered. *Palauastrea* is very similar to *Stylophora*, which forms more tightly rounded heads. *Palauastrea* is also quite similar to *Madracis mirabilis* from the Caribbean.

Lighting Needs	3 - 8
Water Flow	2 - 6
Agressiveness	1
Hardiness	8

Placement

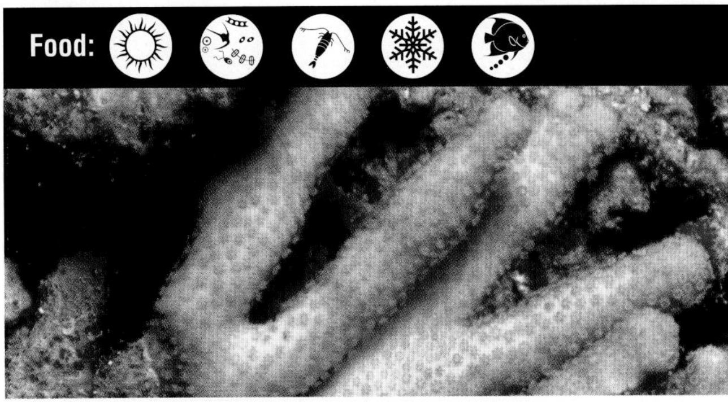

Palauastrea ramosa, Solomon Islands.

Palauastrea ramosa, Solomon Islands.

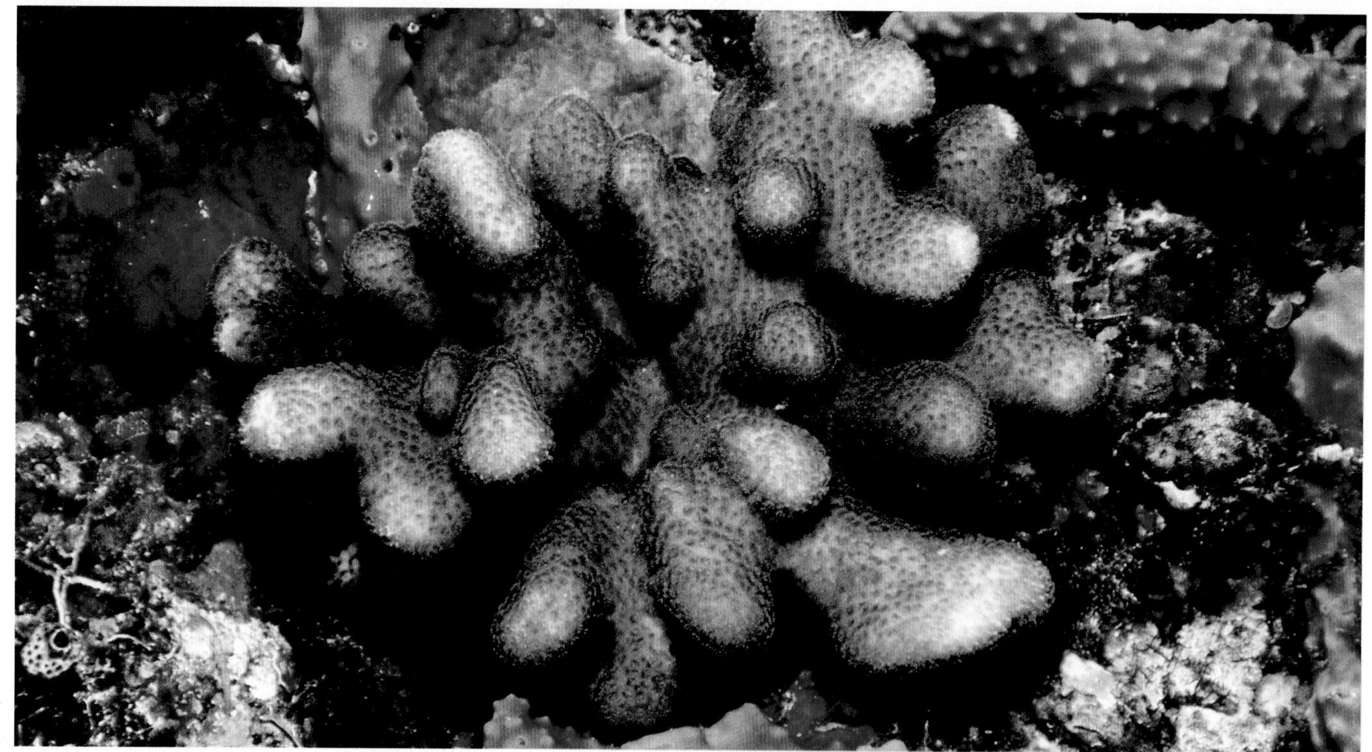

Stylophora pistillata, Solomon Islands.

Stylophora pistillata, Red Sea

Stylophora

Pronunciation: STY-lo-FOR-a

Common Name: Cat's Paw, Birdnest Coral, *Seriatopora*, "Seriatophora"

Region: Red Sea, Indo-Pacific to as far east as Pitcairn Island.

Description: Finger-like branches of varying thickness with blunt tips. Thicker branched specimens are more typical of shallow water high energy reef zones with strong water motion. Thinner branched specimens occur in shallow lagoon environments and deep water. Bright pink, magenta, purple, or orange specimens are from shallow water with bright illumination. Green and brown specimens may also occur in bright light but tolerate lower light levels.

Similar Corals: *Seriatopora caliendrum*, *S. hystrix* (robust form) *Pocillopora damicornis*, *Porites* spp., *Palauastrea ramosa*.

Lighting Needs	4 - 10
Water Flow	4 - 10
Aggressiveness	2
Hardiness	8

Placement

Stylophora sp. with growth form like *Pocillopora eydouxi* on an exposed reef slope, Solomon Islands.

Stylophora pistillata, Aquarium photo, Musee de Oceanographique, Monaco.

Seriatopora

Pronunciation: SEE-ree-AT-oh-POR-uh

Common Name: Needle Coral, Birdsnest coral, Finger coral

Region: Red Sea, Indo-Pacific, to Samoa and some central Pacific localities.

Description: Finely branched colonies with sharply tapered branch tips and polyps aligned in rows. Quite variable growth forms, depending on light and water motion. Colour is variable, including pink, orange, green, yellow, and brown.

Similar Corals: *Seriatopora caliendrum* has blunt tips. *Stylophora pistillata* and *S. hystrix* seem to merge or possibly hybridize. The thick-branched forms of *S. hystrix* may have branches in which the polyps are not clearly aligned in rows, and it is difficult to distinguish them from fine branched *Stylophora pistillata*.

Lighting Needs	5 - 9
Water Flow	4 - 9
Aggressiveness	1
Hardiness	6

Placement

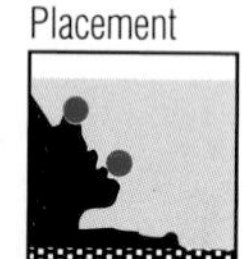

Food:

Thick branched *Seriatopora* sp., center, with finer branched pink *Seriatopora hystrix*, Solomon Islands.

Seriatopora hystrix, Solomon Islands.

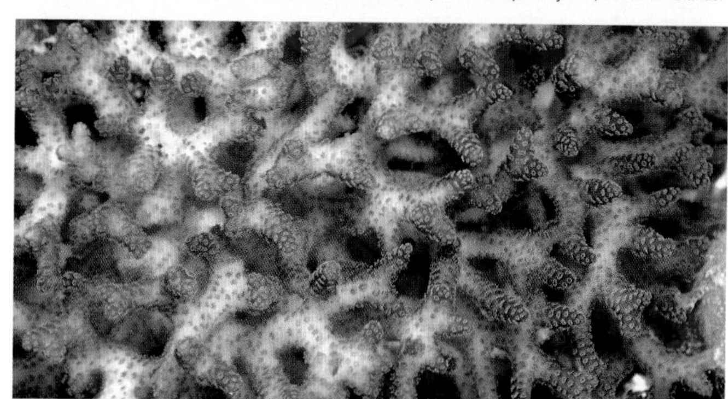

Seriatopora caliendrum, Solomon Islands.

Seriatopora hystrix growing on a shaded vertical wall, Solomon Islands.

Seriatopora caliendrum shown here is easily confused with *Pocillopora damicornis*. Aquarium photo.

Pocillopora

Pronunciation: PO-sill-o-POR-uh (PAW-sill-o-POR-uh, po-SILL-o-por-uh)

Common Name: Birdsnest Coral, Cauliflower Coral

Region: Red Sea, Indo-Pacific, Eastern Pacific

Description: Most *Pocillopora* have thick, heavily calcified branches with bumps (verrucae) all over the surface. They are highly variable, each with distinctive growth forms dependent on environmental conditions, and some being recognizable subspecies (Veron, 1986).

Similar Corals: In aquarium literature *Pocillopora damicornis* has been confused with *Seriatopora caliendrum* (Wilkens, 1986), which it does resemble. It can also be confused with finely branched *Stylophora pistillata*. On reefs *P. eydouxi* superficially resembles *Acropora palifera*.

Lighting Needs		4 - 10
Water Flow		4 - 10
Aggressiveness		2
Hardiness		7

Placement

Food:

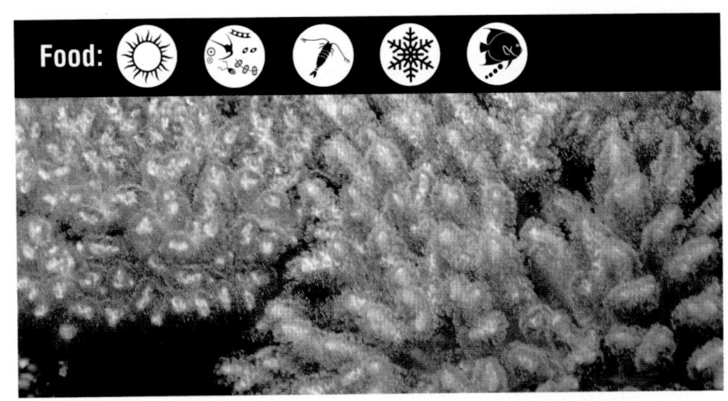

Two color forms of *Pocillopora damicornis* at the Lobbecke Museum, Dusseldorf, Germany.

A particularly colorful *Pocillopora damicornis* on a shallow reef flat, Fiji.

Pocillopora eydouxi, Solomon Islands.

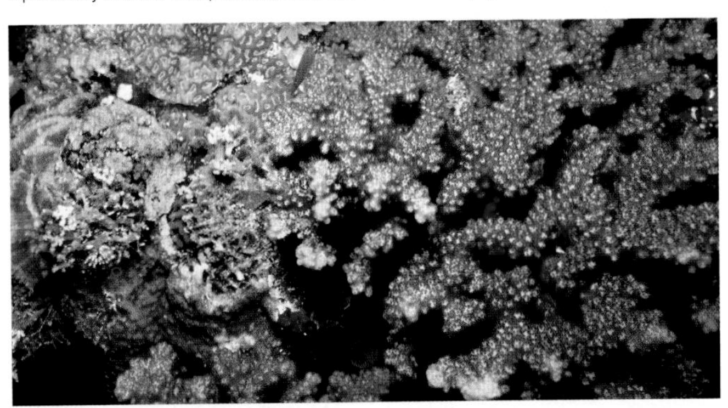

Pocillopora verrucosa, Solomon Islands.

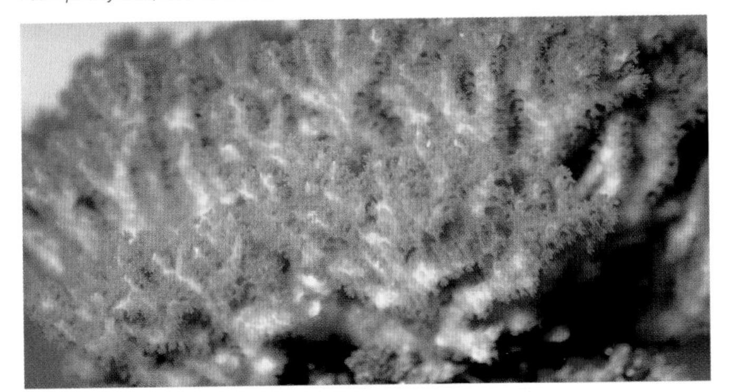

Pocillopora damicornis, aquarium photo. Compare with *Seriatopora caliendrum*.

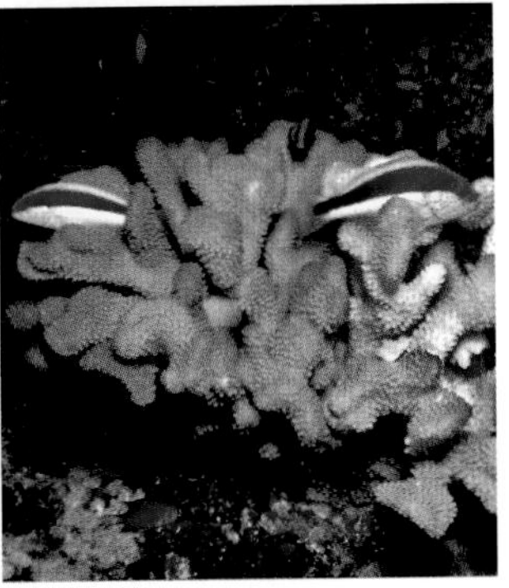

Pocillopora eydouxi, Solomon Islands.

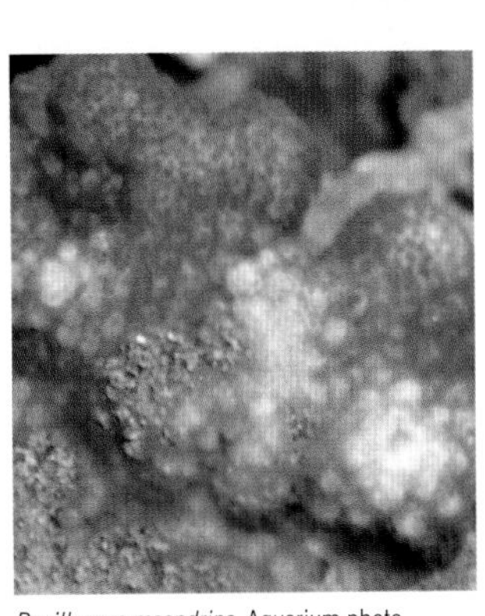

Pocillopora meandrina. Aquarium photo.

Astreopora

Pronunciation: ASS-treo-POR-uh

Common Name: Moon Coral

Region: Red Sea, Indo-Pacific

Description: Colonies dome-shaped, encrusting, foliaceous, or forming thick flat plates. The polyps are immersed or conical, widely spaced as in *Turbinaria.* Polyps generally extend at night only.

Similar Corals: Most similar to *Turbinaria* spp. *Astreopora* spp. have a more porous, lightweight skeleton than *Turbinaria* spp. *Turbinaria* spp. generally have expanded polyps during the day. Domed colonies also resemble *Favia* spp.

Lighting Needs	3 - 8
Water Flow	4 - 9
Aggressiveness	1
Hardiness	8

Placement

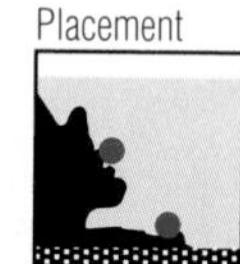

Astreopora sp., Aquarium photo.

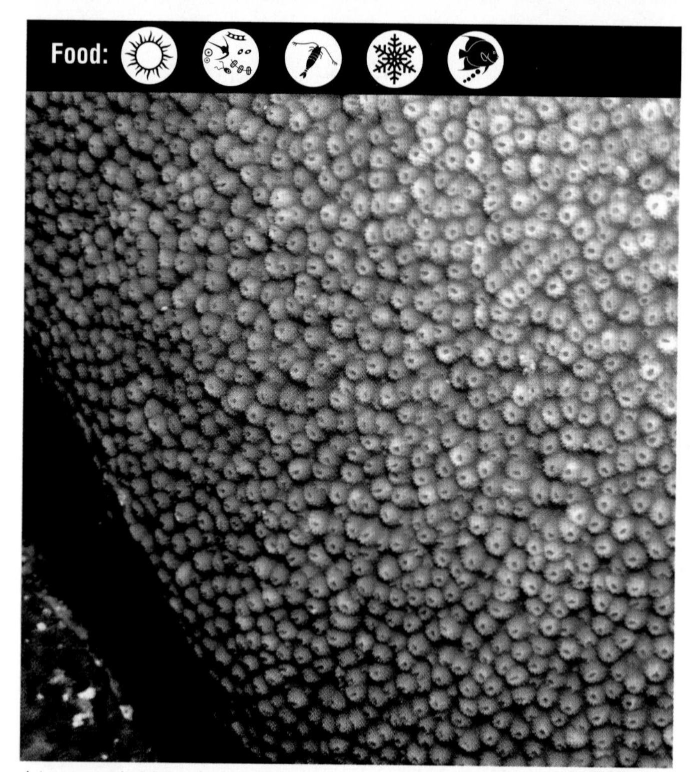

Astreopora myriophthalma, Solomon Islands.

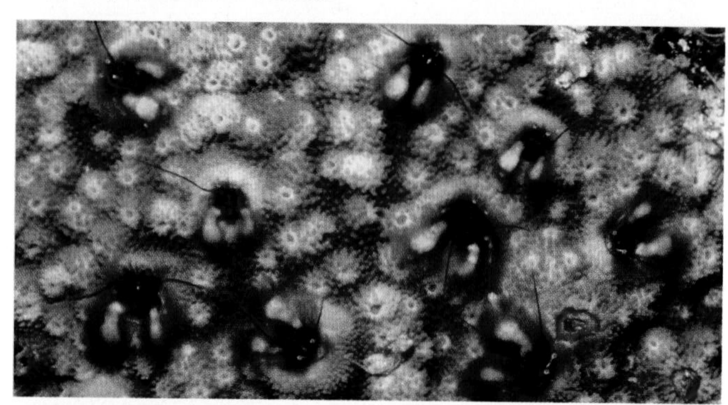

Astreopora listeri with commensal filter feeding hermit crabs, Solomon Islands.

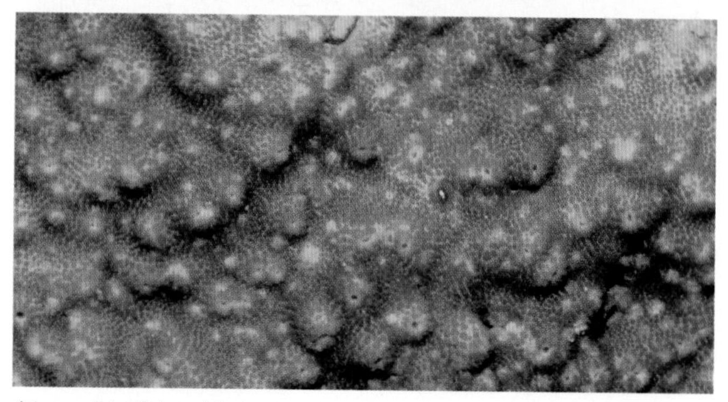

Astreopora listeri, Solomon Islands.

Acropora

Pronunciation: AK-ro POR-a, (a-KROP-ora)

Common Name: Staghorn Coral, Antler Coral

Region: Pacific, Indian, Red Sea, Caribbean

Description: Terminal (axial) polyps at branch tips usually large, distinct, and pale or brightly colored. When branches fuse into plates the growing edge is composed of many terminal polyps. Some have thick branches with pale tips composed of many terminal polyps. Indo-Pacific and Red Sea species may be vivid blue, pink, purple, orange, green, or yellow. Caribbean species are golden brown with white growing tips.

Similar Corals: *Anacropora, Montipora, Paraclavarina, Hydnophora, Pocillopora, Seriatopora,* and *Stylophora* spp. form similar branchy bushes with pale branch tips. *Cyphastrea decadia* has branches with axial corallites.

Lighting Needs	4 - 10
Water Flow	4 - 10
Aggressiveness	3
Hardiness	7

Placement

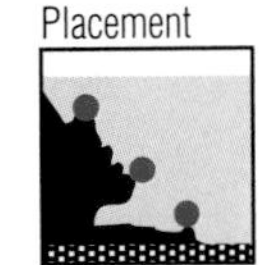

Acropora valida photographed at the New York Aquarium for Wildlife Conservation.

Acropora palmata. Key largo, Florida.

Acropora muricata (= *formosa*), Solomon Islands.

Acropora muricata (= *formosa*). "Stüber's Acropora." Aquarium Photo, Berlin Germany.

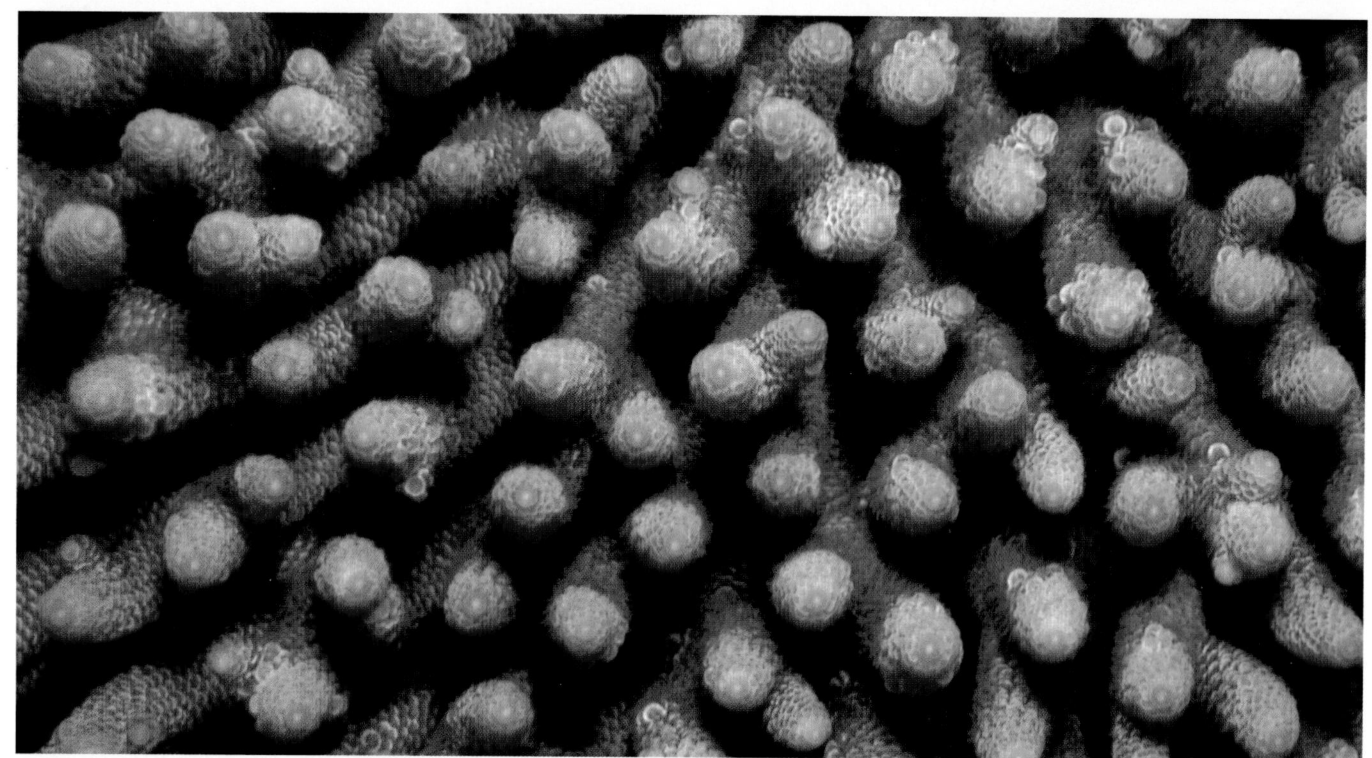

Acropora millepora is among the most colorful species in the genus, often fluorescent purple, orange or green with contrasting branch tips.

Acropora gemmifera and the similar looking *A. monticulosa* are residents of areas with strong water movement and bright light.

Acropora cuneata, aquarium photo.

Lighting Needs		3 - 10
Water Flow		4 - 10
Aggressiveness		1
Hardiness		6

Placement

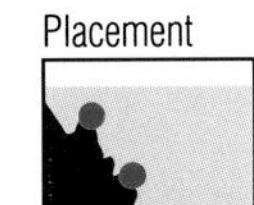

Acropora brueggemanni, Solomon Islands.

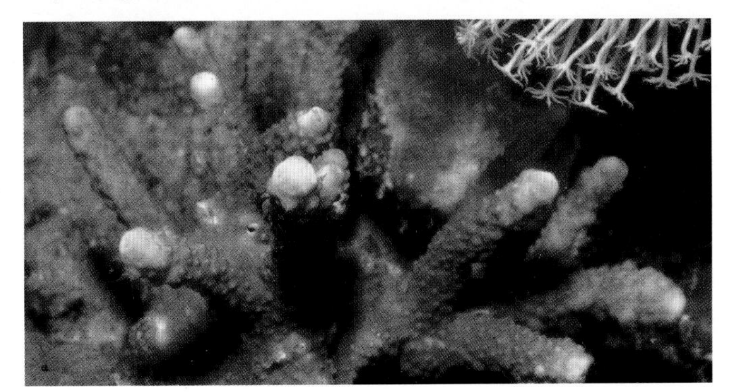

Acropora brueggemanni in deep water. Solomon Islands.

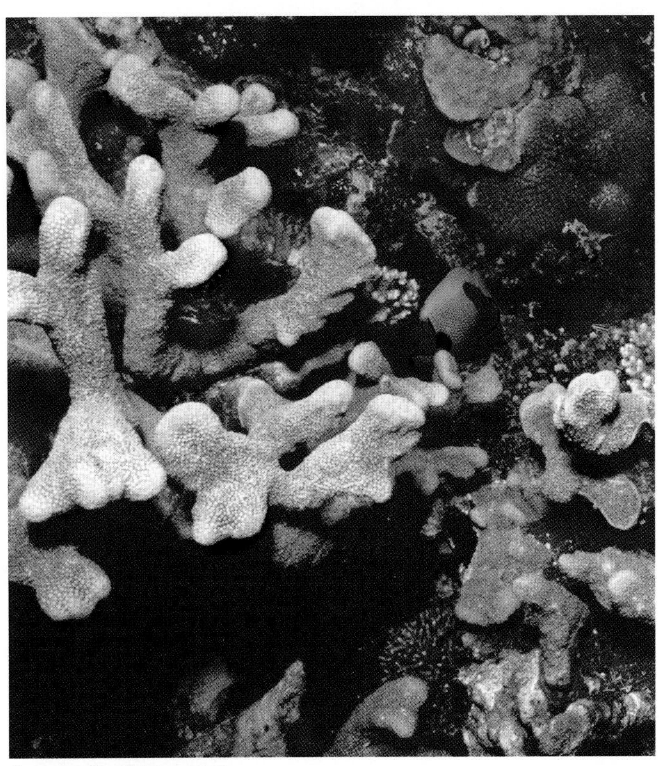

Acropora palifera, Solomon Islands.

Acropora brueggemanni is not always easy to distinguish from A. *palifera*. Solomon Islands.

Acropora florida, Solomon Islands.

Very colorful young *Acropora* sp. Solomon Islands.

Acropora granulosa. Solomon Islands.

Acropora florida. Solomon Islands.

Acropora divaricata. Solomon Islands. Resident fish are an important source of localized pollution (=nutrition) for corals in nutrient poor water. The waste makes them grow!

Acropora palmata with *A. cervicornis*-like projecting fingers on its surface. Key Largo, Florida.

Attribute	Rating
Lighting Needs	5 - 10
Water Flow	4 - 10
Aggressiveness	2
Hardiness	3

Placement

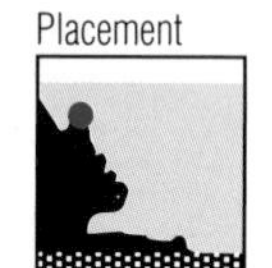

Acropora cervicornis. Key Largo, Florida.

Attribute	Rating
Lighting Needs	4 - 10
Water Flow	4 - 10
Aggressiveness	2
Hardiness	4

Placement

Acropora granulosa. Solomon Islands.

Attribute	Rating
Lighting Needs	5 - 9
Water Flow	5 - 10
Aggressiveness	3
Hardiness	7

Placement

Acropora humilis. Solomon Islands.

Attribute	Rating
Lighting Needs	4 - 10
Water Flow	4 - 10
Aggressiveness	2
Hardiness	4

Placement

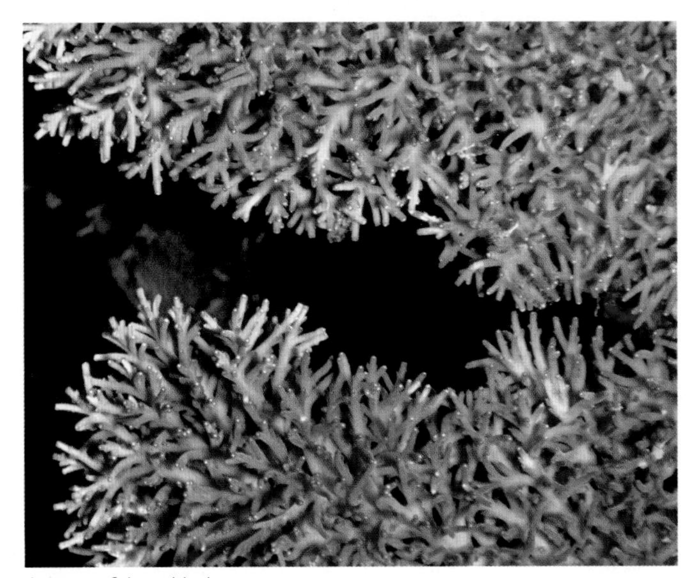

Acropora sp. Solomon Islands.

Lighting Needs	4 - 8
Water Flow	4 - 8
Aggressiveness	2
Hardiness	5

Placement

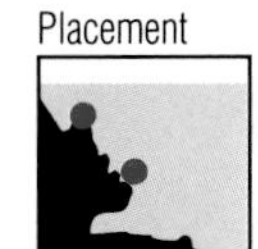

Acropora stoddarti, a distinctive species. Solomon Islands.

Lighting Needs	3 - 7
Water Flow	2 - 7
Aggressiveness	2
Hardiness	7

Placement

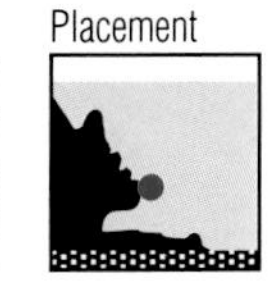

Acropora longicyathus. Solomon Islands.

Lighting Needs	4 - 9
Water Flow	4 - 8
Aggressiveness	2
Hardiness	6

Placement

Acropora longicyathus. Solomon Islands.

Lighting Needs	5 - 8
Water Flow	4 - 9
Aggressiveness	2
Hardiness	5

Placement

Anacropora
Pronunciation: an-AK-ro-POR-a (ana-KROP-ora)

Common Name: *Acropora*, Staghorn Coral

Region: Indian Ocean to Western Pacific.

Description: Brittle thin branches with widely spaced corallites and tapered, pointed branch tips. Corallites project, giving the branches a slightly spiny appearance. The polyps are like those of *Montipora*, but are more widely spaced.

Similar Corals: *Montipora digitata* has polyps are more densely arranged, the tips of its branches do not taper so sharply, and the branches have a smooth, velvety appearance compared to the spiny appearance of *Anacropora*. Aquarium specimens of *Acropora microphthalma* strongly resemble *Anacropora*, but have a terminal polyp on each branch.

Placement

Lighting Needs	3 - 8
Water Flow	1 - 6
Aggressiveness	1
Hardiness	6

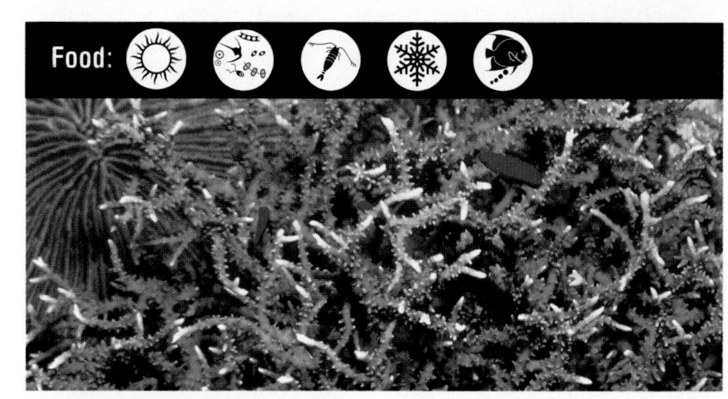

Anacropora, Solomon Islands.

Thick branched *Anacropora*, Solomon Islands.

Two species of *Anacropora*, Solomon Islands.

Montipora
Pronunciation: MON-tee-POR-uh (mon-TIP-or-uh)

Common Name: Cabbage Coral, Lettuce Coral, Finger Coral, Digitata, Velvet Finger Coral, Velvet Rock

Region: Red Sea and Indo-Pacific lagoons, reef flats and protected upper reef slopes. Usually in very shallow water with strong illumination. Aquarium Specimens are from Fiji, Solomon Is., and Indonesia.

Description: Foliaceous, laminar, encrusting, massive, or branchy colonies. Very lightweight fragile skeleton. Small polyps in depressions over colony surface. Coenosteum often with bumps or ridges.

Similar Corals: Similar to *Porites* spp. The calyces in *Porites* are full of septa, while *Montipora* calyces are more empty.

Placement

Lighting Needs	3 - 8
Water Flow	1 - 6
Aggressiveness	1
Hardiness	6

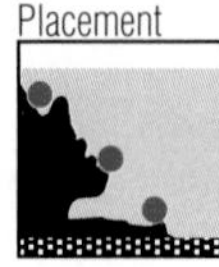

Montipora cf. *confusa* seems to mimic the anemone *Cryptodendrum adhaesivum*, Solomon Islands.

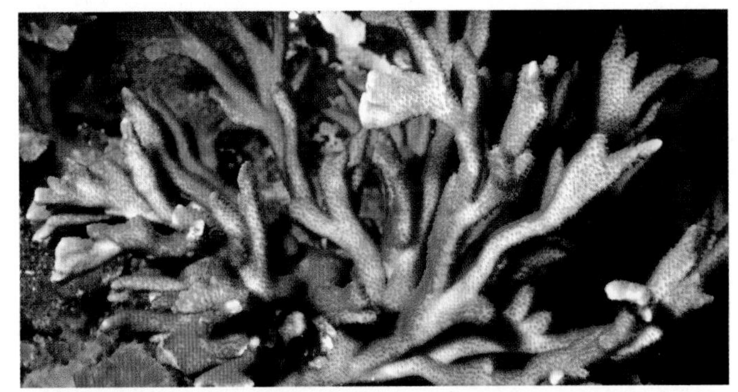

Montipora digitata, green colony adjacent to orange colony. Aquarium photo, Brooklyn, New York.

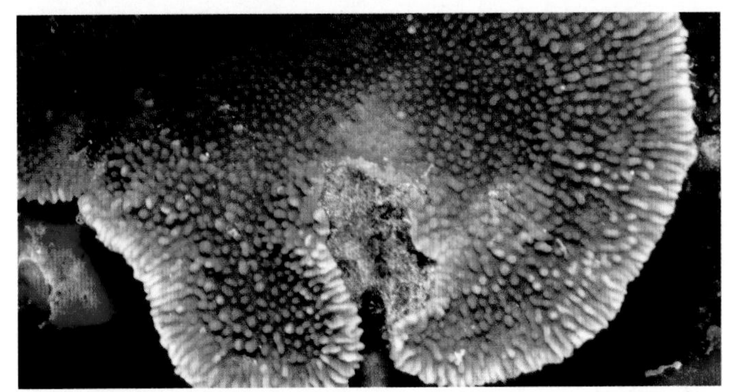

Montipora danae, Solomon Islands.

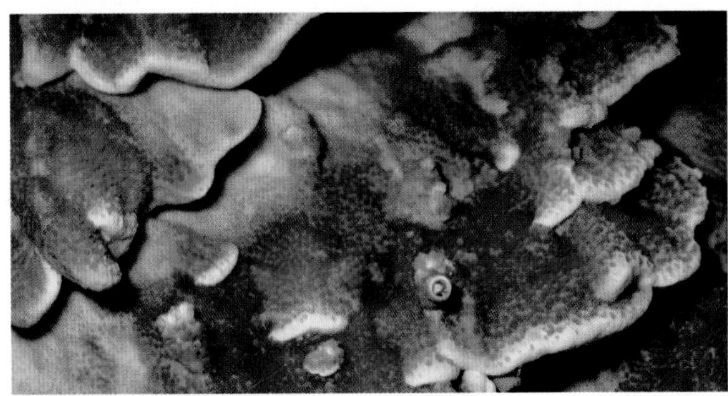

Montipora sp. Löbbecke Museum and Aquazoo, Dusseldorf, Germany.

Montipora sp. in the aquarium of Tony Vargas.

Montipora sp. Long Beach Aquarium.

Montipora digitata, purple morph. It needs bright light to maintain this color. Aquarium photo.

Montipora cf. *hispida*. Solomon Islands.

An extremely colorful *Montipora* sp. Solomon Islands.

Porites

Pronunciation: por-I-teez

Common Name: Finger Coral, Jewel Stone, Jeweled Finger, Jeweled Toe.

Region: Red Sea, Indian, Pacific, Atlantic, Caribbean.

Description: Branching, encrusting or dome shaped. Polyps are tiny. Colour brown, yellow, green, or a combination of these. Sometimes with UV enhanced blue, pink or purple pigments. Often associated with "Christmas tree" fan worms.

Similar Corals: *Porites rus* in particular resembles some species of *Montipora*, but the corallites are larger than in *Montipora* and they are filled with septa. Those of *Montipora* have inward projecting septal teeth (Veron, 1986). *Palauastrea ramosa* is similar to *Porites cylindrica*, the latter having more densely spaced corallites and branches that taper more toward the tip.

Lighting Needs	5 - 10
Water Flow	2 - 10
Aggressiveness	2
Hardiness	7

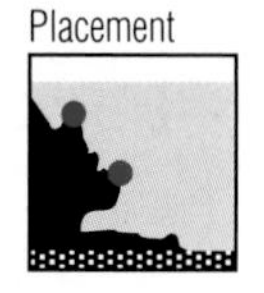

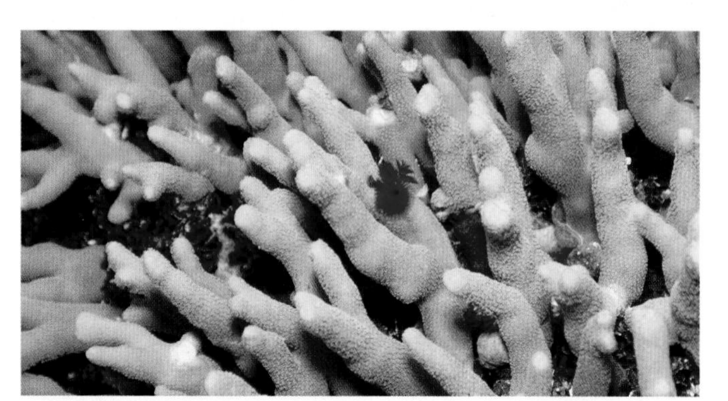

Porites cylindrica, Solomon Islands.

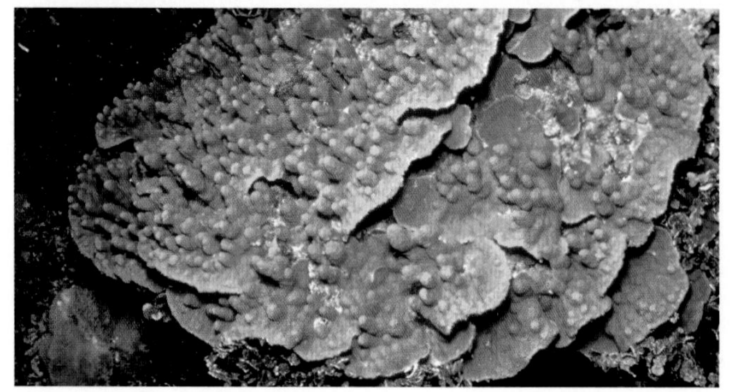

Porites lichen, Solomon Islands.

Porites astreoides, Key Largo, Florida.

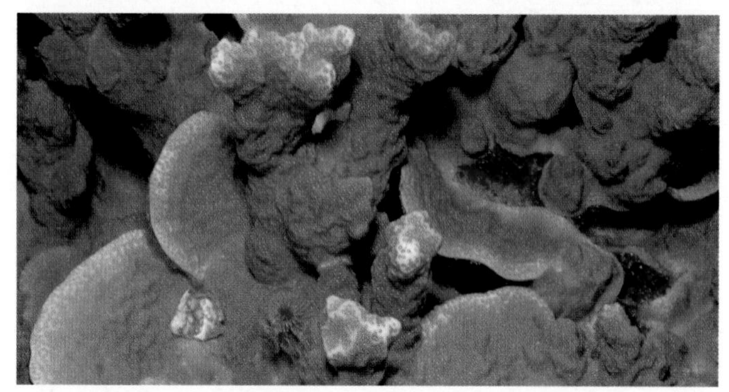

Porites rus colonies are composed of upright branches and flat plates. Solomon Islands.

Porites sp. adorned with commensal "Christmas Tree" worms. Solomon Islands.

Porites porites, Bahamas.

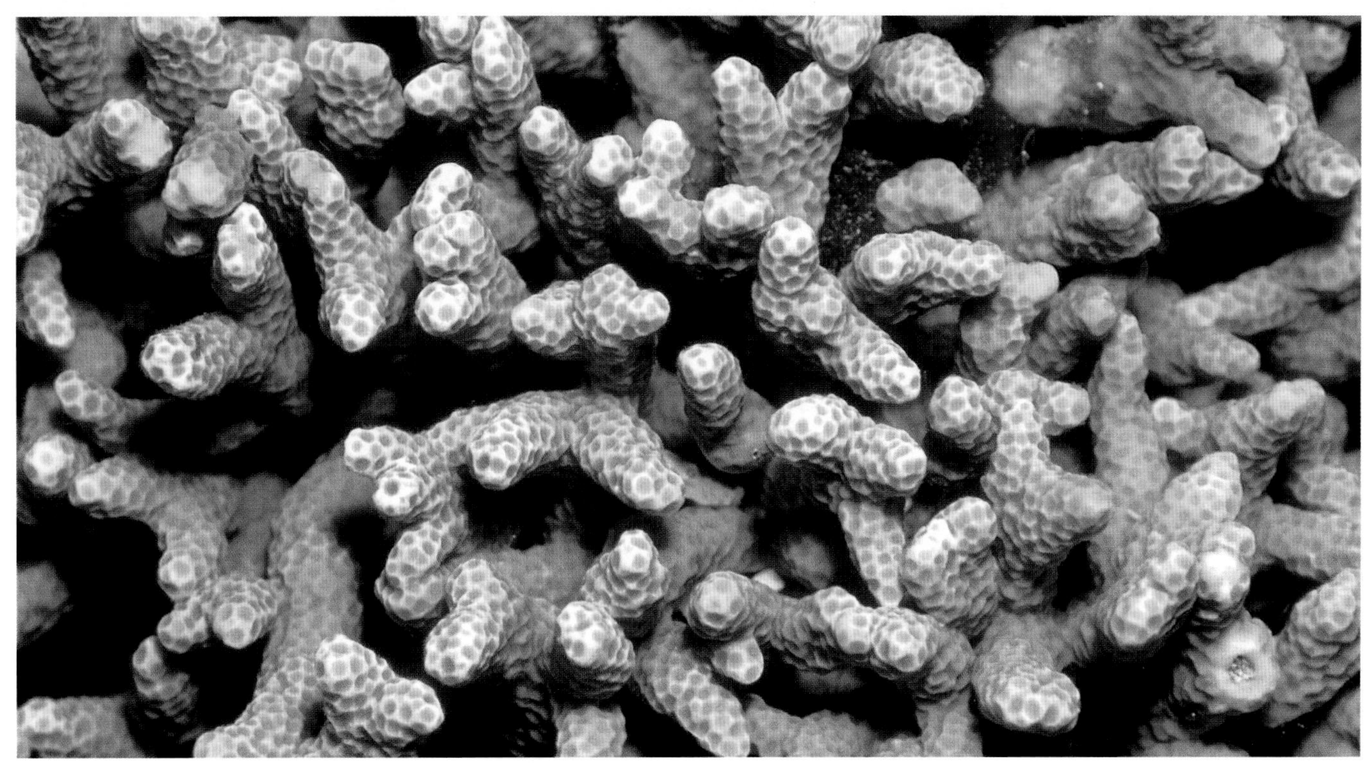

Porites nigrescens, Solomon Islands.

Alveopora
Pronunciation: AL-vee-oh-POR-a

Common Name: Daisy Coral, Flowerpot coral (Branching)

Region: Red Sea, Indian Ocean to central Pacific.

Description: Usually branching but sometimes massive or encrusting colonies, with very porous lightweight skeletons. The polyps are large and in most species extend dramaticaly long tubular columns. There are twelve tentacles, usually with blunt tips.

Similar Corals: *Goniopora* species have similar long tubular polyps, but with 24 tentacles each.

Lighting Needs	2 - 6
Water Flow	0 - 4
Aggressiveness	3
Hardiness	7

Placement

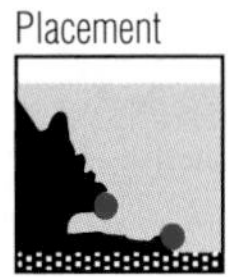

Food:

Alveopora catalai. Solomon Islands.

Alveopora gigas. Aquarium photo.

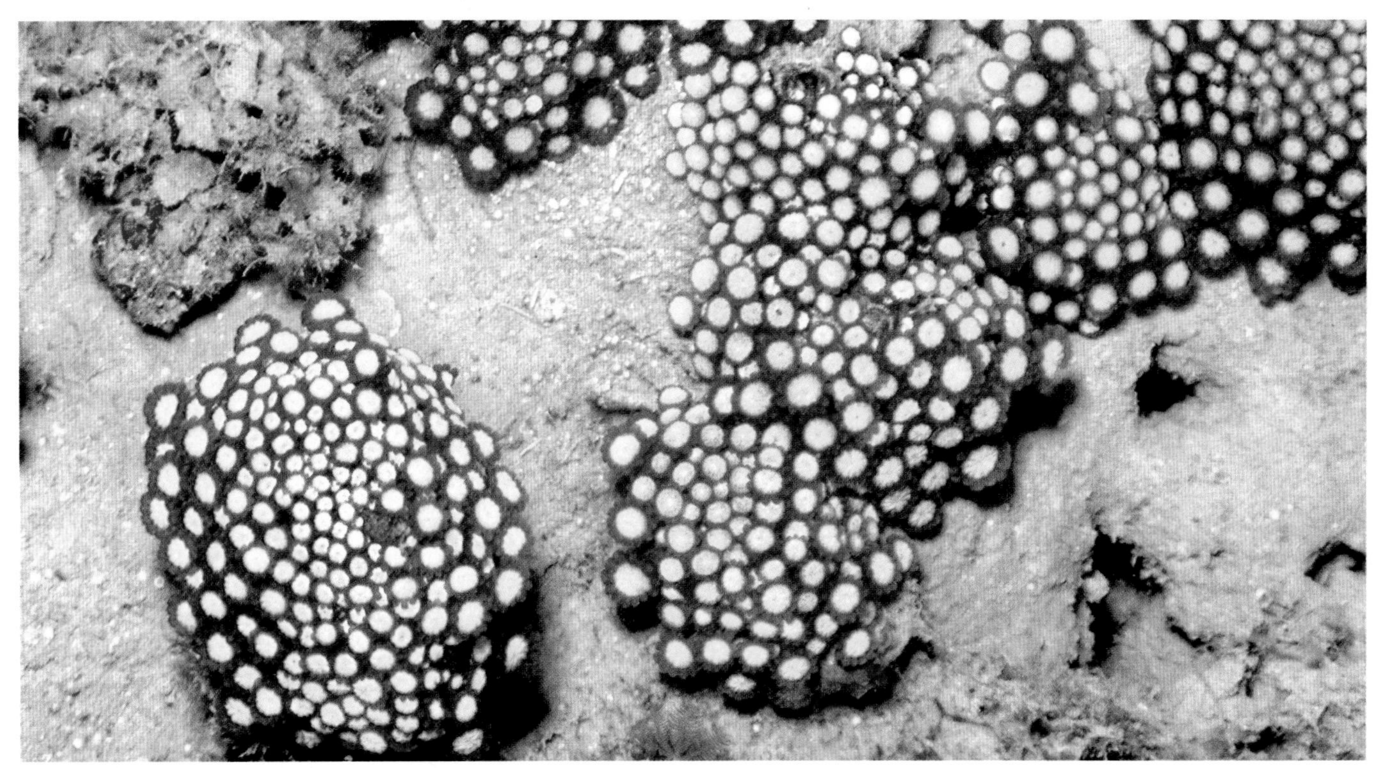

Alveopora sp. Solomon Islands.

Alveopora catalai. Solomon Islands.

Goniopora

Pronunciation: GO-nee-oh-POR-uh (GAW-nee-oh-POR-uh)

Common Name: Daisy Coral, Flowerpot coral

Region: Red Sea to Central Pacific

Description: Colonies massive, branched, or free-living. Polyps extend long tubular columns (to more than 40 cm) and have 24 tentacles each.

Similar Corals: *Alveopora* spp., which have 12 tentacles per polyp.

Food:

aGoniopora stokesi, aquarium photo.

Placement

Lighting Needs	4 - 9
Water Flow	3 - 9
Aggressiveness	6
Hardiness	3

Goniopora sp. Aquarium photo

Placement

Lighting Needs	5 - 9
Water Flow	3 - 8
Agressiveness	4
Hardiness	2

Goniopora sp. Aquarium photo

Placement

Lighting Needs	5 - 9
Water Flow	4 - 9
Agressiveness	6
Hardiness	3

Branched *Goniopora* cf. *pandoraensis*. Indonesia. Aquarium photo.

Rating	Value
Lighting Needs	2 - 8
Water Flow	0 - 5
Aggressiveness	4
Hardiness	8

Placement

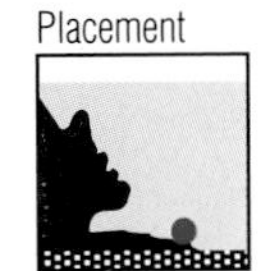

Beautiful red *Goniopora* sp. from Bali. Note formation of sweeper tentacles with acrospheres.

Rating	Value
Lighting Needs	3 - 8
Water Flow	2 - 8
Aggressiveness	6
Hardiness	8

Placement

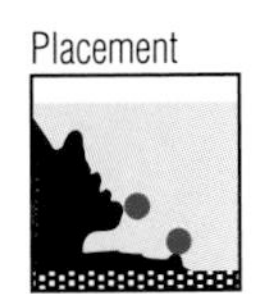

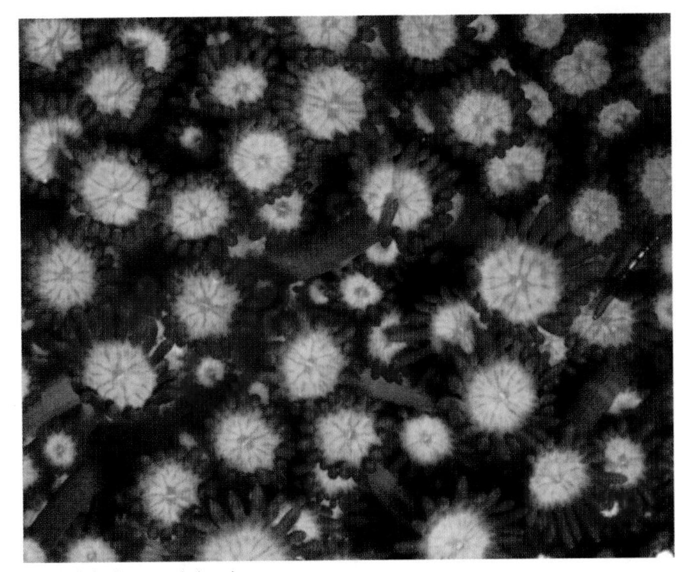

Branched *Goniopora* sp. Indonesia.

Rating	Value
Lighting Needs	3 - 8
Water Flow	0 - 5
Agressiveness	4
Hardiness	8

Placement

Goniopora sp., Solomon Islands.

Rating	Value
Lighting Needs	4 - 8
Water Flow	2 - 8
Agressiveness	6
Hardiness	5

Placement

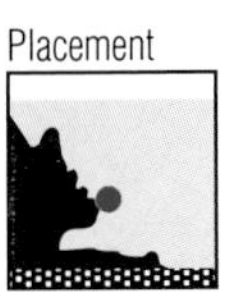

Siderastrea

Pronunciation: SI-der-ass-TREE-uh (SI-der-ASS-tree-uh)

Common Name: Star, Golf Ball, Starlet, Honeycomb Coral

Region: Caribbean, Brazil, Red Sea, Indian Ocean, Eastern Pacific.

Description: Usually small encrusting or dome shaped massive colonies with small cerioid corallites. Some species can grow quite large, forming "bommies" more than 1.5 metres tall and at least 2 metres across. Also forms free-living round colonies that look like golf balls.

Similar Corals: Similar to *Stephanocoenia* in the Caribbean. *Pseudosiderastrea*, a Western Pacific genus, has larger polyps generally, with septa that fuse. *Siderastrea radians* is an extremely variable species. In the author's opinion, the Brazillian "endemic" is likely a form of *S. radians*.

Lighting Needs	3 - 10
Water Flow	3 - 10
Aggressiveness	2
Hardiness	6

Placement

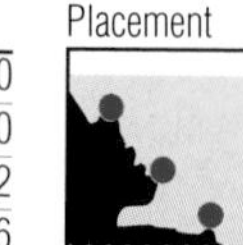

Food:

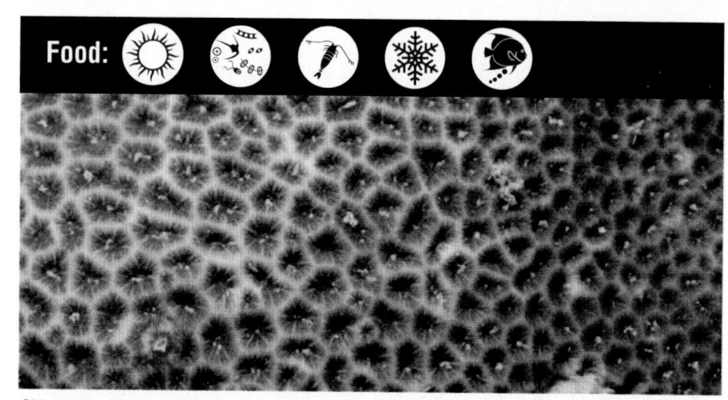

Siderastrea radians. Florida. Polyps on the left are like *Pseudosiderastrea*, on the right they are normal.

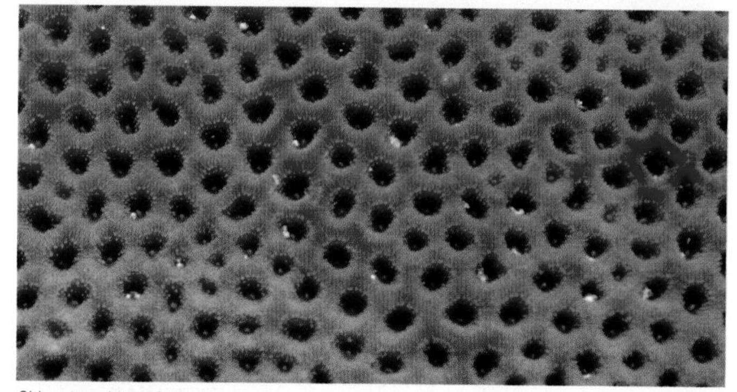

Siderastrea siderea, Bahamas.

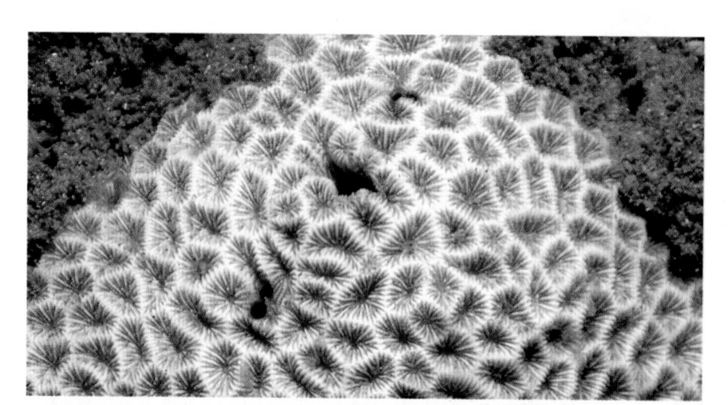

Pseudosiderastrea tayamai, Solomon Islands. Not very different from *Siderastrea* spp.

Siderastrea radians. Florida. Note how the polyps on the round colony differ from its neighbor's.

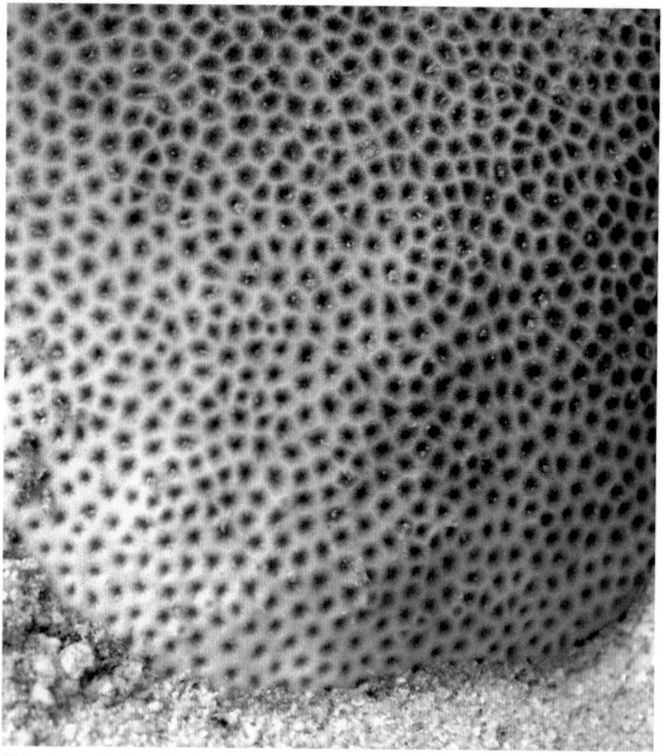

Siderastrea sp. Red Sea. Eilat, Israel.

Psammocora
Pronunciation: SAM-oh-KOR-uh (sam-MOK-caw-ruh)

Common Name: Cat's paw

Region: Red Sea to Eastern Pacific

Description: Massive, encrusting, columnar, foliaceous, or branchy colonies with very small shallow corallites. Some species form free living nodular "coraliths" that roll like tumble weeds accross the bottom.

Similar Corals: Similar to *Pavona* spp. and especially *Coscinaraea* spp.

Placement

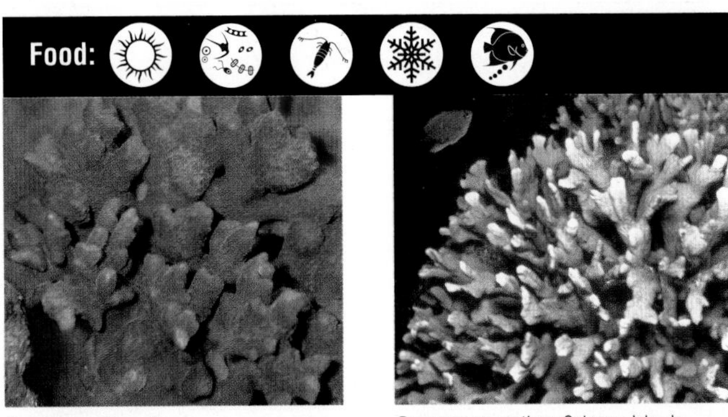

Psammocora cf. *contigua*

Psammocora contigua, Solomon Islands.

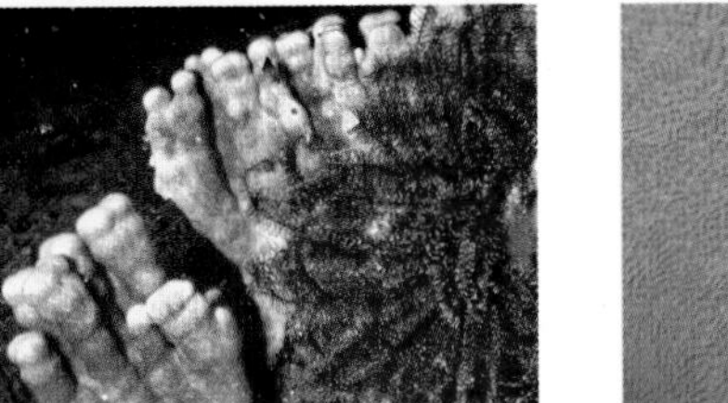

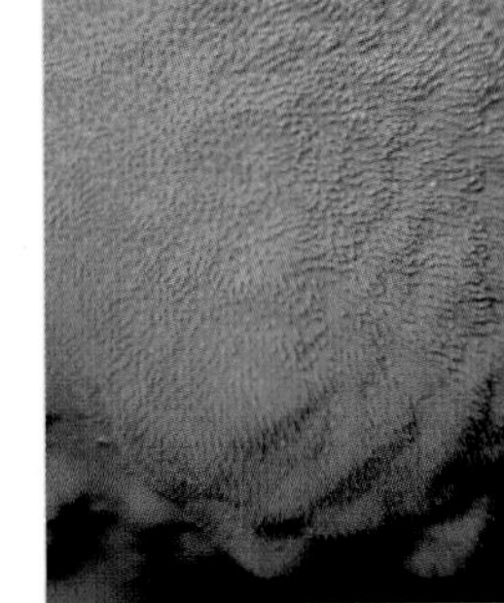

Psammocora digitata, Solomon Islands.

Psammocora sp. Aquarium photo.

Coscinaraea
Pronunciation: KO-sin-uh-REE-uh

Common Name: Plate coral, Finger coral

Region: Central Pacific to Red Sea

Description: Massive, encrusting, laminar, or columnar colonies with shallow corallites, between *Psammocora* and *Pavona* in appearance.

Similar Corals: Laminar colonies resemble *Leptoseris*. Most species are easily confused with *Pavona* spp. and *Psammocora spp*.

Lighting Needs	3 - 8
Water Flow	2 - 8
Agressiveness	3
Hardiness	6

Placement

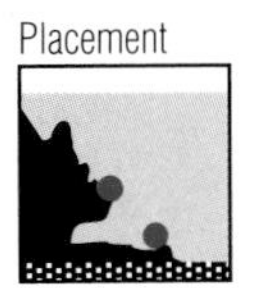

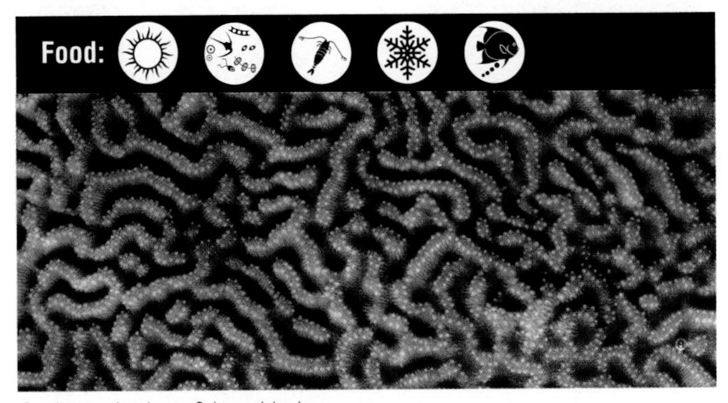

Coscinaraea cf. *columna*. Solomon Islands.

Coscinaraea sp. Red Sea.

Pavona

Pronunciation: puh-VO-nuh

Common Name: Lettuce coral, Cactus coral, Potato chip coral

Region: Red Sea and Indian Ocean to Eastern Pacific

Description: Mostly "leafy" foliaceous colonies with polyps on both sides of the "leaves." Some species encrusting, laminar, or massive. Corallites with are small and shallow, interconnected by prominent septo-costae.

Similar Corals: Most similar to *Leptoseris*, *Coscinaraea*, and *Agaricia*.

Lighting Needs	3 - 9
Water Flow	3 - 9
Aggressiveness	7
Hardiness	9

Placement

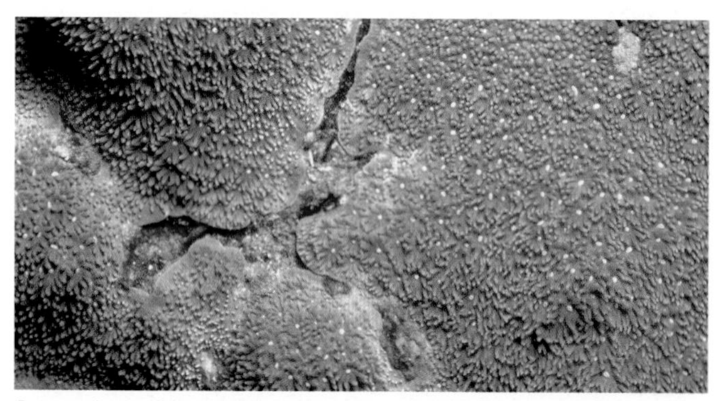

Pavona explanulata, Solomon Islands.

Pavona decussata is often confused with *P. cactus*. *Pavona decussata* has more obvious tentacles.

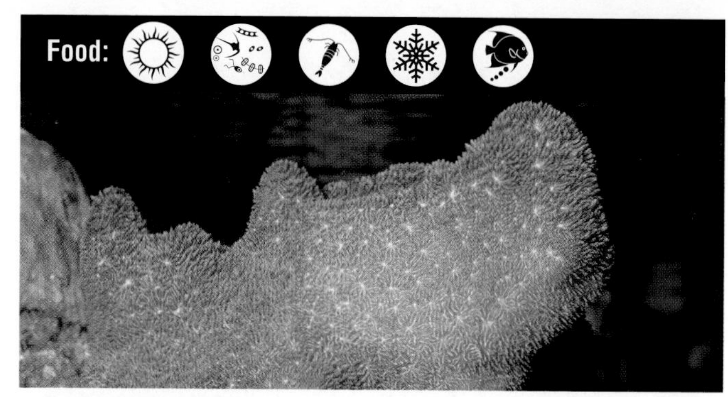

Pavona sp. Aquarium photo.

Pavona venosa in Ron Mascarin's aquarium. Note how different the lower portion looks from the top.

Pavona cactus. Bruce Carlson dubbed it the "Potato Chip" coral. Solomon Islands.

Agaricia

Pronunciation: AG-uh-REE-see-uh

Common Name: Lettuce, Leaf, Plate, Sheet, Scroll coral

Region: Caribbean, Gulf of Mexico, Atlantic, Brazil. Possibly undescribed species in the Western Pacific, see photo.

Description: Encrusting, laminar, foliaceous, sometimes massive colonies typically with polyps in discontinuous valleys in reticulated patterns, sometimes with long valleys.

Similar Corals: Foliaceous and laminar colonies with long valleys resemble *Pachyseris*, an Indo-Pacific genus. Overall quite similar to *Pavona* spp. and *Leptoseris* spp.

Lighting Needs		3 - 9
Water Flow		2 - 9
Aggressiveness		1
Hardiness		7

Placement

Food:

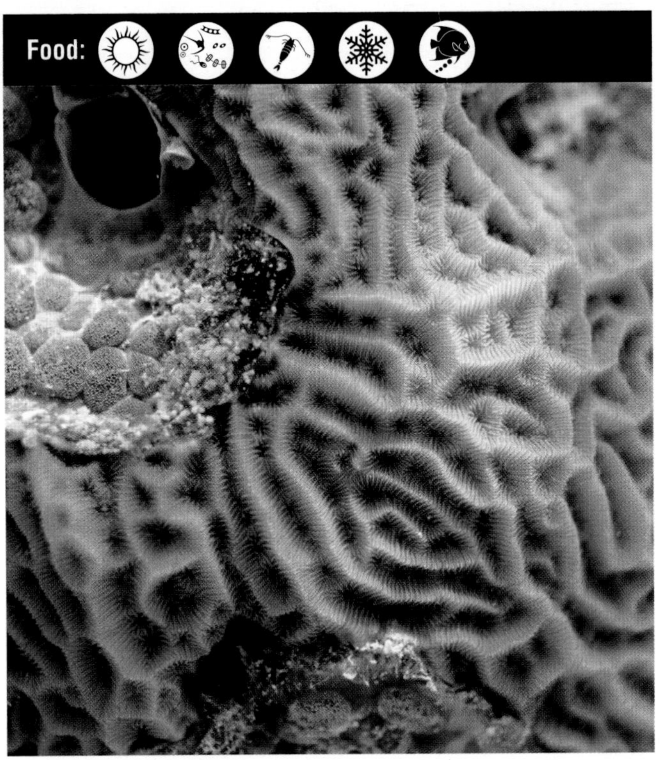

Agaricia agaricites, Nassau, Bahamas.

Agaricia lamarcki, Bahamas.

The author found this undescribed *Agaricia* sp. in the Solomon Islands!

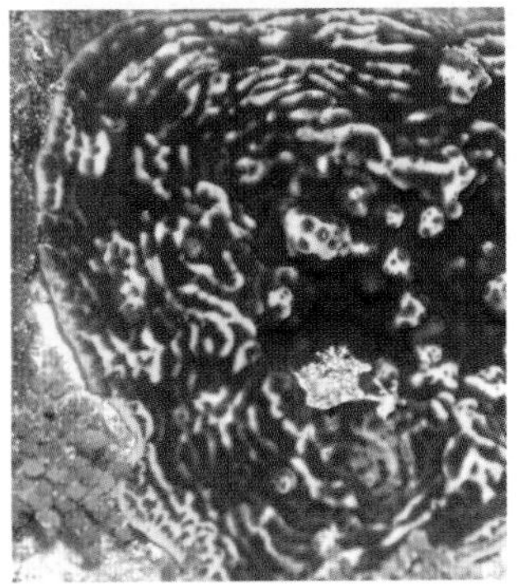

Agaricia fragilis, Florida Keys.

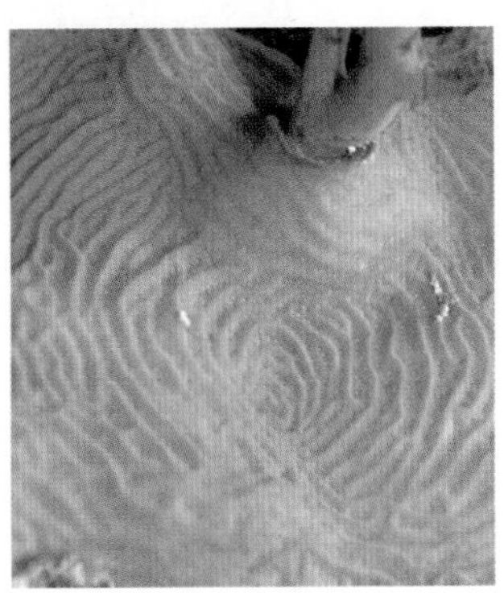

Agaricia sp., Bahamas.

Pachyseris

Pronunciation: PAK-ee-SEE-riss

Common Name: Phonograph, Lettuce, Leaf, Plate, Sheet, Scroll coral, Rugosa coral

Region: Red Sea to central Pacific

Description: Laminar unifacial colonies with concentric ridges and valleys that run parallel to the edge of the corallum. Also branching bifacial colonies with concentric or irregular ridges.

Similar Corals: Most similar in appearance to *Agaricia* spp.

Lighting Needs	3 - 8
Water Flow	1 - 8
Aggressiveness	1
Hardiness	8

Placement

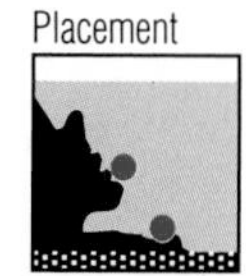

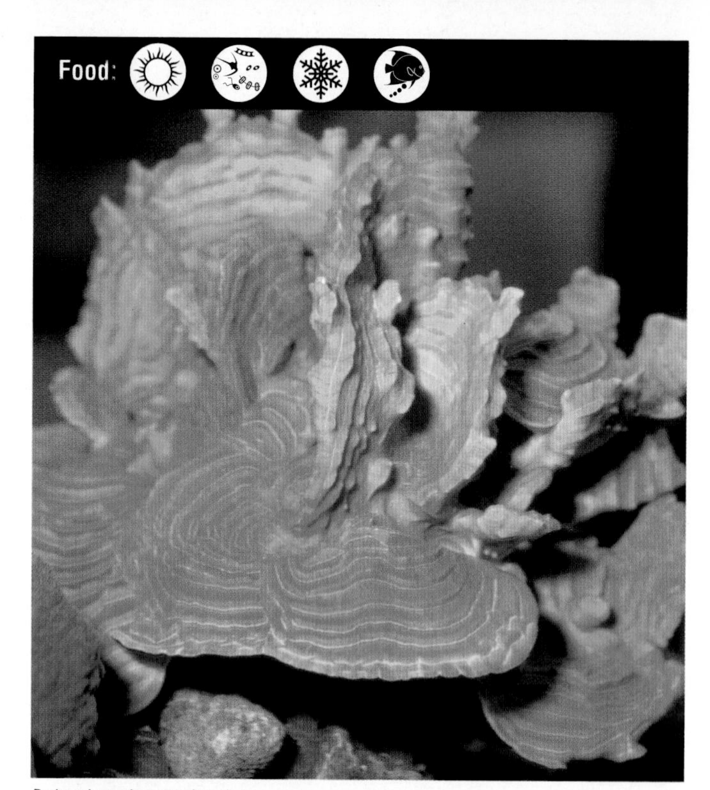

Pachyseris speciosa, aquarium photo.

Pachyseris rugosa, composed of contorted bifacial plates.

Pachyseris foliosa, Solomon Islands.

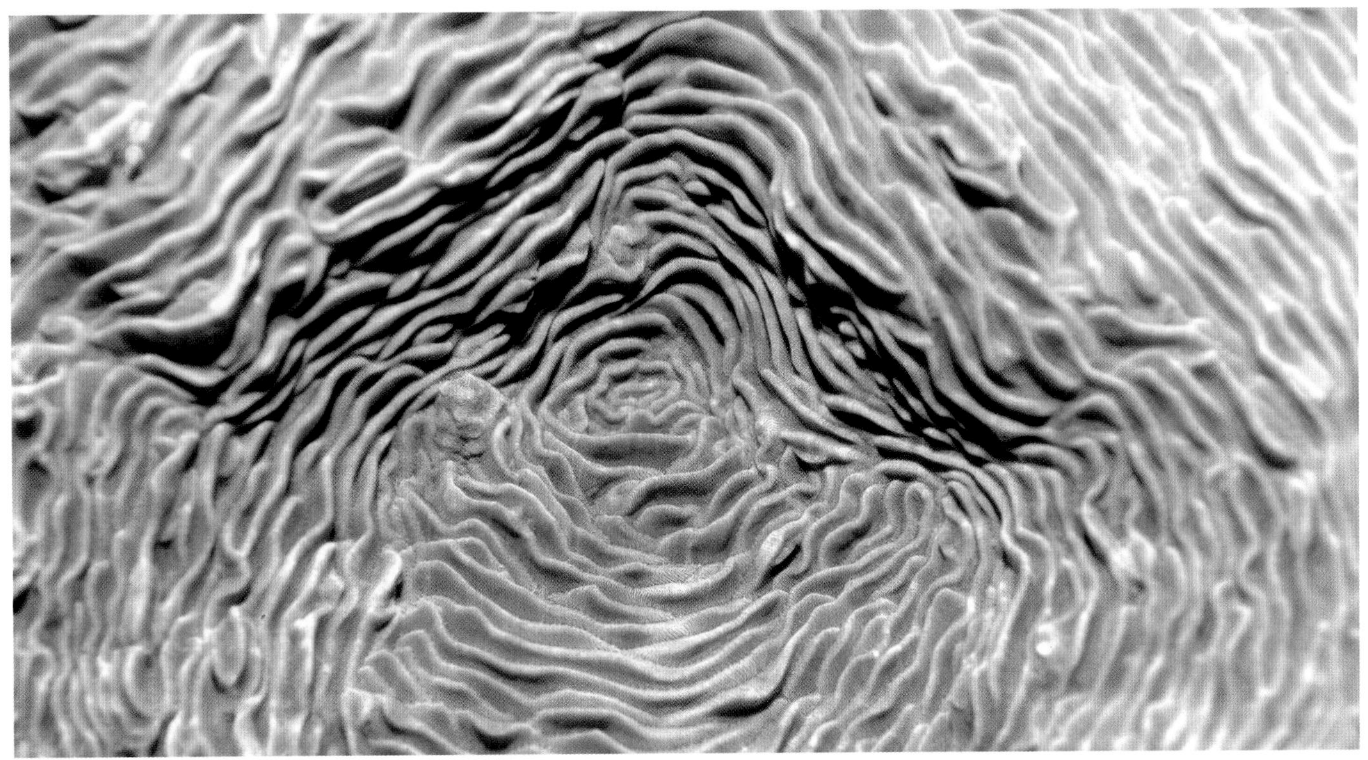

Pachyseris rugosa, Solomon Islands.

Pachyseris foliosa, beautiful! Solomon Islands.

Leptoseris

Pronunciation: LEPT-o-SEE-riss

Common Name: Lettuce, Leaf, Plate, Sheet, Scroll coral

Region: Caribbean, Gulf of Mexico, Atlantic, Red Sea to Eastern Pacific

Description: Unifacial foliaceous, laminar, or encrusting colonies, with corallites typically larger than the similar looking *Pavona* and *Agaricia*.

Similar Corals: *Leptoseris gardineri* is similar to *Pavona cactus*, but the former is unifacial. *Leptoseris mycetoseroides* is similar to *Agaricia* spp.

Lighting Needs	3 - 8
Water Flow	1 - 9
Aggressiveness	2
Hardiness	7

Placement

Leptoseris cuculata, Bahamas.

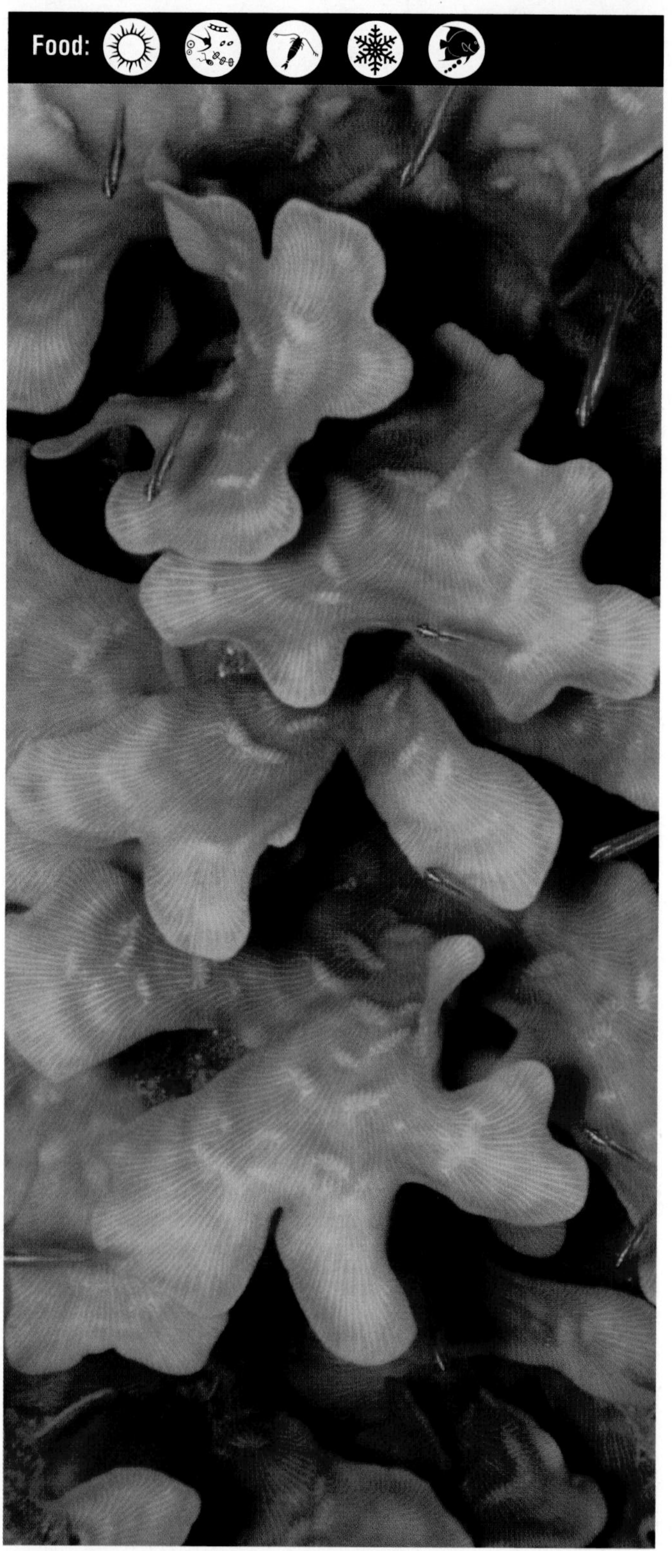

Leptoseris gardineri, Solomon Islands.

Leptoseris gardineri, Solomon Islands.

Leptoseris papyracea, Solomon Islands.

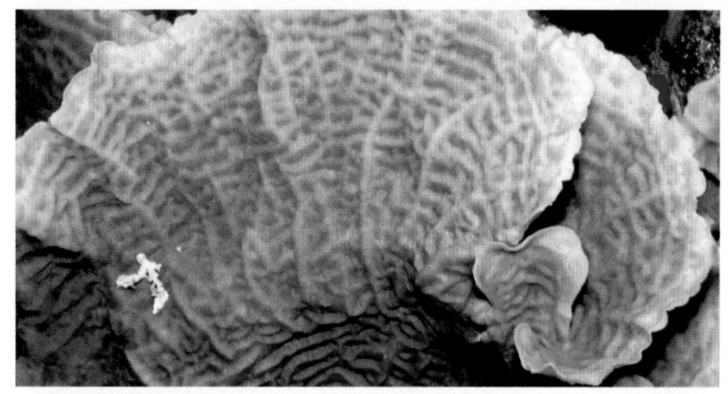

Leptoseris yabei, Solomon Islands.

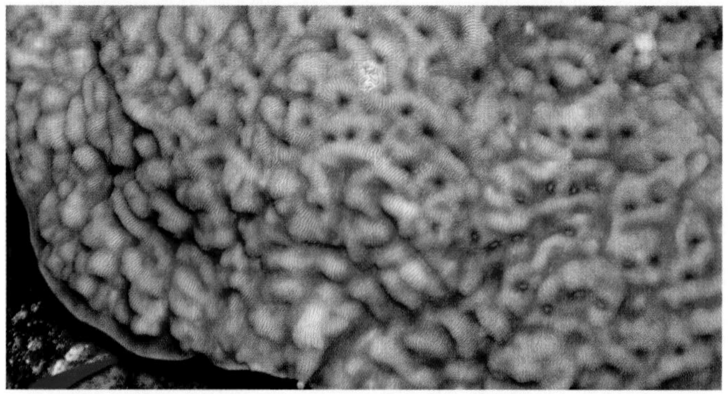

Leptoseris sp., Solomon Islands.

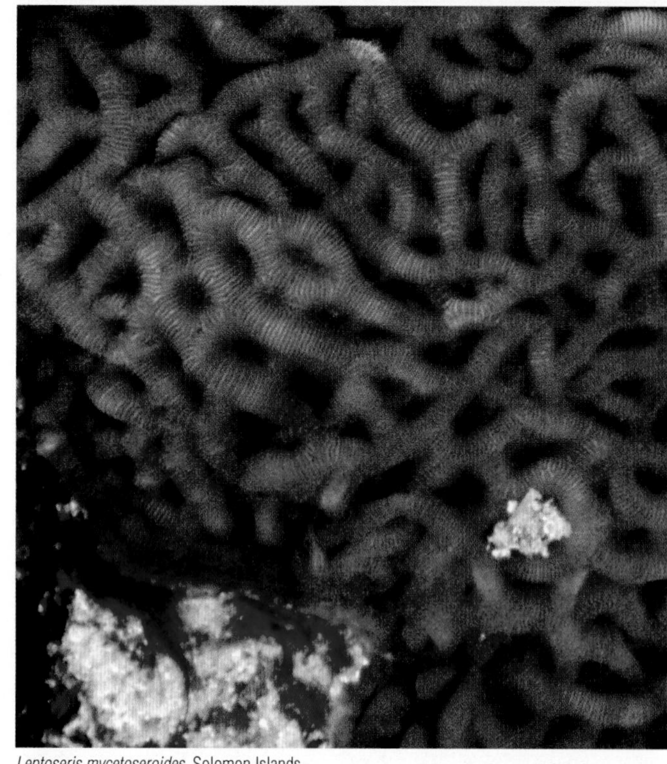

Leptoseris mycetoseroides, Solomon Islands.

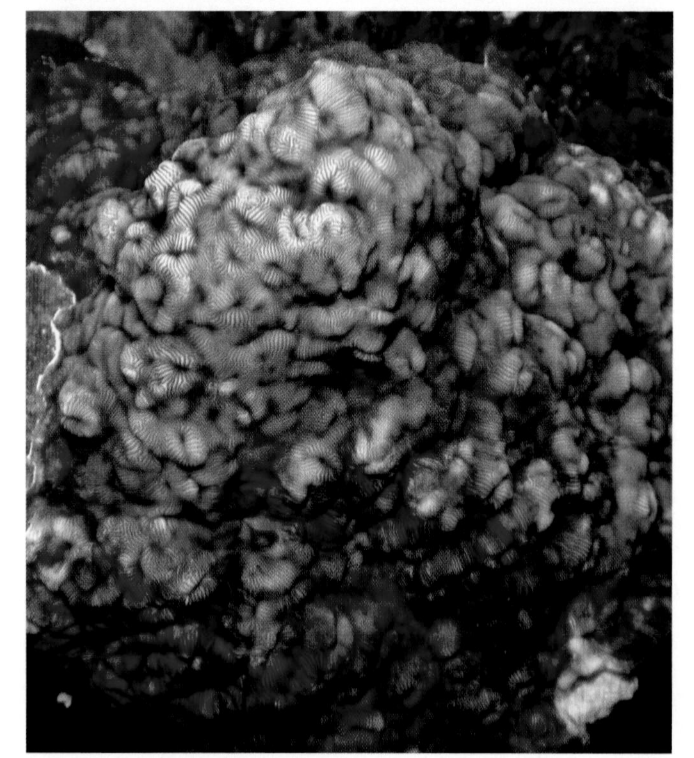

Leptoseris sp. with red pigment, Solomon Islands.

Leptoseris explanata, Solomon Islands.

Gardineroseris

Pronunciation: GAR-din-eh-ro-SEE-riss

Common Name: Favites, Honeycomb coral

Region: Red Sea to Eastern Pacific

Description: Massive or encrusting colonies, with laminar margins where the light is indirect. Corallites or groups of corallites in pits separated by high ridges that give the appearance of a cerioid skeleton like Favites spp.

Similar Corals: Remotely resembles Faviid corals because of the cerioid appearance.

Lighting Needs		4 - 9
Water Flow		4 - 10
Aggressiveness		3
Hardiness		7

Placement

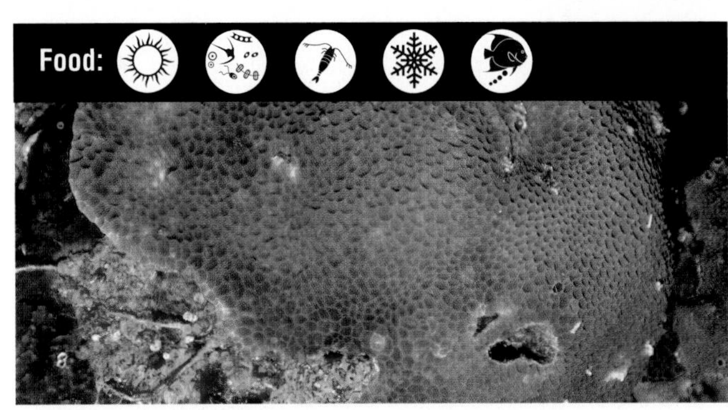

Gardineroseris planulata Solomon Islands.

Gardineroseris planulata Solomon Islands, detail of corallites.

Coeloseris

Pronunciation: SEE-loh-SEER-iss

Common Name: None, but likely to be confused with *Goniastrea, Leptastrea,* or *Favites.*

Region: Western Pacific

Description: Massive or encrusting with cerioid polyps superficially much like *Goniastrea.*

Similar Corals: *Goniastrea retiformis, Leptastrea, Favites.*

Lighting Needs		4 - 9
Water Flow		4 - 8
Aggressiveness		3
Hardiness		6

Placement

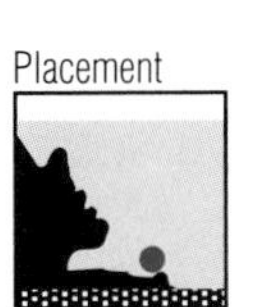

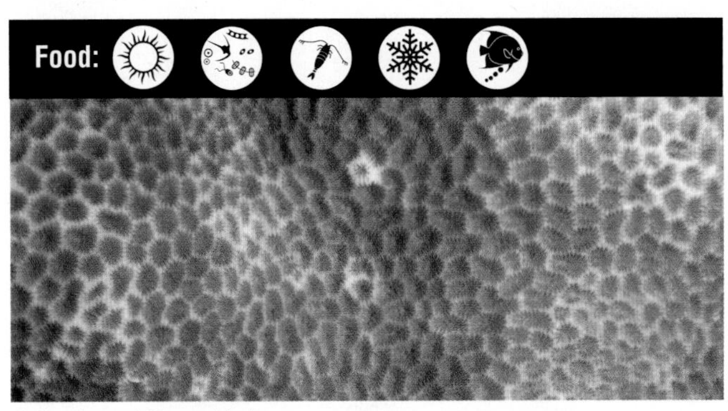

Coeloseris mayeri, Solomon Islands.

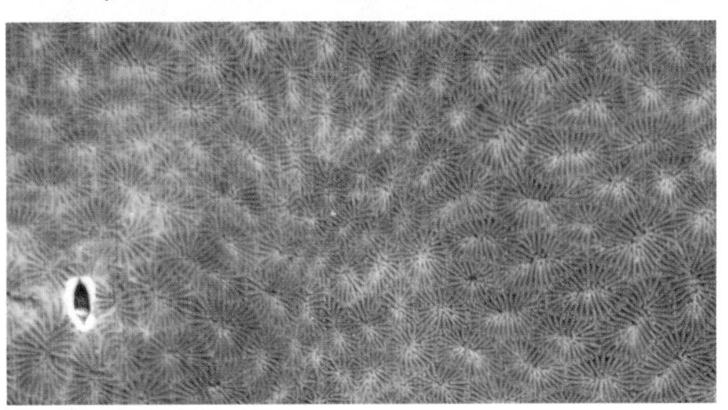

Coeloseris mayeri, Solomon Islands.

Podabacia

Pronunciation: POH-duh-BAY-see-uh

Common Name: Plate Coral

Region: Red Sea to south central Pacific

Description: Encrusting thin laminar unifacial colonies. Typically very pale cream color, sometimes yellow or greenish. Broken sheets may be found free living on loose rubble.

Similar Corals: Free living pieces may be confused with *Halomitra pileus* or *Sandalolitha robusta*, which have similar corallite shape. *Lithophyllon* has the same colony form, but is smaller and usually more darkly pigmented.

Lighting Needs	3 - 8
Water Flow	3 - 9
Aggressiveness	3
Hardiness	7

Placement

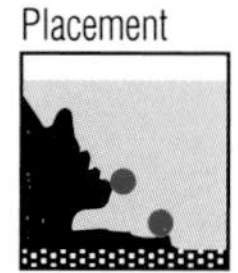

Food:

A free-living *Podabacia* sp. at Hagenbecks Tierpark, Hamburg, Germany.

Typical laminar growth of *Podabacia crustacea*, Red Sea. Photographed at Coral World, Eilat.

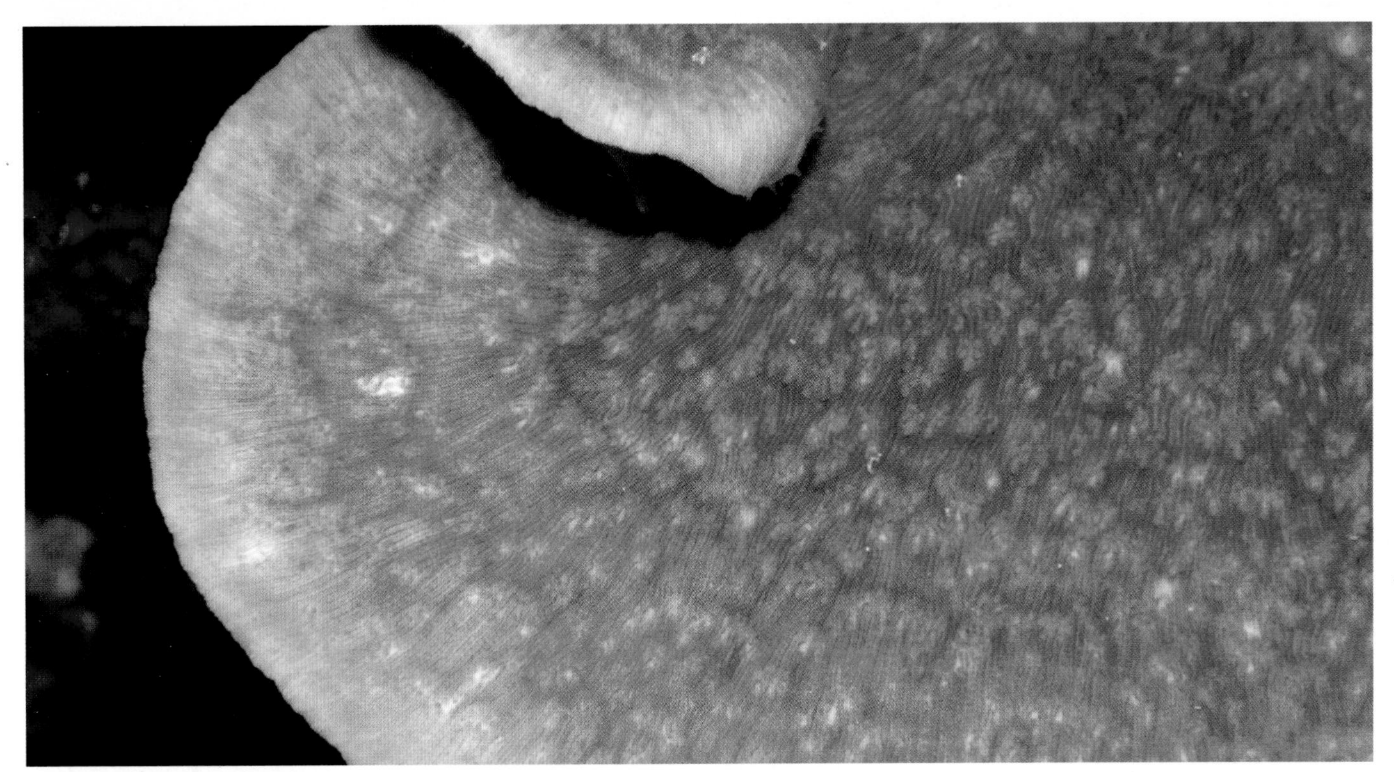

Podabacia motuporensis, Solomon Islands.

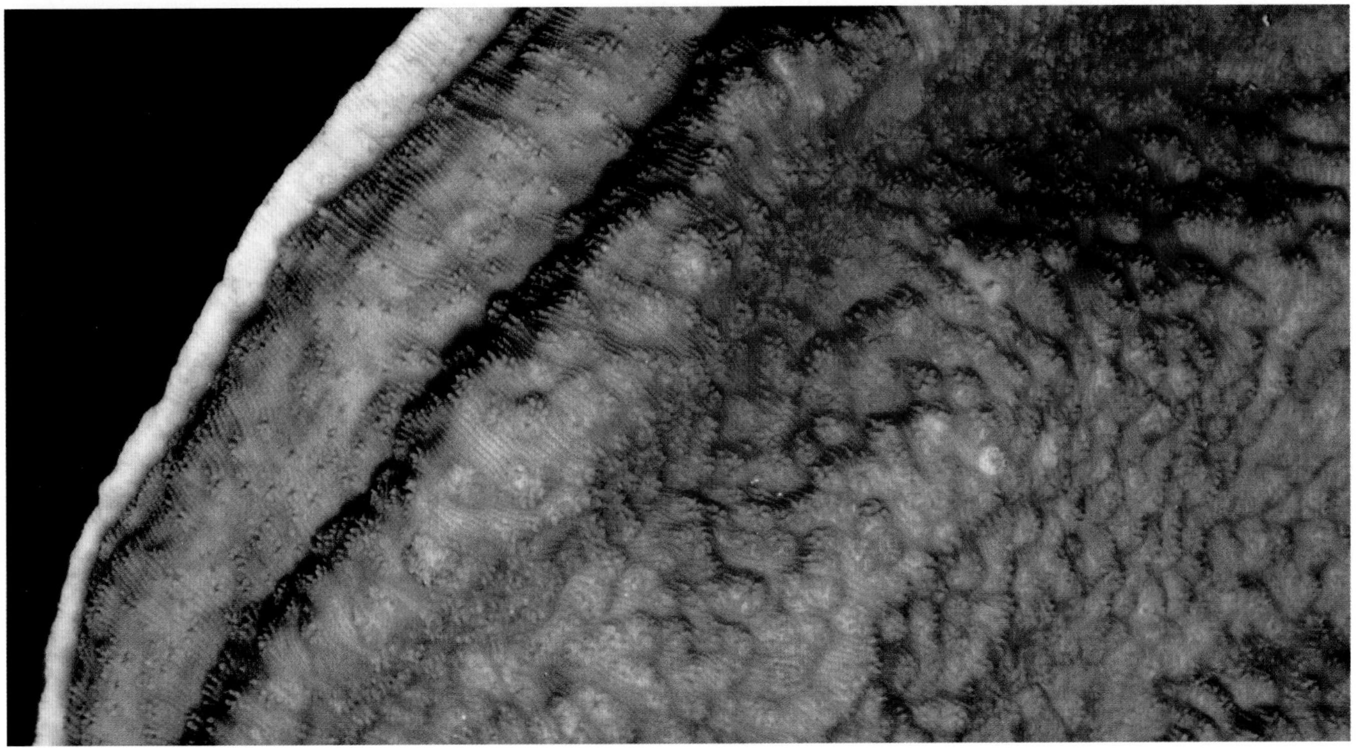

Podabacia motuporensis, Solomon Islands.

Halomitra

Pronunciation: HAL-o-MY-tra

Common Name: Helmet coral, Bonnet coral, Mushroom coral, Dome coral, Plate Coral

Region: East Africa to the central Pacific

Description: Dome shaped free-living colonies with a thin skeleton and widely spaced corallites. No axial furrow. Colour is typically brown with bright pink or purple margin. Mouth areas often whitish, contrasting with the brown.

Similar Corals: Most similar to *Sandalolitha*, but has a less dense skeleton with polyps more widely spaced, and more prominent septo-costae. Free-living *Podabacia* pieces strongly resemble *Halomitra*.

Lighting Needs	4 - 8
Water Flow	1 - 9
Aggressiveness	3
Hardiness	8

Placement

Halomitra pileus, aquarium photo. Compare to the free-living *Podabacia*.

Halomitra pileus has a thin skeleton which breaks easily. This specimen has reproduced vegetatively by breaking.

Sandalolitha
Pronunciation: SAN-duh-lo-LEE-thuh

Common Name: Helmet coral, Mushroom coral, Dome coral, Plate Coral

Region: Western Pacific to central Pacific

Description: Free-living dome shaped or circular colonies with a thick skeleton and closely spaced corallites. No axial furrow. Colour is typically brown or green, sometimes with bright pink or purple margin. Mouth areas often whitish.

Similar Corals: *Halomitra* spp. have more widely spaced corallites and a thinner skeletal construction. Compared to *S. robusta*, *Sandalolitha dentata* has longer and sharper teeth on the septa (Hoeksema, 1989). The diference between *Sandalolitha* and *Halomitra* seems much like the difference between *Lithactinia* and *Polyphyllia.*

Lighting Needs		4 - 8
Water Flow		1 - 9
Aggressiveness		4
Hardiness		8

Green *Sandalolitha robusta* on a protected, level reef slope. Solomon Islands.

Sandalolitha robusta surface detail. Solomon Islands.

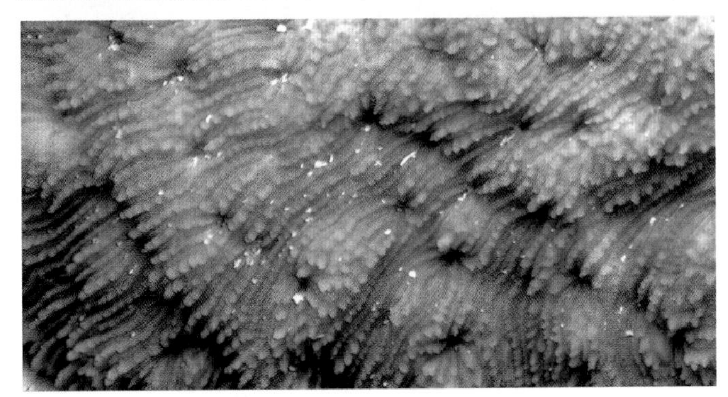

Sandalolitha dentata surface detail. Solomon Islands.

Typical color form of *Sandalolitha robusta* on a steep reef slope. Solomon Islands.

Polyphyllia
Pronunciation: PAW-lee-FILL-ee-uh

Common Name: Slipper coral, Mole coral, Sea mole, Tongue coral, Plate coral

Region: Madagascar to central Pacific at least as far as Samoa.

Description: Free-living elongate, oval, X, or Y - shaped coralla. Axial furrow often indistinct. Corallite centers evenly distributed. Tentacles expand during the day. Two species, *P. talpina* and *P.* (= *Lithactinia*) *novaehiberniae*. A possible 3rd species (see photo) may be just an ecomorph of *P. talpina*.

Similar Corals: *Herpolitha*, which has a more prominent axial furrow and shorter, more sparse tentacles. In aquaria *Herpolitha*'s tentacles may become elongate, making the difference between it and *Polyphyllia* less distinct.

Lighting Needs	3 - 9
Water Flow	1 - 9
Aggressiveness	4
Hardiness	10

Placement

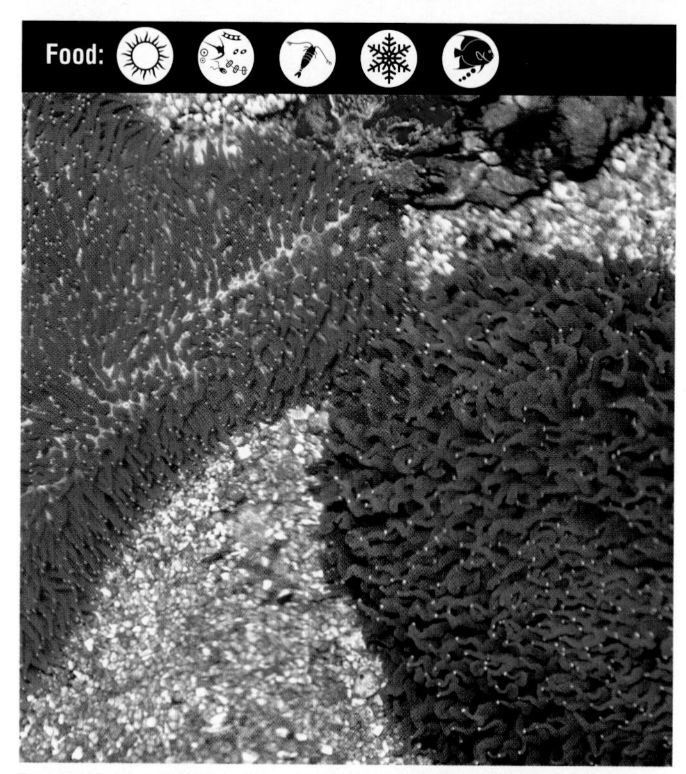

Two species? of *Polyphyllia*. One with broad corallum and fat tentacles, the other narrow & thin.

Lithactinia
Pronunciation: LITH-ack-TIN-ee-uh

Common Name: Helmet coral, Bonnet coral, Dome coral, Sea mole, *Polyphyllia*

Region: Solomon Islands, Fiji, Tonga, Samoa, Far Eastern New Guinea, New Caledonia.

Description: Dome shaped, round, or elongate coralla with thin skeleton. Tentacles expanded during the daytime give furry appearance like *Polyphyllia*. Corallum often with scars showing where breakage occurred, and broken fragments may grow into large coralla without secondary centers.

Similar Corals: Most similar to *Polyphyllia talpina*, which has a heavier skeleton. Their ranges do not overlap. See Lamberts, (1984). Often confused with *Halomitra* because of the shape and thin skeleton. Hoeksema (1989) and Veron (1993) consider *Lithactinia* synonymous with *Polyphyllia*.

Lighting Needs	2 - 8
Water Flow	1 - 8
Aggressiveness	3
Hardiness	6

Placement

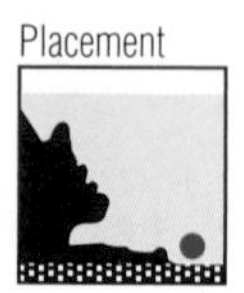

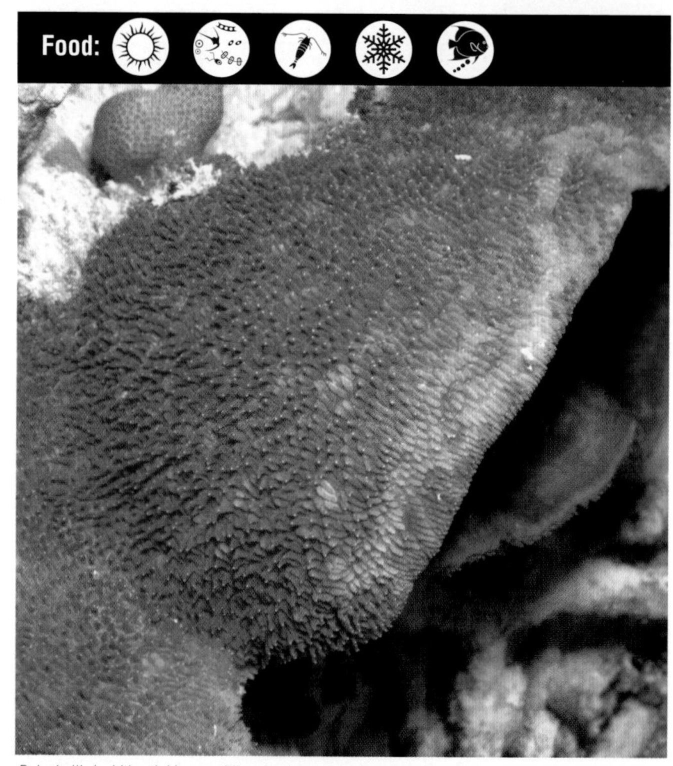

Polyphyllia (= *Lithactinia*) *novaehiberniae*, large unbroken specimen. Solomon Islands.

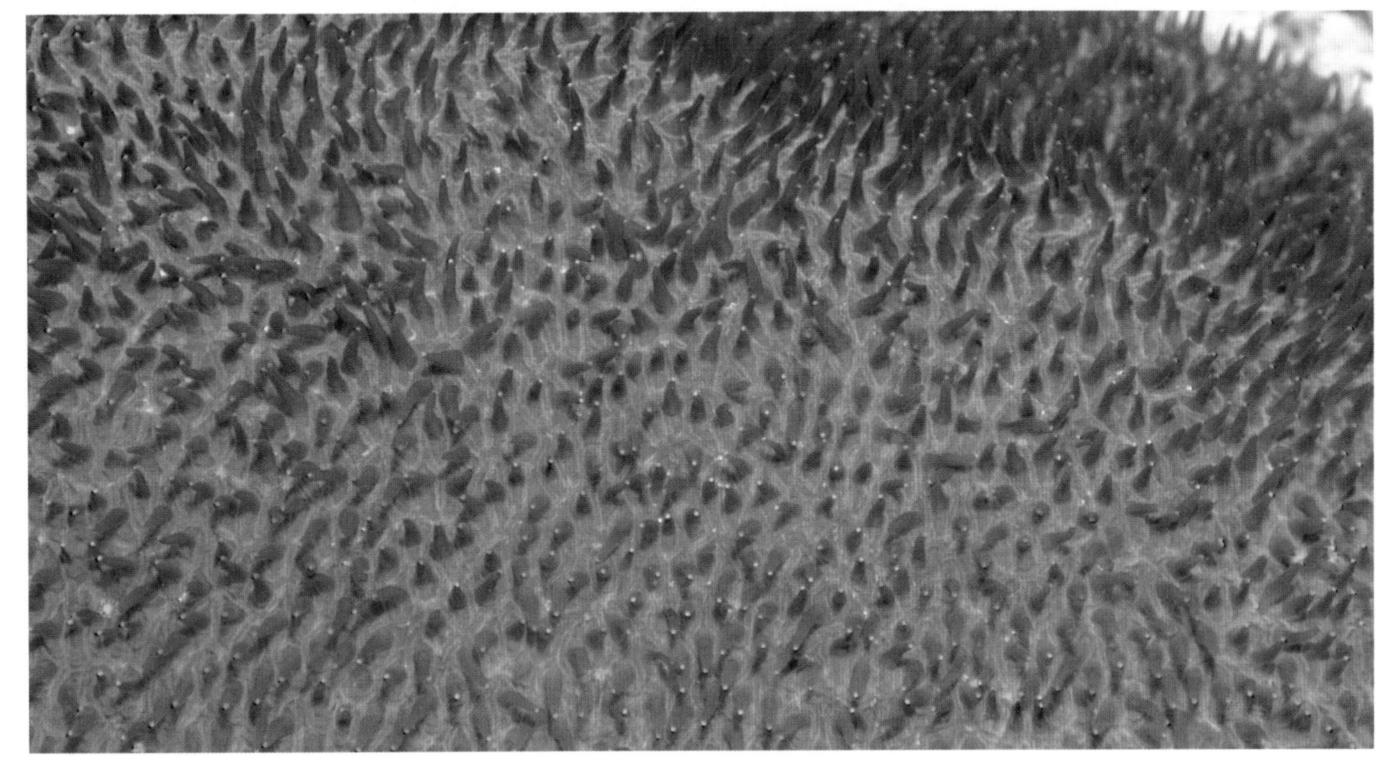

Polyphyllia (= *Lithactinia*) *novaehiberniae*, surface detail of a smaller specimen. Solomon Islands.

Diaseris

Pronunciation: DYE-uh-SEE-riss

Common Name: None

Region: Red Sea to Eastern Pacific

Description: Free-living solitary flat irregular disk shaped corals with thin fragile skeleton that has numerous fracture zones. Commonly with several mouths along zones of fracture. Colonies reproduce asexually by breaking into several wedge-shaped segments.

Similar Corals: Similar to *Cycloseris* spp., which are usually more symmetrical than *Diaseris* and usually have just one central mouth.

Lighting Needs	2 - 8
Water Flow	0 - 9
Aggressiveness	1
Hardiness	8

Placement

Food:

Diaseris distorta from the Galapagos Is. Aquarium photo.

Lithophyllon
Pronunciation: LITH-o-FILL-on

Common Name: Encrusting *Fungia*

Region: Eastern edge of Indian Ocean, Japan, to as far east as Samoa.

Description: Encrusting, laminar, unifacial, usually small colonies with septo-costae similar to those of *Diaseris.* Sometimes forms large colonies.

Similar Corals: Small colonies look like attached *Fungia.* Large colonies are similar to *Podabacia,* which is also encrusting and laminar, but has more prominent septo-costae. *Cantharellus* spp. form similar attached colonies.

Lighting Needs	3 - 8
Water Flow	2 - 10
Aggressiveness	1
Hardiness	6

Placement

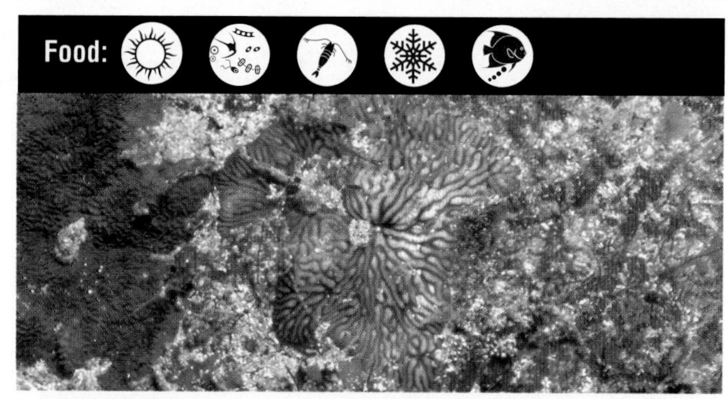

Lithophyllon cf. *mokai* can be confused with *Cantharellus*, Solomon Islands.

Lithophyllon sp. Aquarium photo, Tokyo Sealife Park, Japan.

Cycloseris
Pronunciation: SI-klo-SEE-riss

Common Name: *Fungia,* Mushroom coral, Plate coral

Region: Red Sea to Eastern Pacific

Description: Free-living disk shaped, oval, or dome shaped colonies with a central mouth. The underside is smooth.

Similar Corals: Similar to *Fungia* spp. *Cycloseris* spp. are smaller than *Fungia* spp, and have smoother undersides.

Lighting Needs	2 - 8
Water Flow	0 - 7
Aggressiveness	2
Hardiness	6

Placement

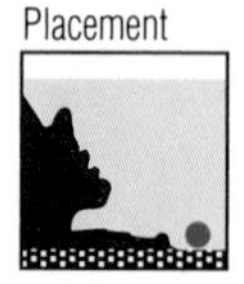

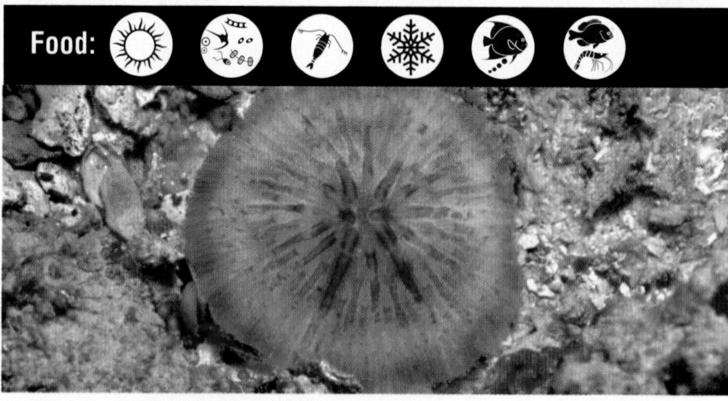

Cycloseris cf. *patelliformis.* Solomon Islands.

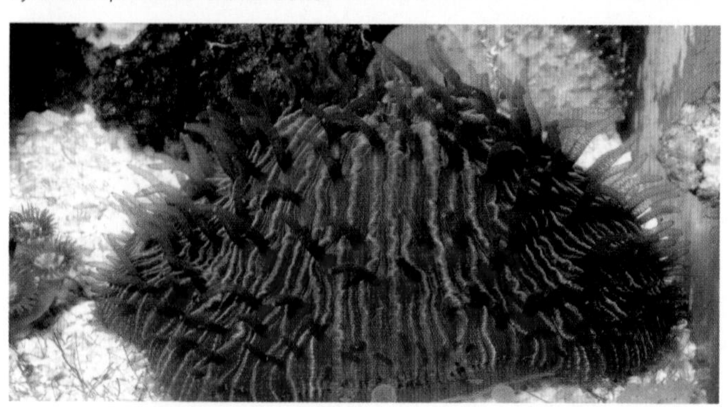

Cycloseris erosa from Indonesia. Aquarium photo.

Fungia granulosa. Solomon Islands.

Fungia granulosa. Small polyps are red, with skeleton like *Cycloseris tenuis*.

Fungia granulosa skeleton.

Cycloseris sp. left, and *Cycloseris patelliformis*, right, from the Solomon Islands.

Small *Fungia* spp. look like *Cycloseris* spp.

Cycloseris cf. *sinensis*. Fiji.

Cycloseris cf. *hexagonalis*

Fungia

Pronunciation: FUN-dgee-uh

Common Name: Plate coral, Mushroom coral

Region: Red Sea and East Africa to central Pacific

Description: Free-living (except juveniles, which begin as attached polyps, and *F. moluccensis*, which is encrusting) flat or dome shaped usually circular or oval colonies with a central mouth. Sometimes elongate.

Similar Corals: Similar to *Cycloseris* and *Herpolitha*.

Lighting Needs	3 - 10
Water Flow	1 - 10
Aggressiveness	4
Hardiness	8

Placement

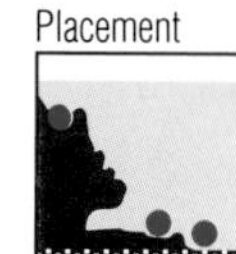

Fungia cf. *klunzingeri*. Solomon Islands.

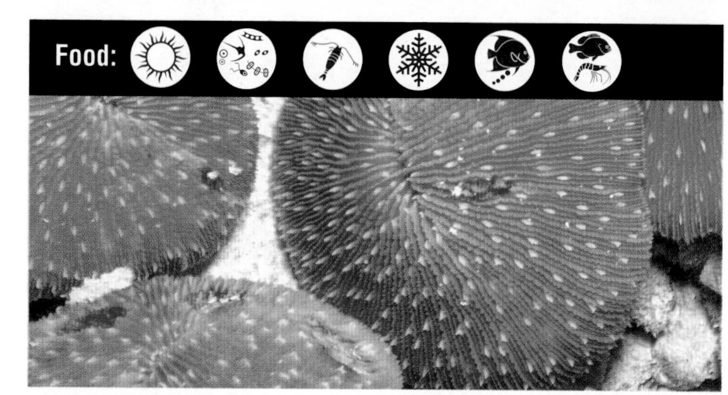

Fungia danai. Solomon Islands.

Fungia spp. Solomon Islands.

The mouth of a colorful *Fungia*.

Herpolitha

Pronunciation: HER-po-LEETH-uh

Common Name: Tongue coral, Slipper coral, Mole coral

Region: Red Sea to South Central Pacific

Description: Colonies elongate, tongue-shaped, with rounded (*H. limax*) or pointed (*H. weberi*) ends. Sometimes shaped like Y, T, or X. Axial furrow with mouths may extend to corallum ends. Secondary mouths sparse on rest of corallum. Primary septa on *H. weberi* are longer.

Similar Corals: Similar to *Polyphyllia*, which has a less distinct axial furrow, secondary centers evenly distributed over its surface, and more numerous, long tentacles all over its surface. In aquaria *Herpolitha* may develop elongate tentacles and become very similar to *Polyphyllia*.

Lighting Needs	3 - 9
Water Flow	1 - 10
Aggressiveness	3
Hardiness	10

Placement

Herpolitha weberi. Aquarium photo. Note development of long tentacles like *Polyphyllia*.

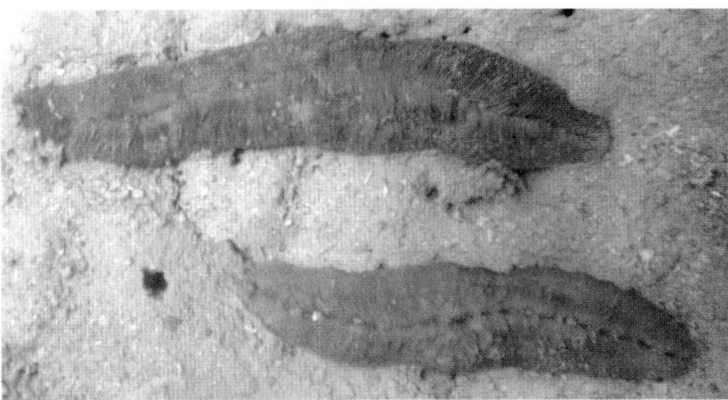

Herpolitha limax. Whitsunday Is., Australia.

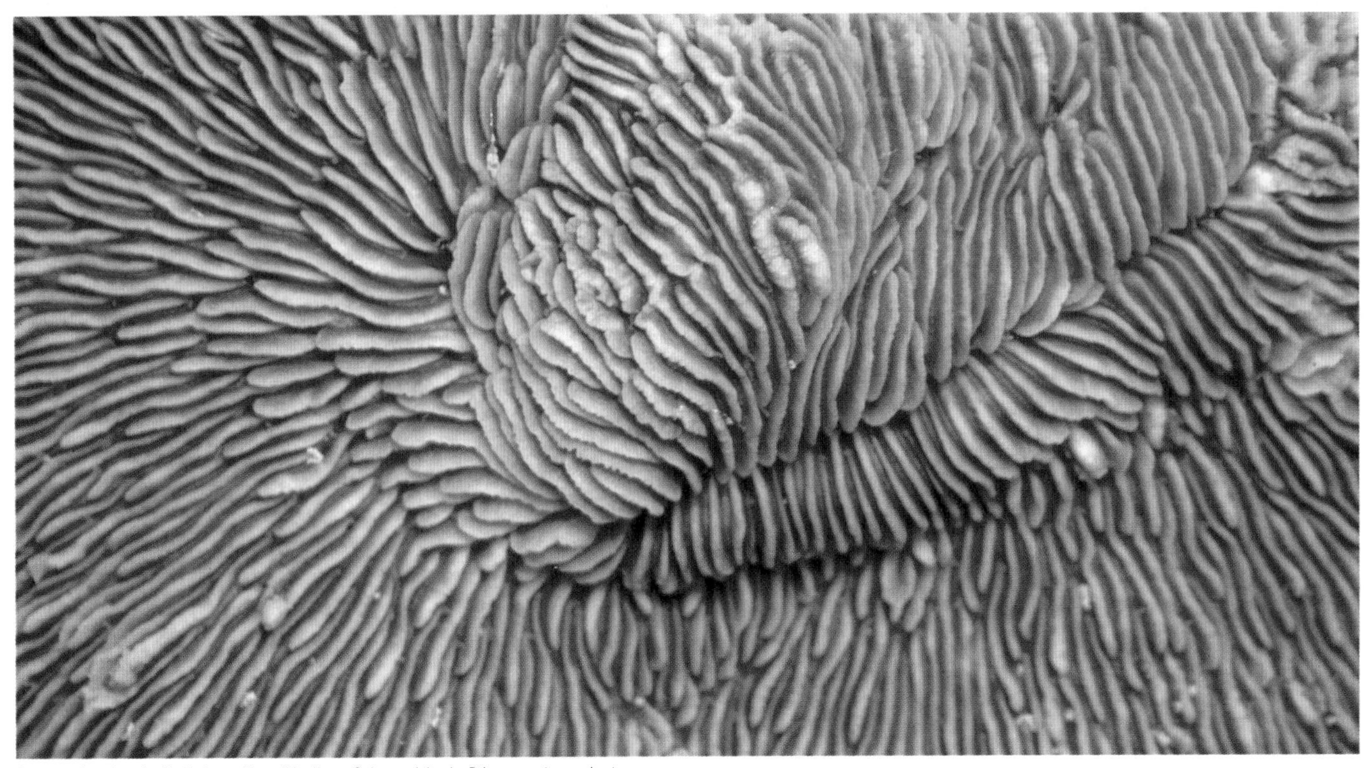

Closeup of surface detail of a large *Herpolitha limax.* Solomon Islands. Primary septa are short.

Ctenactis
Pronunciation: tee-NACK-tiss

Common Name: Tongue coral

Region: Red Sea to Japan and the south central Pacific

Description: Elongate heavy corallum with strongly developed septal teeth and costal spines. *Ctenactis echinata* has a single mouth inside a short axial furrow and *Ctenactis crassa* has several mouths located in an axial furrow that extends almost to the corallum ends. *Ctenactis albitentacula* has distinctive whitish tentacles.

Similar Corals: Similar to *Herpolitha*, but with much more prominent teeth on its surface. Broken or irregularly shaped *C. echinata* are easily mistaken for *Zoopilus echinatus*.

Lighting Needs		3 - 9
Water Flow		2 - 10
Aggressiveness		4
Hardiness		6

Placement

Ctenactis echinata, Solomon Islands. Note characteristic large-toothed septa.

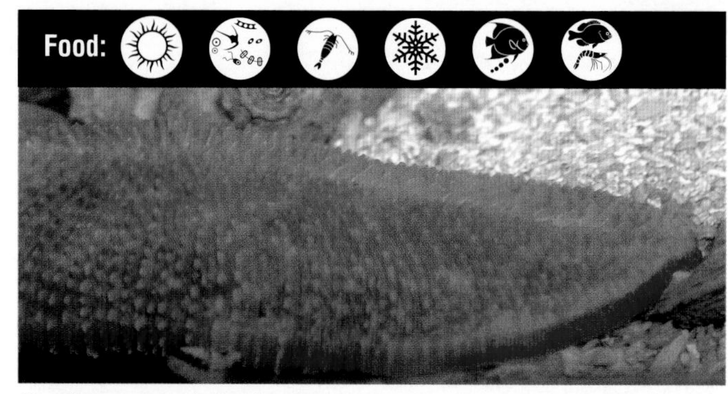

Ctenactis crassa, Indonesia. Aquarium photo.

Ctenactis albitentaculata, Solomon Islands.

Zoopilus

Pronunciation: zo-PY-luss

Common Name: Plate coral

Region: Western Pacific to at least as far east as the Marshall Islands and Fiji, but rare or absent from Australia.

Description: Free living disks or domes with *Ctenactis*-like spines. The skeletal construction is quite thin and brittle. In some locations *Zoopilus echinatus* forms dense congregations of small individuals produced asexually by breakage. The skeletons show the fractures, with regrowth of septa in new directions. In other locations *Zoopilus echinatus* forms large solitary domes similar in appearance to *Halomitra*.

Similar Corals: *Halomitra, Ctenactis, Lithactinia*

Lighting Needs	2 - 8
Water Flow	2 - 8
Aggressiveness	2
Hardiness	6

Placement

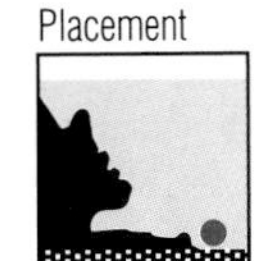

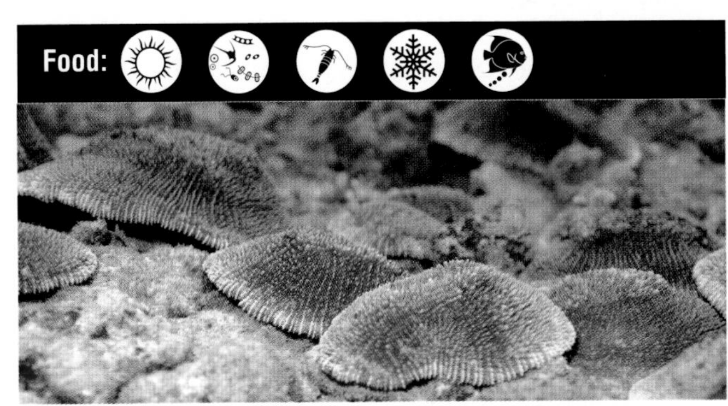

Reef slope shingle of living and dead *Zoopilus*, shown to the author by Dr. Bruce Carlson. Suva, Fiji.

The skeleton of *Zoopilus echinatus*.

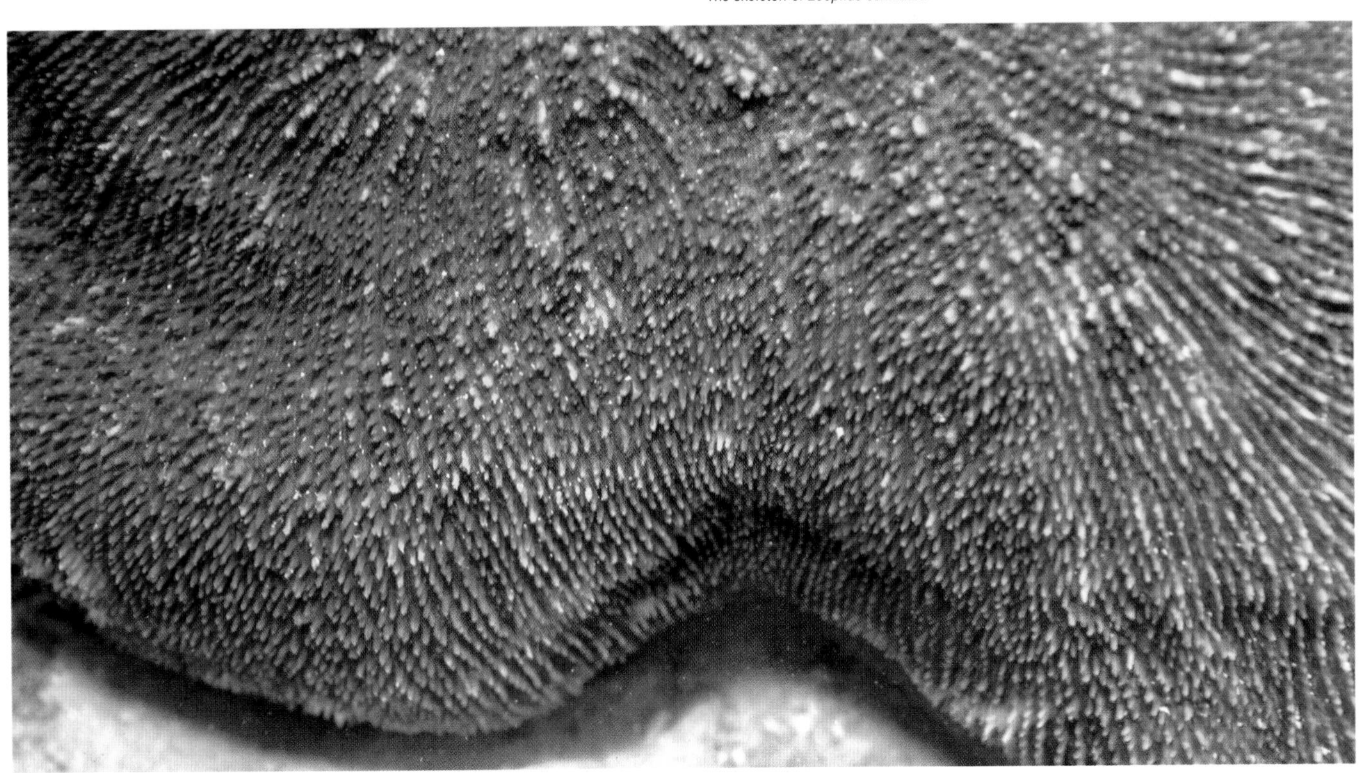

Portion of a very large *Zoopilus*. Solomon Is.

Heliofungia
Pronunciation: HEE-lee-o-FUN-dgee-uh

Common Name: Plate coral,

Region: Southeastern Indian Ocean to Western Pacific, Australia north to the Ryukyu Islands.

Description: Solitary free-living flat plate with large central mouth and long tubular tentacles with pale or brightly colored tips. Juveniles are attached.

Similar Corals: The skeleton is very similar to *Fungia* spp., but the polyp is most similar to *Euphyllia* spp. It is the author's opinion that *Heliofungia actiniformis* is more closely related to *Euphyllia* spp. than to *Fungia* spp. The opinion that *Heliofungia* might be a free-living relative of *Euphyllia* spp. contradicts the current taxonomic placement of this genus.

Lighting Needs	4 - 9
Water Flow	2 - 8
Aggressiveness	4
Hardiness	5

Placement
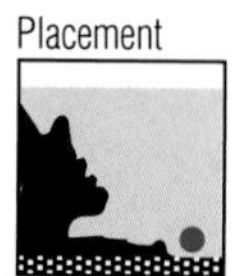

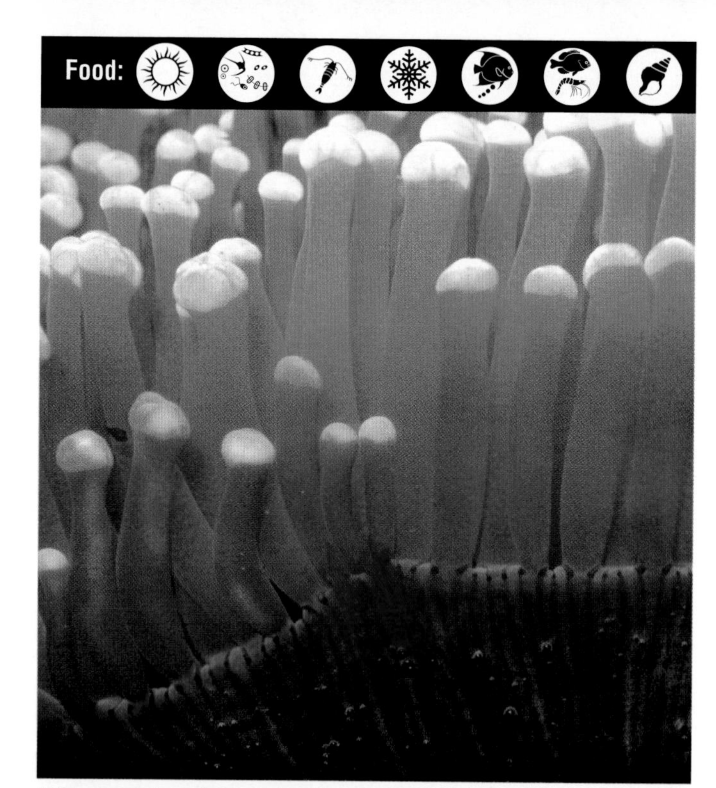

Heliofungia actiniformis photographed against the front glass of an aquarium.

Heliofungia actiniformis, Solomon Islands.

Heliofungia actiniformis with tentacles like *Euphyllia divisa.* Musee Oceanographique de Monaco.

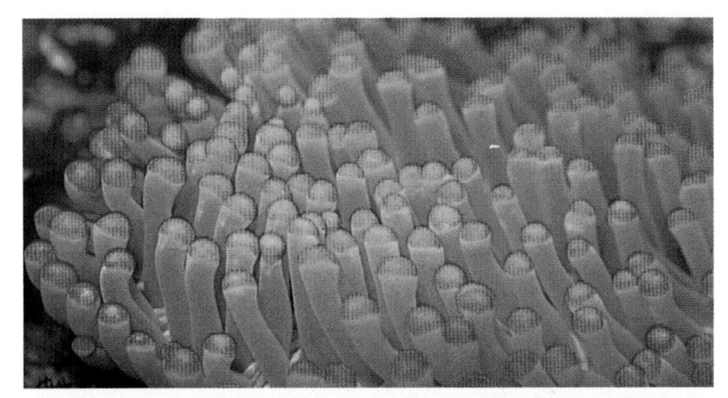

Heliofungia actiniformis with pink-tipped tentacles, like *Catalaphyllia jardinei.* Aquarium photo.

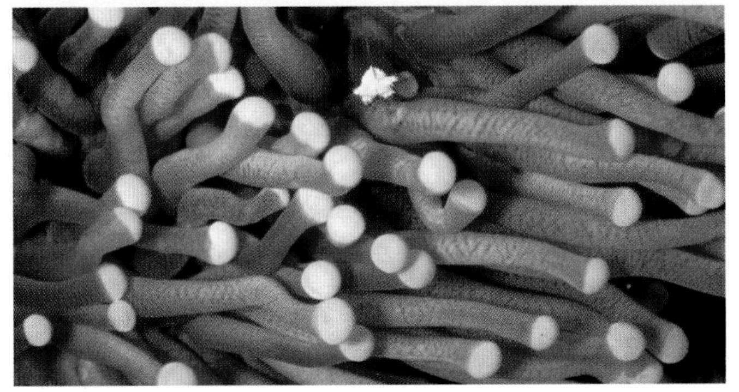

Heliofungia actiniformis often harbours commensal shrimps.

Heliofungia actiniformis, small polyps still attached. Compare to *Euphyllia glabrescens*, below.

Euphyllia

Pronunciation: yu-FILL-ee-uh

Common Name: Torch coral, Hammer coral, Anchor coral, Frogspawn coral, Fine Grape coral, Whiskers

Region: Red Sea to Samoa

Description: Phaceloid to flabello-meandroid colonies with large polyps expanded during the daytime. The distinctions between species is unclear as the skeletons are often the same, and polyp characters may be shared or mixed.

Similar Corals: *Euphyllia* spp. are similar to *Plerogyra, Nemenzophyllia, Catalaphyllia,* and *Heliofungia.*

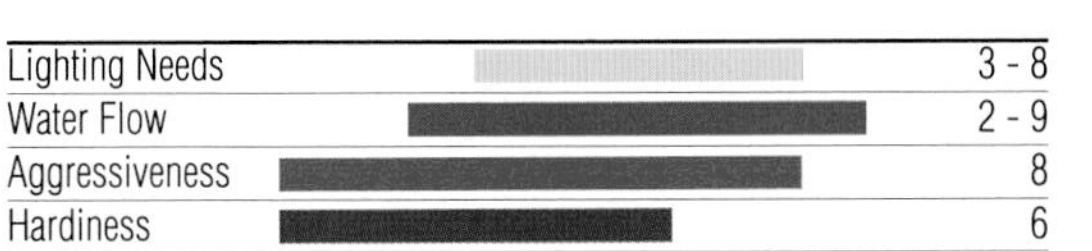

Placement

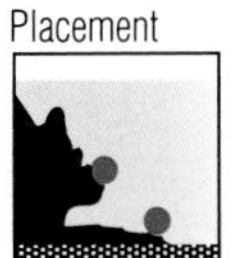

Euphyllia glabrescens from Indonesia. Aquarium photo.

Euphyllia glabrescens, showing typical skeleton. Aquarium Photo, Aquatropics, New Jersey.

E. glabrescens with flabellomeandroid skeleton. The skeleton of this specimen is like that of *E. ancora*.

Portrait of a strikingly colored *Euphyllia glabrescens*. Solomon Islands.

A new species of *Euphyllia*. The polyps are similar to but smaller than *E. glabrescens*. Note skeleton.

A green specimen of the new species of *Euphyllia*. Aquarium Photo, Aquatropics, New Jersey.

Euphyllia cristata. Solomon Is. During the day it resembles *Eusmilia fastigiata* from the Caribbean.

The same colony at night with polyps expanded. Now it resembles *E. glabrescens*.

Another apparently new species of *Euphyllia*, similar to *E. glabrescens*. The polyps are remarkably similar to those of *Duncanopsammia axifuga* ! See Putterbaugh and Borneman, (1996). Aquarium Photo.

A perfect mimic of *Duncanopsammia axifuga*, this *Euphyllia* sp. has not been described.

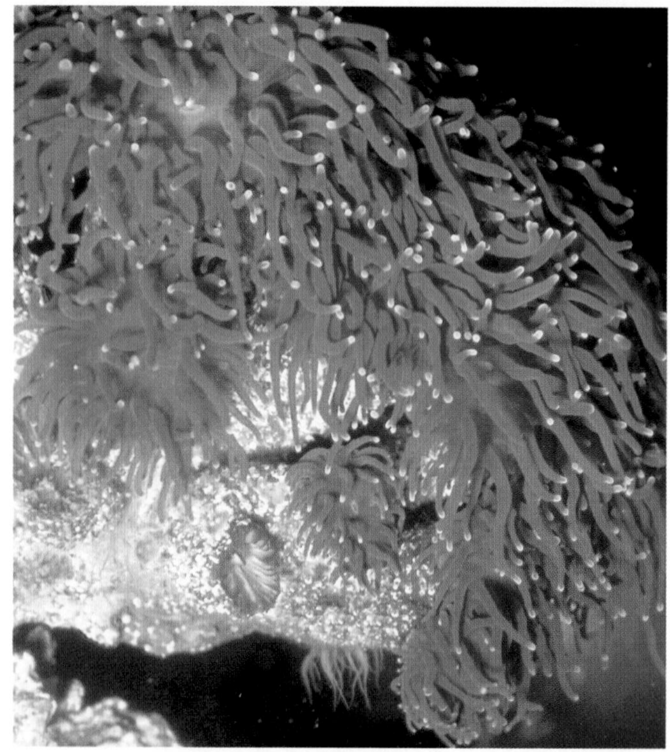

A large colony of the same *Euphyllia* sp., note skeleton. Aquarium photo, Long Beach Aquarium.

Euphyllia parancora from Indonesia. Aquarium photo. Note thin tubular corallites.

Distinctive polyp of the fine-branched *Euphyllia parancora*. Note striped oral disc, like *Heliofungia*.

Euphyllia parancora from Indonesia. Aquarium photo.

Euphyllia paradivisa has polyps like *E. divisa*, but a phacelloid skeleton.

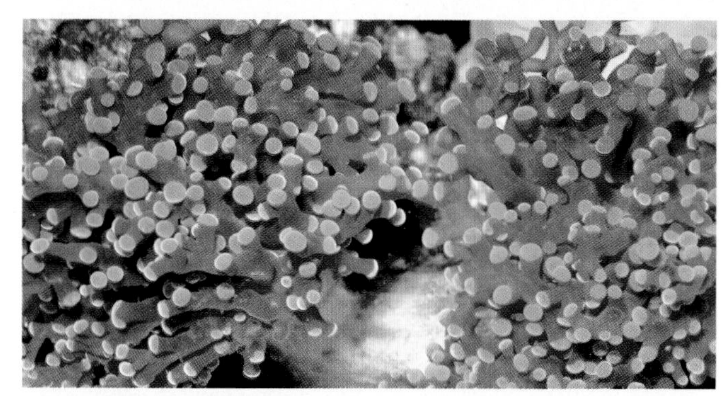

Euphyllia paradivisa, polyps expanded.

A rare phacelloid form of *Euphyllia ancora*. Compare to *E. parancora*. The skeleton is like *E. paradivisa*.

Colony with "hybrid" polyps like both *Euphyllia parancora* and *E. paradivisa*. The skeleton is like *E. parancora*.

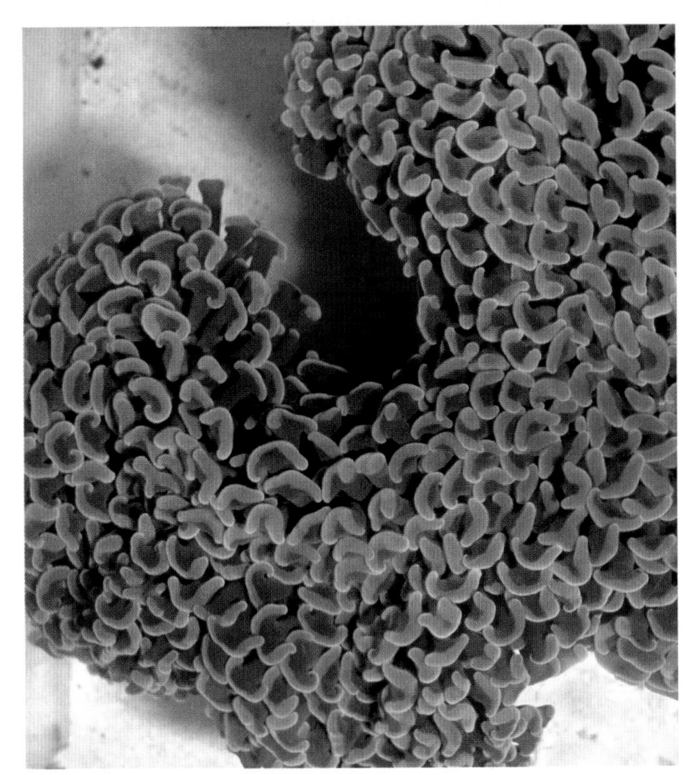

Euphyllia ancora. Note flabellomeandroid skeleton.

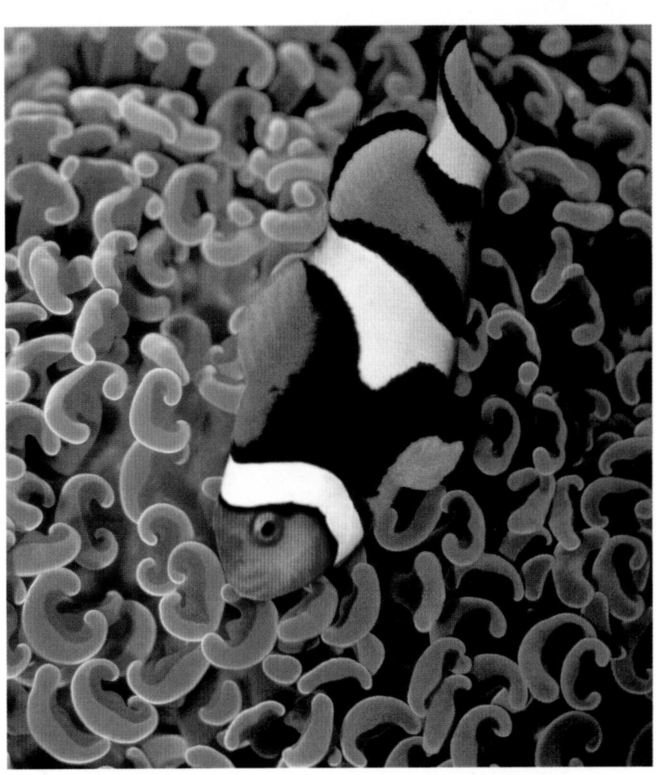

A Percula clownfish adopts *Euphyllia ancora* as a substitute host "anemone" in an aquarium.

"Mish-mosh." *Euphyllia ancora* and *E. divisa* characteristics in the polyps of two adjacent colonies.

Euphyllia divisa has among the most beautiful of all polyps with its translucent "frogspawn" tentacles.

Euphyllia yaeyamaensis has a phacelloid skeleton and more compact tentacles than *E. paradivisa*.

Euphyllia yaeyamaensis, Solomon Islands.

Catalaphyllia
Pronunciation: kuh-TAH-luh-FILL-ee-uh

Common Name: Elegance, Wonder, Ridge coral

Region: Aldabra Is. in the Indian Ocean to southern Japan and Vanuatu.

Description: Flabellomeandroid colonies typically free-living or embedded in soft substrates. Small specimens with cone-shaped skeleton. Valleys are deeply v-shaped. Polyp is large and fleshy with long tubular tentacles with pale, often bright pink ball-shaped tips.

Similar Corals: *Heliofungia actiniformis* and *Euphyllia glabrescens* also have tubular tentacles with ball-shaped tips. *Catalaphyllia jardinei* has color forms (grey with white tips and brown with yellow tips) that match *H. actiniformis* and *E. glabrescens*.

Lighting Needs	3 - 8
Water Flow	2 - 8
Aggressiveness	8
Hardiness	8

Placement

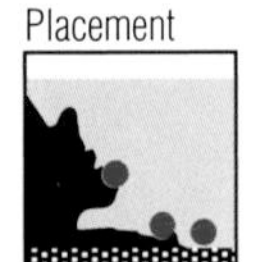

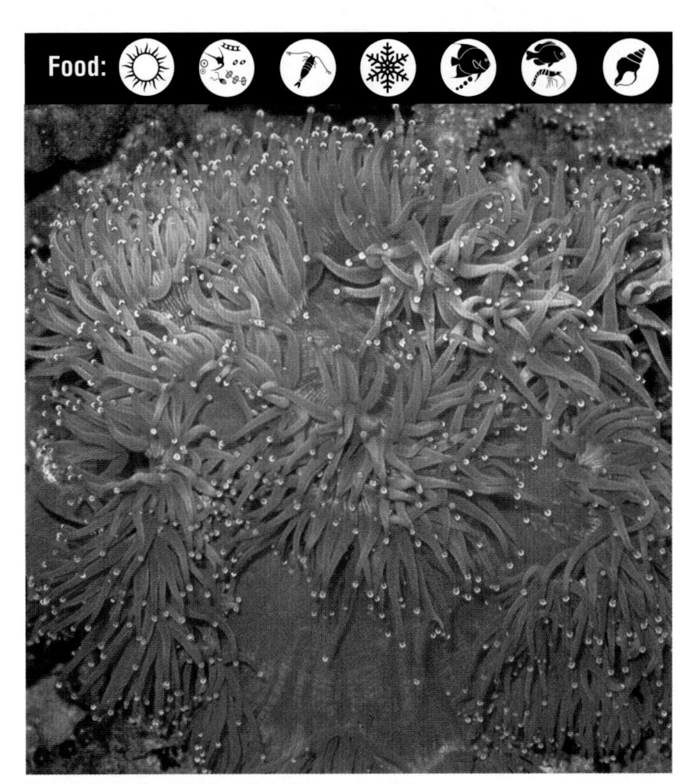

The typical coloration of *Catalaphyllia jardinei*, aquarium photo.

C. jardinei with bifurcated tentacles like those of *Euphyllia divisa*.

Catalaphyllia jardinei, partially contracted. Aquarium photo. Note flabellomeandroid skeleton.

Plerogyra

Pronunciation: PLEH-ro-JAI-ruh

Common Name: Bubble coral, Grape coral, Octobubble

Region: Red Sea, Indian Ocean to central Pacific.

Description: Colonies flabellomeandroid or phaceloid with large, smooth-edged exsert septa. Polyps extend grape-like vesicles during the day, tentacles expand at night.

Similar Corals: *Physogyra*, which has a meandroid colony form and smaller vesicles

Lighting Needs	3 - 8
Water Flow	0 - 5
Aggressiveness	7
Hardiness	8

Placement

Plerogyra cf. *eurysepta*, Solomon Islands.

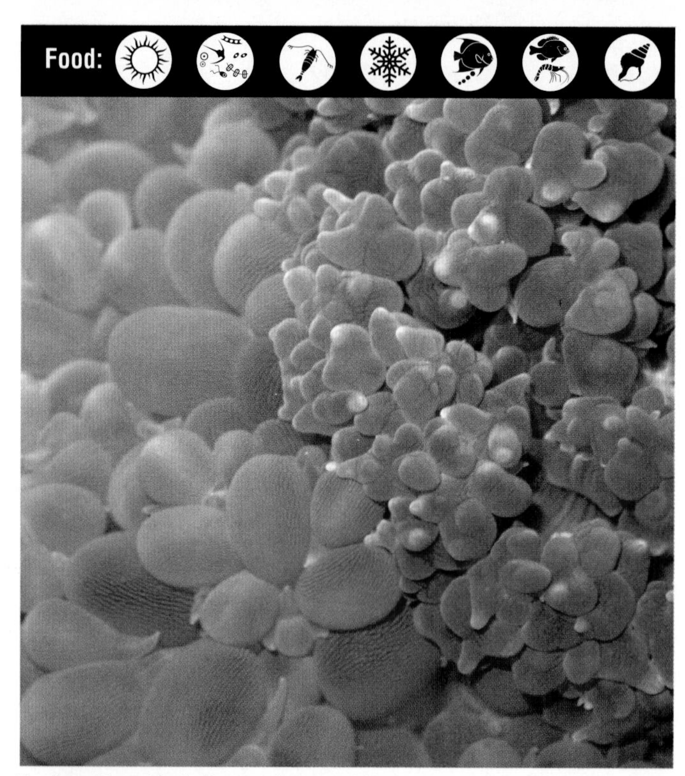

The shape of the vesicles in *Plerogyra sinuosa* is variable.

Fluorescent green *Plerogyra sinuosa*. Aquarium photo.

Night-time appearance of *Plerogyra sinuosa*, feeding tentacles expanded. Aquarium photo.

Plerogyra sinuosa. Eilat Israel. A large flabellomeandroid colony.

Plerogyra cf. *simplex.* Aquarium Center, Randallstown, Maryland.

Plerogyra cf. *simplex.* Skeleton similar to the mystery "*Physogyra.*" Aquarium photo.

P. simplex skeleton, quite like *Nemenzophyllia.*

Damaged flabellomeandroid *P. simplex.*

Physogyra

Pronunciation: FI-zo-JAI-ruh

Common Name: Bubble coral, Grape coral, Octobubble

Region: Red Sea, Indian Ocean to central Pacific.

Description: Meandroid massive or laminar colonies. Space between valleys is (usually) filled with lightweight very porous coenosteum. Bubble-like vesicles extended during the day, tentacles extend at night. *Physogyra exerta* has tubular rather than bubble shaped vesicles.

Similar Corals: Similar to *Plerogyra*

Lighting Needs	3 - 9
Water Flow	3 - 8
Aggressiveness	6
Hardiness	5

Placement

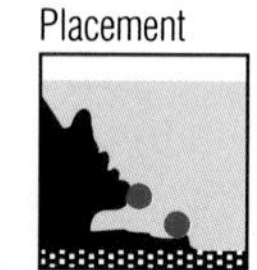

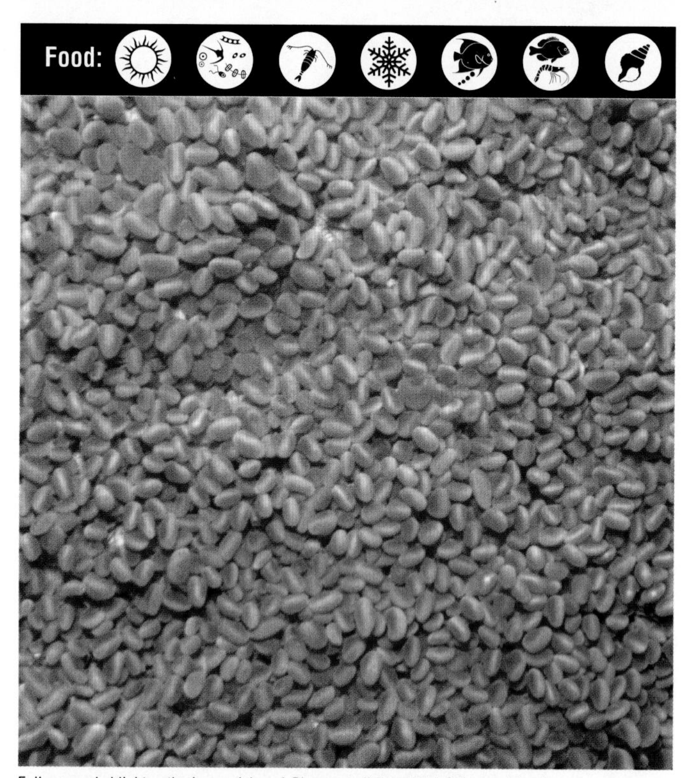

Fully expanded light-gathering vesicles of *Physogyra lichtensteini*, Solomon Islands.

Physogyra exerta, polyps contracted. Solomon Islands.

Physogyra exerta has elongated tubular vesicles. Solomon Islands.

Physogyra lichtensteini. Note the appearance of the meandroid polyps. Solomon Islands.

Physogyra lichtensteini, feeding tentacles expanded at night. Solomon Islands.

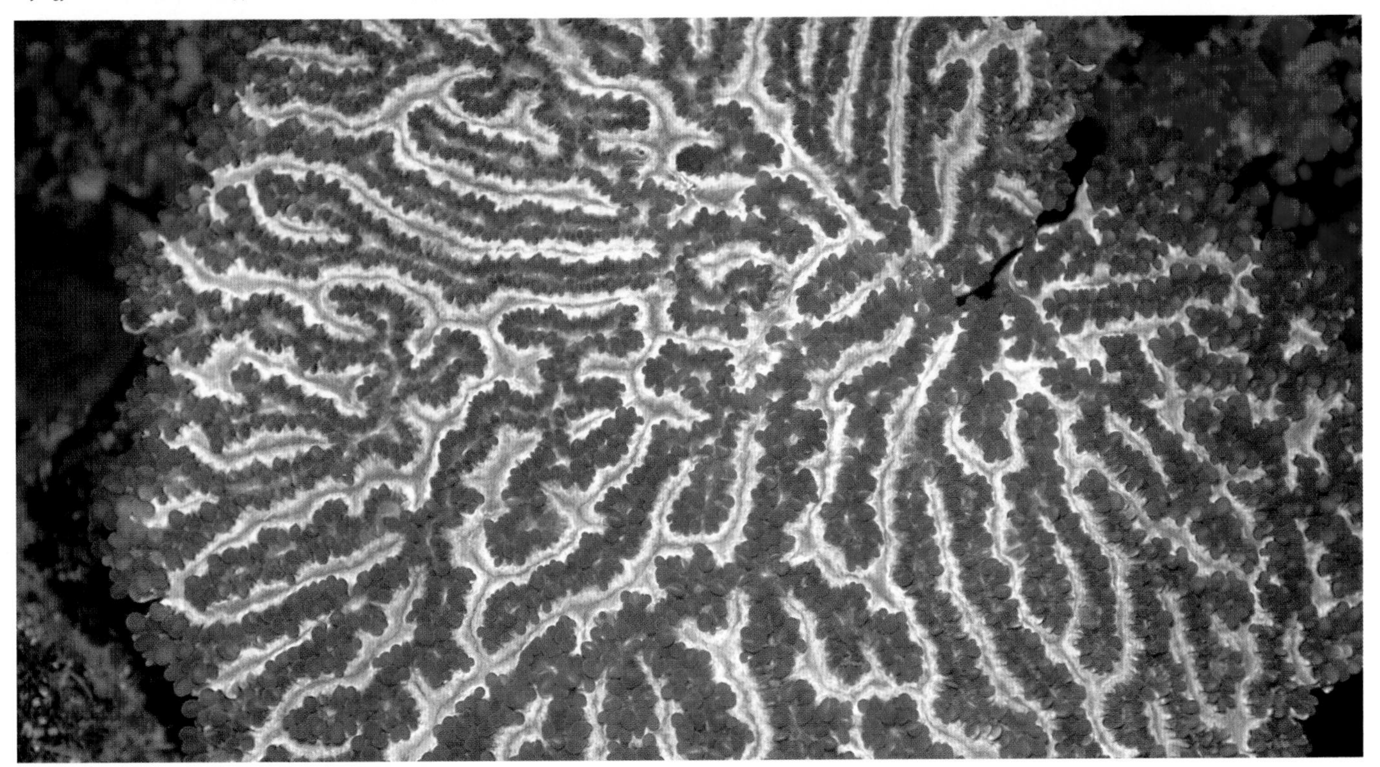

Physogyra sp. on a reef wall in the Solomon Islands.

Mystery coral: A new *Physogyra* species or new genus. To fully appreciate how not-*Plerogyra*-like this coral is, one must have a sense of scale. Note the mangrove leaves around this colony.

The mystery coral seems to be a *Physogyra* without the characteristic blistery coenosteum.

Closeup of the colony above, with greenish color. Note septa visible in each vesicle, as in *Physogyra*.

Closeup of the colony at bottom left. The fully expanded polyps of this mystery coral have small vesicles, more like *Physogyra* than *Plerogyra*. Solomon Islands.

Polyps contracted to reveal a skeleton with form similar to that of *Nemenzophyllia* and virtually identical to *Plerogyra simplex*.

Nemenzophyllia

Pronunciation: ne-MEN-zo-FILL-ee-uh

Common Name: Fox Coral, Ridge Coral

Region: Philippines, Indonesia, New Guinea, Solomon Is.

Description: *Nemenzophyllia turbida* has a thin, approximately 1 cm wide skeleton with flabello-meandroid growth. The walls are very fragile and paper thin. When the polyp is expanded it looks like a corallimorpharian. It has no tentacles at all, and a mantle-like surface. The mouths are numerous along the central portion of the meandering polyp. When fully expanded the polyp becomes "fluffy" looking, and some areas may be so swollen that they appear almost like the inflated ribs on a beach raft.

Similar corals: The skeleton is essentially identical with that of a species of *Plerogyra*, and the unidentified new species of *Physogyra* shown in this book.

Lighting Needs	2 - 7
Water Flow	0 - 3
Aggressiveness	3
Hardiness	7

Placement

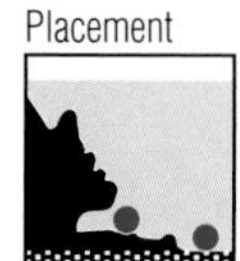

Nemenzophyllia turbida, Solomon Islands.

Nemenzophyllia turbida and *Plerogyra sinuosa*, aquarium photo.

Skeleton of *Nemenzophyllia turbida*.

Nemenzophyllia turbida, with commensal shrimp. Solomon Islands.

Meandrina
Pronunciation: MEE-an-DRY-nuh

Common Name: Butterprint Brain coral

Region: Caribbean, Brazil

Description: Colonies massive, columnar, or free-living with meandroid corallites. One form is laminar in shallow water and columnar in deep clear water. It has narrower valleys than mound form, probably a separate species. There are two free living forms, f. *danae*, which has a continuous central valley and f. *brasiliensis*, which does not.

Similar Corals: Free-living colonies resemble *Manicina*. In aquaria the free-living forms develop a mop of tentacles that remain expanded during the day, making them look very much like *Polyphyllia*.

Lighting Needs	3 - 9
Water Flow	3 - 9
Aggressiveness	6
Hardiness	7

Placement

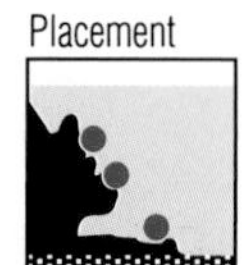

Meandrina meandrites f. *danae.*

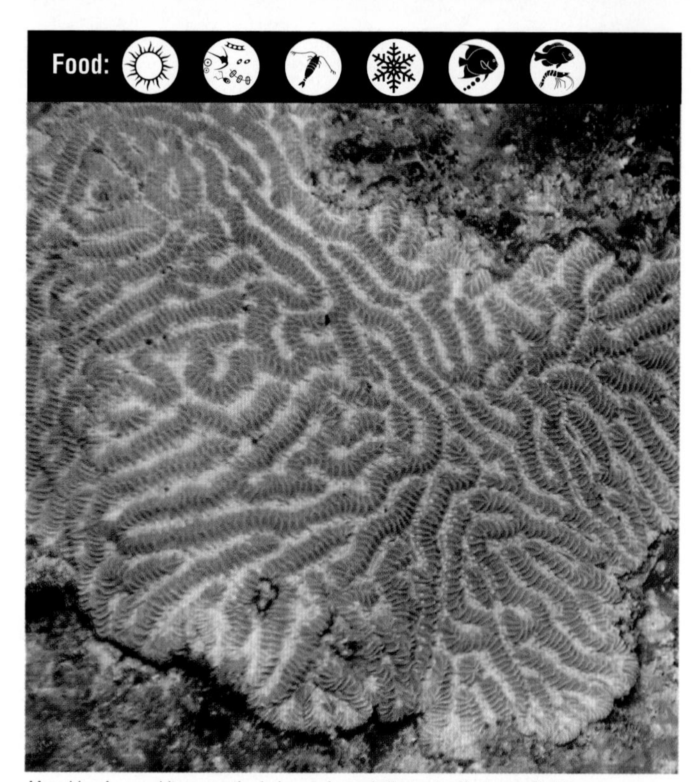

Meandrina cf. *meandrites* encrusting/columnar form, shallow water. Key Largo, Florida.

Meandrina cf. *meandrites* encrusting/columnar form, deep water. Nassau, Bahamas.

Meandrina cf. *meandrites* mound form, shallow water. Key Largo, Florida.

Meandrina cf. *meandrites* polyps expanded at night.

Eusmillia

Pronunciation: yooz-MILL-ee-uh

Common Name: Flower coral, Smooth Flower coral

Region: Caribbean

Description: Phacelloid to Flabellomeandroid colonies with polyps very similar in behavior and form to those of *Meandrina meandrites*. The current taxonomical status of this coral is in the Family Caryophylliidae. In the author's opinion this coral belongs in the Meandrinidae, and so in this book it is placed adjacent to *Meandrina*.

Similar Corals: The skeleton is similar to *Plerogyra simplex* from the Indo-Pacific. The living coral is most like *Meandrina meandrites*.

Lighting Needs	3 - 8
Water Flow	4 - 9
Aggressiveness	3
Hardiness	5

Placement

Eusmillia fastigiata.

Gyrosmilia

Pronunciation: JAI-ro-ZMILL-ee-uh

Common Name: Brain coral

Region: Red Sea primarily, but also reported from a single specimen in Japan (Veron, 1993). May be more widely distributed.

Description: Encrusting to massive meandroid colonies.

Similar Corals: Similar to *Meandrina meandrites* from the Caribbean. *Gyrosmilia* has more narrow valleys. There is a small, encrusting, darkly pigmented shallow water form that lives in shaded regions on vertical walls in the vicinity of Eilat. It may be an ecomorph only, or a separate species.

Lighting Needs	3 - 8
Water Flow	3 - 9
Aggressiveness	6
Hardiness	7

Placement

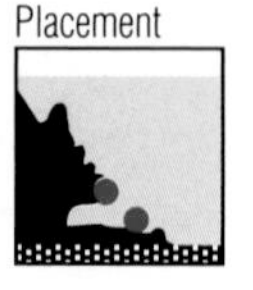

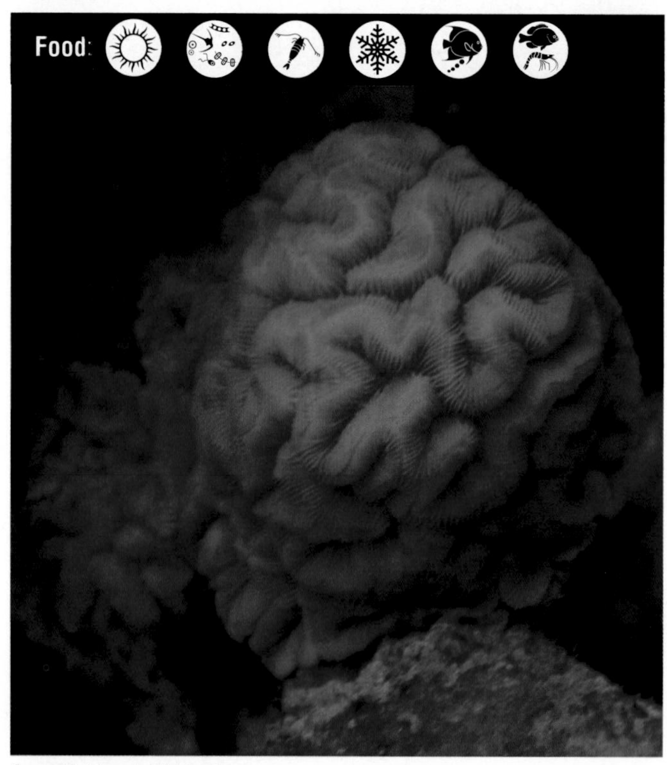

Gyrosmilia interrupta, Eilat, Israel.

Dichocoenia

Pronunciation: DI-ko-SEE-nee-uh

Common Name: Star Coral, Elliptical Star coral

Region: Caribbean

Description: Small dome shaped massive colonies. Columnar or laminar in deep water. Corallites plocoid, to submeandroid. Two species are commonly observed, *D. stokesii* and *D. stellaris.* The latter has smaller polyps with fewer septa. Some authorities consider the two species synonymous. The author considers them distinct. *D. stokesii* is highly varible. A rare giant form in the Florida Keys may be an undescribed species. Another form has cerioid polyps. See photos.

Similar Corals: Small *D. stokesii* may be confused with *Favia fragum.*

Lighting Needs	4 - 9
Water Flow	3 - 9
Aggressiveness	2
Hardiness	7

Placement

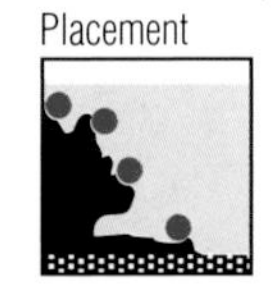

Typical *Dichocoenia stokesii.* New Providence Is., Bahamas.

Dichocoenia stellaris. Key Largo, Florida.

An atypical *Dichocoenia stokesii,* with elongate polyps. New Providence Is., Bahamas.

Dichocoenia cf. *stokesii* special form with cerioid polyps, closeup detail of polyps with inflated "vesicles" over the septa.

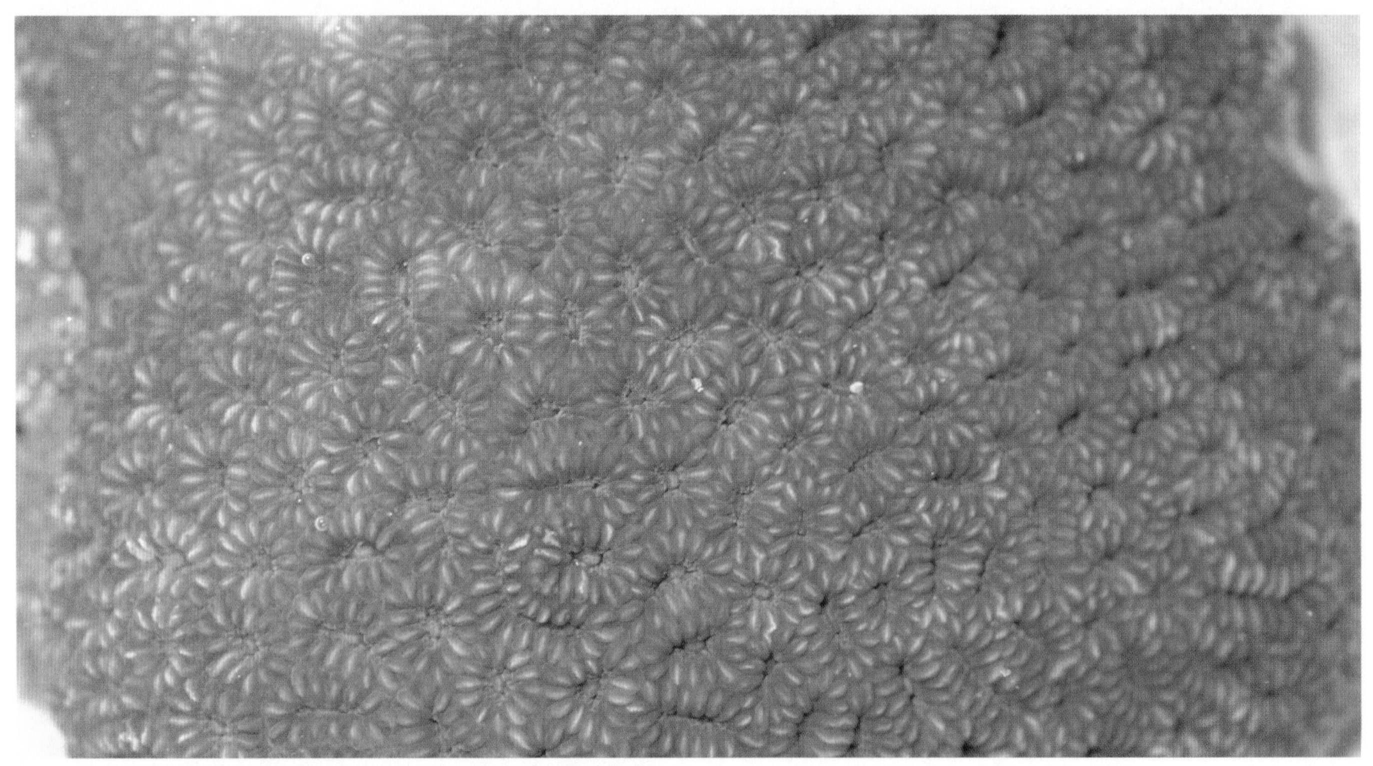

Dichocoenia cf. *stokesii* with cerioid polyps. This form is common from Miami to Palm Beach Florida.

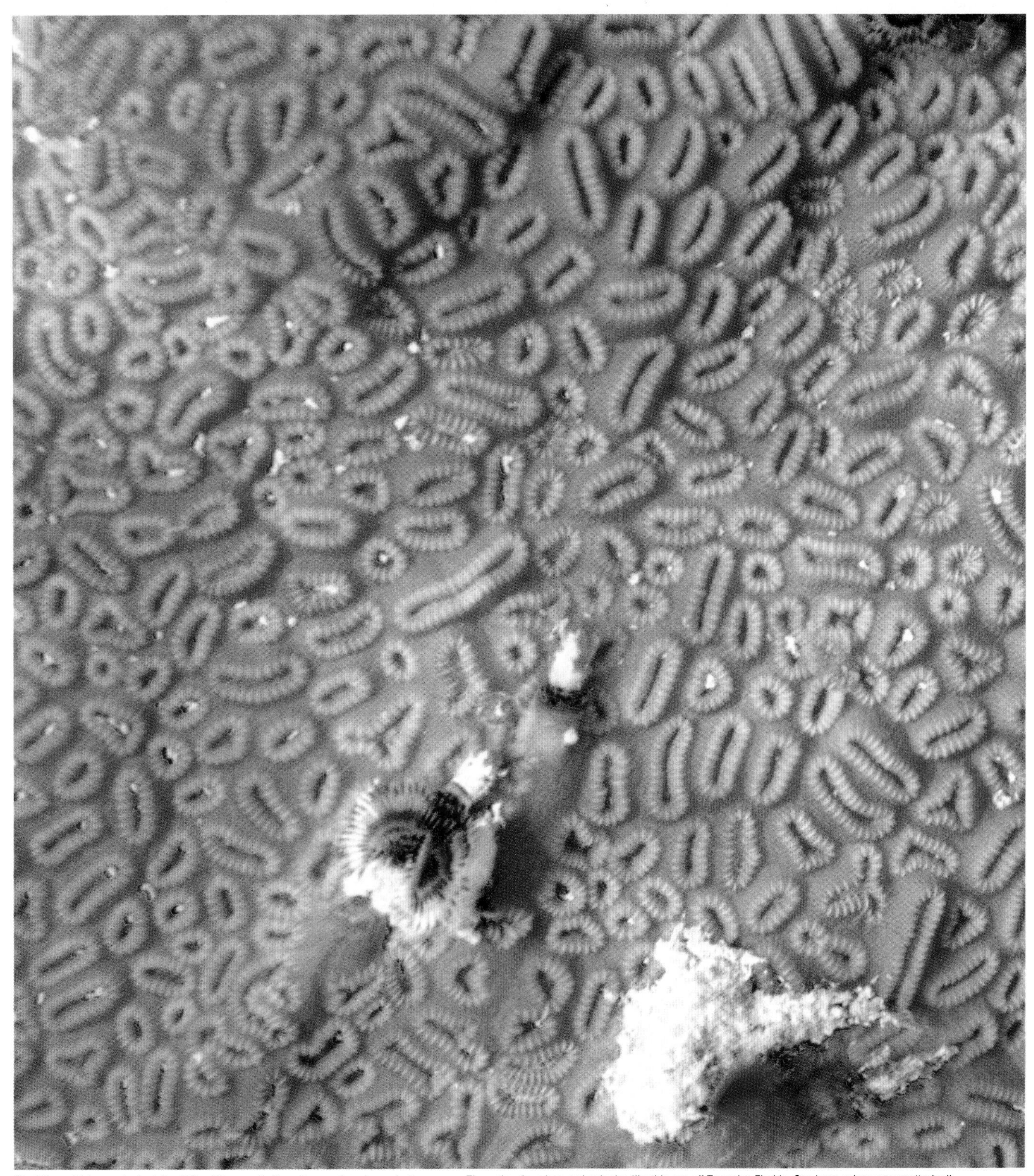

Giant form, *Dichocoenia* cf. *stokesii.* Corallites are 2 - 3 cm long, colony is nearly 1 m across. The author found several colonies like this one off Tavernier, Florida. One large colony was unattached!

Dendrogyra
Pronunciation: DEN-dro-JAI-ruh

Common Name: Pillar coral

Region: Caribbean

Description: Columnar and encrusting colonies with meandroid corallites. Tentacles fully expanded during the day give columns a furry appearance.

Similar Corals: Columnar *Meandrina* resembles *Dendrogyra.*

Lighting Needs	4 - 10
Water Flow	4 - 9
Aggressiveness	4
Hardiness	5

Placement

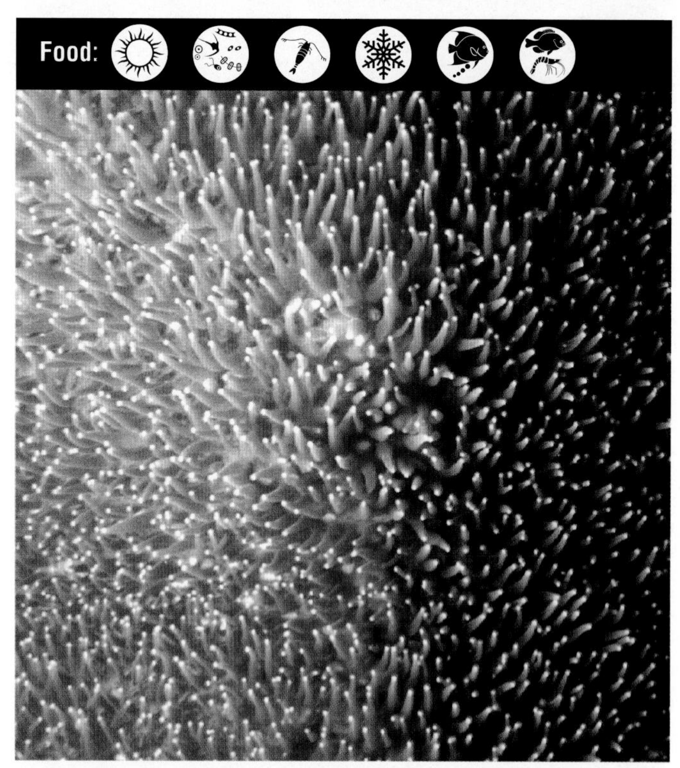

Dendrogyra cylindrus has bushy tentacles expanded during the day. Key Largo, Florida

Dendrogyra cylindrus, Key Largo, Florida

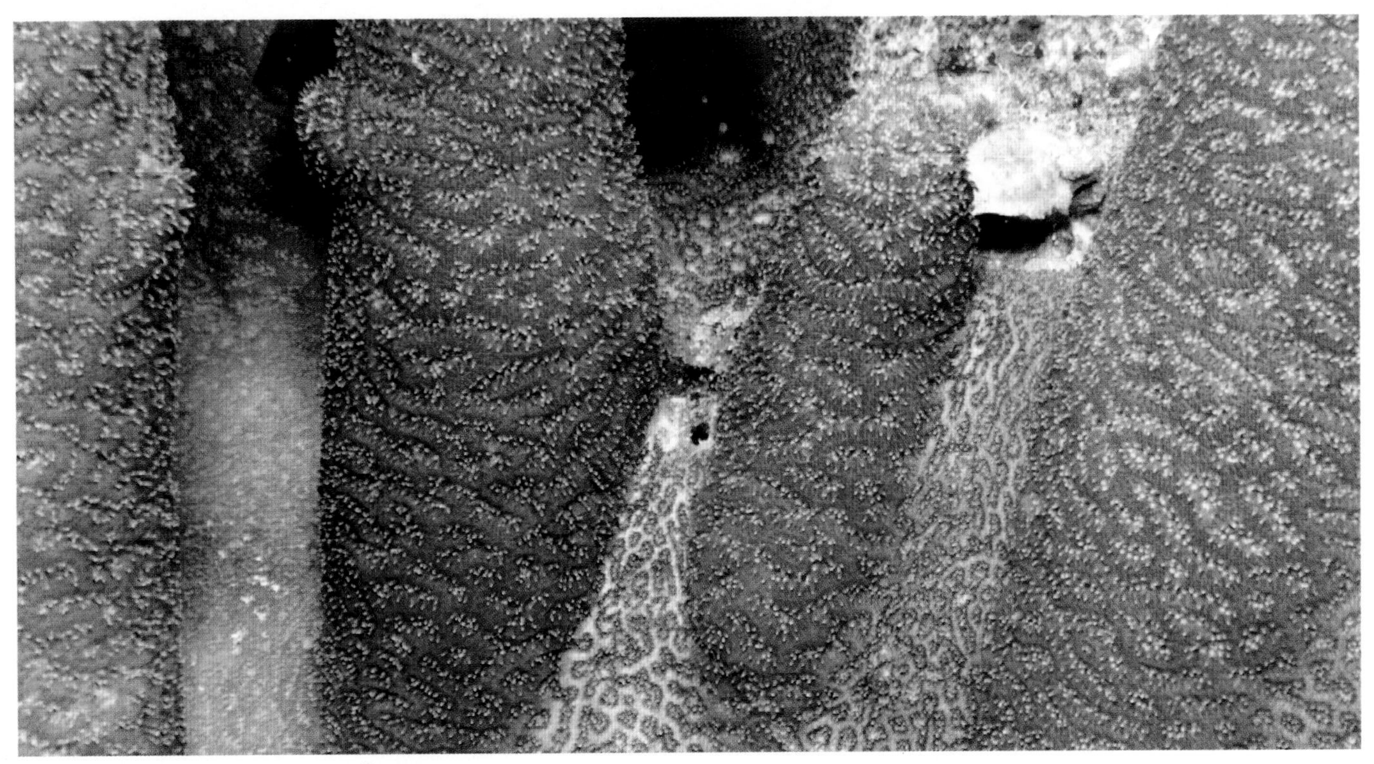

Dendrogyra cylindrus, polyps contracted to show corallite structure.

Dendrogyra cylindrus, Key Largo, Florida

Galaxea

Pronunciation: guh-LAX-ee-uh

Common Name: Crystal coral, Starburst coral

Region: Red Sea and Indian ocean to Japan and South central Pacific

Description: Massive, encrusting or columnar colonies with cylindrical corallites separated by very porous, brittle, lightweight blistery coenosteum. Corallites project beyond the coenosteum. Corallites with very exsert septa.

Similar Corals: *Acrhelia*. In the author's opinion, *Galaxea* and *Acrhelia* seem more closely related to corals like *Euphyllia* and *Physogyra* than to *Oculina* spp.

Lighting Needs	4 - 9
Water Flow	4 - 9
Aggressiveness	7
Hardiness	7

Placement

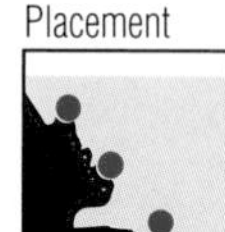

Food:

Galaxea astreata, Solomon Islands.

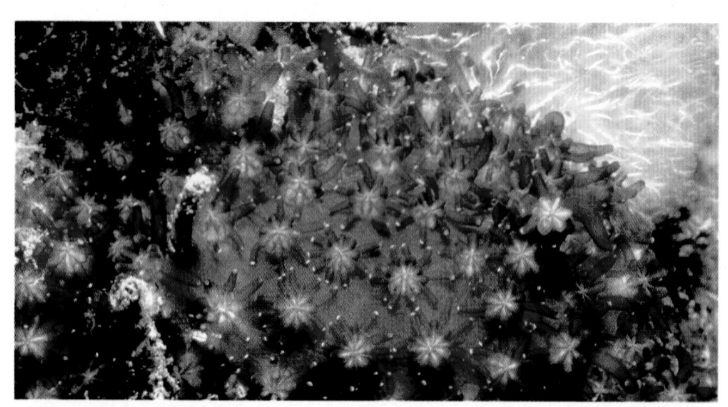

Galaxea paucisepta, Solomon Islands.

Galaxea fascicularis, Solomon Islands.

Artificially propagated *G. fascicularis* hang like rock candy at the Musee de Oceanographique, Monaco.

Acrhelia

Pronunciation: uh-KRELL-ee-uh

Common Name: Bush coral

Region: East Indian ocean, Western Pacific to Marshall and Gilbert Islands.

Description: Colonies arborescent and bushy. Septa very exsert.

Similar Corals: Veron (2000) Made *Acrhelia* a synonym of *Galaxea,* and showed that there are several arborescent species in the genus, including *Acrhelia horrescens.*

Lighting Needs	4 - 9
Water Flow	4 - 9
Aggressiveness	4
Hardiness	6

Placement

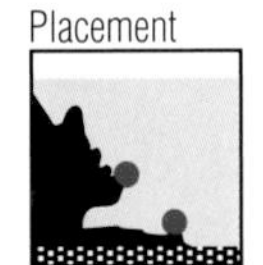

Galaxea (= Acrhelia) horrescens. Solomon Islands.

Galaxea (= Acrhelia) horrescens. Solomon Islands.

Cladocora

Pronunciation: KLAD-o-KOR-uh

Common Name: Ivory Tube coral

Region: Caribbean, Gulf of Mexico, Mediterranean

Description: Small branched clump shaped colonies, each branch ending with a corallite. Sometimes loose in seagrass beds or on soft substrates, sometimes attached on hardbottom. The Gulf of Mexico encrusting form appears distinct from the form found throughout the Caribbean.

Similar Corals: The relationship to *Solenastrea* and *Oculina* is apparent when the living colonies are observed. In some references they are placed in different families: *Solenastrea* and *Cladocora* in faviidae, *Oculina* in oculinidae. In the author's opinion *Solenastrea, Oculina,* and *Cladocora,* belong to the same family.

Lighting Needs	4 - 9
Water Flow	2 - 8
Aggressiveness	1
Hardiness	6

Placement

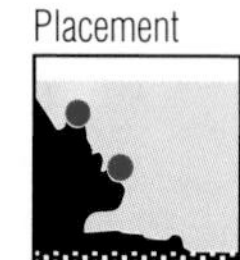

Cladocora cf. *arbuscula*, typical form found throught the Caribbean and south Florida.

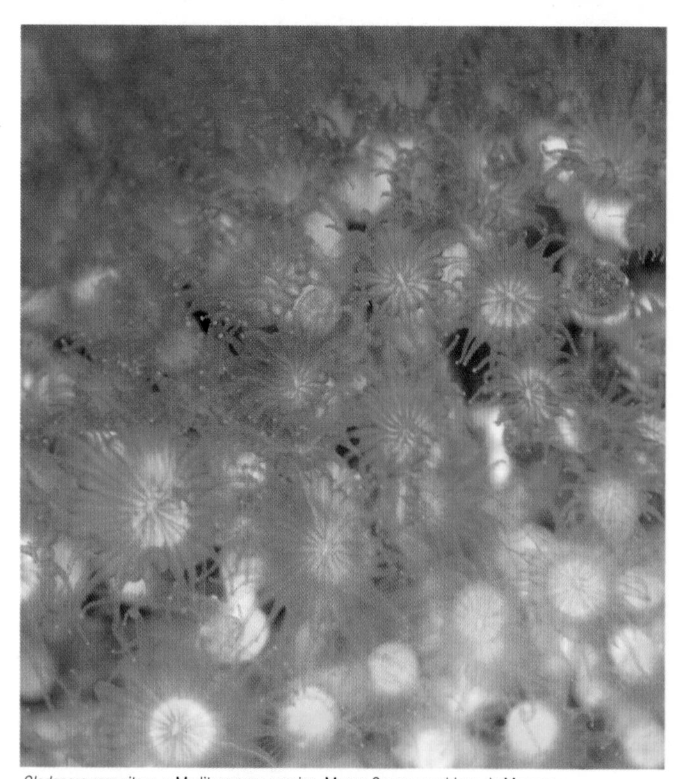

Cladocora caespitosa, a Mediterranean species. Musee Oceanographique de Monaco.

Cladocora cf. *arbuscula*, Gulf of Mexico & north Florida encrusting form. Compare this with *Oulastrea.*

Cladocora, Riverbanks Zoo & Aquarium.

Cladocora, encrusting form, Miami Beach.

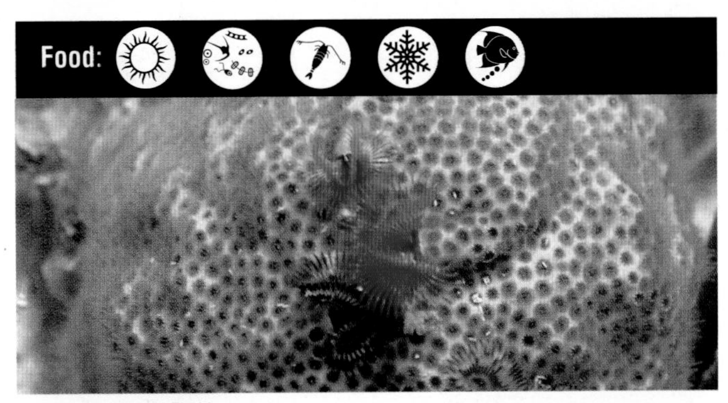

Solenastrea bournoni, Florida.

Solenastrea hyades, Florida.

Solenastrea

Pronunciation: SO-len-ASS-tree-uh

Common Name: Star coral, Knobby Star coral, Smooth Star coral, Lobed Star coral, Stump coral, Eyed coral

Region: Florida, Caribbean

Description: Massive dome shaped or columnar colonies with small circular corallites

Similar Corals: Most similar to Oculina spp., also similar to *Cladocora caespitosa* from the Mediterranean.

Lighting Needs	4 - 8
Water Flow	3 - 9
Aggressiveness	2
Hardiness	7

Placement

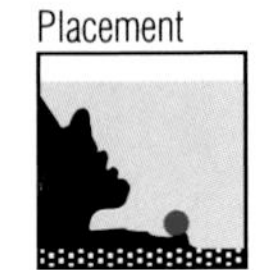

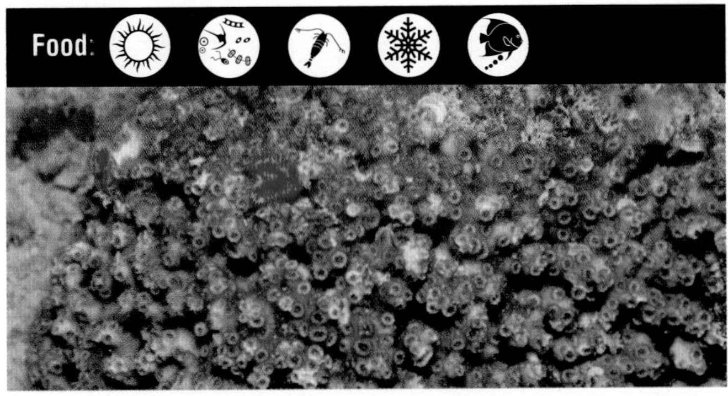

Oculina diffusa, a compactly branched colony. Miami Beach, Florida.

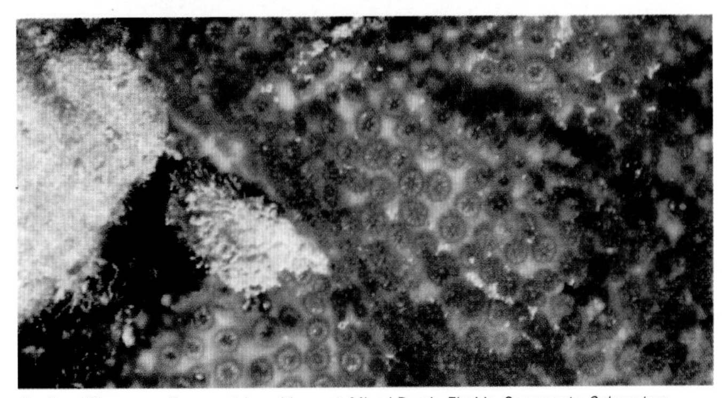

Oculina diffusa encrusting a metal machine part. Miami Beach, Florida. Compare to *Solenastrea*.

Oculina

Pronunciation: AW-kyu-LINE-uh

Common Name: Ivory Bush coral, Ivory Tree coral

Region: Atlantic, Gulf of Mexico, Caribbean, Mediterranean, Eastern Pacific, New Zealand.

Description: Encrusting to ramose and bushy colonies with corallites and polyps like those of *Solenastrea* and *Cladocora*. There are zooxanthellate and non-zooxanthellate species.

Similar Corals: Like a branched *Solenastrea*. Encrusting colonies of *Oculina* are most similar to *Solenastrea*. In the author's opinion, *Oculina* does not belong in the same family as *Galaxea* (both are considered oculinidae). *Solenastrea*, *Oculina*, and *Cladocora* seem most closely related.

Lighting Needs	4 - 8
Water Flow	3 - 9
Aggressiveness	2
Hardiness	7

Placement

Oulastrea

Pronunciation: OO-lass-TREE-uh

Common Name: None

Region: Western Pacific, from Northwest Australia, Indonesia to Japan, and the Solomon Islands

Description: Small encrusting colonies with black skeleton and contrasting white septa.

Similar Corals: *Oulastrea crispata* resembles *Favia fragum* from the Caribbean in size and habitat. Living polyps are much like *Cladocora*.

Lighting Needs	4 - 8
Water Flow	3 - 9
Aggressiveness	2
Hardiness	7

Placement

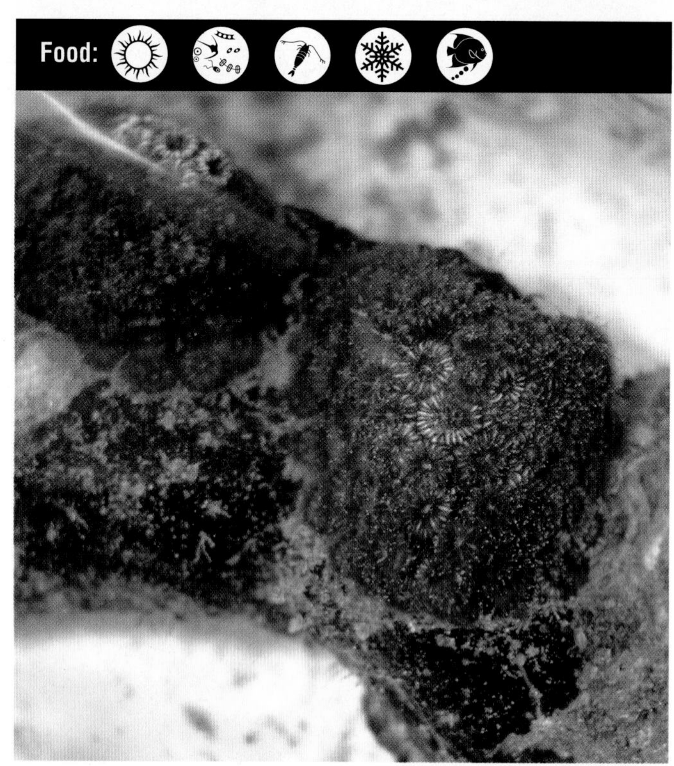

Oulastrea crispata.

Leptastrea

Pronunciation: LEP-tuh-STREE-uh

Common Name: Crust coral

Region: Red Sea, Indian Ocean to central Pacific.

Description: Colonies massive, encrusting, or dome-shaped. Corallites are cerioid to plocoid.

Similar Corals: *Leptastrea transversa* is similar to *Goniastrea* and *L. inaequalis* is similar to *Montastrea.*

Lighting Needs	3 - 9
Water Flow	3 - 9
Aggressiveness	2
Hardiness	9

Placement

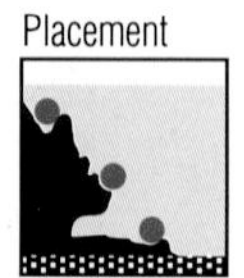

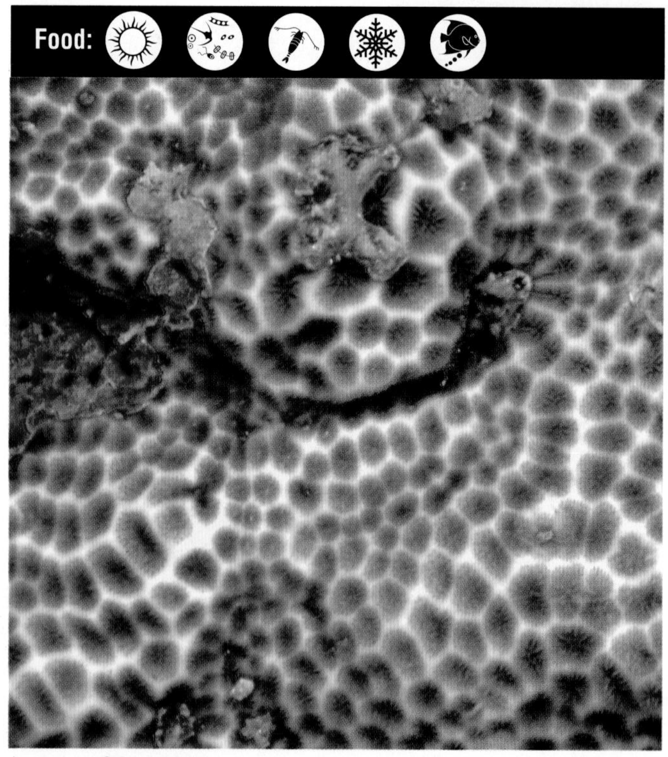

Leptastrea sp. Solomon Islands.

Leptastrea pruinosa, Solomon Islands.

Leptastrea pruinosa, Solomon Islands.

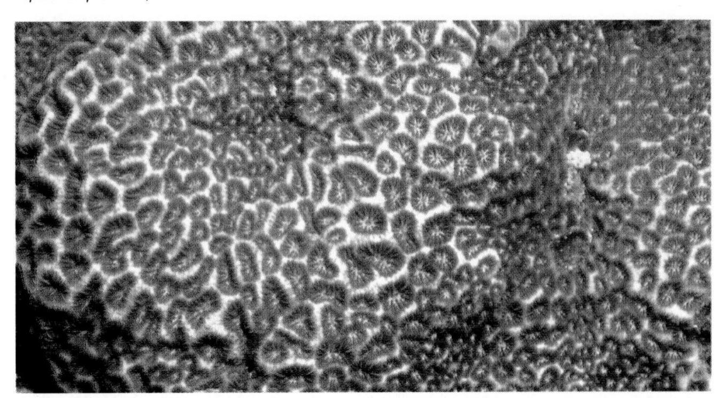
Leptastrea sp., Solomon Islands.

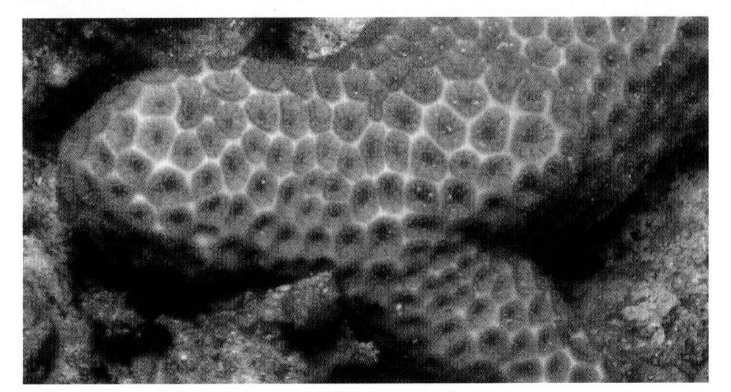
Leptastrea sp., Solomon Islands.

Leptastrea inaequalis, Red Sea. Eilat Israel.

Cyphastrea

Pronunciation: SI-fass-TREE-uh

Common Name: Knob coral, Lesser Knob coral

Region: Red Sea, Indian Ocean to central Pacific.

Description: Massive or encrusting colonies, usually, with one species forming branches.

Similar Corals: Encrusting colonies look like small *Montastrea.* The branchy species resembles *Acropora* spp. because it has axial corallites.

Rating	Value
Lighting Needs	3 - 9
Water Flow	3 - 9
Aggressiveness	3
Hardiness	7

Placement

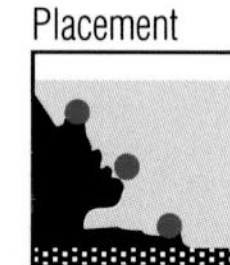

Cyphastrea serailia, Solomon Islands.

Cyphastrea decadia, Solomon Islands.

Cyphastrea serailia, Solomon Islands.

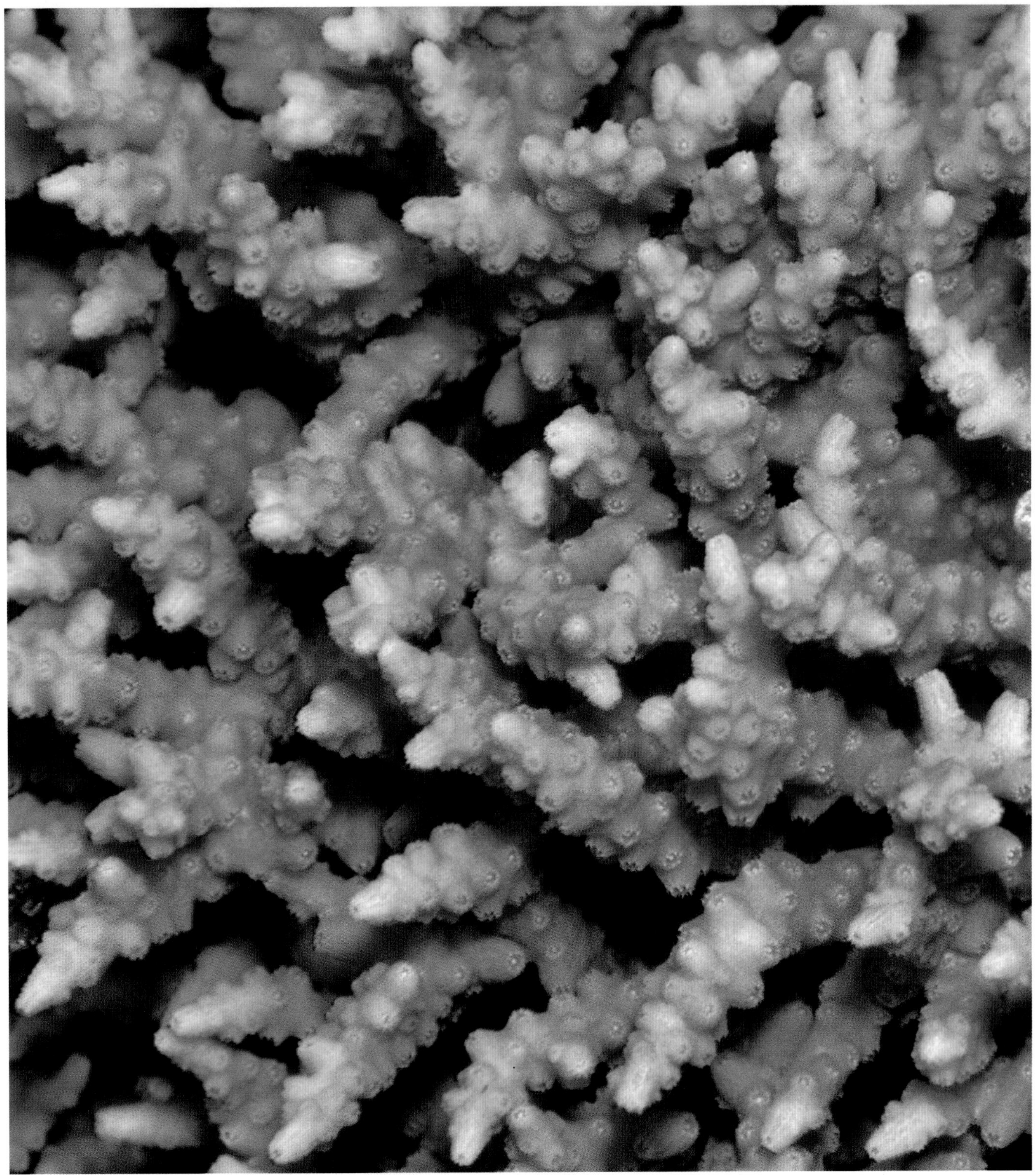

Cyphastrea decadia, Solomon Islands.

Echinopora

Pronunciation: ee-KI-no-POR-uh

Common Name: Hedgehog coral

Region: Red Sea, Indian Ocean to central Pacific.

Description: Foliaceous, arborescent, laminar, or massive colonies with small plocoid corallites

Similar Corals: May be confused with *Oxypora* and especially *Echinophyllia.*

Lighting Needs	4 - 9
Water Flow	4 - 9
Aggressiveness	2
Hardiness	6

Placement

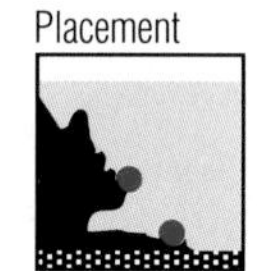

Food:

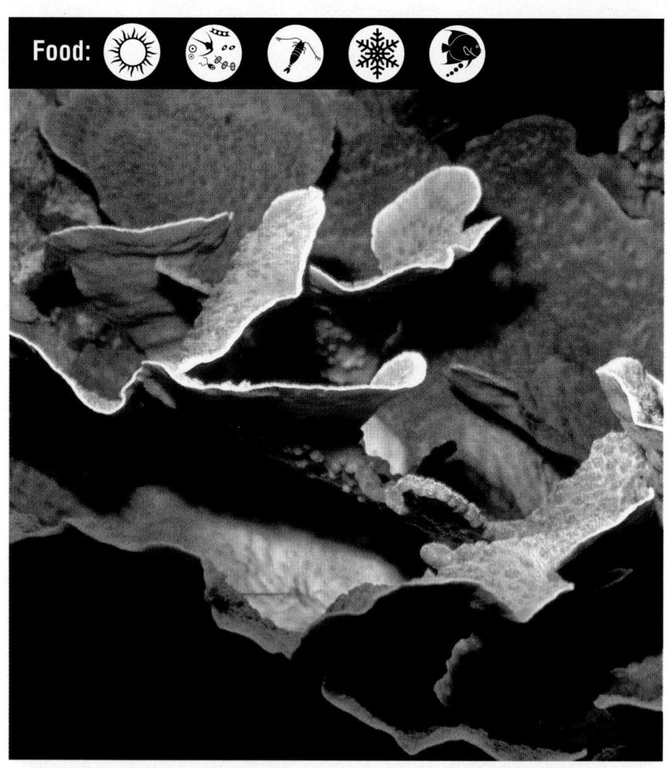

Echinopora lamellosa, Aquarium Photo, Löbbecke Museum and Aquazoo, Düsseldorf, Germany.

Echinopora lamellosa, Solomon Islands.

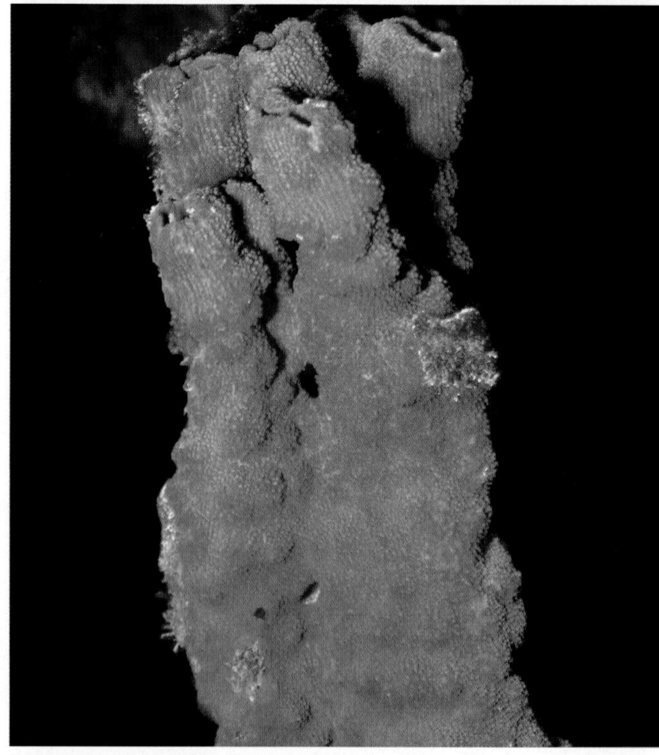

Echinopora lamellosa or possibly *E. ashmorensis*, Aquarium photo.

Echinopora mammiformis, Solomon Islands.

Echinopora horrida, Solomon Islands.

Trachyphyllia
Pronunciation: TRAY-kee-FILL-ee-uh

Common Name: Open Brain coral, Rose coral, *Wellsophyllia*

Region: Red Sea, Indian Ocean, Western Pacific, Japan, Australia, Solomon Islands.

Description: Free-living flabello-meandroid corals with fleshy polyps often brightly colored.

Similar Corals: Similar in habitat and form to *Manicina areolata* from the Caribbean. *Wellsophyllia* has been synonymized with *Trachyphyllia.* The name referred to colonies in which adjacent valleys become fused. *Manicina* also has different forms that parallel those of *Trachyphyllia.* See Borel Best and Hoeksema (1987) and Veron and Hodgson (1988).

Lighting Needs	3 - 9
Water Flow	0 - 7
Aggressiveness	2
Hardiness	8

Placement

Food:

Colorful round *Trachyphyllia geoffroyi* could be confused with *Scolymia* and *Cynarina.*

Trachyphyllia geoffroyi, a large specimen with convoluted valleys. Aquarium photo.

Trachyphyllia geoffroyi often has a figure eight shape. Aquarium photo.

The skeleton of a similarly shaped specimen, used to be called *Trachyphyllia* (=*Wellsophyllia*) *radiata.*

The skeleton of a similarly shaped specimen. Note pronounced paliform lobes here.

A distinctive form of *Trachyphyllia* from Bali. The corallum is flattened and quite like a fungiid.

Manicina
Pronunciation: MAN-iss-SEE-nuh

Common Name: Rose coral

Region: Caribbean

Description: Free-living flabello-meandroid coral found on soft bottoms inside reefs and seagrass flats. Sometimes attached on reef.

Similar Corals: An attached hemispherical form, f. *mayori*, known by the common name "Tortugas Rose Coral" (Humann, 1993) grows to a much larger size and is difficult to distinguish from *Colpophyllia*.

Rating	Value
Lighting Needs	3 - 10
Water Flow	0 - 8
Aggressiveness	2
Hardiness	8

Placement

Trachyphyllia sp. from the Solomon Islands. A very distinctive form.

Trachyphyllia geoffroyi, comes in an array of color patterns.

Food:

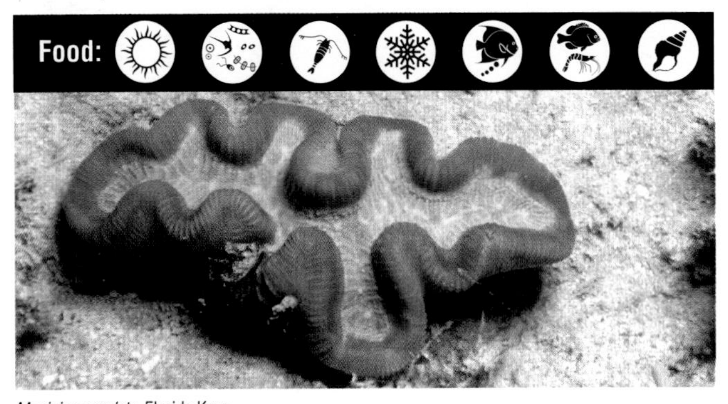

Manicina areolata, Florida Keys.

Manicina areolata f. *mayori*.

Manicina areolata, Florida Keys.

Colpophyllia

Pronunciation: KOLL-po-FILL-ee-uh

Common Name: Boulder Brain coral, Giant Brain coral

Region: Caribbean

Description: Massive dome shaped colonies with meandroid or cerioid corallites.

Similar Corals: Resembles *Oulophyllia* from the Red Sea and Indo-Pacific. Also small colonies are quite similar to *Manicina* and may be difficult to distinguish in the field. *Colpophyllia* exhibits mimicry, with one form having white stripes that make it look like *Meandrina meandrites.* Another form that occurs on shaded slopes and bridge pilings is colored and shaped like *Mycetophyllia danaana*.

Lighting Needs	4 - 9
Water Flow	3 - 8
Aggressiveness	3
Hardiness	8

Placement

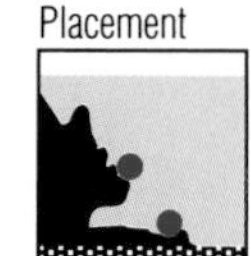

Colpophyllia natans, Key Largo, Florida.

Compare this young *Colpophyllia* with the striped *Manicina* on the previous page.

Compare this *Colpophyllia* with the mound form of *Meandrina.* It is a mimic.

Colpophyllia that mimics *Mycetophyllia danaana.* Some are orange and green like their model.

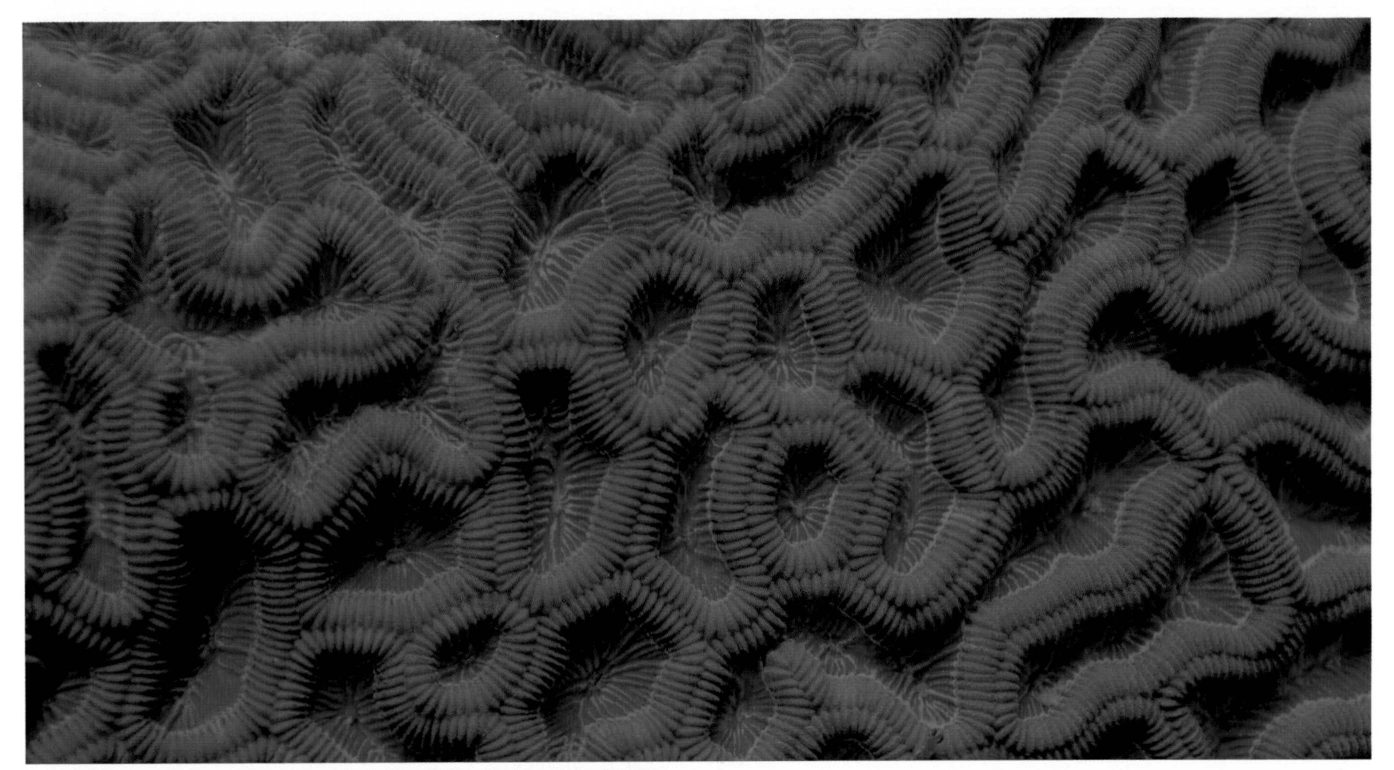
Colpophyllia natans with closed valleys, photographed without flash to show fluorescence. Bahamas.

Colpophyllia natans, photographed without flash (truth: because flash malfunctioned!) Bahamas.

Oulophyllia

Pronunciation: OO-lo-FILL-ee-uh

Common Name: Brain coral, Closed Brain coral

Region: Red Sea, Indian Ocean, Western Pacific, Japan, east to Samoa

Description: Massive dome shaped colonies with meandroid or cerioid corallites. *Oulophyllia crispa* has wide, v-shaped valleys. *Oulophyllia bennettae* has mostly cerioid corallites.

Similar Corals: Resembles *Colpophyllia* from the Caribbean in appearance and habitat. Like *Oulophyllia*, *Colpophyllia* also has both meandroid and cerioid forms, but in *Colpophyllia* they are considered to be variations of one species. At least one species of *Pectinia* resembles *Colpophyllia* so strongly that it has been overlooked by taxonomists. See below and in Chapter Four.

Lighting Needs	4 - 8
Water Flow	4 - 9
Aggressiveness	4
Hardiness	9

Placement

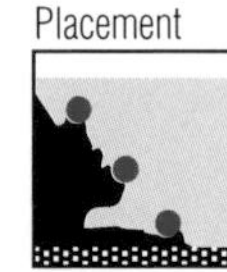

Oulophyllia bennettae. Solomon Islands.

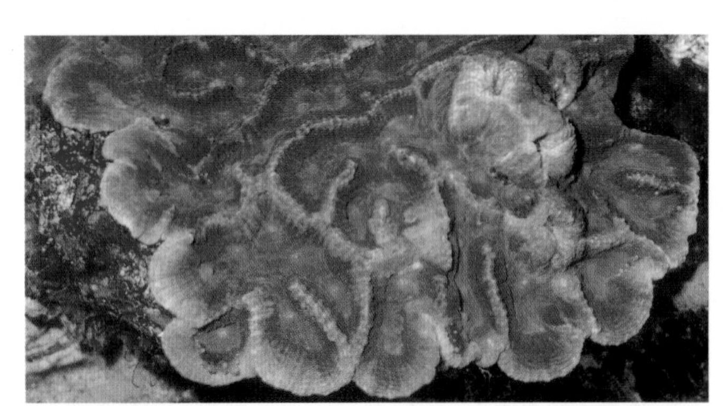

Oulophyllia sp. Japan. Aquarium photo, Blue Harbor, Osaka.

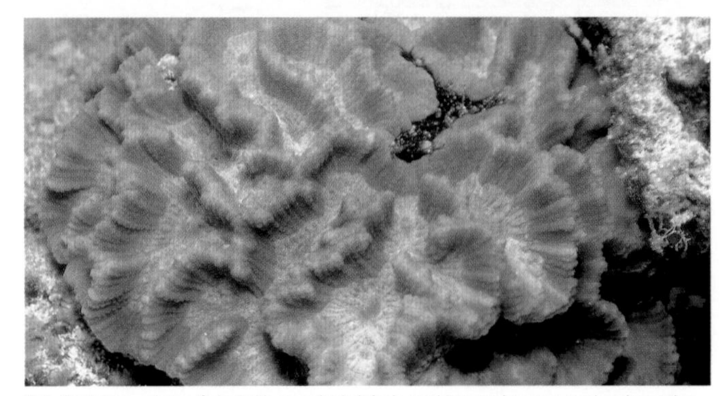

This *Pectinia* sp. mimics *Oulophyllia* so perfectly it fools coral taxonomists even on close inspection.

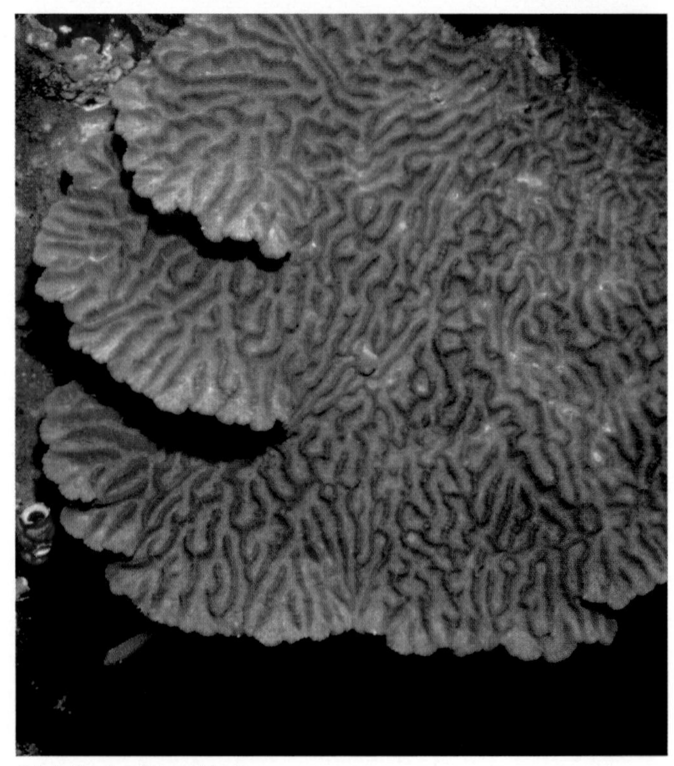

Oulophyllia crispa. Solomon Islands.

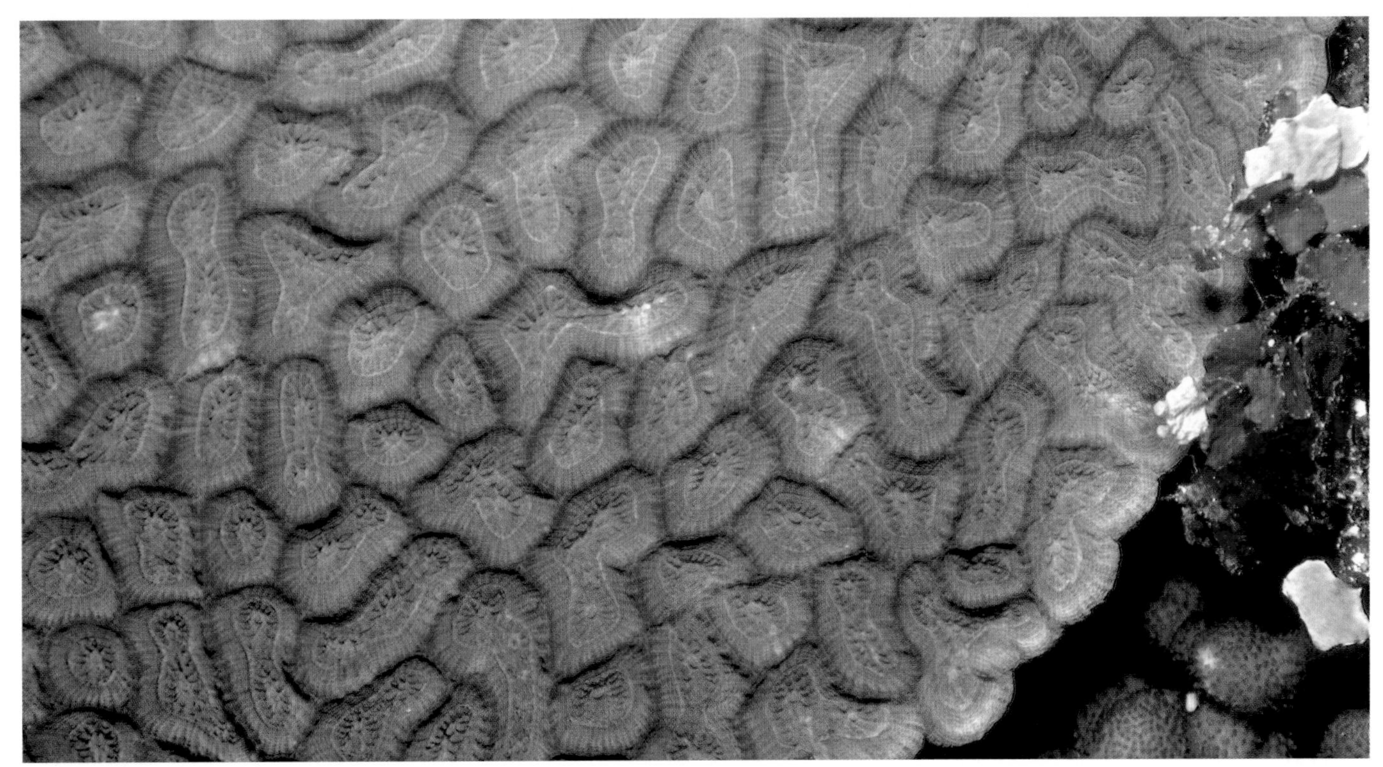

Oulophyllia bennettae. Solomon Islands.

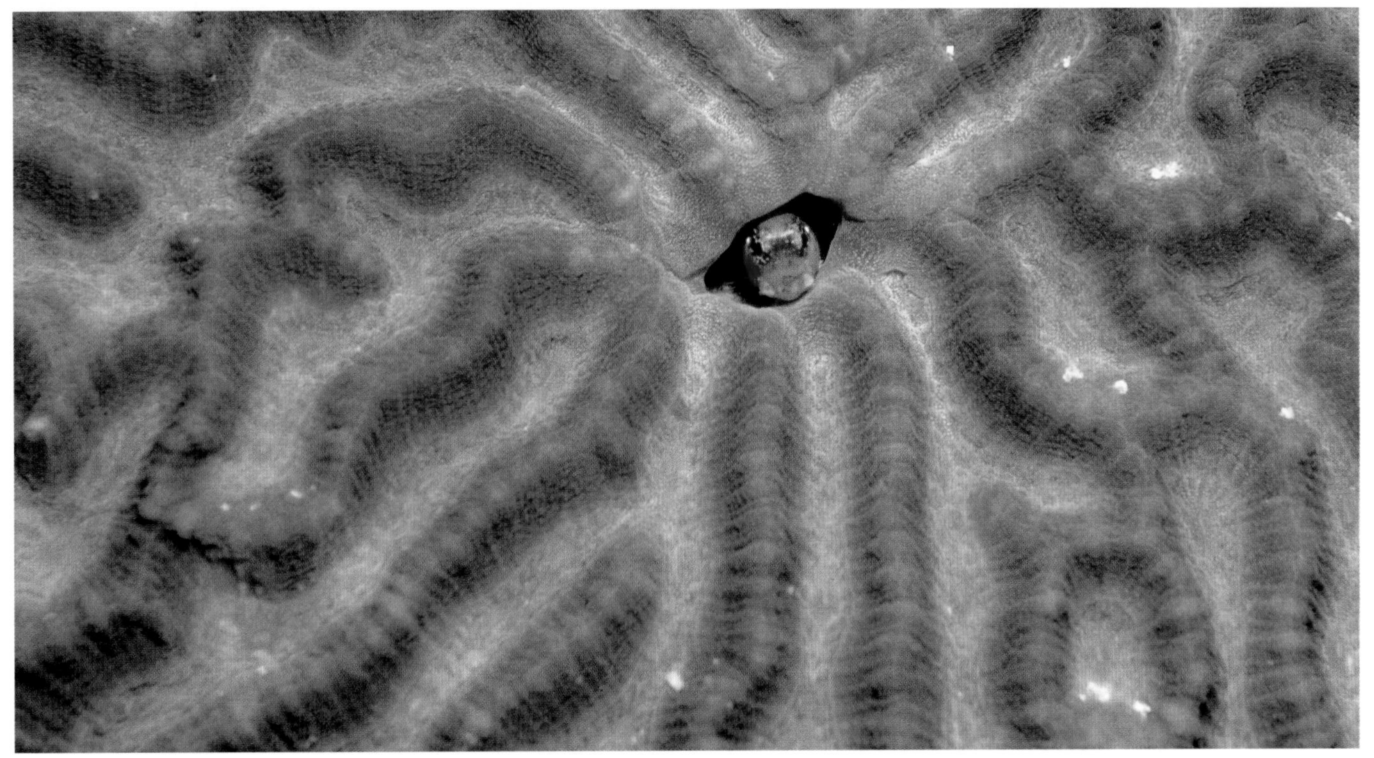

Oulophyllia crispa, home to a blenny in the Solomon Islands.

Caulastrea

Pronunciation: CAWL-ass-TREE-uh (cawl-ASS-tree-uh)

Common Name: Bullseye coral, Candy coral, Trumpet coral

Region: East Africa, Indian Ocean, Japan, Marshall Islands east to south central Pacific.

Description: Phacelloid to occasionally flabello-meandroid (see *C. tumida* in Veron, 1986). Corallites with numerous fine septa.

Similar Corals: Fully expanded colonies look like *Favia* spp. May also be confused with *Blastomussa*.

Lighting Needs	3 - 9
Water Flow	2 - 9
Aggressiveness	4
Hardiness	9

Placement

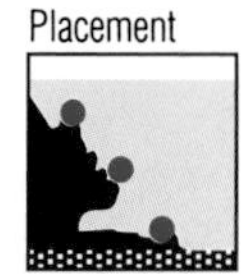

Caulastrea furcata in Doug Robbins' aquarium, Brooklyn, New York.

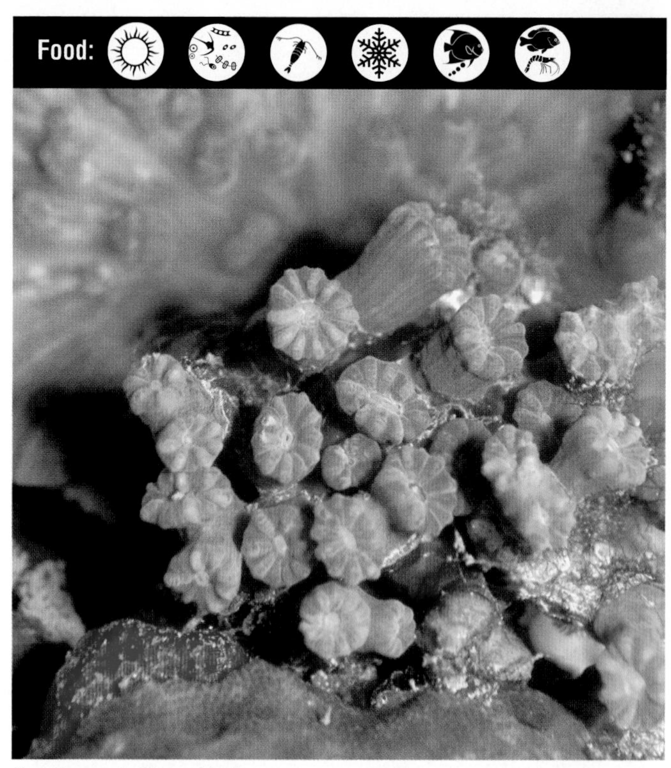

Caulastrea curvata, Solomon Islands.

Caulastrea curvata.

Damaged *Caulastrea tumida*, Japan. Note the characteristic solid skeleton below the short corallites.

Caulastrea cf. *curvata* can be colored the same as *C. furcata*.

Erythrastrea
Pronunciation: eh-RITH-raz-TREE-uh

Common Name: Brain coral

Region: Red Sea

Description: Flabello-meandroid with thin walls. Polyps are like *Caulastrea.*

Similar Corals: Esssentially like *Caulastrea* with very elongated corallites. The author does not see a reason to separate this genus from *Caulastrea.*

Lighting Needs	4 - 9
Water Flow	3 - 9
Aggressiveness	4
Hardiness	8

Placement

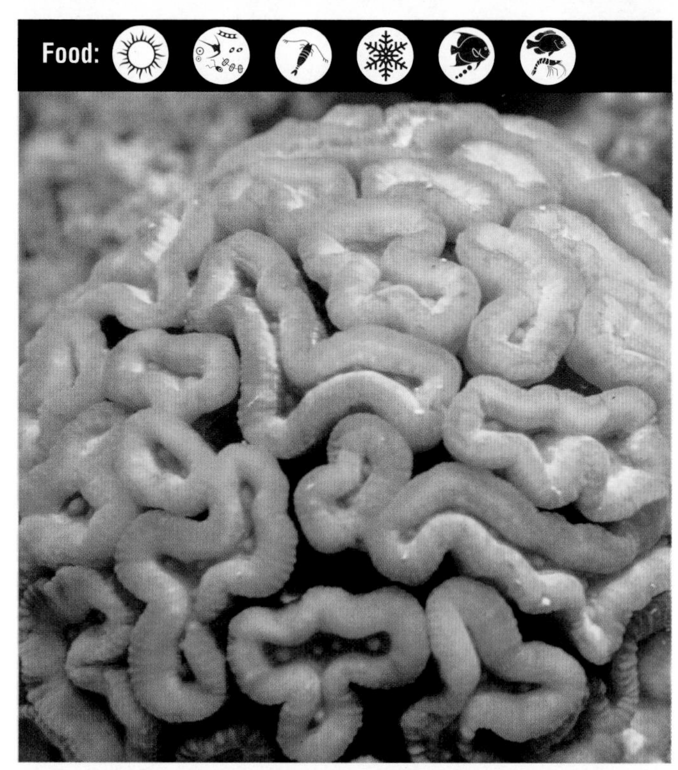

Erythrastrea sp. Eilat, Israel.

Erythrastrea sp. Eilat, Israel.

Montastrea

Pronunciation: MONT-az-TREE-uh (mont-ASS-tree-uh)

Common Name: Star coral, Moon coral

Region: Caribbean, West Africa, East Africa, Red Sea, Indian Ocean to central Pacific.

Description: Massive colonies with plocoid corallites. Daughter polyps formed by extratentacular budding.

Similar Corals: Indo-Pacific *Favia* spp. mostly seem to belong to the same genus as *Montastrea* spp., while the nominal species, *F. fragum* from the Caribbean, seems distinct.

Lighting Needs	3 - 9
Water Flow	3 - 9
Aggressiveness	8
Hardiness	9

Placement

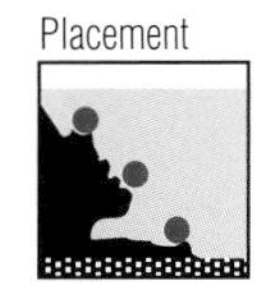

Unknown *Montastrea* sp., possibly *M. annuligera*.

Montastrea curta, Kushimoto, Japan.

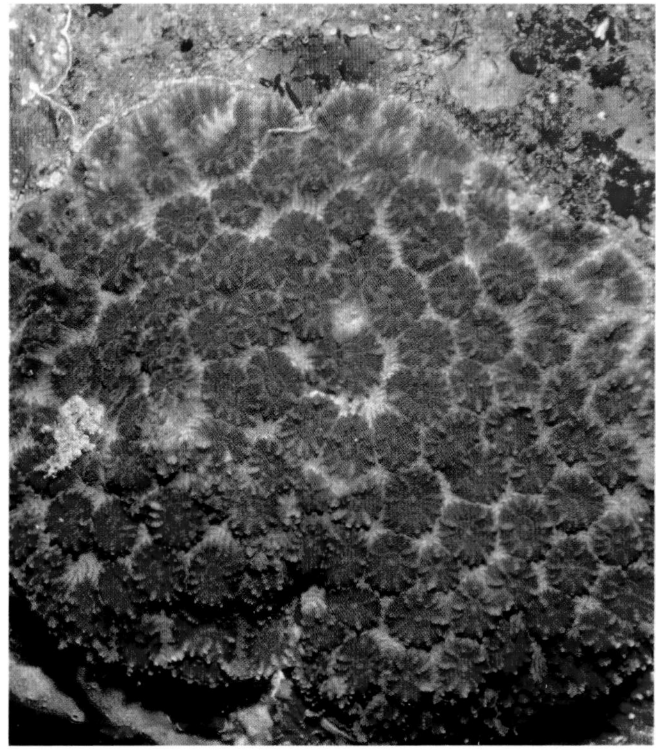

Montastrea cf. *annuligera*.

Montastrea annularis, Key Largo, Florida.

Montastrea cavernosa, Miami Beach, Florida.

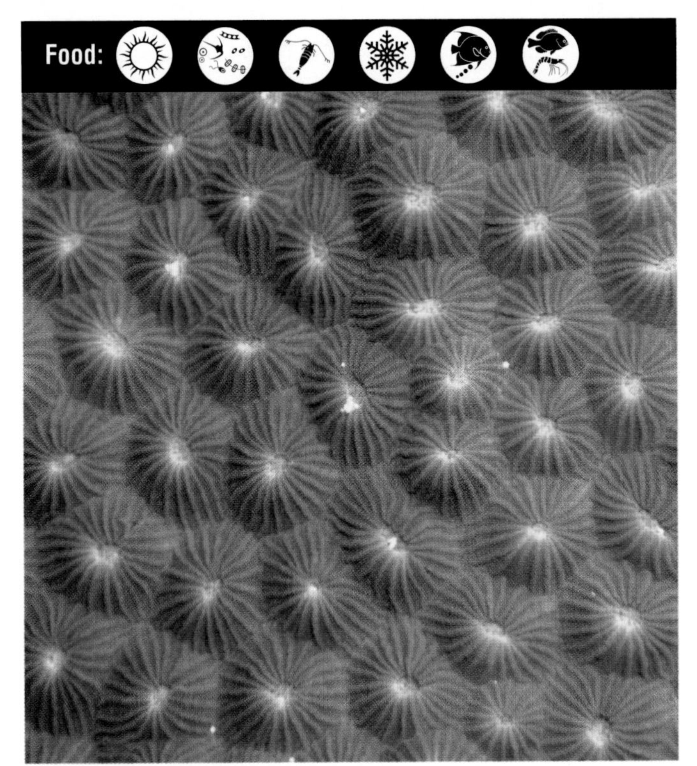

Diploastrea heliopora, Solomon Islands.

Diploastrea

Pronunciation: DIP-lo-az-TREE-uh

Common Name: Moon Coral

Region: Red Sea, Indian Ocean, Western Pacific, Japan, east to Samoa

Description: Massive dome-shaped colonies growing to enormous size (several meters in diameter). Colony surface is even, corallites are plocoid and regularly arranged.

Similar Corals: Resembles *Montastrea cavernosa* from the Caribbean, and *Favia leptophyllia* from Brazil.

Lighting Needs	3 - 9
Water Flow	3 - 9
Aggressiveness	8
Hardiness	9

Placement

Diploastrea heliopora at night with expanded polyps. Solomon Islands.

Favia
Pronunciation: FAY-vee-uh

Common Name: Honeycomb coral, Moon coral, Closed Brain coral, Worm coral

Region: Caribbean, Brazil, West Africa, Red Sea, East Africa, Indian Ocean, east to Hawaii and Easter Island.

Description: assive or encrusting usually dome-shaped colonies with monocentric plocoid corallites. Daughter corallites usually but not always formed by intratentacular division.

Similar Corals: Favites corallites are more typically cerioid and divide unequally. *Barabattoia* spp. have projecting (plocoid) corallites.

Lighting Needs	4 - 9
Water Flow	3 - 10
Aggressiveness	8
Hardiness	8

Placement

Favia fragum, Florida Keys.

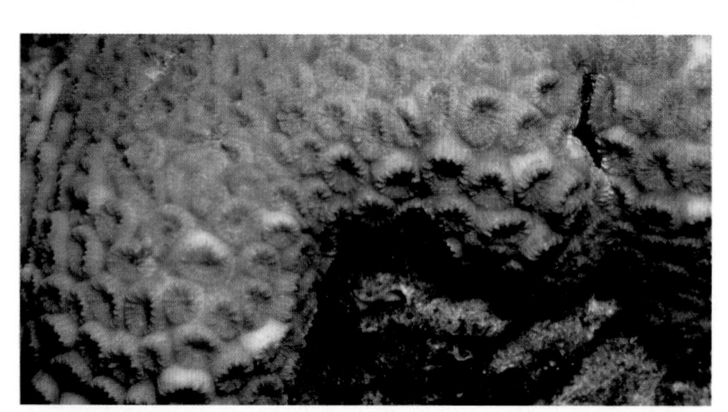

Barabattoia spp. are essentially like plocoid *Favia* spp.

Favia sp.

Favia rotundata

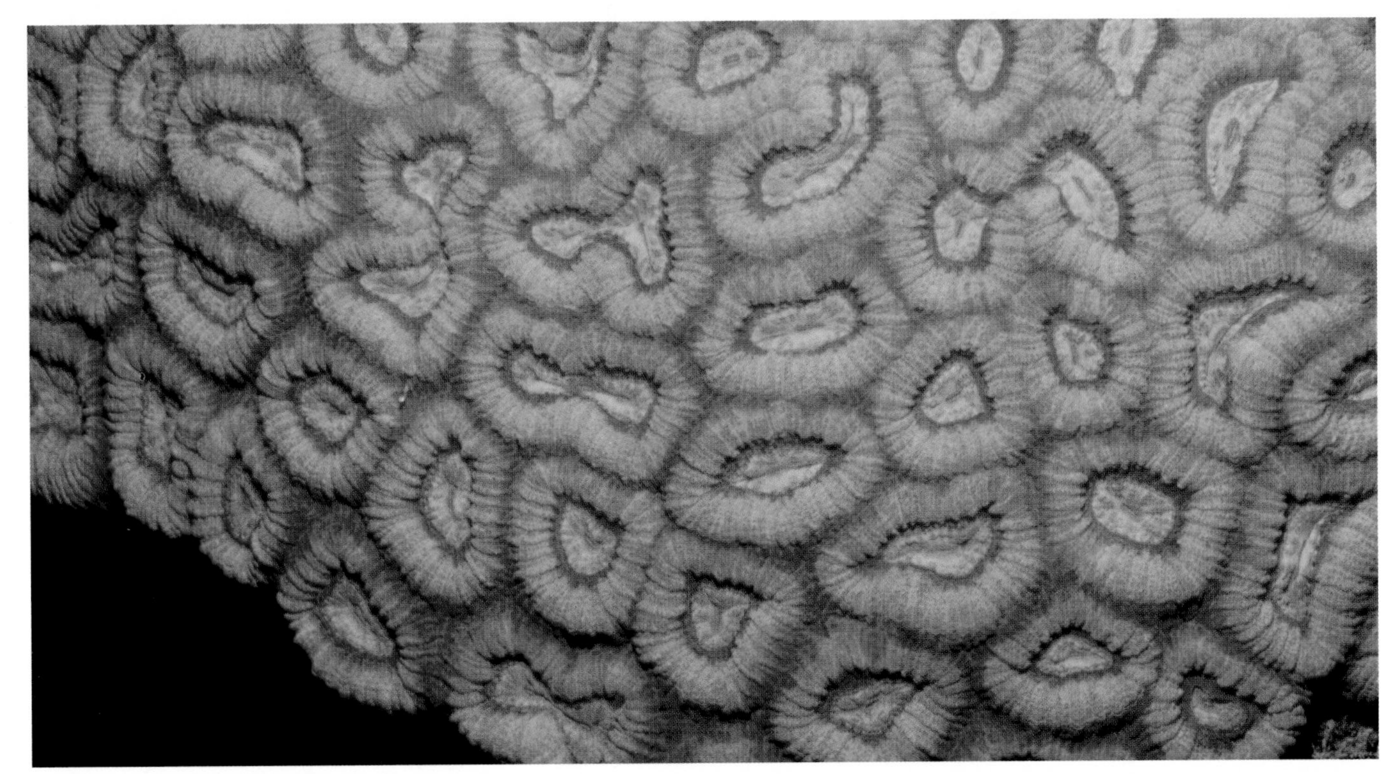

Favia sp.

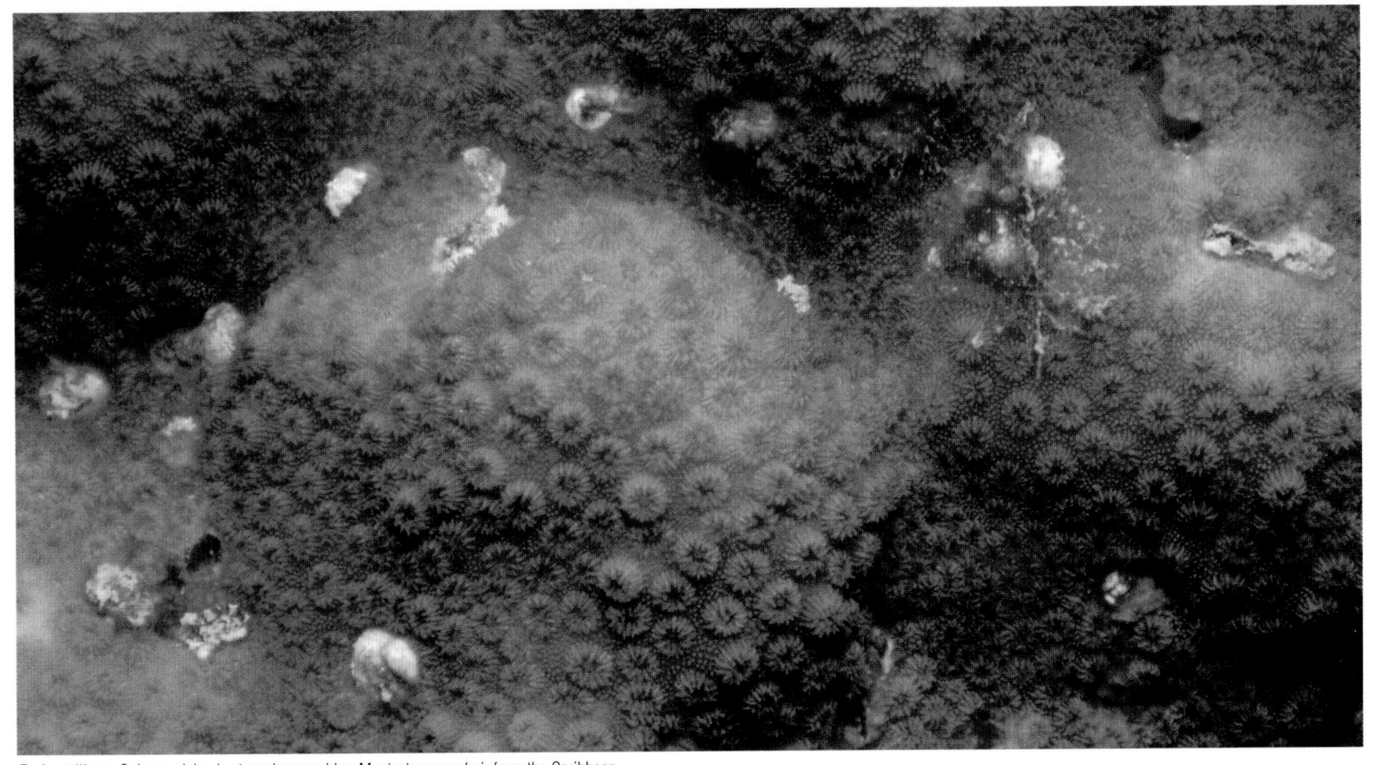

Favia stelligera, Solomon Islands strongly resembles *Montastrea annularis* from the Caribbean.

Favites
Pronunciation: fuh-VI-teez

Common Name: Moon coral, Honeycomb coral, Closed Brain coral, Worm coral

Region: Red Sea, Indian Ocean, Western Pacific, Japan, east to the Line and Tuamotu Islands.

Description: Encrusting or Massive colonies with mostly cerioid corallites giving a honeycomb appearance.

Similar Corals: *Favia* and *Goniastrea*. *Goniastrea* has prominent paliform lobes

Lighting Needs	4 - 9
Water Flow	3 - 10
Aggressiveness	8
Hardiness	8

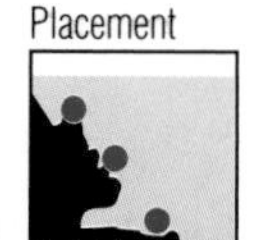

Favites sp. from the Red Sea. Musee de Oceanographique, Monaco.

Favites halicora forms knobby growths.

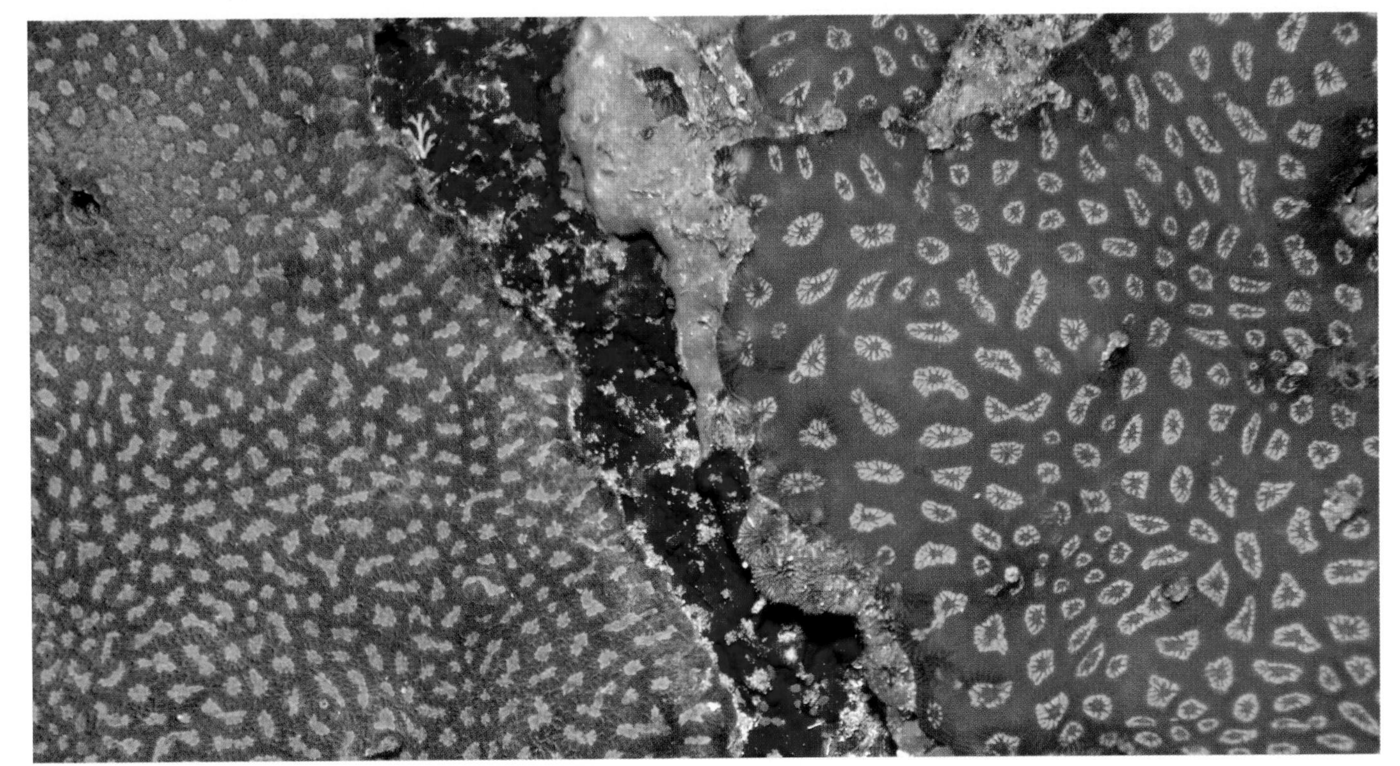

Favites cf. *pentagona*, left and *Favites abdita*, right. Solomon Islands.

Plesiastrea

Pronunciation: PLEE-zee-az-TREE-uh

Common Name: Knob coral

Region: Red Sea, East Africa, Indian Ocean, Persian Gulf, Japan, to central Pacific. Also in temperate water in southern Australia.

Description: Massive or encrusting flat or dome shaped colonies with plocoid monocentric corallites approximately 3 mm in diameter.

Similar Corals: Quite similar to *Montastrea* and *Cyphastrea*.

Food:

Plesiastrea versipora, Kushimoto, Japan.

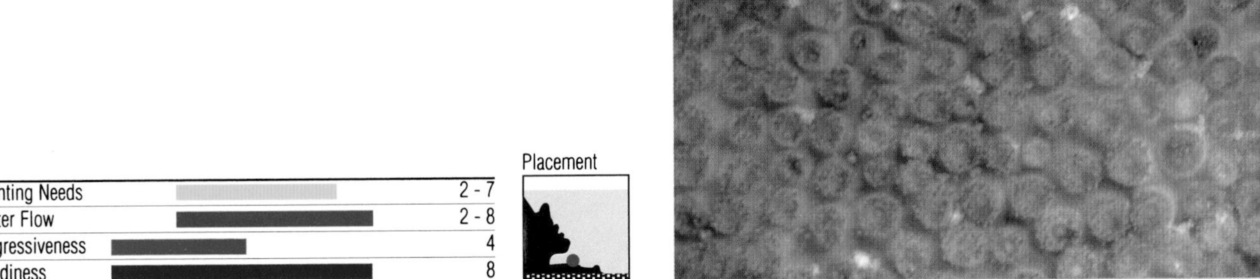

Plesiastrea versipora, Eilat, Israel.

Goniastrea
Pronunciation: GO-nee-ass-TREE-uh

Common Name: Honeycomb coral, Closed Brain coral, Worm coral

Region: Red Sea, Persian Gulf, Indian Ocean, to central Pacific

Description: Massive colonies with cerioid or meandroid corallites. *Goniastrea pectiniata* forms columns.

Similar Corals: *Diploria* of the Caribbean is quite like a meandroid *Goniastrea.* Living colonies are similar to *Leptoria, Platygyra* and *Favites.* The well developed paliform lobes of the skeleton in *Goniastrea* is an important distinguishing character. *Goniastrea pectiniata* could be confused with *Australogyra* and *Merulina.*

Lighting Needs	4 - 10
Water Flow	4 - 10
Aggressiveness	4
Hardiness	6

Placement

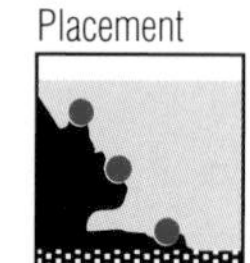

Food:

Goniastrea sp., on a shallow reef top, Red Sea.

Goniastrea pectiniata, Solomon Islands.

Goniastrea palauensis, Whitsunday Islands, Australia.

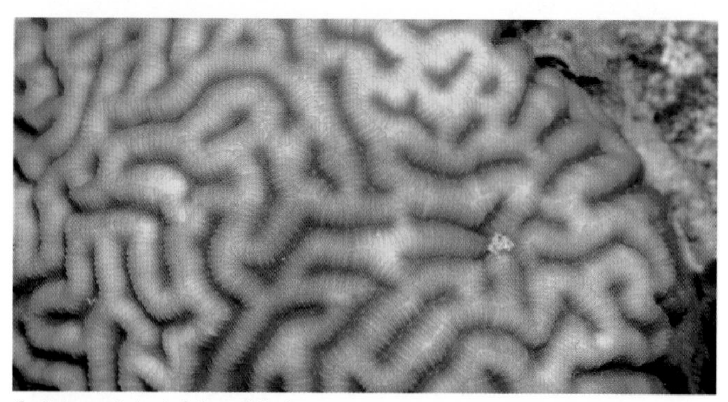

Goniastrea australensis, Solomon Islands.

Goniastrea retiformis, Solomon Islands.

Goniastrea sp., Solomon Islands.

Diploria
Pronunciation: dip-PLOR-ee-uh

Common Name: Brain coral

Region: Caribbean

Description: Massive or encrusting colonies with meandroid corallites usually, sometimes with cerioid corallites.

Similar Corals: Similar to meandroid forms of *Goniastrea and Platygyra* of the Red Sea and Indo-Pacific. Occasionally forms cerioid colonies or portions of colonies. These look like corals in the wrong ocean! Fossil records of *Goniastrea* from the West Indes (see Veron, 1986) may be *Diploria.*

Lighting Needs	4 - 10
Water Flow	4 - 9
Aggressiveness	4
Hardiness	7

Placement

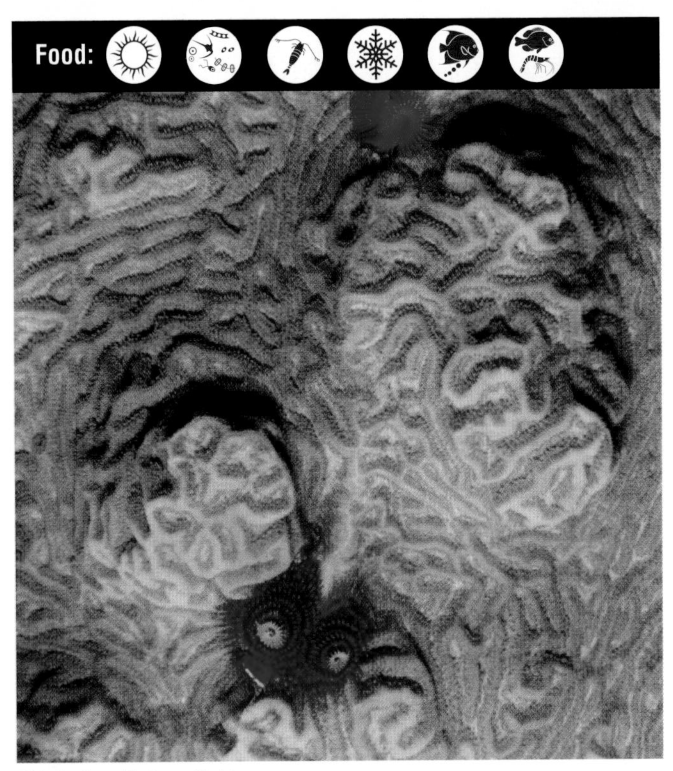

Diploria clivosa, Key Largo, Florida

Diploria strigosa, Key Largo, Florida

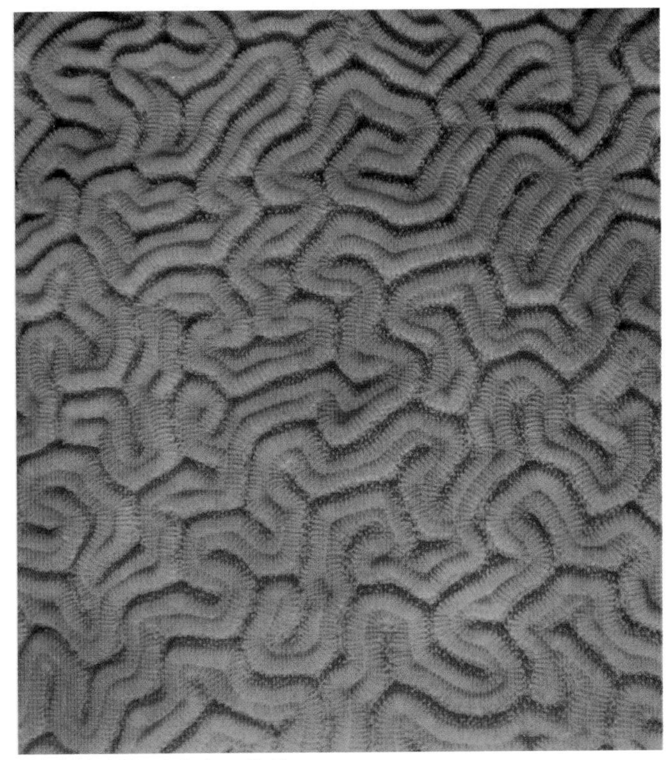

Diploria labyrinthiformis, Key Largo, Florida

Leptoria
Pronunciation: lep-TOR-ee-uh

Common Name: Brain coral, Closed Brain coral

Region: Red Sea and Indian Ocean to Japan and east to the south central Pacific.

Description: Massive colonies with very meandroid corallites. Septa very uniformly spaced like stairs on a ladder.

Similar Corals: Similar to *Platygyra* and *Goniastrea*.

Lighting Needs	5 - 9
Water Flow	4 - 9
Aggressiveness	4
Hardiness	6

Placement

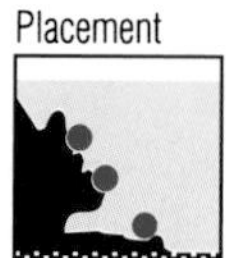

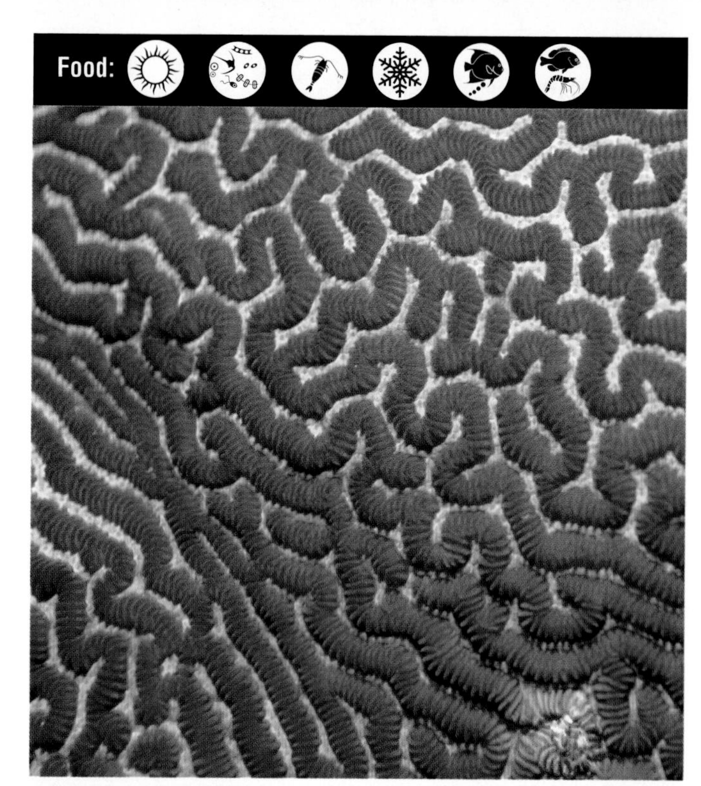

Leptoria phrygia, Solomon Islands.

Leptoria phrygia, Solomon Islands.

Platygyra

Pronunciation: PLA-tee-JAI-ruh

Common Name: Brain coral, Closed Brain coral, Worm coral

Region: Red Sea and Indian Ocean to Japan and east to the south central Pacific.

Description: Massive or encrusting colonies with meandroid to occasionally cerioid corallites.

Similar Corals: Similar to *Goniastrea* and *Leptoria.* The differences are most clearly seen in the skeletal structure. Aquarists confuse *Oulophyllia* with *Platygyra.* The former has wider valleys. *Australogyra* is essentially like a branchy *Platygyra,* but living *Australogyra* "behaves" like *Hydnophora* and *Paraclavarina* of the family Merulinidae.

Lighting Needs	3 -10
Water Flow	4 - 9
Aggressiveness	7
Hardiness	9

Placement

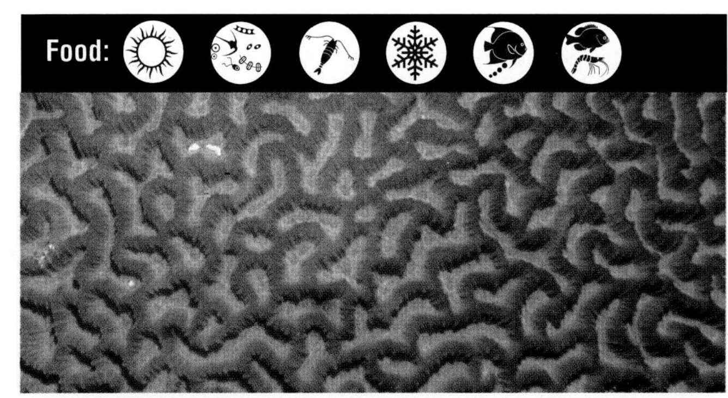

Platygyra sinensis. Solomon Islands.

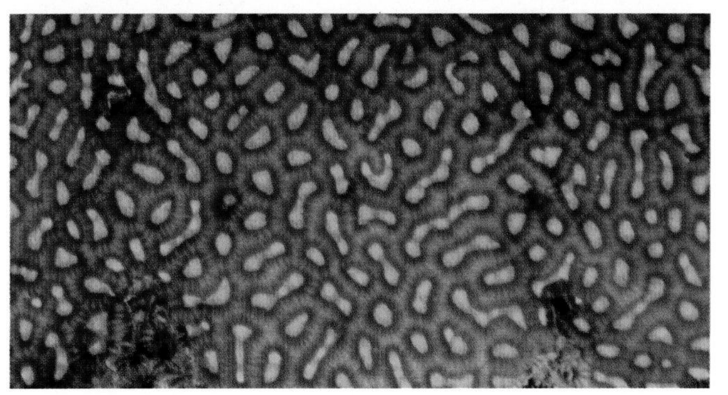

Platygyra pini. Solomon Islands.

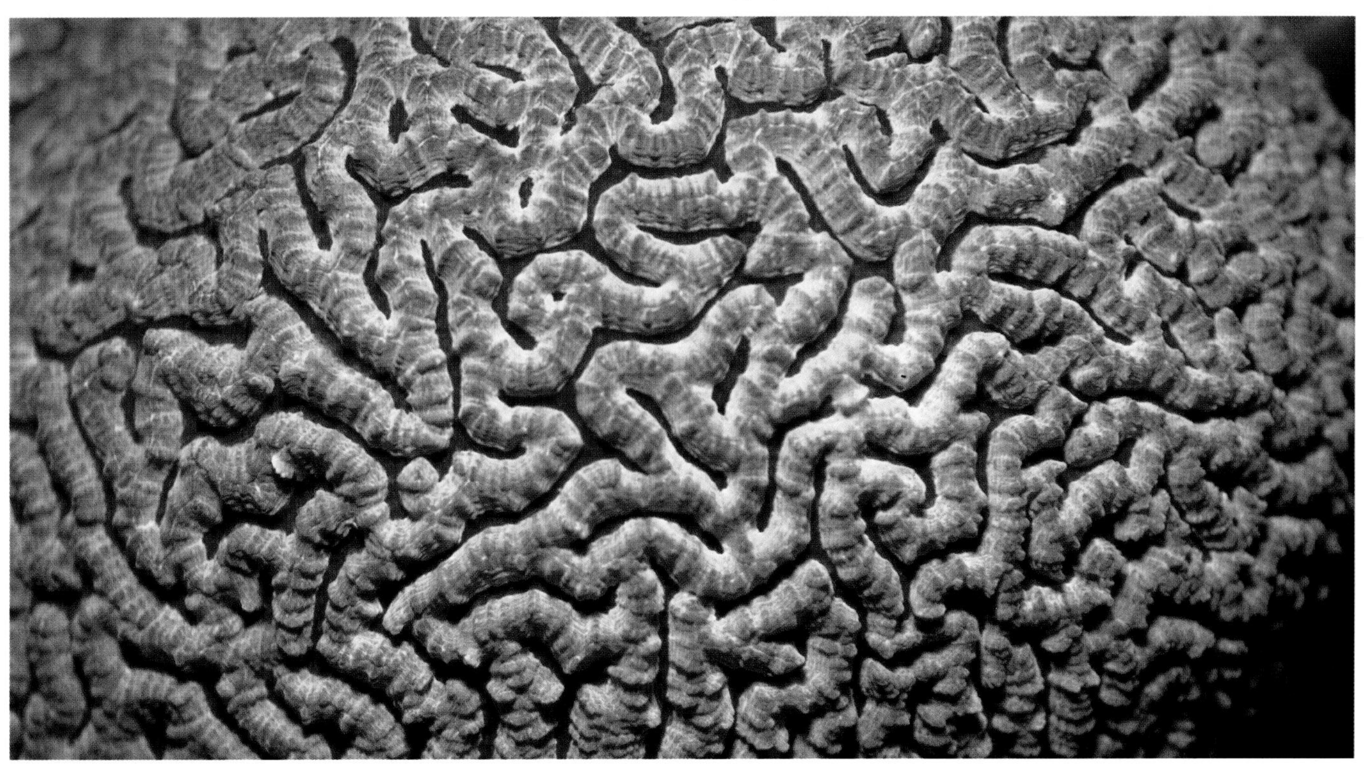

Platygyra sp. Solomon Islands.

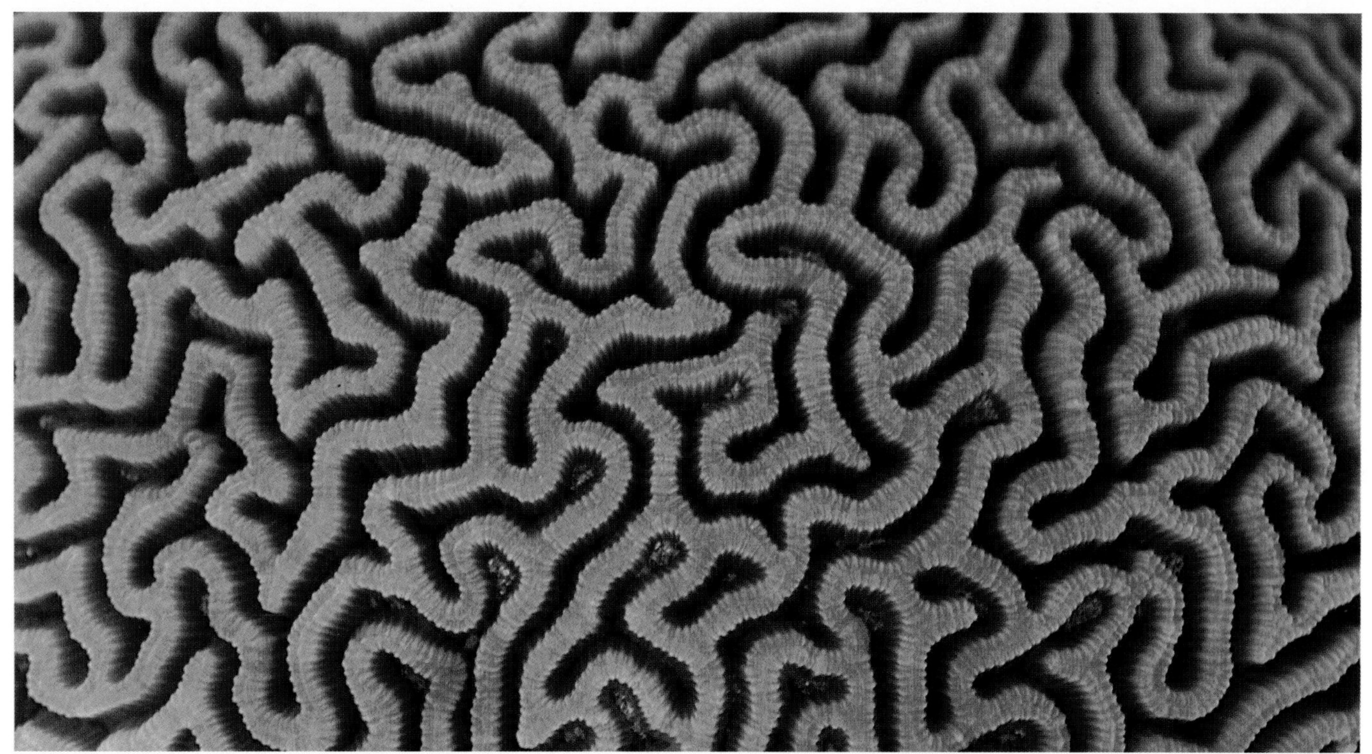

Platygyra sp. from the Red Sea. Specimens with such sinuous labrynths are easily confused with Leptoria.

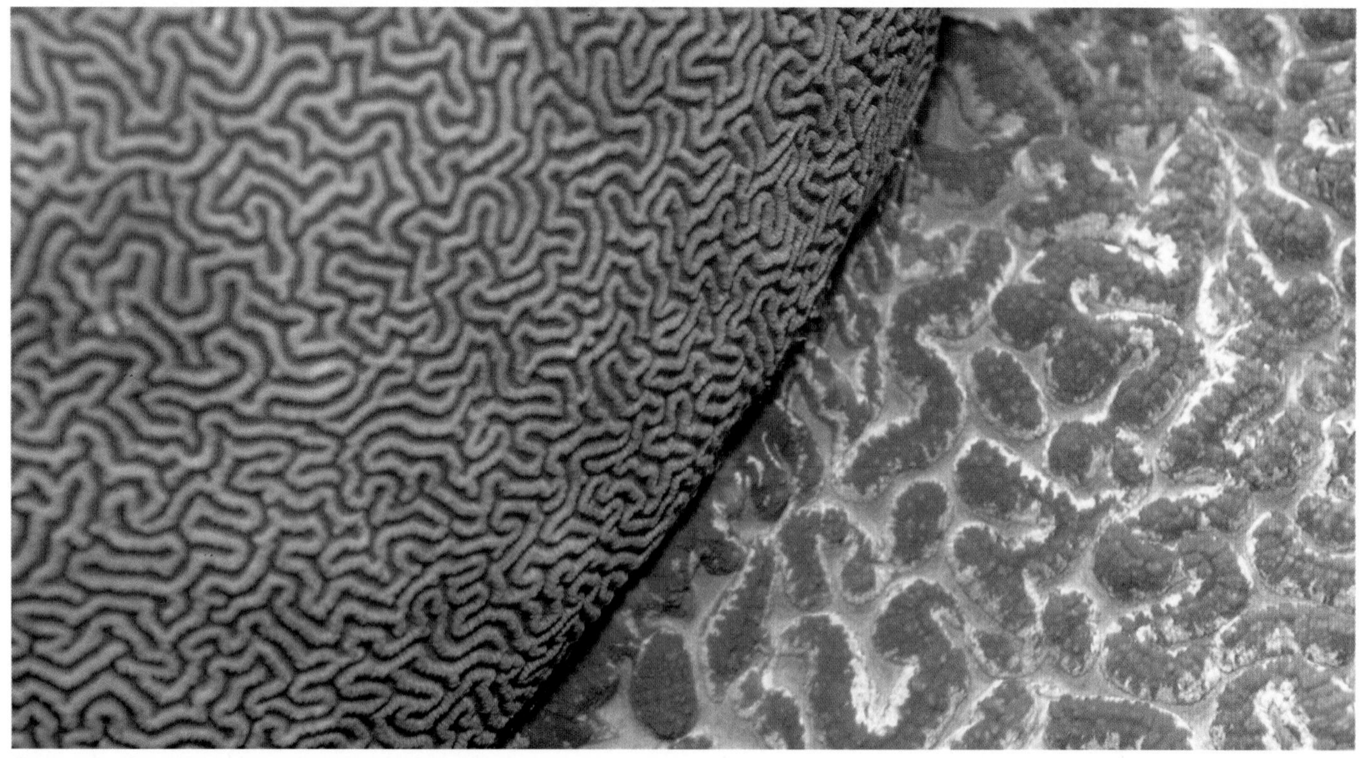

Platygyra sp. left, *Symphyllia* sp. right. A meeting of the minds. Solomon Islands.

Merulina

Pronunciation: MEHR-yoo-LINE-uh (MEH-roo-LINE-uh)

Common Name: Lettuce Coral, Cabbage Coral

Region: Red Sea and Indian Ocean to Japan and east to the south central Pacific.

Description: Colonies foliaceous, laminar, columnar, or arborescent, often showing all of these characteristics within one colony. Short valleys spread fanwise from colony center on laminar plates, becoming contorted on branches.

Similar Corals: Branched portions resemble *Hydnophora* and *Paraclavarina.* Laminar portions resemble *Scapophyllia,* which does not have fanwise spreading valleys.

Lighting Needs	4 - 10
Water Flow	4 - 9
Aggressiveness	2
Hardiness	7

Placement

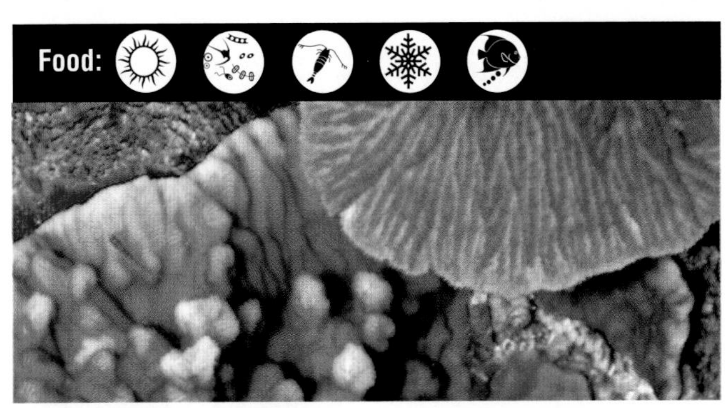

Merulina ampliata, below, *Merulina scabricula* above it. Solomon Islands.

Portion of *M. ampliata* with contorted branches.

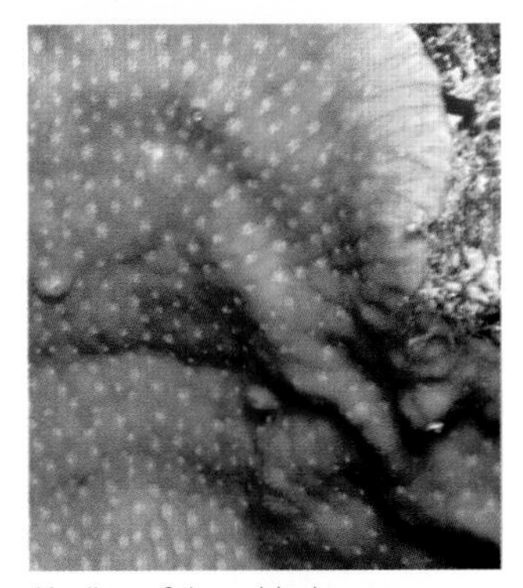

Merulina sp. Solomon Islands.

Australogyra

Pronunciation: OSS-truh-lo-JAI-ruh

Common Name: Horn Coral, *Hydnophora*, Antler Coral.

Region: Australia, New Guinea, Solomon Islands, Indonesia, Philippines, Vietnam.

Description: Encrusting flat plates with robust upright contorted branches that have sharp tips. Polyps are cerioid to meandroid.

Similar Corals: Quite similar to *Hydnophora* superficially, but considered a close relative of *Platygyra,* family Faviidae. In the author's opinion *Australogyra* belongs in the family Merulinidae, closest to *Paraclavarina. Goniastrea pectiniata* is similar to *Australogyra* and especially to *Merulina.* It may also belong to the Merulinidae, though this is not its current taxonomic placement either.

Lighting Needs	4 - 9
Water Flow	4 - 9
Aggressiveness	2
Hardiness	3

Placement

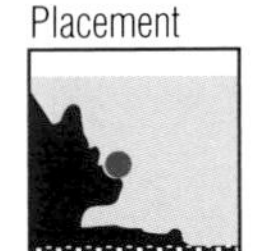

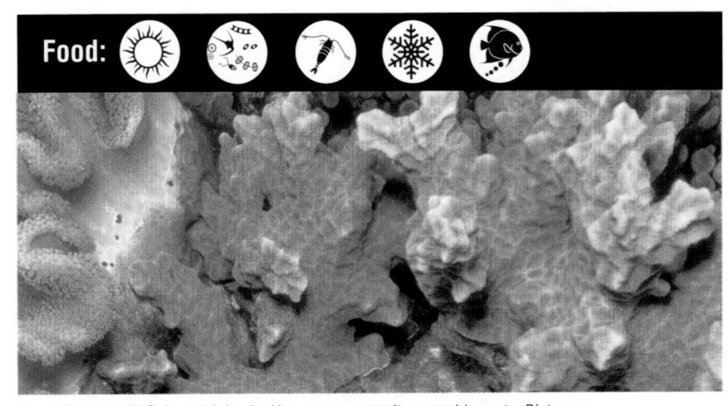

Australogyra zelli, Solomon Islands. Here one can see its resemblance to *Platygyra*.

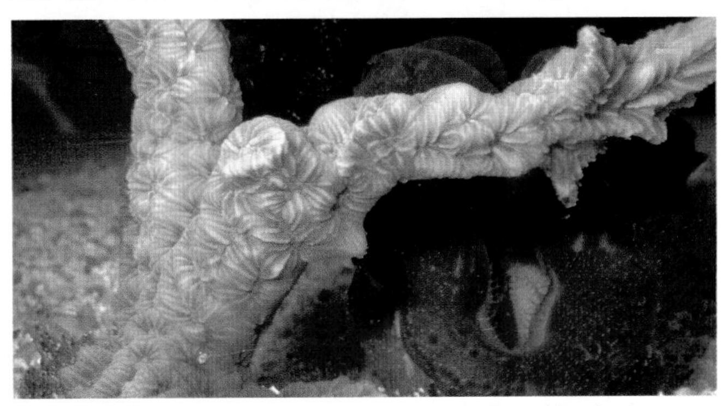

Australogyra zelli, closeup detail showing strong similarity to *Hydnophora* and *Paraclavarina*.

Scapophyllia

Pronunciation: SKAP-oh-FILL-ee-uh

Common Name: Pillar coral, Brain coral.

Region: Western Pacific to Eastern Indian Ocean.

Description: Colonies with columns rising from encrusting laminar base. The valleys are meandroid and sinuous.

Similar Corals: Most similar to *Merulina* which has shorter valleys that spread out fanwise. Also similar to *Leptoria* which has meandroid valleys but does not form upright columns.

Placement

Lighting Needs	4 - 9
Water Flow	5 - 9
Aggressiveness	4
Hardiness	5

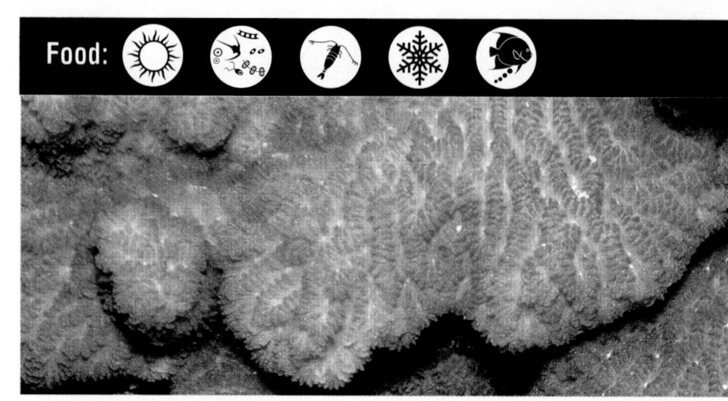

Scapophyllia cylindrica, closeup detail. Solomon Islands.

Scapophyllia cylindrica, Solomon Islands.

Hydnophora

Pronunciation: HIDE-no-FOR-uh (HID-no-FOR-uh, hid-NOF-or-uh)

Common Name: *Acropora*, Horn coral, Branch coral, Fluorescent coral.

Region: Indo-Pacific, Red Sea.

Description: Colonies massive, encrusting or arborescent. Sometimes the branches of *Hydnophora rigida* are more rounded in cross section and the hydnophores are less distinct, the latter form apparently a product of environmental effects (i.e. strong water motion). *Hydnophora excesa* has branches about twice as thick as those of *H. rigida.*

Similar Corals: Some forms of *H. rigida* are very similar to *Paraclavarina triangularis. Australogyra zelli* is similar to branchy *Hydnophora* spp., but lacks hydnophores.

Placement

Lighting Needs	5 - 9
Water Flow	5 - 9
Aggressiveness	4
Hardiness	6

Food:

The Orangespot filefish feeding on *Hydnophora rigida*. Solomon Islands.

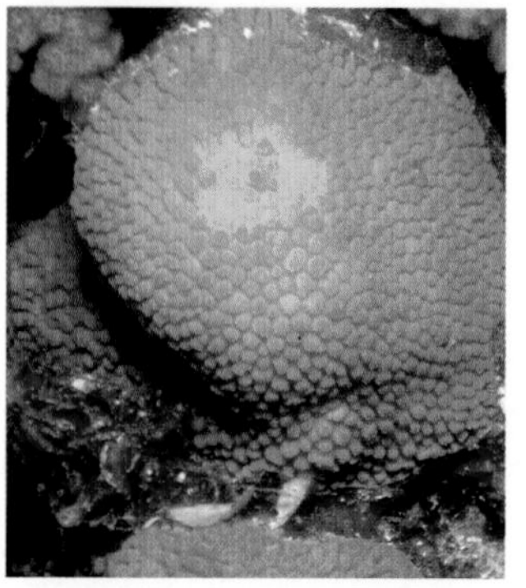

Hydnophora microconos, Solomon Islands.

Small *Hydnophora exesa*, Solomon Islands

Hydnophora pilosa. Aquarium photo.

Paraclavarina
Pronunciation: PAH-ra-KLAV-uh-RINE-uh

Common Name: Horn Coral, Night-Blooming *Australogyra.*

Region: Western Pacific, Australia, New Guinea, Solomon Islands In turbid lagoons.

Description: Colonies of anastomosing branches approximately 1 cm in diameter that are triangular in section. Corallites are in short, shallow velleys like grooves on the branches. The calcification is dense and the skeletal elements of the corallites are fused into a solid structure.

Similar Corals: Most similar to *Hydnophora rigida,* which usually has hydnophores on its branches. One form of *H. rigida* does not have hydnophores, and it has corallites quite similar to those of *Paraclavarina.* Also similar to *Australogyra zelli* and *Pectinia teres,* which grow in the same habitat.

Rating	Value
Lighting Needs	3 - 7
Water Flow	2 - 8
Aggressiveness	2
Hardiness	5

Placement

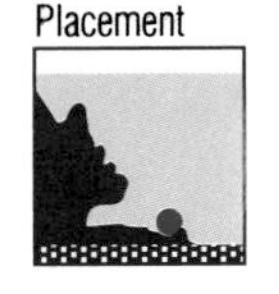

Hydnophora rigida. Solomon Islands. Under low light conditions it has this form.

Hydnophora grandis is very similar to *H. rigida*, but has slightly thicker branches. Aquarium photo.

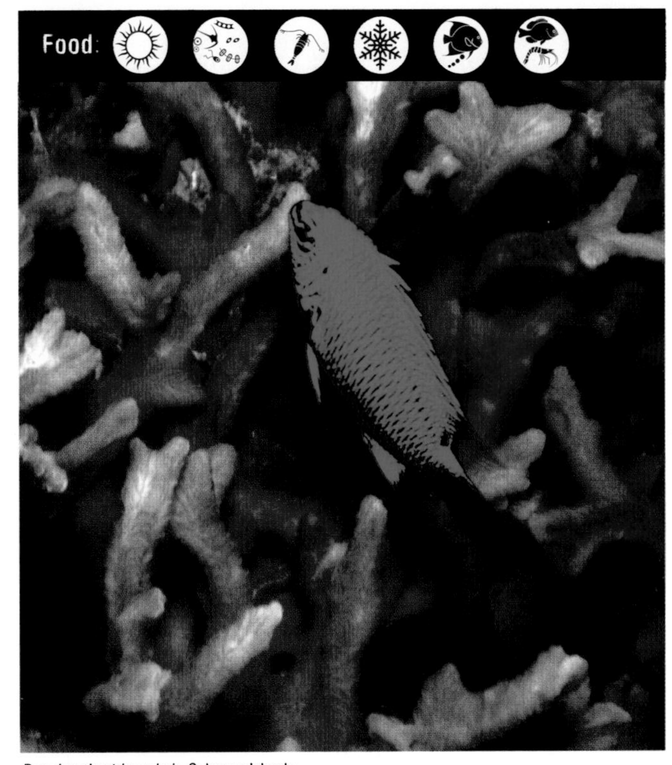

Paraclavarina triangularis, Solomon Islands.

Pectinia

Pronunciation: pek-TIN-ee-yuh

Common Name: *Pectinia*, Lettuce Coral, Hibiscus coral, Carnation Coral, Cabbage Coral, Spiny Cup coral

Distinguishing Characteristics: Colonies like ruffled leaves with thin, sharp ridges or long spires in the center of the colony. Some colonies are branchy (see for example *P. teres*). Corallites widely spaced and not very distinctive. Colours include brown, gray, purple, green, yellow, sometimes red.

Similar Corals: *Physophyllia* is essentially like *Pectinia* but forms flat plates, see Veron, 1986. At least one form of *Pectinia* looks like *Oulophyllia*.

Region: Indo-Pacific, Red Sea. More abundant in turbid water on fringing reefs, lagoons or on reef slopes, but also present on outer barrier reefs.

Lighting Needs	3 - 8
Water Flow	2 - 9
Aggressiveness	2
Hardiness	6

Placement

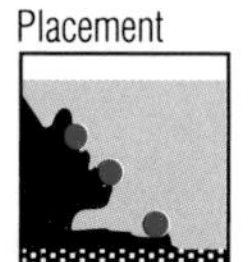

Pectinia paeonia. Solomon Islands. This form looks like *Sinularia dura.*

Pectinia lactuca. Solomon Islands.

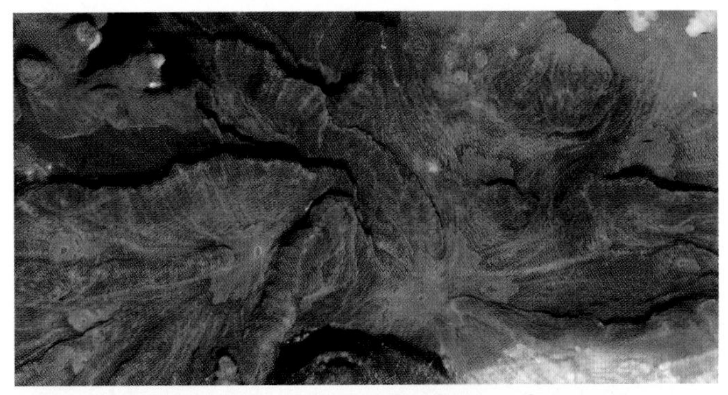

Extremely colorful *Pectinia* sp. from Japan. Display aquarium Blue Harbor, Osaka, Japan.

This *Pectinia* sp. *mimics Oulophyllia crispa*. Solomon Islands.

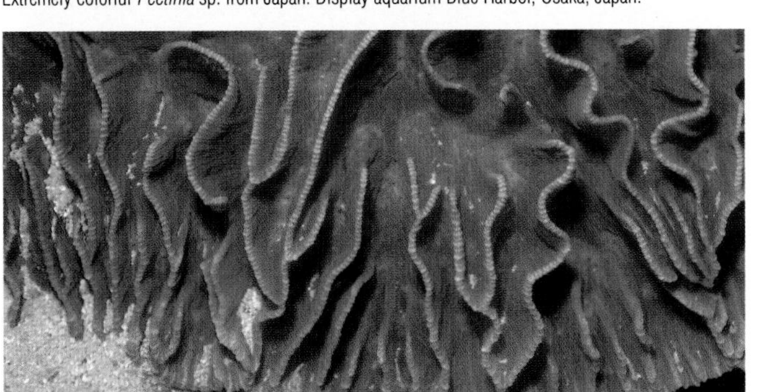

Pectinia cf. *lactuca*, large colony. Solomon Islands.

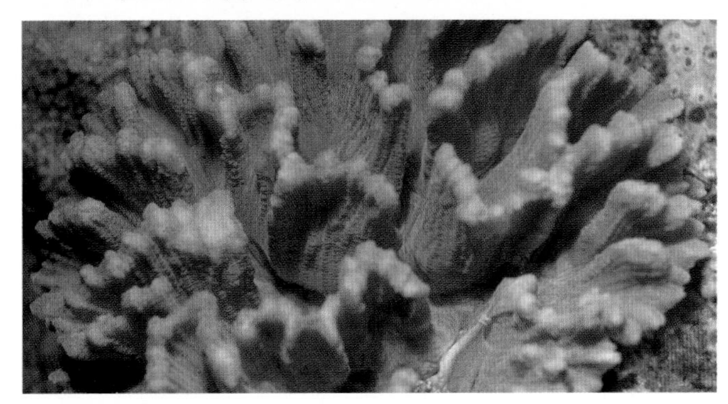

Pectinia paeonia. Solomon Islands.

Pectinia sp. small colony. Aquarium photo, display aquarium Sea Dwelling Creatures.

Pectinia teres. Solomon Islands.

Blue *Pectinia paeonia*. Solomon Islands.

Pectinia sp. Solomon Islands.

Mycedium

Pronunciation: my-SEE-dee-um

Common Name: Mycedium, Plate Coral, Green-eyed Cup

Region: Red Sea, Indo-Pacific as far east as Tahiti

Description: Laminar or foliaceous colonies with widely spaced corallites. The corallites face outward to the perimeter of the colony and project off the thin plate-like skeleton like little noses (Veron, 1986). Costae form relatively smooth outward radiating lines that reach the perimeter of the corallum. The perimeter of the corallum has a rolled appearance, less dentate than similar-looking *Oxypora*.

Similar Corals: *Oxypora* has shallow corallites thar are not inclined like noses, and a spiny appearance due to the teeth on its costae. In *Echinophyllia* the costae have distinctive teeth.

	Range
Lighting Needs	3 - 7
Water Flow	2 - 7
Aggressiveness	2
Hardiness	6

Placement

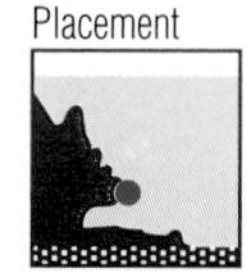

Mycedium elephantotus. Solomon Islands.

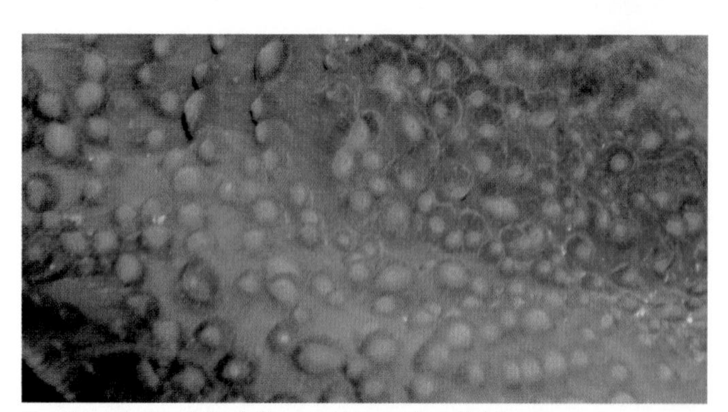

Mycedium elephantotus. Lobbecke Museum and Aquazoo, Dusseldorf, Germany.

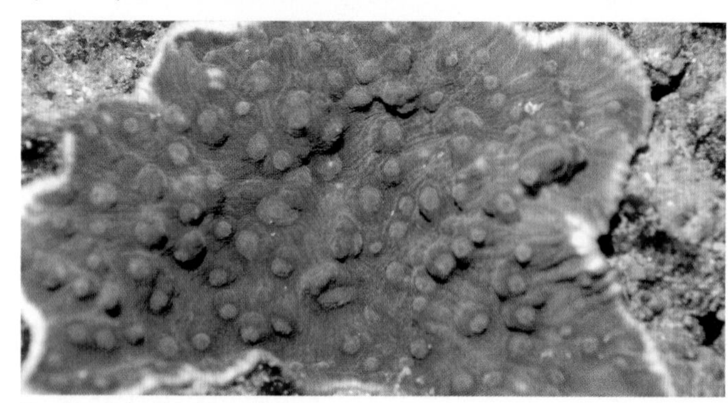

Mycedium elephantotus. Solomon Islands.

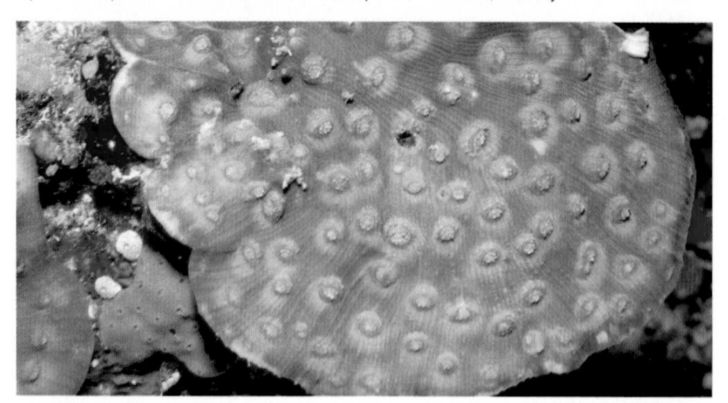

Mycedium elephantotus. Solomon Islands.

Mycedium robokaki. Solomon Islands.

Oxypora

Pronunciation: OX-ee-POR-uh

Common Name: Lettuce coral, Porous Lettuce coral, Green Eyed Cup coral

Region: Red Sea and Indian Ocean to Japan and east to the south central Pacific.

Description: Foliaceous colonies with rough texture. Corallites not strongly inclined. The edges of the colony are dentate.

Similar Corals: Similar to *Mycedium*, *Echinopora* and *Echinophyllia*.

Lighting Needs	3 - 9
Water Flow	2 - 9
Aggressiveness	2
Hardiness	6

Placement

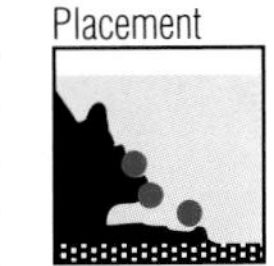

Mycedium robokaki. Solomon Islands.

Oxypora glabra. Solomon Islands.

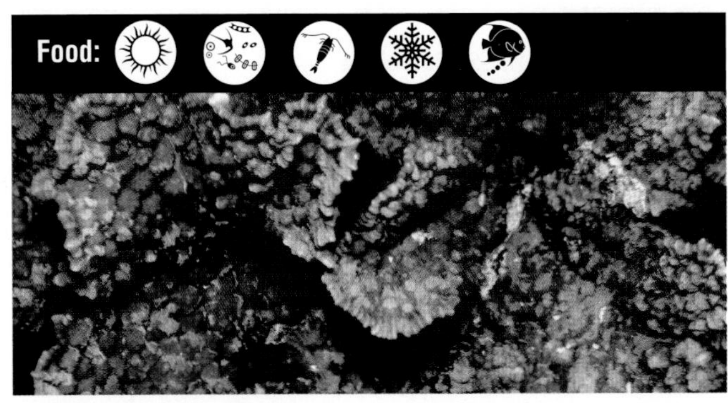

Mycedium mancaoi. Solomon Islands.

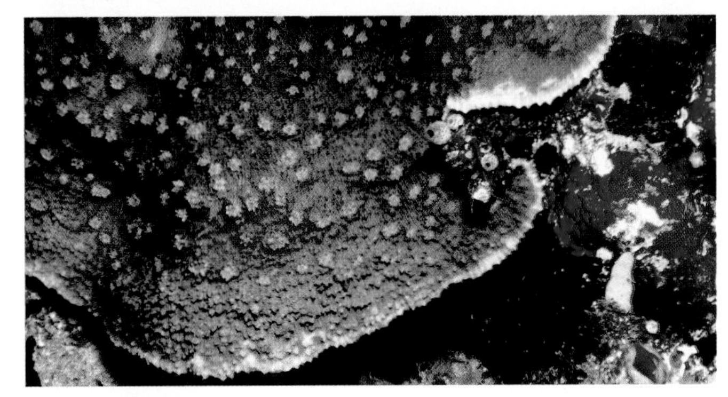

Oxypora lacera. Solomon Islands.

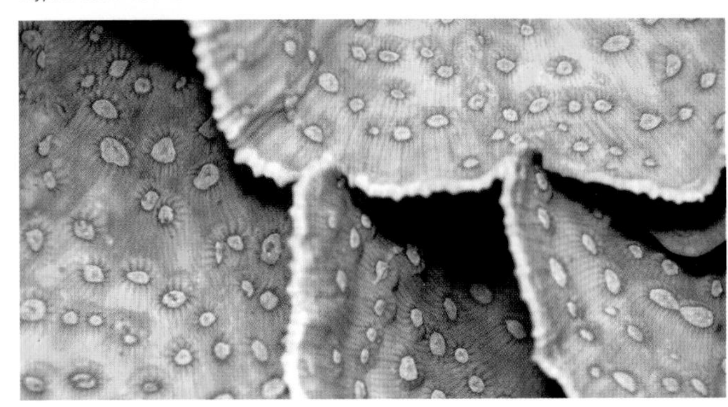

Color variation of Mycedium robokaki. Solomon Islands.

First polyp of *Oxypora glabra.* Solomon Islands.

Echinophyllia
Pronunciation: ee-KI-no-FILL-ee-uh

Common Name: Lettuce coral, Hedgehog coral

Region: Red Sea and Indian Ocean to Japan and east to the south central Pacific.

Description: Laminar, foliaceous, or encrusting colonies with immersed to tubular round corallites and spiny texture.

Similar Corals: Laminar colonies readily confused with *Oxypora, Mycedium,* and *Echinopora.* Young *Echinophyllia echinata* and *E. nishihirai* may resemble *Scolymia.*

Lighting Needs	3 - 8
Water Flow	2 - 9
Aggressiveness	4
Hardiness	7

Placement

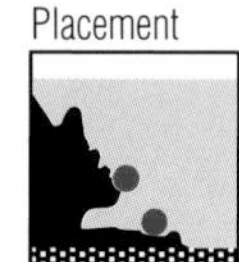

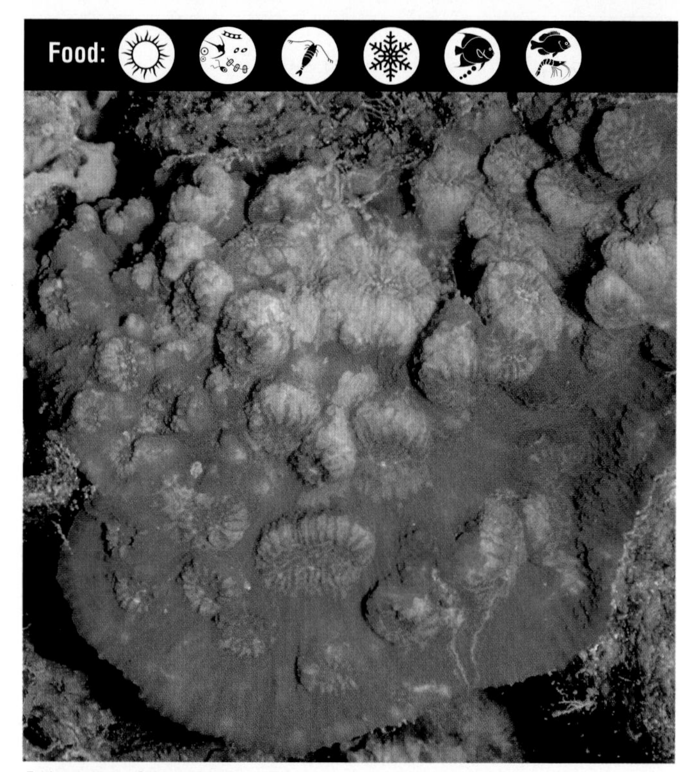

Echinophyllia sp. Solomon Islands.

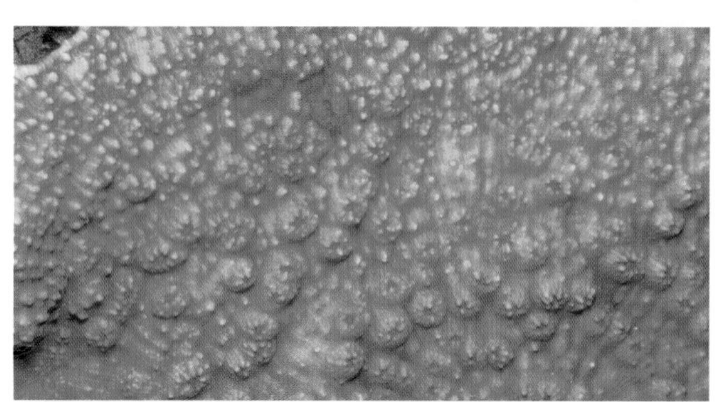

Echinophyllia sp. Solomon Islands.

Echinophyllia cf. *echinata.* Sea Dwelling Creatures' display aquarium.

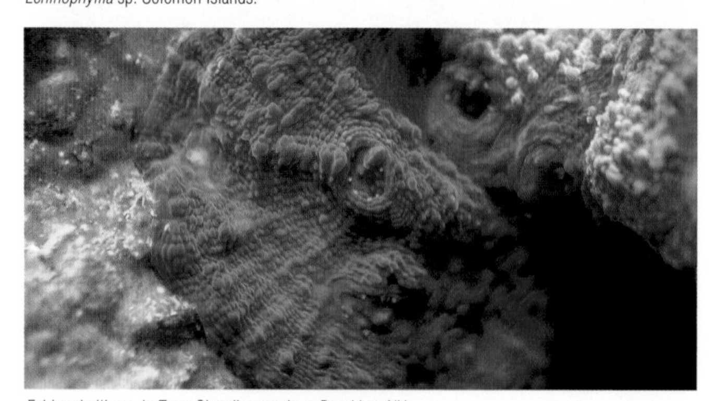

Echinophyllia sp. in Terry Siegel's aquarium, Brooklyn, NY.

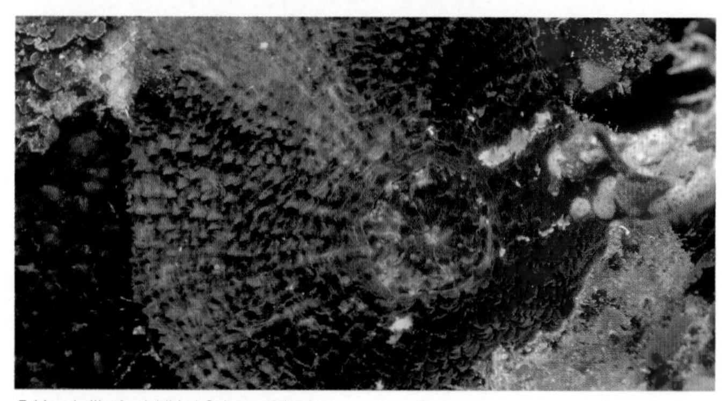

Echinophyllia cf. *nishihirai.* Solomon Islands.

Acanthastrea
Pronunciation: AK-an-THASS-tree-uh

Common Name: Pineapple coral, Artichoke coral, Starry cup coral, *Favia*

Region: Red Sea and Indian Ocean to Japan and east to the south central Pacific.

Description: Massive flattened, encrusting, or dome-shaped colonies with cerioid or subplocoid corallites with tall sharp teeth on the septo-costae.

Similar Corals: Similar to *Isophyllastrea rigida* from the Caribbean. Also similar to *Mussismilia braziliensis* and *M. hispida* from Brazil. Superficially resembles Faviids, but the spiny skeleton of mussids distinguishes it readily. Some species with big polyps are very like *Symphyllia*, some resemble *Blastomussa wellsi*, and others *Echinophyllia*.

Lighting Needs	3 - 9
Water Flow	3 - 10
Aggressiveness	6
Hardiness	7

Placement

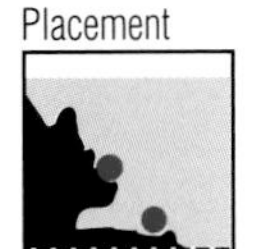

Food:

Acanthastrea echinata, Solomon Islands.

Acanthastrea lordhowensis looks like *Blastomussa*. St. George's Aquarium, Sydney, Australia.

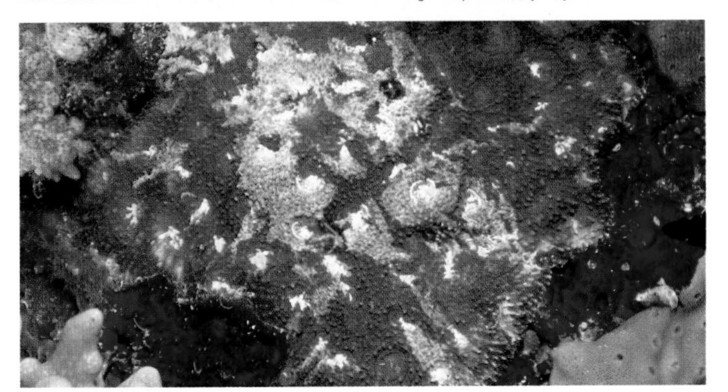

This cryptic coral could be an *Echinophyllia* sp. or an *Acanthastrea* sp., Solomon Islands.

Acanthastrea sp. that resembles *Favia* spp. Solomon Islands.

Isophyllastrea

Pronunciation: I-so-FILL-ass-TREE-uh

Common Name: Pineapple coral, Rough Star Coral, Polygonal coral

Region: Caribbean

Description: Small hemispherical dome shaped colonies with polygonal shaped calyces. Septal teeth give rough texture. Polyps fleshy, approximately 15mm in diameter, usually monocentric, but sometimes with more than one center per valley.

Similar Corals: Very similar to *Acanthastrea* from the Red Sea and Indo-Pacific. Also similar to *Mussismilia braziliensis* and *M. hispida* from Brazil. Veron (2000) makes *Isophyllastrea* a synonym of *Isophyllia.*

Lighting Needs	3 - 9
Water Flow	3 - 9
Aggressiveness	6
Hardiness	6

Placement

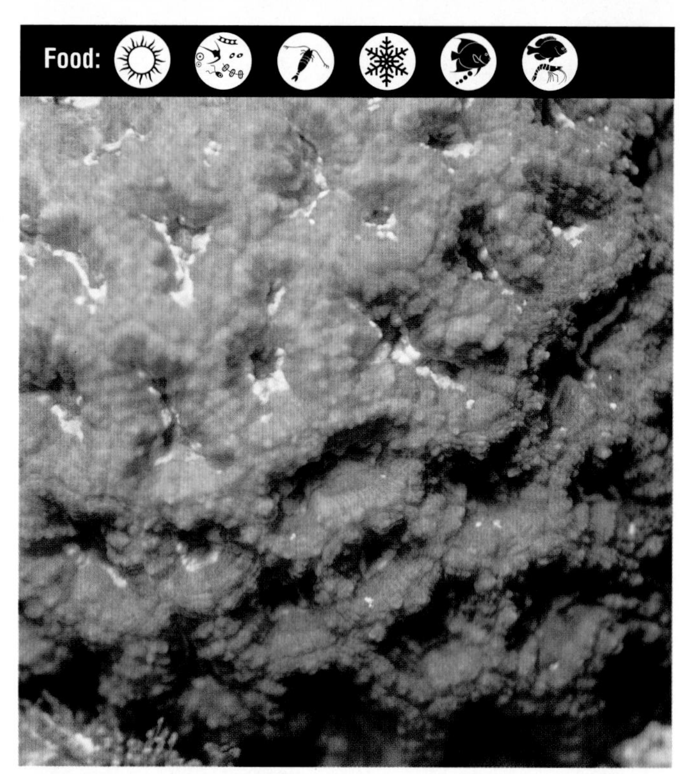

Isophyllia (= *Isophyllastrea*) *rigida*, Bahamas.

Mussismilia

Pronunciation: MUSS-is-MILL-ee-uh

Common Name: Flower Coral

Region: Brazil

Description: Three species, *Mussismilia hartti*, which is phacelloid, with large polyps, *Mussismilia braziliensis*, which is cerioid with small polyps, and *M. hispida*, which is cerioiod to subplocoid with polyps of irregular shape, sized intermediate between the other two. All are endemic to Brazil.

Similar Corals: Similar to *Acanthastrea* from the Red Sea and Indo-Pacific, and *Isophyllastrea rigida* from the Caribbean. *Mussismilia hartti* is superficially similar to *Lobophyllia corymbosa* from the Red Sea and Indo-Pacific.

Lighting Needs	4 - 8
Water Flow	3 - 8
Aggressiveness	6
Hardiness	6

Placement

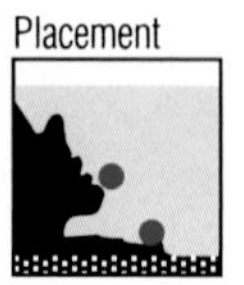

Mussismillia hartti.

Mussismillia hispida in the aquarium of J. C. Basso, Sao Paulo, Brazil.

Isophyllia

Pronunciation: I-so-FILL-ee-uh

Common Name: Cactus coral, Sinuous cactus coral, Brain coral

Region: Caribbean

Description: In Florida, the Bahamas, and northern Caribbean usually small hemispherical meandroid domes up to 25 cm across, with wide valleys. With large septa and sharp teeth. Very fleshy polyps expand to hide sharp skeleton. In the southern Caribbean (around Panama) colonies may be much larger, up to more than 1 meter across, with more narrow valleys. This latter form is extremely like *Symphyllia.*

Similar Corals: This genus strongly resembles *Symphyllia* from the Red Sea and Indo-Pacific. Sometimes colonies are not meandroid but cerioid instead. These may be confused with *Isophyllastrea.*

		Placement
Lighting Needs	3 - 10	
Water Flow	3 - 9	
Aggressiveness	8	
Hardiness	7	

Food:

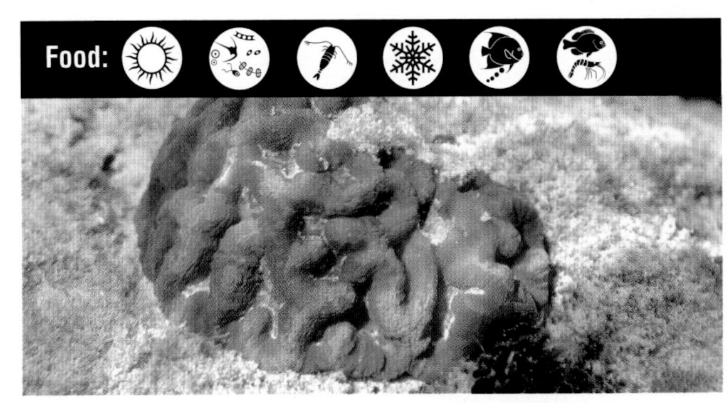

Isophyllia sinuosa. Bahamas.

Isophyllia sinuosa. Bahamas.

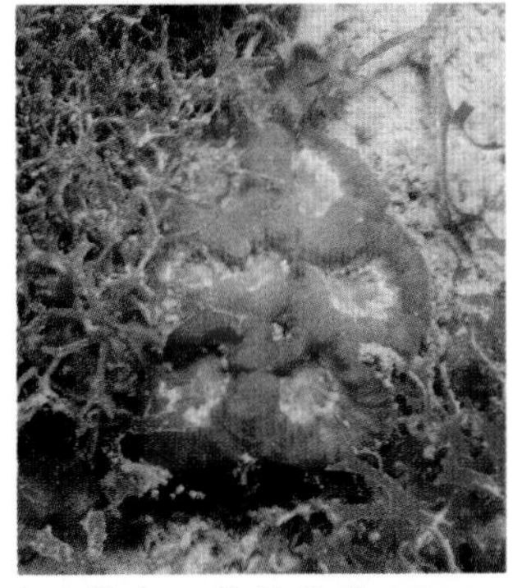

Isophyllia sinuosa. Florida. Small specimen.

Symphyllia

Pronunciation: sim-FILL-ee-uh

Common Name: Brain coral, Open Brain coral

Region: Red Sea, Indian Ocean, Japan, Australia, to south central Pacific.

Description: Meandroid massive colonies with wide valleys. Tops of walls with a groove, usually. Large septa have long sharp teeth.

Similar Corals: Similar to *Isophyllia* from the Caribbean. *Symphyllia valenciennesii* is similar to *Lobophyllia* and small specimens of it may also be confused with *Scolymia.*

		Placement
Lighting Needs	3 - 9	
Water Flow	2 - 9	
Aggressiveness	8	
Hardiness	8	

Food:

Symphyllia radians. Aquarium photo.

Symphyllia agaricia. Solomon Islands.

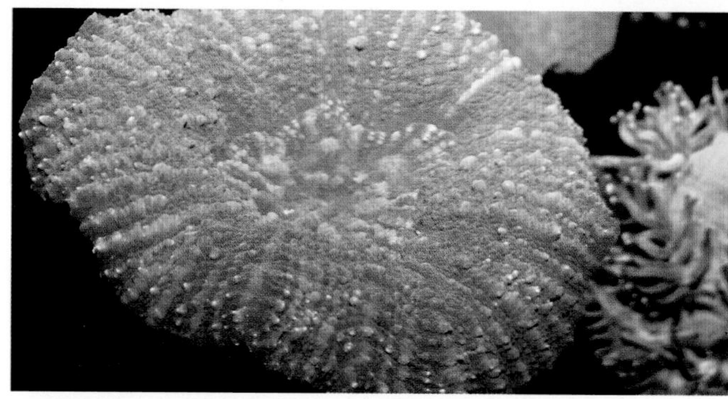

Symphyllia valenciennesii, small polyp, which resembles *Scolymia.* Aquarium photo.

Mature *Symphyllia valenciennesii*, Aquarium Photo.

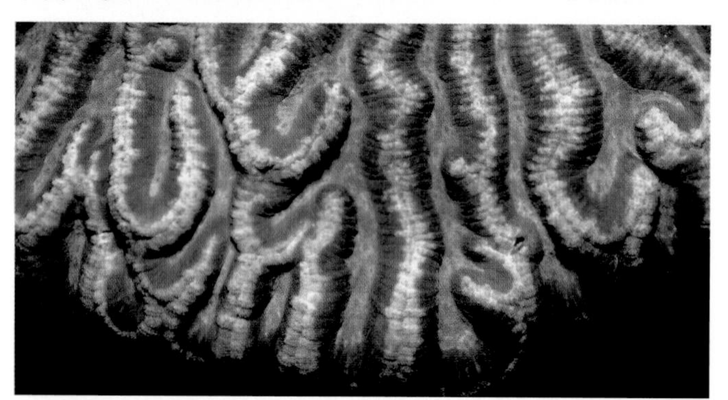

Symphyllia radians. Solomon Islands.

Small *Symphyllia valenciennesii*, resemble another uncommon coral, *Lobophyllia robusta.*

Symphyllia recta. Solomon Islands.

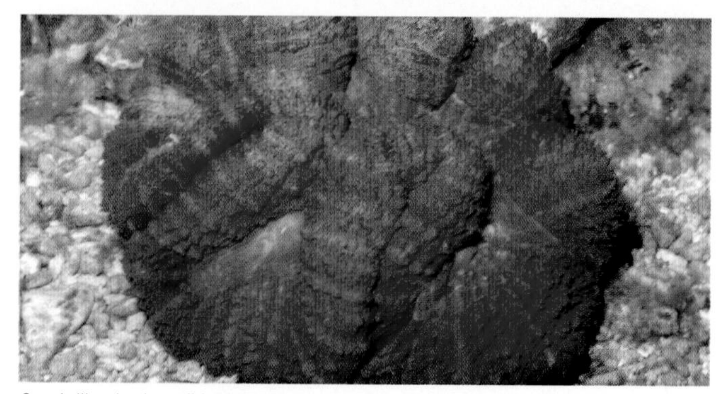

Symphyllia valenciennesii, Lobbecke Museum and Aquazoo, Dusseldorf, Germany.

Mycetophyllia

Pronunciation: my-SEE-to-FILL-ee-uh

Common Name: Ridged Cactus coral

Region: Caribbean

Description: Flat plates or irregular encrusting mounds with scalloped edges and ridges that run around colony edge and toward center.

Similar Corals: *Colpophyllia* has a form that mimics *Mycetophyllia danaana.*

Lighting Needs		3 - 8
Water Flow		3 - 8
Aggressiveness		3
Hardiness		7

Placement

Food:

Mycetophyllia aliciae, large colony in shallow water. Florida Keys.

Mycetophyllia aliciae. First polyp.

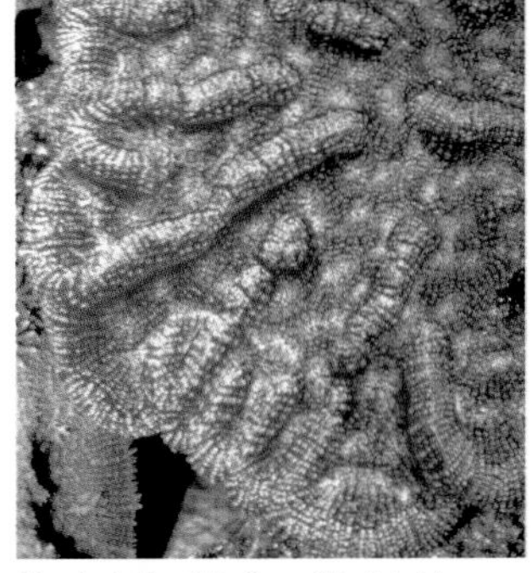

Mycetophyllia aliciae forms thin flat plates.

Mycetophyllia danaana. Florida Keys.

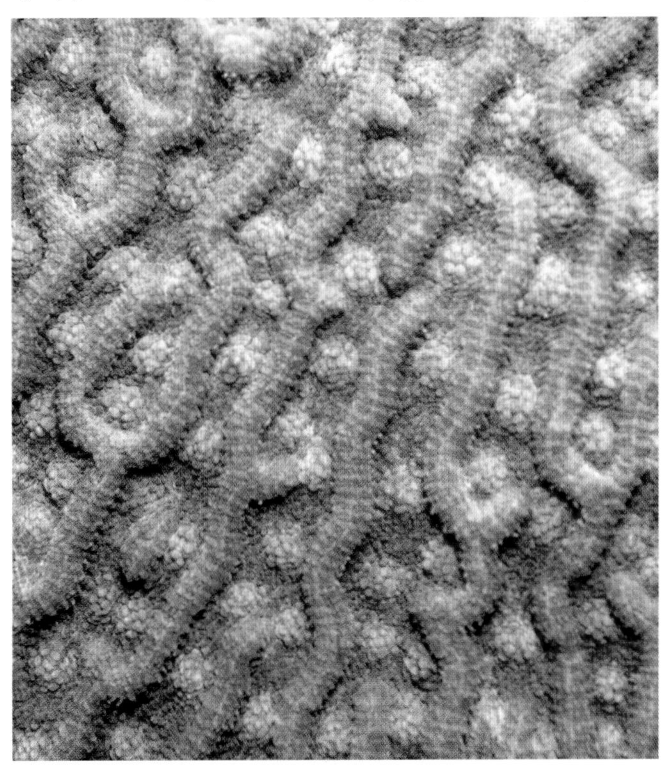

Mycetophyllia ferox. Florida Keys.

Lobophyllia

Pronunciation: LO-bo-FILL-ee-uh

Common Name: Flower coral, Colored Brain coral, Carpet Brain coral

Region: Red Sea, Indian Ocean to Japan and south central Pacific.

Description: Colonies phacelloid to flabello-meandroid. Large corallites with numerous long septal teeth and fleshy polyps.

Similar Corals: *Mussa angulosa* from the Caribbean, *Mussismilia* from Brazil.

Lighting Needs	3 - 8
Water Flow	2 - 8
Aggressiveness	8
Hardiness	8

Placement

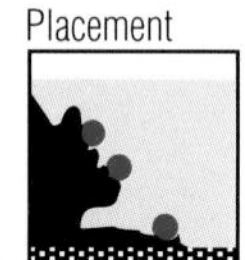

Lobophyllia hemprichii, Solomon Islands.

Lobophyllia hemprichii, Waikiki Aquarium, Honolulu, Hawai'i.

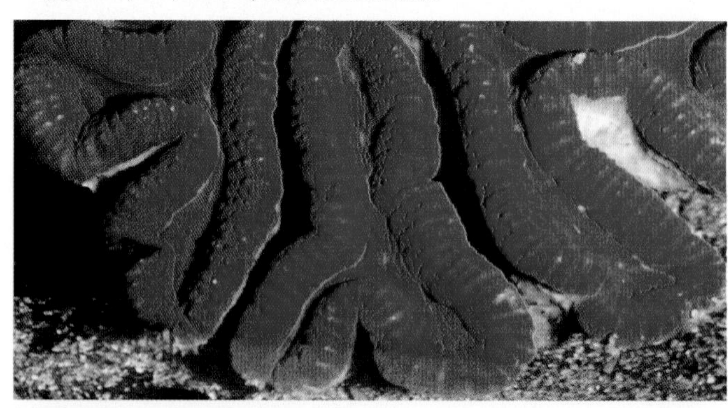

Lobophyllia hemprichii, polyps contracted. Aquarium photo.

Lobophyllia hemprichii, polyp with pimply texture. aquarium photo.

Lobophyllia diminuta, Solomon Islands.

Lobophyllia hataii, aquarium photo.

Mussa

Pronunciation: MUSS-uh (MOOSE-uh)

Common Name: Flower coral

Region: Caribbean

Description: Phacelloid colonies with large fleshy polyps. Septa with numerous spiny teeth.

Similar Corals: Most similar to *Lobophyllia* from the Red Sea and Indo Pacific.

Lighting Needs	3 - 8
Water Flow	3 - 8
Aggressiveness	3
Hardiness	6

Placement

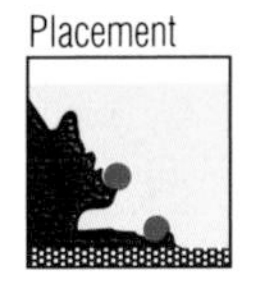

Lobophyllia corymbosa, aquarium photo.

Mussa angulosa, Bahamas.

Scolymia
Pronunciation: SKO-lee-MY-uh

Common Name: Artichoke coral

Region: Caribbean, Brazil, Indian, Western Pacific, south central Pacific

Description: Usually solitary large polyps, sometimes with secondary centers or dividing to form clusters of polyps. Primary septa with large regular teeth.

Similar Corals: Small *Lobophyllia, Mussa,* and *Mycetophyllia. Scolymia* do not expand as dramatically as *Cynarina. Scolymia australis* forms thick, tall skeletons up to 10 cm in diameter, with polyps like *Lobophyllia hemprichii. Scolymia vitiensis* may form flat plates up to 30 cm in diameter with skeletal characteristics like *Fungia. Scolymia vitiensis* also forms colonies with multiple centers that cannot easily be distinguished from the closely related *Australomussa.*

Lighting Needs	3 - 8
Water Flow	2 - 8
Aggressiveness	6
Hardiness	6

Placement

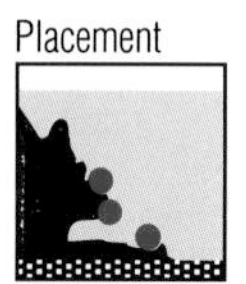

Scolymia vitiensis. Solomon Islands.

This could be *Australomussa rowleyensis* or *S. vitiensis* with multiple centers. Solomon Islands.

Scolymia vitiensis in Greg Schiemer's Aquarium.

Scolymia wellsi from Brazil, polyp deflated.

Lighting Needs		3 - 7
Water Flow		2 - 8
Aggressiveness		1
Hardiness		4

Placement

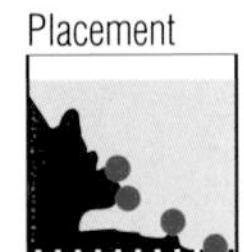

Scolymia wellsi from Brazil, polyp fully inflated.

Scolymia australis. A rare red and green specimen from the Whitsunday Islands, Australia.

Lighting Needs		3 - 8
Water Flow		2 - 8
Aggressiveness		2
Hardiness		5

Placement

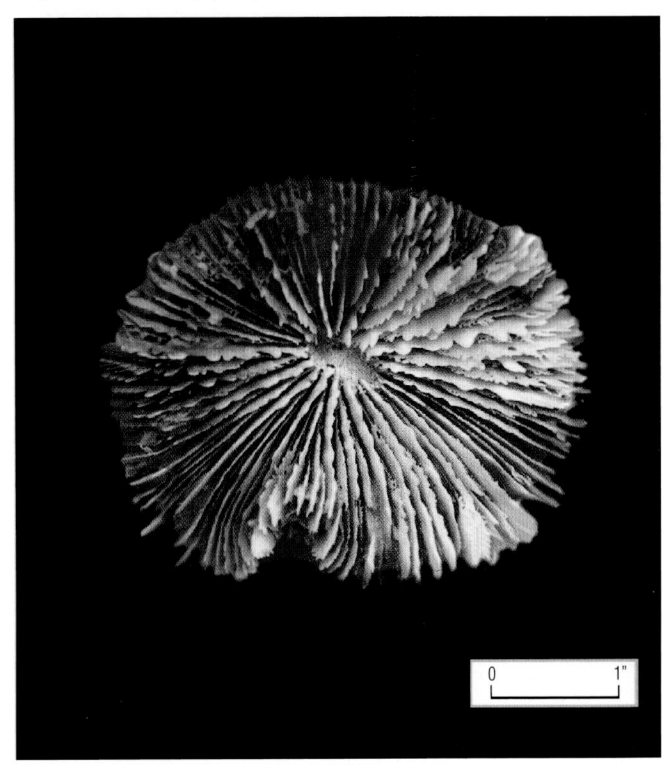

The skeleton of the same *Scolymia australis*, which died from an injury after five years in captivity.

Cynarina

Pronunciation: SY-nuh-REE-nuh

Common Name: Meat, Knob, or Doughnut coral, *Scolymia*

Region: Red Sea to Japan and south to Kermadec, Fiji

Description: Three distinct forms are probably separate species. All occur in Indonesia and expand a very large fleshy polyp, sometimes exceeding 35 cm in diameter. *Cynarina lacrymalis* has transparent tissue that forms bubble-like vesicles. Its skeleton reaches a maximum diameter of about 10 cm, having thick primary septa with large, often conical teeth. Pallus-like inner lobes are well developed, forming a distinctly separate rise in the center of the corallite. Another form of *Cynarina* does not form bubble-like vesicles, has thicker, opaque tissue, and a skeleton with diameter to at least 15 cm. The skeleton has thinner septa than those of *C. lacrymalis* and does not have distinct pallus-like inner lobes. This form was described as *Carophyllia deshayesiana* by Michelin (1850), and later by Wells (1937) as *Acanthophyllia deshayesiana*. See Wells (1964). Borel Best and Hoeksema (1987) describes the third species as *Indophyllia macassarensis*. The genus *Indophyllia* was described from fossils by Gerth (1921).

Similar Corals: *Cynarina* (= *Acanthophyllia*) *deshayesiana* is often confused with *Scolymia*. *Cynarina* (=*Indophyllia*) *macassarensis* has transparent tissue like *C. lacrymalis*. Veron (pers. comm., 1996) believed that the distinct looking *C. lacrymalis* and *Acanthophyllia deshayesiana* belong to one highly variable species only, *C. lacrymalis*. It is possible that in some localities the forms are not distinct. In Japan the author observed that the skeletons are the same for the quite different polyp forms. In the author's opinion the forms are distinct in Indonesia. See Veron (1995) for an explanation of speciation and coral taxonomy.

Lighting Needs	2 - 8
Water Flow	0 - 5
Aggressiveness	1
Hardiness	10

Placement

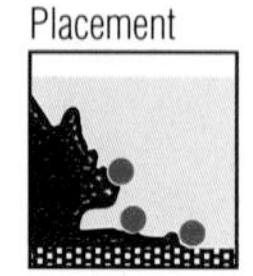

One of the most beautiful corals, *C. lacrymalis* in the Solomon Islands. Note visible "dog-tooth" septa.

Fluorescent Red *Cynarina lacrymalis*. Solomon Islands.

Extreme development of vesicles in *C. lacrymalis*. Doug Robbins' aquarium, Brooklyn, New York.

Two varieties of *Cynarina lacrymalis* skeletons. Note typical size and the presence of pallus-like lobes.

A lovely green *C. lacrymalis* in the aquarium of David Saxby, London England.

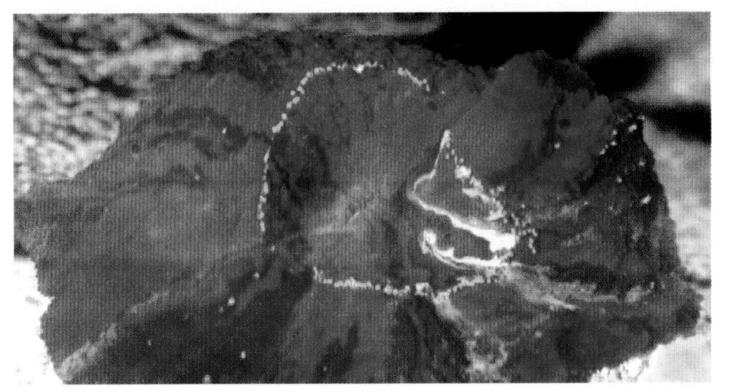
Cynarina deshayesiana can be extremely colorful, and is hardy in aquariums.

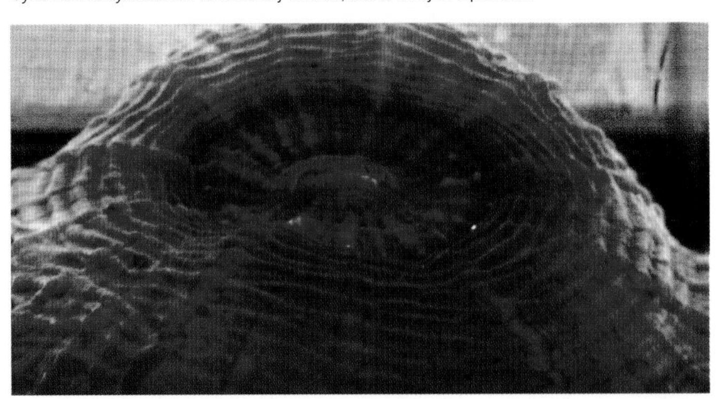
Cynarina (= *Indophyllia*) *macassarensis* appears intermediate between *C. deshayesiana* & *C. lacrymalis*.

Skeletons of *Cynarina* (= *Indophyllia*) *macassarensis*.

Compare this *C. deshayesiana* with the photo of *Scolymia australis*. Confusion is easy to understand.

The polyp of *C. deshayesiana* may develop a texture, as in *Lobophyllia hemprichii*.

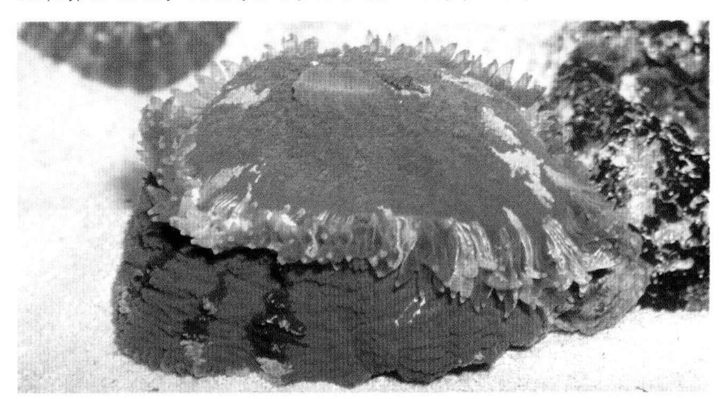
At night the *C. deshayesiana* polyp deflates and the tentacles extend, ready to capture prey.

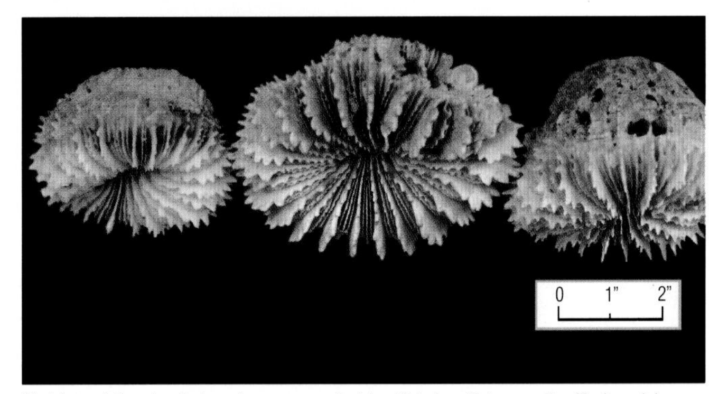

Skeletons of *Cynarina deshayesiana* may span to at least 5 inches. Note: no pallus-like inner lobes.

Blastomussa
Pronunciation: BLASS-toh-MUSS-uh

Common Name: Pineapple coral, Branched cup coral

Region: Red Sea to central Pacific

Description: Phacelloid to plocoid colonies with fleshy polyps that expand during the day and cover the skeletal structure. Corallites with one center each. *Blastomussa merleti* has corallites about 5 mm in diameter, *Blastomussa wellsi* has corallites about 15 mm or more in diameter.

Similar Corals: Colonies that are brown with green centers resemble *Caulastrea* . The latter is also phacelloid, but has corallites that often have more than one center.

Lighting Needs	2 - 7
Water Flow	1 - 7
Aggressiveness	3
Hardiness	8

Placement

Food:

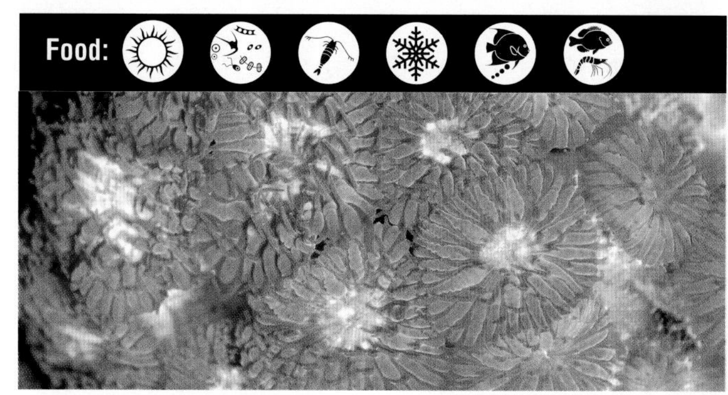

Blastomussa merleti. Aquarium photo.

Skeletal structure of *B. merleti*, upper left.

Blastomussa merleti, Red Sea. Like *Caulastrea*.

A stunning *B. wellsi*, Aquarium photo.

The skeleton of *Blastomussa wellsi*.

Blastomussa wellsi. Aquarium photo.

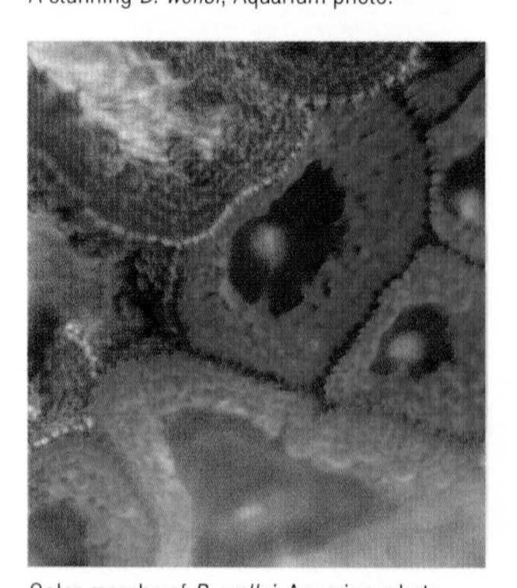

Color morphs of *B. wellsi*, Aquarium photo.

A colorful polyp of *B. wellsi*, Aquarium photo.

Blastomussa wellsi and *Scolymia vitiensis*, Solomon Islands.

Turbinaria
Pronunciation: TER-bin-AIR-ee-uh

Common Name: Scroll coral, Vase coral, Cup coral, Pagoda coral, Ruffled Ridge coral

Region: Red Sea, Indian Ocean, Japan to south central Pacific.

Description: Colonies typically foliaceous, but may also be massive, columnar, or branchy. Polyps are circular and immersed to tubular. Skeletal construction is dense and heavy.

Similar Corals: Aquarists sometimes confuse *Turbinaria* with *Montipora*. The latter is of a much more porous and delicate construction, with smaller polyps.

Lighting Needs	3 - 9
Water Flow	4 - 9
Aggressiveness	1
Hardiness	9

Placement

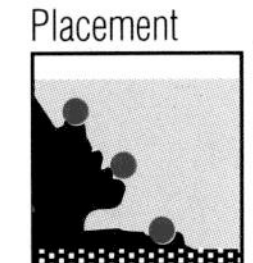

Food:

Turbinaria mesenterina, Red Sea.

Turbinaria cf. *frondens*, Solomon Islands

Turbinaria sp. Aquarium Photo.

Turbinaria stellulata, Solomon Islands

Turbinaria reniformis, Solomon Islands.

Turbinaria peltata, Solomon Islands.

Turbinaria peltata, Solomon Islands.

Duncanopsammia
Pronunciation: DUN-can-op-SAM-ee-uh

Common Name: "Whiskers"

Region: Australia, New Guinea, and eastern Indonesia (Veron, 1986).

Description: Large, fleshy polyps held at the end of a branchy dendroid skeleton. Has symbiotic zooxanthellae. Colour is grayish green or brown, sometimes bright fluorescent green.

Similar Corals: Similar to *Turbinaria heronensis*, which has thinner branches and smaller polyps. Borneman, (1996) confuses a similar-looking *Euphyllia* sp.with this species. Also resembles Elegance coral, *Catalaphyllia jardinei*, when fully expanded. When closed, *D. axifuga* resembles *Tubastraea micrantha*.

Lighting Needs	2 - 9
Water Flow	3 - 9
Aggressiveness	3
Hardiness	9

Placement

Duncanopsammia axifuga. Aquarium photo.

Duncanopsammia axifuga.

Tubastraea

Pronunciation: TOOB-ass-TREE-uh (too-BASS-tree-uh)

Common Name: Orange Cup coral, Turret coral, Orange Sun Polyp, Branching Octopus coral

Region: Caribbean, Red Sea, Indian, Pacific

Description: Colonies with tubular corallites

Similar Corals: *Balanophyllia, Dendrophyllia*

Lighting Needs	0
Water Flow	5 - 10
Aggressiveness	1
Hardiness	5

Placement

Tubastraea faulkneri with *T. micrantha* at night, Solomon Islands.

Tubastraea diaphana. Aquarium photo.

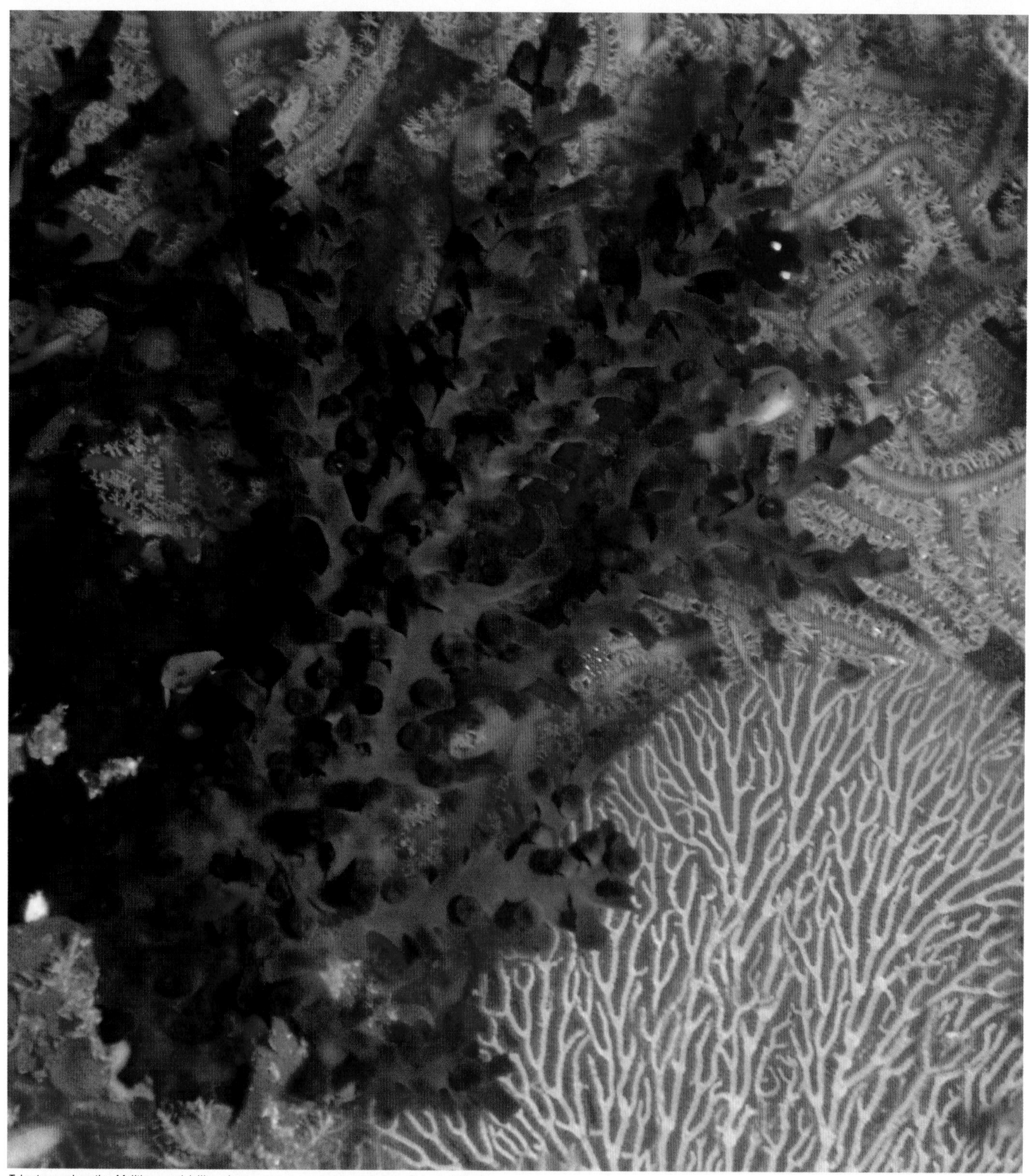

Tubastraea micrantha, *Melithaea*, and *Iciligorgia* on a current swept steep reef slope. Solomon Islands.

Chapter One

Dendrophyllia

Pronunciation: DEN-dro-FILL-ee-uh

Common Name: Turret coral

Region: Cosmopolitan

Description: Tube shaped corallites, colonies colored orange, salmon, brown, or green.

Similar Corals: *Tubastraea.* Distinguishable by skeletal features of mature polyps, see Veron (1986).

Placement

Lighting Needs	0
Water Flow	4 - 10
Aggressiveness	2
Hardiness	6

Dendrophyllia sp. Solomon Islands.

Balanophyllia

Pronunciation: BAL-uh-no-FILL-ee-uh

Common Name: Turret coral

Region: Cosmopolitan

Description: Usually solitary but sometimes forming small clumps of attached polyps. Ahermatypic. Brightly colored polyps in shades of orange, magenta, or red

Similar Corals: *Tubastraea* and *Dendrophyllia*

Placement

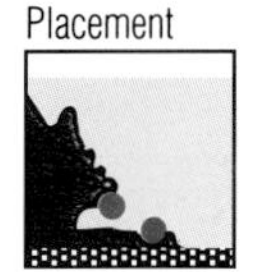

Lighting Needs	0
Water Flow	3 - 9
Aggressiveness	2
Hardiness	6

Balanophyllia sp. photographed at the Waikiki Aquarium.

Soft Corals

Soft corals are a diverse group of animals that includes Sea pens, sea fans, sea whips, and fleshy soft corals, as well as the Organ Pipe, Blue, and Red Precious coral that form hard skeletons.

Like stony corals, soft corals belong to the Class Anthozoa, but they differ from stony corals because they have eight tentacles per polyp, hence they belong to the Subclass Octocorallia (Alcyonaria). Exceptions to the eight tentacle rule occur only as rare mutations or aberrent individual polyps (see Sprung and Delbeek, 1997). Another characteristic of most soft coral polyps is the presence of side branchlets called pinnules on each tentacle. The pinnules make the tentacles look like little feathers or palm fronds. Presently these pinnules are considered to be a characteristic of the tentacles of all soft corals. This is not the case. While it is well known that some soft corals have extremely reduced pinnules, a few tropical species have no pinnules at all, and some have fused pinnules, which give the tentacles a paddle-like appearance. Some of these special polyped soft corals are featured in this book.

Another feature of soft corals is the presence of minute, spiny or sand-like skeletal elements known as sclerites (spicules to some folks, though the latter term is used more often for the skeletal spines in sponges). Soft coral sclerites are made of calcite, a form of calcium carbonate. Taxonomists use them to identify soft corals because the different groups and species have characteristically shaped sclerites.

Colony shape is sometimes useful for identifying soft corals. Some, however, share the same form while being only distantly related and some have completely different colony forms though closely related.

While the perception of coral reefs seems to focus on their construction by the stony corals, scleractinia, the octocorals are equally important members of the reef community. Though most don't leave much behind but sandy sclerites when they die, in life the mass of soft corals often rivals that of the stony corals, so they are important reef habitat. Additionally, some soft corals contribute significantly to the solid reef structure with calcareous skeletons, fused sclerites, and thick horn-like holdfasts.

Heliopora
Pronunciation: HEE-lee-oh-PORE-uh

Common Name: Blue coral, blue fire coral

Region: Red Sea, Indian Ocean to Samoa.

Description: This monotypic "soft" coral has a hard skeleton made of calcium carbonate and colored blue by special iron salts. Colonies may be encrusting, laminar, columnar, or form upright flattened plates. The living tissue is usually brown, but sometimes it is pale blue.

Similar Corals: *Montipora spongodes* and *Millepora* spp. resemble *Heliopora*. *Heliopora* has eight tentacles on each polyp.

Placement

Lighting Needs	3 - 10
Water Flow	2 - 10
Agressiveness	2
Hardiness	9

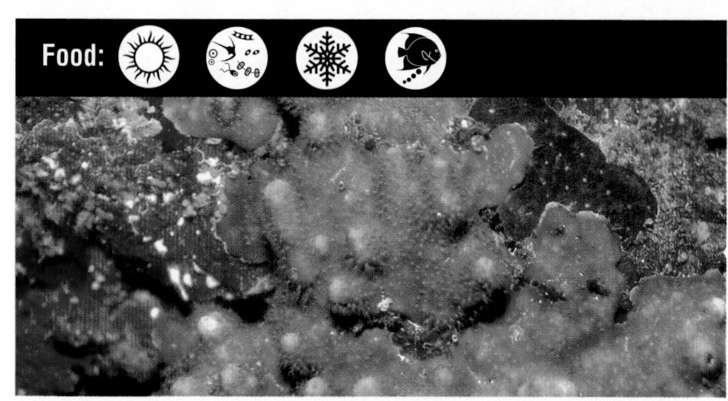

Heliopora coerulea closeup showing the eight-tentacled polyps, Solomon Islands.

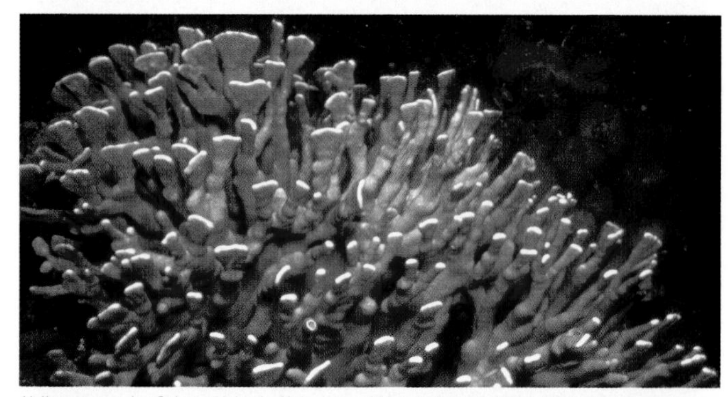

Heliopora coerulea, Solomon Islands. Note exposed blue skeleton on broken blade, bottom center.

Clavularia
Pronunciation: clav-u-LAIR-ee-uh

Common Name: Clove Polyp, Glove polyp, Waving hand polyp, or *Anthelia* (especially in Germany)

Region: Indonesia, Melanesia, Philippines, Australia

Description: Cylindrical upright stiff tube-like calyces sprout from a common ribbon-like creeping stolon that adheres to the substrate. Anthocodiae can completely retract into the calyces. Tentacles large and feathery with distinct pinnules. More than 40 species described. References: Tixier-Durivault (1964); Weinberg (1986); Williams (1992)

Similar Corals: *Anthelia* spp. have similar polyps, and the two genera are often confused. *Anthelia* deflates only and cannot retract its polyps the way *Clavularia* does. When *Clavularia* is closed one sees the round heads of each closed calyx. One form of organ pipe coral, *Tubipora* sp. has giant polyps nearly indistinguishable from *Clavularia*.

Placement

Lighting Needs	3 - 9
Water Flow	1 - 9
Agressiveness	4
Hardiness	7

Clavularia sp. showing retracted and opened polyps, and a few stolons. Solomon Islands.

This spectacular green *Clavularia* species was quite common in some areas in the Solomon Islands. It also occurs in Indonesia, and the polyps may have flourescent orange tips.

Clavularia sp. with a polyp diameter of about 5 cm (2 in)! Solomon Islands.

A distinctive species of Clavularia from the Solomon Islands.

Scientific Name: Undescribed

Common Name: Clove polyp, Glove Polyp, Star polyp, *Xenia, Anthelia,* Unidentified Stoloniferan number One, *Acrossota,* Paddle-tentacles

Region: Indonesia, especially Bali.

Description: Flattened, paddle shaped tentacles about 1/16 to 1/8 inch wide. The pinnules are fused. Encrusts with creeping stolons like *Clavularia.* Dr. Phil Alderslade examined specimens and noted that they seem like *Acrossota liposclera* described by Bourne in 1914, but Bourne's original specimens of have been lost, and his description is not very definitive. It is impossible to determine if this is the same coral, so it will be given a new genus name. There seem to be two species. (P. Alderslade pers. comm.), They differ by pinnule counts.

Similar Corals: The polyps look similar to "brown star polyp" *Pachyclavularia violacea,* but the flattened tentacles are distinctive. *Tubipora* has two forms with Paddle shaped tentacles.

Lighting Needs	2 - 8
Water Flow	2 - 9
Agressiveness	2
Hardiness	8

Placement

One species holds its tentacles roughly perpendicular to the polyp axis.

The fused pinnules are clear to see in this close-up photo of the other species of this coral.

Scientific Name: Undescribed

Common Name: Clove Polyp, Unidentified Stoloniferan Number Two

Region: Indonesia, especially Bali

Description: Polyps have cylindrical tentacles, without pinnules, on creeping stolons that are most similar to "Clove polyp" (page 149). Sprung and Delbeek (1997) call this species "Unidentified Stoloniferan Number Two." Colour light brown to coppery. In older colonies the stolons fuse into a brittle, thickened mat.

Similar Corals: The polyps look similar to "brown star polyp" *Pachyclavularia violacea*, but they are on stolons. *Tubipora* has one form with tentacles lacking pinnules, but it has whitish polyps.

Lighting Needs	4 - 10
Water Flow	4 - 9
Agressiveness	4
Hardiness	7

Placement

Food:

This new stoloniferan from Bali Indonesia has polyps completely devoid of pinnules.

Coelogorgia sp.

Pronunciation: SEE-lo-GOR-gee-uh

Common Name: None

Region: Western Pacific, Indian Ocean, Red Sea.

Description: A root-like stolon attaches the upright branches to the substrate. New polyps arise from stalks, and bud off of other polyps. Branches often pinnate, pale brown to lavender with brown polyps. .

Similar Corals: *Coelogorgia* is easily confused with *Carijoa* and *Telesto*. In *Carijoa* individual branches are formed by a tall axial polyp with many short lateral polyps budding off the side. In *Coelogorgia* new polyps often bud off of other polyps, thereby forming new branches (P. Alderslade, pers. comm.). The species of *Coelogorgia* seen in the aquarium trade contains zooxanthellae.

Lighting Needs	3 - 9
Water Flow	4 - 9
Agressiveness	2
Hardiness	9

Placement

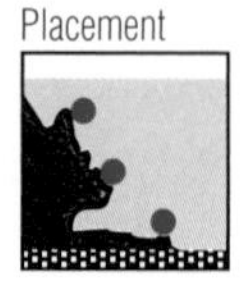

Food:

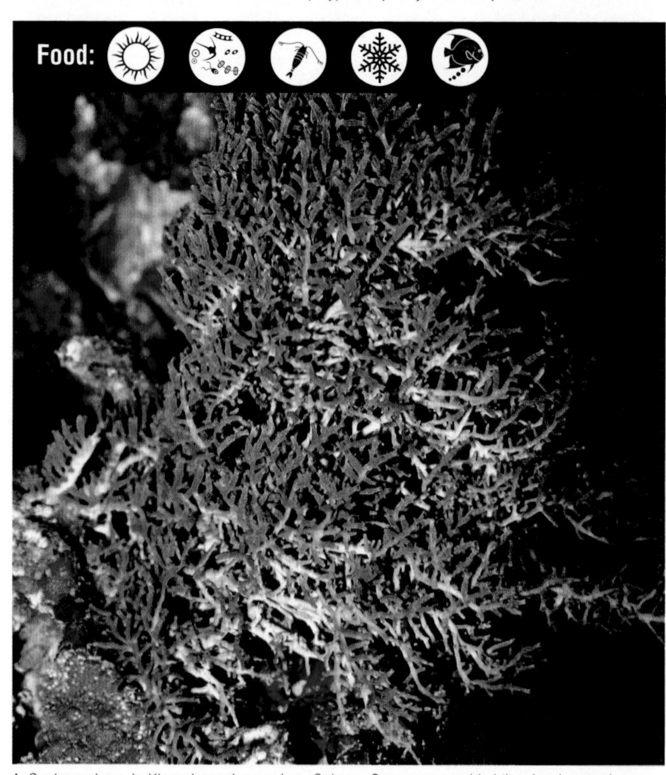

A *Coelogorgia* sp. in Klaus Jansen's aquarium, Cologne Germany resembled the alga *Laurencia*.

Coelogorgia cf. *palmosa* photographed at Vivarium Karlsruhe, Karlsruhe, Germany.

***Carijoa* sp.**
Pronunciation: carry-YO-a (cari-JO-a)

Common Name: none

Region: East Africa to Hawaii, Caribbean.

Description: Colonies of upright branches connected by stolons from which new axial polyps emerge. A root-like stolon attaches the branches to the substrate. Stalk-like branches form by the growth of a single axial polyp off of which daughter polyps bud. Daughter polyps do not bud off of other daughter polyps. Stalks mostly singular and long with infrequent branching. Pale brown or pinkish with white polyps. Often the stalks are encrusted with a commensal sponge that makes the colonies brilliant orange, yellow, or purple. The polyps are always white, and do not contain zooxanthellae.

Similar Corals: *Coelogorgia* is easily confused with *Carijoa*. In *Coelogorgia* new polyps often bud off of other polyps, forming many new branches.

Lighting Needs	0
Water Flow	3 - 10
Agressiveness	1
Hardiness	3

Placement

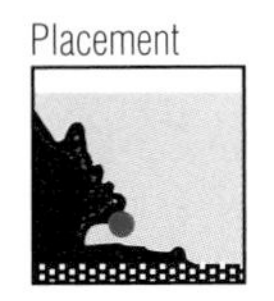

Food:

Carijoa spp. are common around the mouths of caves, in shipwrecks and on pilings in harbors.

Tubipora
Pronunciation: TOO-bee-POR-a (TUBE-ih-por-uh)

Common Name: Organ-pipe coral, Pipe-organ coral

Region: Red Sea, East Africa, Japan, to the Marshall Islands

Description: Skeleton distinctive, being reddish to maroon and composed of long tubes with connecting terraces. Polyps white, gray, brown or green. Although *Tubipora* is considered monotypic (Veron, 1986), *T. musica* being the only species recognized, it is likely that the different forms are different species. Some may even belong to different genera.

Similar Corals: The polyps may easily be confused with those of *Clavularia*, *Briareum*, and *Pachyclavularia*. One form that lacks pinnules has polyps like those of the stony coral *Alveopora*, distinguishable only by the fact that *Alveopora* has twelve tentacles and *Tubipora* only eight. Another form has flattened tentacles that look like paddles because the pinnules are fused.

Lighting Needs	5 - 9
Water Flow	4 - 9
Agressiveness	1
Hardiness	6

Placement

Tubipora from Fiji with medium sized polyps. Aquarium photo, Living Seas, Chicago.

The "paddle tentacle" variety of *Tubipora*, has fused pinnules. Solomon Islands.

Tubipora with no pinnules! The polyps are remarkably similar to those of *Alveopora*. Solomon Islands.

View of a large colony of the *Tubipora* with no pinnules. Solomon Islands.

Tubipora with giant polyps very similar to those of *Clavularia*. Solomon Islands.

Tubipora with small polyps like those of *Briareum*. Aquarium photo of colony from Indonesia.

Briareum
Pronunciation: bry-AIR-ee-um

Common Name: Green Star Polyp, Star Polyps, *Xenia,* Corky Sea Fingers, Encrusting Gorgonian, Briareum

Region: Caribbean, Western Pacific, possibly Red Sea.

Description: The form commonly called "green star polyp" usually has brilliant green polyps with small (less than 1/16 inch), pale green or whitish center. Polyps occasionally just brown or gray. Encrusting sheet is usually deep purple, but sometimes is brownish or light tan. *Briareum asbestinum* is a beautiful soft coral from the Caribbean that may form flat crusts, knobby crusts, upright branches like a gorgonian but without a horny skeleton, or it may encrust (and kill) other gorgonians, using the skeleton for support.

Similar Corals: *Erythropodium* spp., *Pachyclavularia* spp. In the Caribbean *Briareum asbestinum* is often confused with similar-looking but unrelated *Erythropodium caribaeorum.* There are two forms (probably species) of *Briareum* in the Caribbean, one basically encrusting; the other forming upright branches that have not encrusted over another gorgonian. The sheet or encrusting form has erroneously been given the name *Erythropodium polyanthes* Duchassaing and Michelotti (see Bayer, 1961). It is also possible that there is more than one encrusting species in the Caribbean as there are differences in the size and colour of polyps and pinnule development, as well as the thickness and consistency of the encrusting sheets (pers. obs.). See West, Harvell, and Walls (1993), and Brazeau and Harvell (1994) for additional information about variability in this species. *Pachyclavularia violacea* ("Brown Star Polyp") is easily distinguished. It has a very large bright center on each polyp (ca. 1/16 to 1/8 inch), and when the polyps close they leave tall projecting tubular calyces that are dark purple (a synonymous name is *Pachyclavularia erecta*). When the similar "Green Star Polyp," *Briareum* sp. closes, the calyces are only slightly projecting. Either genus can have brown, green, or gray polyps. The distinction between Indo-Pacific *Pachyclavularia* and *Briareum* species is not always obvious.

Lighting Needs	3 - 10
Water Flow	5 - 10
Agressiveness	7
Hardiness	9

Placement

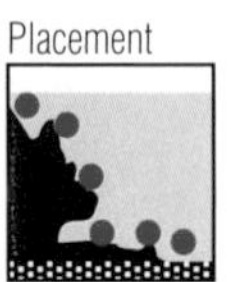

Compare the appearance of *Briareum asbestinum* (L) to *Erythropodium caribaeorum* (R).

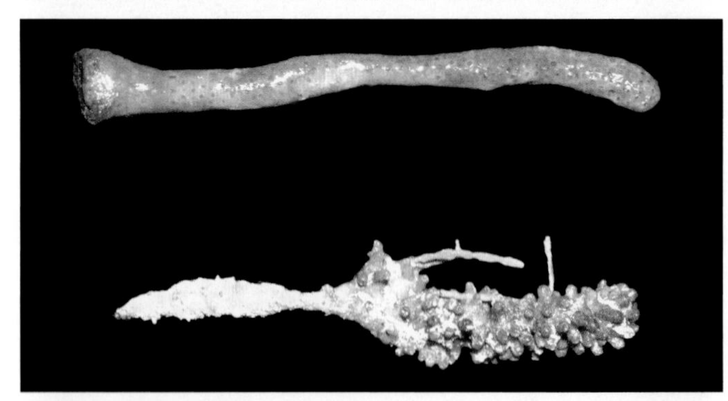

Briareum cf. *asbestinum*, erect form above and an encrusting form with tubular calyces, Florida.

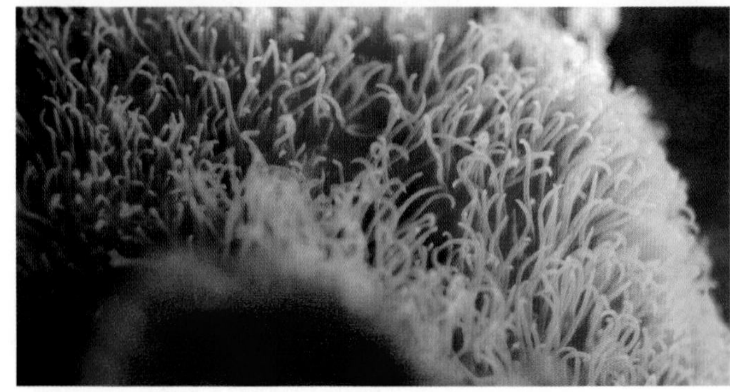

Fluorescent green "Star Polyp," *Briareum* sp. from Indonesia. Aquarium photo.

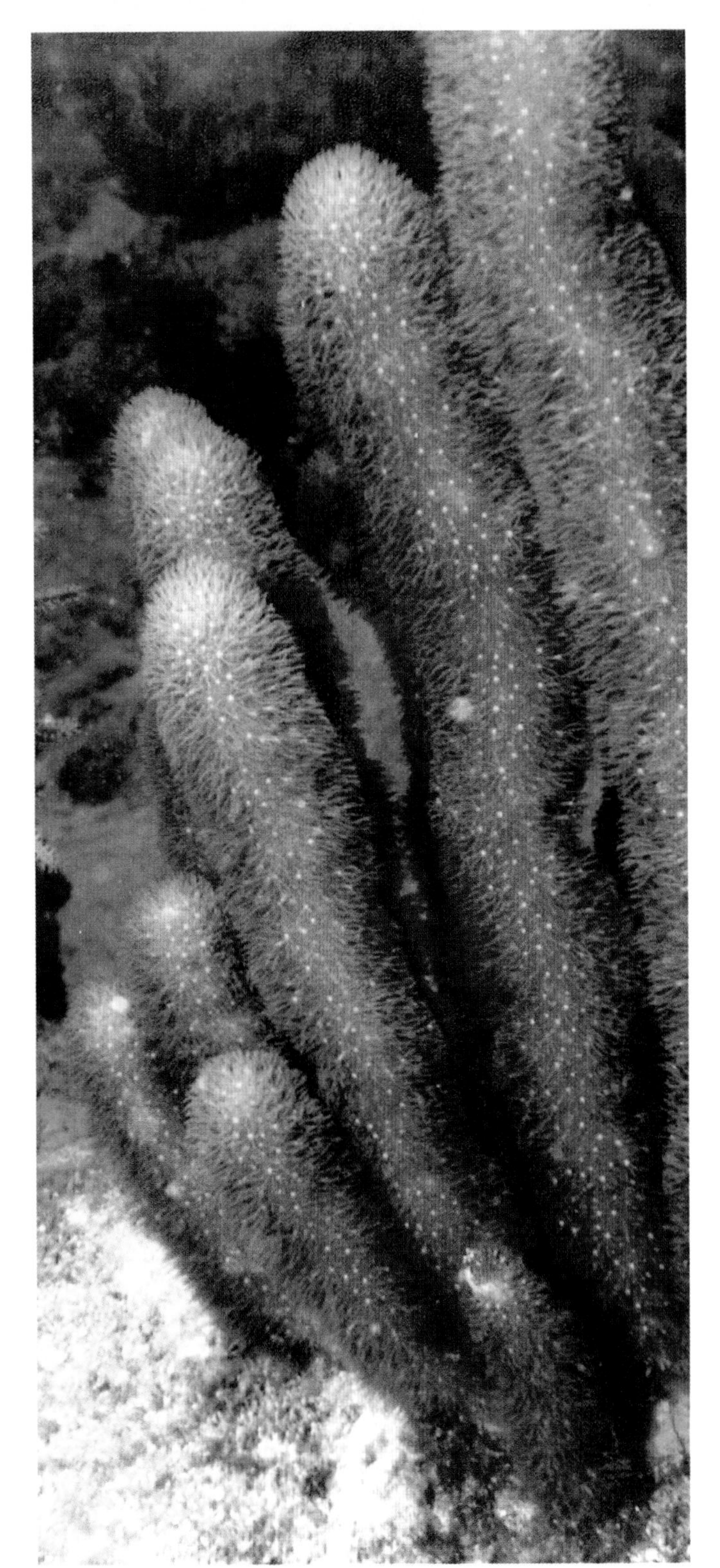

Briareum cf. *asbestinum*, erect form. Key Largo, Florida.

Fluorescent green polyped, branchy *Briareum* sp. from Bali Indonesia. Aquarium photo.

Fluorescent green "Star Polyp," *Briareum* sp. from Indonesia. Aquarium photo.

Pachyclavularia violacea

Pronunciation: PACK-ee-CLAV-yu-LAIR-ee-uh VY-oh-LACE-ee-uh

Common Name: Brown Star Polyp, Green Star polyp (green form)

Region: Western Pacific. Australia, Phillippines, New Guinea, Solomon Islands, Indonesia.

Description: Purple encrusting sheets with brown or green polyps. The 1/16 to 1/8 inch centers of the polyps are bright white, green, or yellow. When the polyps close, they leave long projecting calyces. Polyps have some indistinct pinnules.

Similar Corals: *Erythropodium* spp. Fabricius and Aldersalde (2001) makes *Pachyclavularia* a synonym of *Briareum.*

Lighting Needs		3 -9
Water Flow		3 - 10
Agressiveness		8
Hardiness		9

Placement

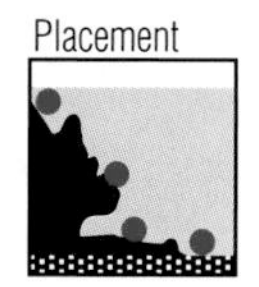

Food:

Briareum (=Pachyclavularia) violacea.

Studeriotes sp.

Pronunciation: STOO-dair-ee-OH-deez

Common Name: "Christmas tree" coral, "French Tickler", *Sphaerella krempfi*

Region: Indonesia, Singapore, Phillipines

Description: A pale, off-white column with large sclerites on the outside. The polyparium consists of straight branches with polyps in paralell circling rows. The branches may be completely withdrawn into the column (rachis) much like an anemone retracts its tentacles. Polyps are brown but do not contain zooxanthellae.

Similar Corals: None

Lighting Needs		0
Water Flow		4 - 9
Agressiveness		1
Hardiness		7

Placement

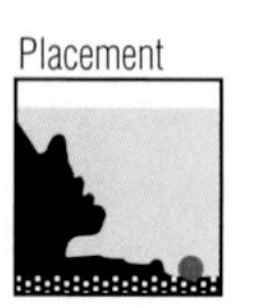

Food:

Studeriotes cf. *longiramosa*. Note stolons around base and attached gravel. Aquarium photo, England.

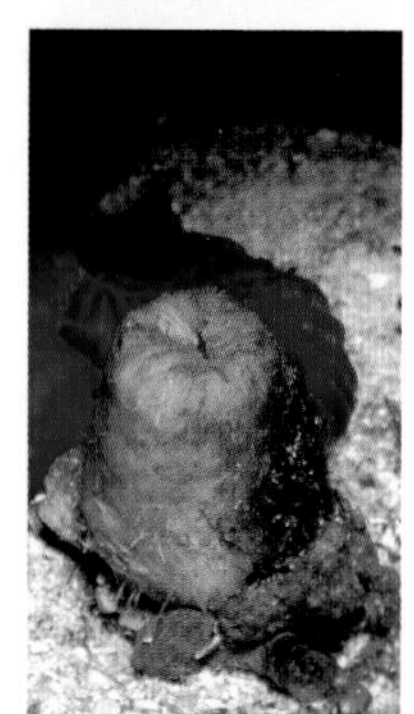

Studeriotes withdrawing its polyparium.

Maasella

Pronunciation: mah-SELL-uh

Common Name: None

Region: Mediterranean. Subtropical to temperate localities.

Description: Colonies consist of short upright connected fingers with the polyps on the tips. The polyparium can be completely withdrawn into the column (branch, in this case) like *Studeriotes*.

Similar Corals: Superficially resembles *Capnella* and *Paralemnalia*.

Placement

Lighting Needs	5 - 9
Water Flow	5 - 9
Agressiveness	2
Hardiness	5

Maasella eduardi photographed in a temperate water aquarium at ZOOMARK Milan, Italy.

Minabea

Pronunciation: MIN-uh-BEE-uh

Common Name: None

Region: Western Pacific

Description: Small red or orange tough finger-like colonies found on steep walls especially under ledges. Produces large transparent polyps at night.

Similar Corals: *Minabea aldersladei* looks similar to *Nephthyigorgia* at first glance, but it is not branchy and has a smoother texture.

Placement

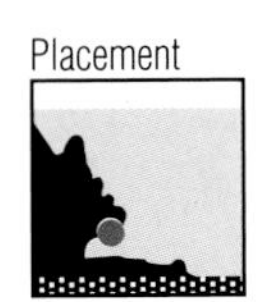

Lighting Needs	0
Water Flow	5 - 9
Agressiveness	2
Hardiness	7

Minabea aldersladei, contracted during the daytime. At night it sprouts long translucent polyps.

Klyxum

Pronunciation: CLICKS-um

Common Name: Colt coral, Broccoli coral, Cauliflower coral, *Cladiella*

Region: Red Sea and Indo-Pacific.

Description: *Klyxum* spp. are slippery to the touch, and have polyps that appear to be generated on the lower portions of the stalk, developing as they migrate upward. There are zooxanthellate and non-zooxanthellate forms. Colonies may be erect and branchy or low and encrusting with small branches. Very variable appearance.

Similar Corals: *Klyxum* spp. are quite similar to *Cladiella*, so it is not surprising that confusion exists between these genera. Some slimy species of *Sinularia* are also quite similar to *Klyxum* spp. when expanded. Some expanded *Klyxum* spp. could be confused with *Nephthea*, *Lemnalia*, or *Capnella*, but *Klyxum* spp. is slimy to the touch while the three mentioned nephtheids have a rough texture because of their abundant large sclerites.

Lighting Needs	2 - 9
Water Flow	2 - 9
Agressiveness	4
Hardiness	7

Placement

Typical *Klyxum* sp. "Colt Coral" from Indonesia. Aquarium photo.

This rare variety of *Klyxum* from Indonesia is similar to *Cladiella* spp. Aquarium photo.

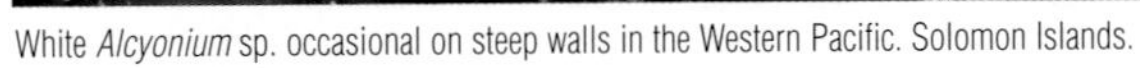
White *Alcyonium* sp. occasional on steep walls in the Western Pacific. Solomon Islands.

Blue *Alcyonium* with chocalate brown polyps, Red Sea. Aquarium photo at Coral World, Eilat, Israel.

This *Klyxum*-like soft coral from deep water at "Ghavutu," a turbid lagoon in the Solomon Islands, belongs to a new genus.

Rhytisma
Pronunciation: ri TIZ muh

Region: Red Sea, Mediterranean and Indo-Pacific.

Common Name: Encrusting leather coral

Description: Yellow or brown encrusting thin sheets with long polyps that resemble those of leather corals (*Sarcophyton* spp.). Strong pungent odor when lifted out of water.

Similar Corals: Similar to *Sympodium* superficially.

Lighting Needs	5 - 10
Water Flow	3 - 9
Agressiveness	9
Hardiness	7

Placement

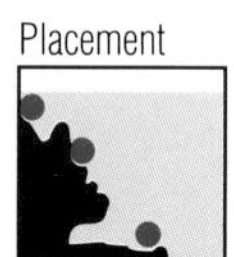

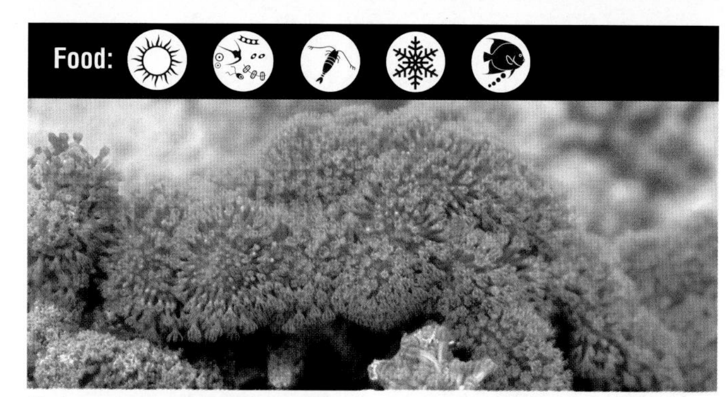

Rhytisma sp. Red Sea. Note mass of eggs of predatory nudibranch, far left.

Indonesian *Rhytisma* sp. Aquar. photo.

Rhytisma sp. Red Sea.

Rhytisma sp. Red Sea. Note mass of eggs of predatory nudibranch, top center.

Cladiella

Pronunciation: KLAH-dee-EL-uh (klah-DYELL-uh)

Common Name: Finger leather, Colt coral, Cauliflower coral, Blushing coral.

Region: Red Sea, Indian Ocean, Western Pacific to Polynesia

Description: Brown polyps contrasting with strikingly paler tissue. When the polyps are expanded the colony looks bushy and brown. When disturbed the polyps contract and the colony blanches white. *Cladiella* spp. are slippery, like a wet bar of soap.

Similar Corals: *Alcyonium, Sinularia.* Examination of the sclerites is required for positive confirmation. *Cladiella* sclerites are distinctively dumbell-shaped. The blanch from brown to white when the polyps close is typical for the genus, but also occurs in a few unrelated nephtheidae, which could easily be mistaken for *Cladiella* based on their appearance.

Lighting Needs	4 - 9
Water Flow	4 - 10
Agressiveness	9
Hardiness	8

Placement

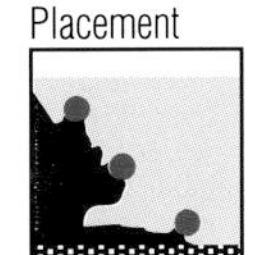

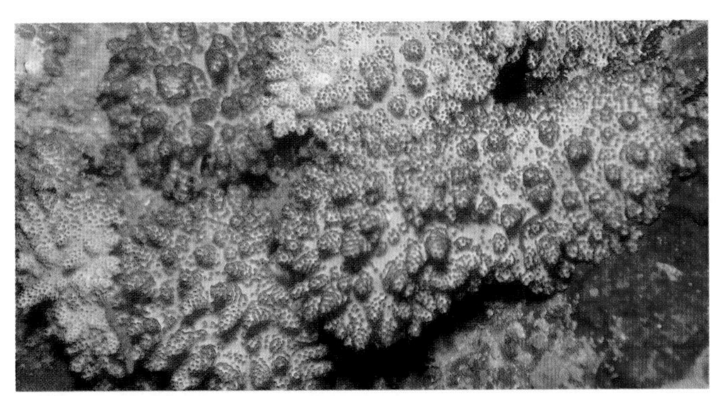

Cladiella sp. Solomon Islands.

The dramatic difference in *Cladiella's* appearance expanded, left versus contracted, right

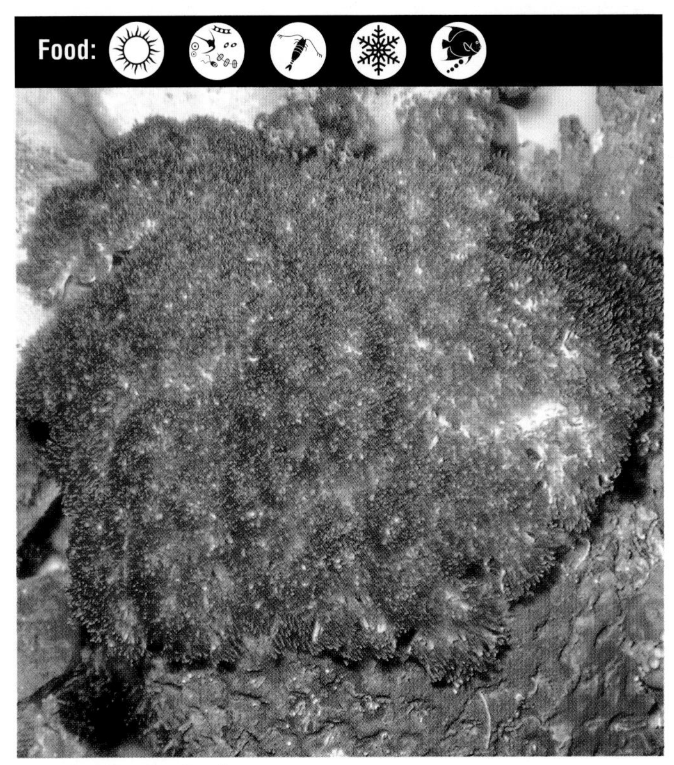

Typical *Cladiella* sp. Aquarium photo.

Though most are low and clumpy, a few *Cladiella* spp. have elongated branches, like *Sinularia* spp.

Sarcophyton
Pronunciation: SAR-ko-FY-tun (SAR-ko-fy-tun, SAR-ko-FEE-tun)

Common Name: Leather coral, Mushroom coral, Toadstool coral

Region: Red Sea and Indo-Pacific

Description: *Sarcophyton* species all look like mushrooms or toadstools, with lovely polyps that extend from the head-like, often convoluted upper surface called a capitulum. Their appearance is highly variable, and the same species from slightly different locations can look radically different. Two types of polyps occur on the capitulum, tubular autozooids which extend tentacles and siphonozooids which look like freckles.

Similar Corals: *Sarcophyton* is most similar to *Lobophytum.*

Lighting Needs	3 -10
Water Flow	4 - 9
Agressiveness	3
Hardiness	8

Placement

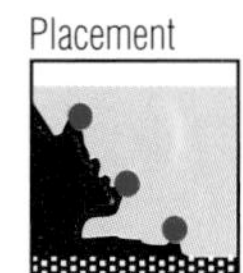

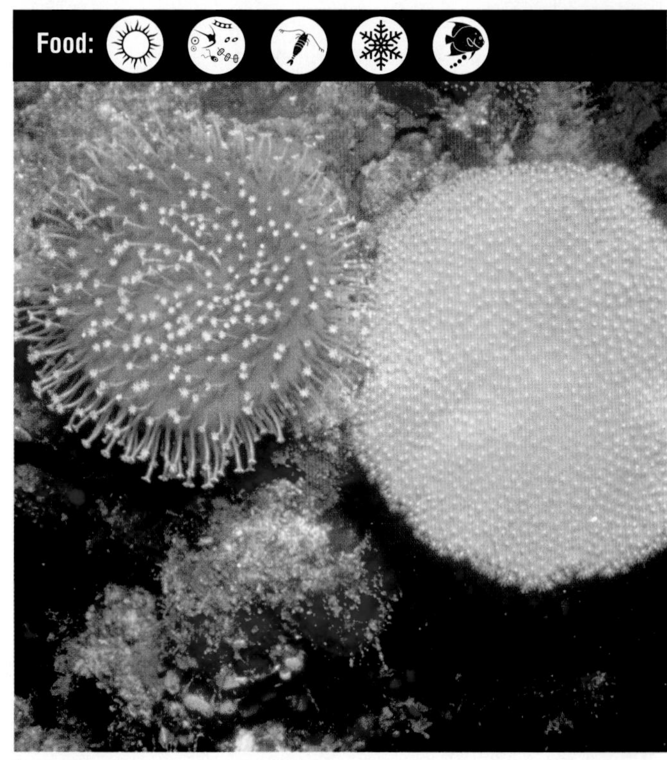

Two species of *Sarcophyton*, Solomon Islands.

Sarcophyton ehrenbergi, aquarium photo.

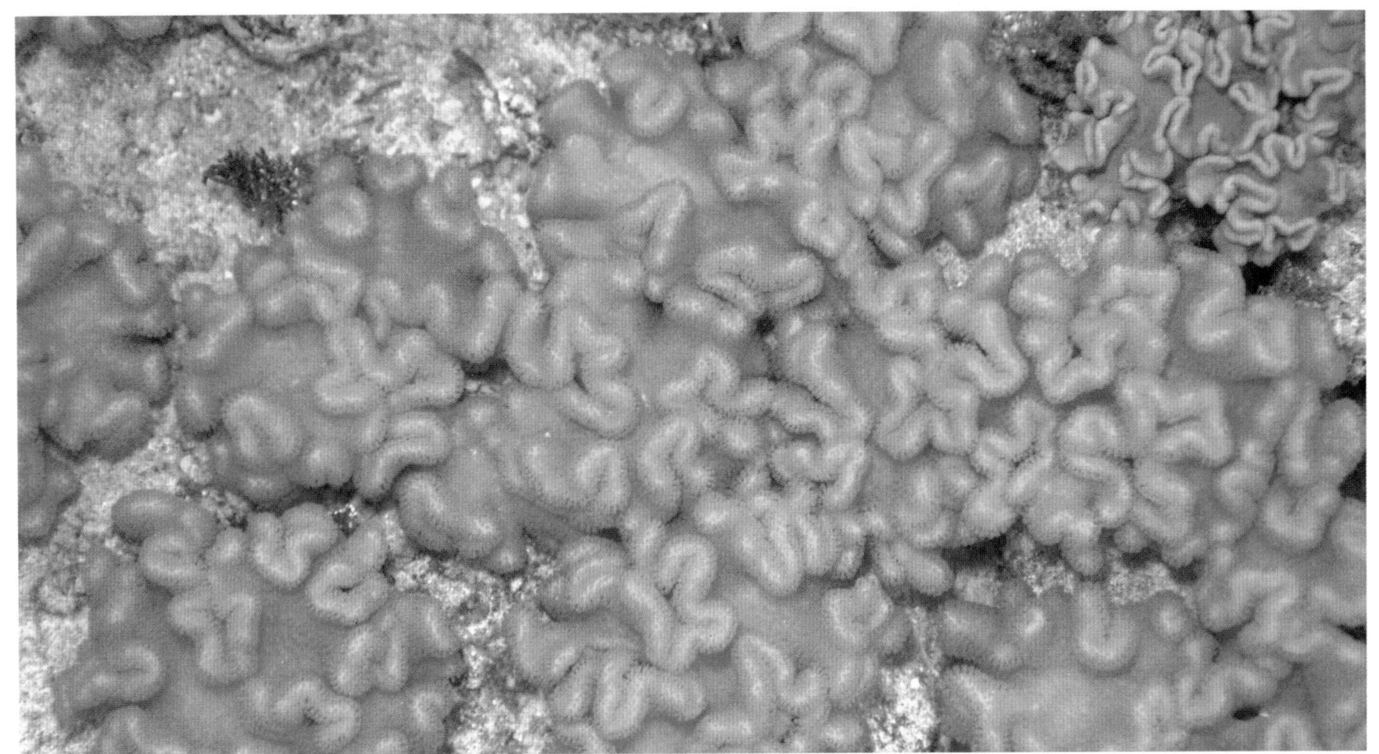

Sarcophyton elegans on a shallow reef top near Bequa, Fiji. It prefers very strong illumination and water movement, much more than any other *Sarcophyton* species.

Sarcophyton elegans is very distinctive, one of very few *Sarcophyton* species identifiable with a photograph.

A fireworks display of *Sarcophyton*, photographed at night in the Solomon Islands.

Lobophytum
Pronunciation: LO-bo-FY-tum

Common Name: Devil's hand, finger leather, "Lobophyton" Please note that the correct spelling of the genus is *Lobophytum.*

Region: Indo-Pacific to Red Sea.

Description: This genus is very closely related to *Sarcophyton*, and some colonies appear essentially the same as members of that genus, like large toadstools, except that in *Lobophytum* the crown has finger-like branches or lobes. Like *Sarcophyton*, *Lobophytum* has two types of polyps, autozooids and siphonozooids.

Similar Corals: *Sarcophyton* spp. Small colonies of *Lobophytum* may not have developed lobes and cannot be distinguished from *Sarcophyton* without examination of the sclerites. The sclerites are not always dramatically different either, and it seems that these two genera intergrade, though there are many species on opposite extremes of the spectrum of differences. *Sinularia* spp. are similar to *Lobophytum*, particularly the massive encrusting species, but *Sinularia* spp. do not have two types of polyps, and they have large robust sclerites around the base

Lighting Needs	3 - 10
Water Flow	3 - 10
Agressiveness	3
Hardiness	10

Placement

Small *Lobophytum* with expanded polyps. Solomon Islands.

Lobophytum sp. from Indonesia. Aquarium Photo.

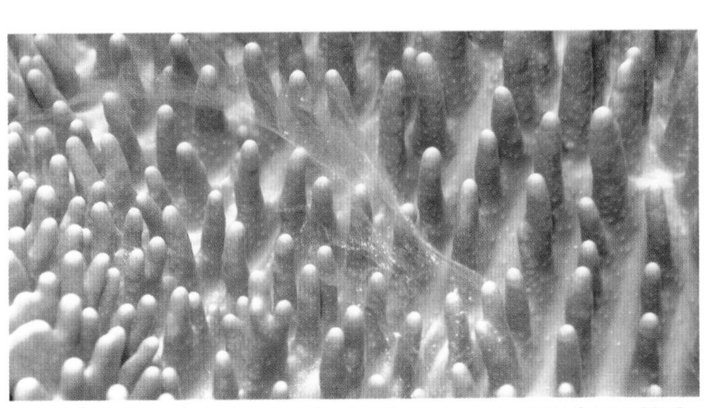

A large *Lobophytum* sp. sheds a waxy film to free its surface of algae and sediment. Solomon Islands.

A rare *Lobophytum* sp. from Indonesia that looks like *Sinularia.* Aquarium Photo, England.

Sinularia
Pronunciation: sin-u-LAIR-ee-uh

Common Name: Finger Leather, Soft finger, Digitate Leather

Region: Indo-Pacific and Red Sea.

Description: The genus *Sinularia* contains many species with very different appearance. Some have fat branches, some have thin branches, some have no branches at all, forming thick encrusting sheets with raised lobes, some are flat like tree fungus. The characteristic that links them is the presence of long robust spicules of characteristic shape around the base of the colony. There are over 100 species of *Sinularia* described.

Similar Corals: Some *Alcyonium* and *Cladiella* species are difficult to distinguish from *Sinularia* superficially. Examination of the sclerites is required for positive distinction. *Dampia* is most similar to *Sinularia dura*. Many *Sinularia* superficially resemble *Lobophytum*. They can be differentiated based on the presence of siphonozoids in *Lobophytum*.

Lighting Needs	3 - 10
Water Flow	3 - 10
Agressiveness	6
Hardiness	8

Placement

Sinularia flexibilis in a calm lagoon environment. Solomon Islands.

Sinularia sp. Red Sea.

Sinularia sp. that looks like *Lemnalia*. Aquarium photo.

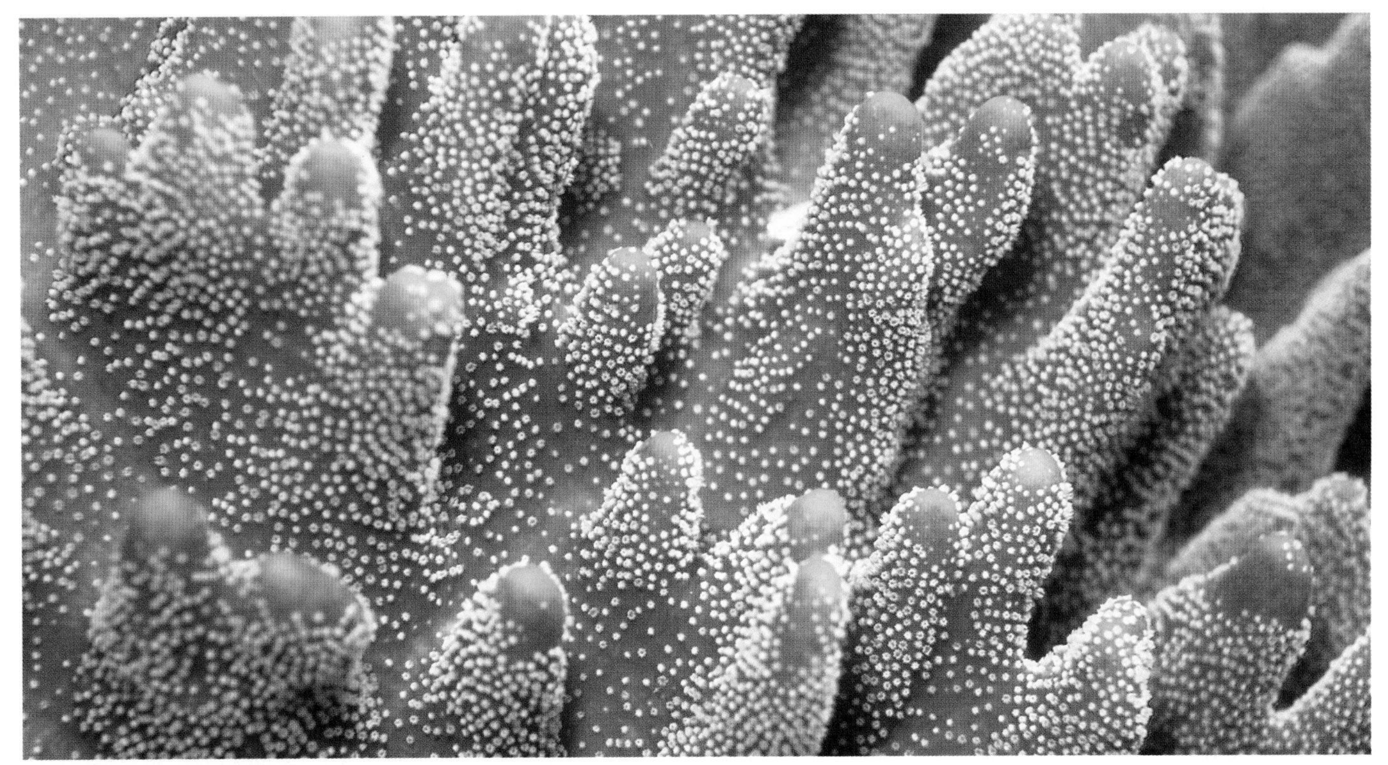

This *Sinularia* sp. looks like a *Lobophytum* sp., note: no siphonozooids. Solomon Islands.

Encrusting *Lobophytum* left, *Sinularia* right on an upper reef slope. Solomon Islands.

Sinularia brassica is distinct from *S. dura*, but may be an ecomorph. See Benayahu et. al. (1998)

Sinularia dura photographed at the Löbbecke Museum in Düsseldorf, Germany.

Dampia
Pronunciation: DAMP-ee-uh

Common Name: Leather coral, *Sinularia dura.*

Region: Western Pacific.

Description: Forms a thick flat encrusting or bowl-shaped colonies, often with upright lobes.

Similar Corals: Very similar to *Sinularia dura*, but grows much larger and has slightly larger and more numerous polyps. *Dampia pocilloporaeformis* was described as a new genus and species (Alderslade, 1983), but may be an aberrant *Sinularia* (P. Alderslade, pers. comm.).

Food:

Dampia pocilloporaeformis is quite similar to *Sinularia dura.*

Lighting Needs	3 - 9
Water Flow	2 - 10
Agressiveness	6
Hardiness	10

Placement

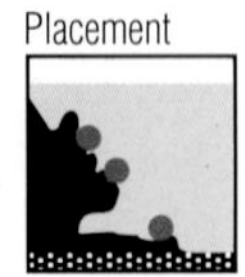

Lemnalia

Pronunciation: lem-NAIL-ee-uh

Common Name: Spaghetti coral, Branch coral, Tree coral, Cauliflower Soft coral

Region: Indo-Pacific from East Africa to parts of Polynesia

Description: *Lemnalia* spp. are arborescent with fine branches and polyps generally without supporting sclerite bundles. To the naked eye the sclerites are not obvious in the stalk.

Similar Corals: *Paralemnalia*, is distinguished by forming encrusting mats with digitiform branches. Several species of *Sinularia* superficially resemble *Lemnalia*. *Lemnalia* does not have the large spindle shaped sclerites of *Sinularia*. The stalks resemble those of *Nephthea* or *Litophyton*, but the polyps are arranged more sparsely.

Lighting Needs	3 - 8
Water Flow	5
Agressiveness	10
Hardiness	3

Placement

A small *Lemnalia* sp. appears to be "in bondage" with commensal brittle stars. Solomon Islands.

Lemnalia sp. at "Mary Island" Solomon Islands.

Lemnalia sp. Solomon Islands.

Paralemnalia
Pronunciation: PAH-ruh-lem-NAIL-ee-uh

Common Name: Finger Leather

Region: Red Sea to Western Pacific and Southern Japan.

Description: *Paralemnalia* spp. form encrusting mats with digitiform branches that bear retractile polyps. Two forms are common, one with branches as wide as a finger, the other with much finer branches. There are numerous species with these forms, and some intermediate in appearance.

Similar Corals: Mature colonies of the thick branch species resemble *Lobophytum* spp., because they develop a round base from which the lobe-like branches protrude. The polyps of the thick branch species are most like those of *Capnella*. The thin-branched species are similar in appearance to some *Sinularia* species, and *Lemnalia* species.

Lighting Needs		3 - 9
Water Flow		4 - 9
Agressiveness		4
Hardiness		7

Placement

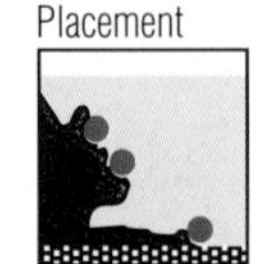

Food:

Paralemnalia sp. from the Red Sea. Photographed at Coral World, Eilat, Israel.

Paralemnalia sp. with thin branches, polyps open. Solomon Islands.

Paralemnalia sp. with thin branches, polyps closed. Solomon Islands.

Another species of *Paralemnalia* with branches of medium thickness. Solomon Islands.

Close-up of species of *Paralemnalia* with branches of medium thickness. Solomon Islands.

"Thick-finger" species of *Paralemnalia* common in the Solomon Islands.

Paralemnalia growing against the glass in an aquarium.

Stereonephthya

Pronunciation: STEH-ree-o-NEF-thee-yuh

Common Name: *Nephthea*, Tree Coral, *Dendronephthya*

Region: East Africa to the Western Pacific.

Description: When the branches of *Stereonephthya* deflate, the bundles of sclerites around the polyps at the branch tips form distinctive spiny bur-like processes. *Stereonephthya* species may be very colourful: A common photosynthetic *Stereonephthya* sp. in Fiji is a magnificent blue-violet.

Similar Corals: *Nephthea*, *Capnella*, and especially *Neospongodes* are most similar to *Stereonephthya*. *Dendronephthya* (*Roxasia* and *Spongodes*), which lack zooxanthellae, are superficially similar to *Stereonephthya*.

Lighting Needs	3 - 9
Water Flow	5 - 9
Agressiveness	3
Hardiness	5

Placement

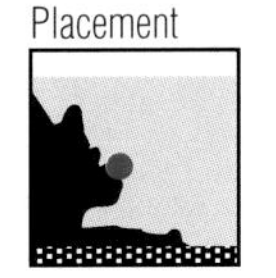

"Thick-finger" species of *Paralemnalia*, polyps closing after being disturbed. Solomon Islands.

Food:

Stereonephthya sp.The deflated branches become stiff and have spiny burr-like tips. Solomon Islands.

Stereonephthya spp. are very spiny. Solomon Islands.

Nephthea

Pronunciation: NEF-thee-uh (nef-THAY-uh)

Common Name: Broccoli coral, Cauliflower coral, *Litophyton arboreum*, "Lithophyton," "Nephthya," "Nepthya," "Nepthea" Note the common mis-spellings. The correct spelling is *Nephthea.*

Region: East Africa, the Red Sea and Indo-Pacific.

Description: Brown, yellow, whitish, occasionally green upright and bushy, arborescent colonies. Non-retractile polyps with supporting bundle of sclerites that do not project much beyond the polyp when closed. Polyps arranged in lobes (catkins). Sclerites irregular, spindle, or caterpillar-like.

Similar Corals: *Neospongodes.* Very similar to *Capnella* spp, but the sclerites are very different. "*Litophyton*" is between *Lemnalia* and *Nephthea* in external appearance, and may simply be slender types of *Nephthea*; the distinction not being very clear. *Stereonephthya* is also arborescent, but it is stiffer than *Nephthea* and has much more obvious sclerites.

Lighting Needs	4 - 10
Water Flow	3 - 9
Agressiveness	2
Hardiness	7

Placement

Nephthea in an aquarium at the Musee de Oceanographique, Monaco.

Exquisite yellow *Nephthea* on a Red Sea Reef, Egypt.

Nephthea in an aquarium at Jago Aquaristik, Berlin, Germany.

Capnella
Pronunciation: kap-NEL-luh

Common Name: Kenya tree, “Nephthya”, Nephthea

Region: East Africa to the Western Pacific, in tropical and temperate localities.

Description: Forms a thick trunk like a tree with beautiful branches that sometimes hang like a weeping willow tree. Some species are lobed. The polyps are like *Nephthea*, *Lemnalia*, and *Litophyton*, but they are larger. Sometimes forms compact flattened colonies with short branches. Colour is gray with brown polyps, sometimes green. Bleached colonies may be yellow.

Similar Corals: *Nephthea* species. Distinguished by the shape of the sclerites. In general, *Capnella* spp. have larger polyps than *Nephthea* spp. *Capnella* spp. superficially resemble *Alcyonium* spp., but are distinguished readily by the latter's slippery texture. *Capnella* spp. have a rough sandpapery feel characteristic of Nephtheidae.

Lighting Needs	2 - 10
Water Flow	2 - 8
Agressiveness	3
Hardiness	9

Placement

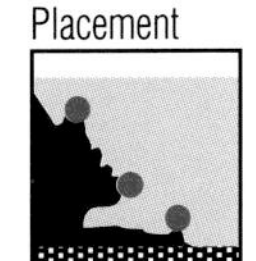

Food:

Typical appearance of *Capnella* when contracted. Note how the polyps lay against the branches.

Capnella imbricata. Aquarium photo, Löbbecke Museum in Düsseldorf, Germany.

Capnella sp. Aquarium photo.

Capnella imbricata. Aquarium photo.

Neospongodes

Pronunciation: NEE-oh-spung-OH-deez

Common Name: Broccoli coral, Cauliflower coral, *Lemnalia*

Region: Western Pacific, Indian Ocean, East Africa, Brazil, Caribbean and South Atlantic

Description: Spicules are conspicuous on all branches. Colonies seldom larger than 10 inches tall. Some *Neospongodes* spp. have zooxanthellae and some do not

Similar Corals: Very similar to *Nephthea* and *Capnella*, but smaller in height and less branchy. It is most similar to *Nephthea* and *Stereonephthya*. The distinctions between *Neospongodes* and *Nephthea* are not very compelling and it may be that revision of this group will cause at least some of the species in this genus to be included in the genus *Nephthea* (P. Alderslade, pers. comm.).

Lighting Needs	3 - 8
Water Flow	5 - 9
Agressiveness	3
Hardiness	4

Placement

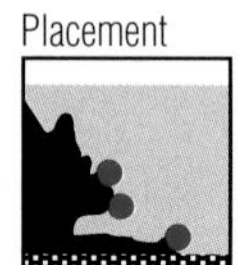

Three color morphs of *Neospongodes* photographed at Wiwi Aquaria, Winterthur Switzerland.

Neospongodes atlantica from Brazil, aquarium photo.

Neospongodes expanded and contracted. Aquarium photo.

Scleronephthya

Pronunciation: SKLEH-ro-NEPH-thee-uh

Common Name: Strawberry corals. Pink/Orange cauliflower

Region: Red Sea to New Guinea, Philippines, Solomon Islands and Micronesia (Gosliner *et al.*, 1996).

Description: Contracted colonies fleshy, lobular with short stalks from which the branches extend. Expanded colonies branchy, polyps without supporting bundles of sclerites. The stalks, branches and tips tend be varying shades of one colour i.e. orange, pink or yellow (Gosliner, *et al.*, 1996).

Similar Corals: Similar to *Neospongodes* and *Dendronephthya*, and the large forms with few sclerites are superficially like *Alcyonium*.

Rating	Value
Lighting Needs	0
Water Flow	5 - 10
Agressiveness	2
Hardiness	5

Placement

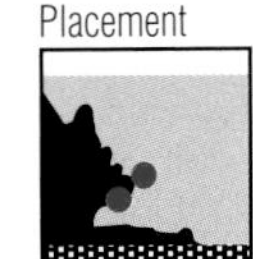

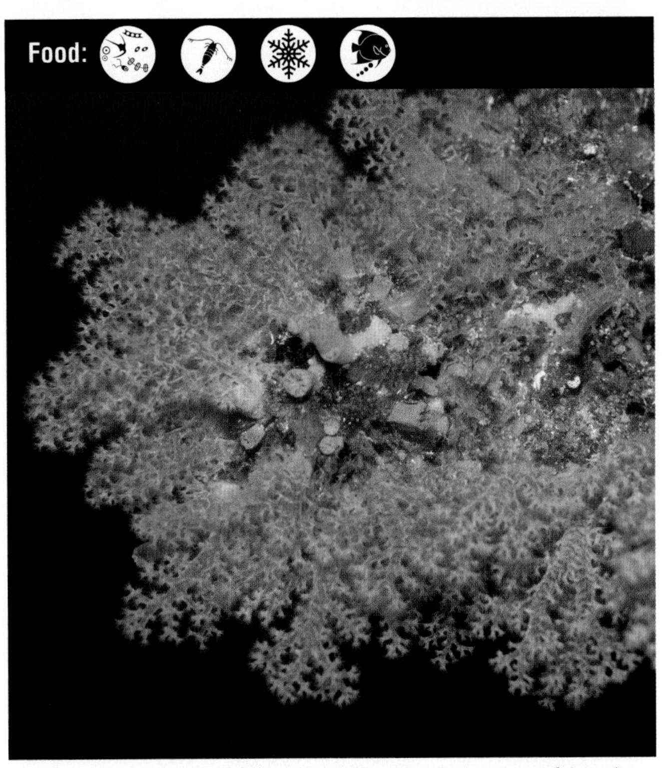

Scleronephthya sp. encrusting a shaded projection off the reef slope in strong current. Solomon Is.

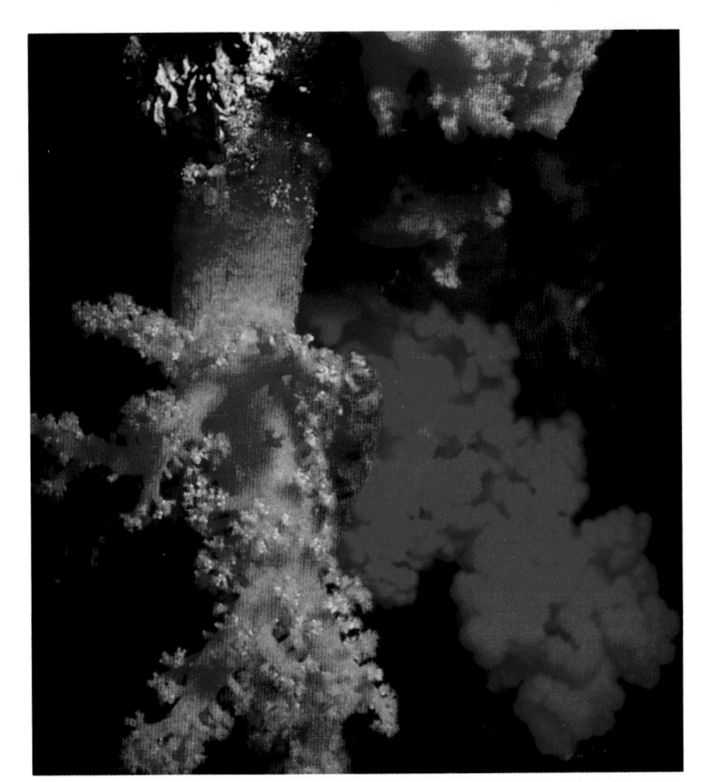

Three distinct species of *Scleronephthya* from Indonesia. Aquarium photo, Country Critters, New York.

A short *Scleronephthya* sp. with obvious sclerites. Solomon Islands.

Tall *Scleronephthya* sp. with few sclerites.

The same species expanded. Solomon Is.

***Dendronephthya* spp.**
Pronunciation: DEN-dro-NEF-thee-uh

Common Name: Strawberry coral, Cauliflower coral, Tree coral, Dendrophyta, Dendronephyta. The latter common names are common contraction/mangling of the genus name.

Region: Red Sea and Indo-Pacific

Description: Branchy soft corals with brightly colored spicules and polyps. Able to expand tremendously with water or deflate into a small spiny blob. Spicules afford a rough texture. Not photosynthetic.

Similar Corals: Similar to *Scleronephthya*, *Nephthyigorgia*, and *Stereonephthya*.

Lighting Needs		0
Water Flow		4 - 9
Agressiveness		2
Hardiness		1

Placement

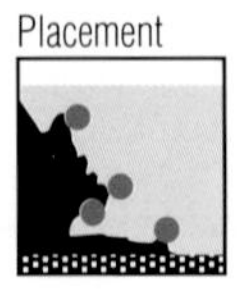

Food:

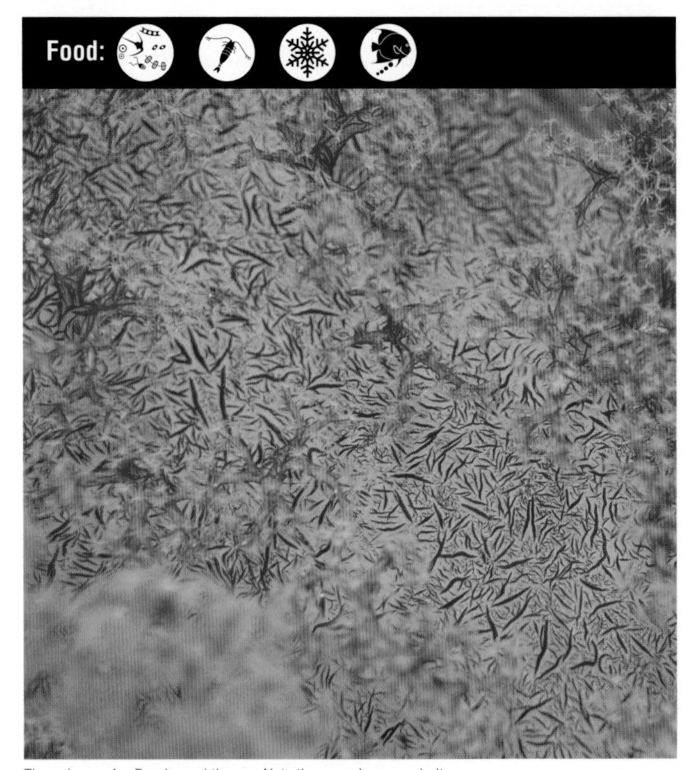

The column of a *Dendronephthya* sp. Note the conspicuous sclerites.

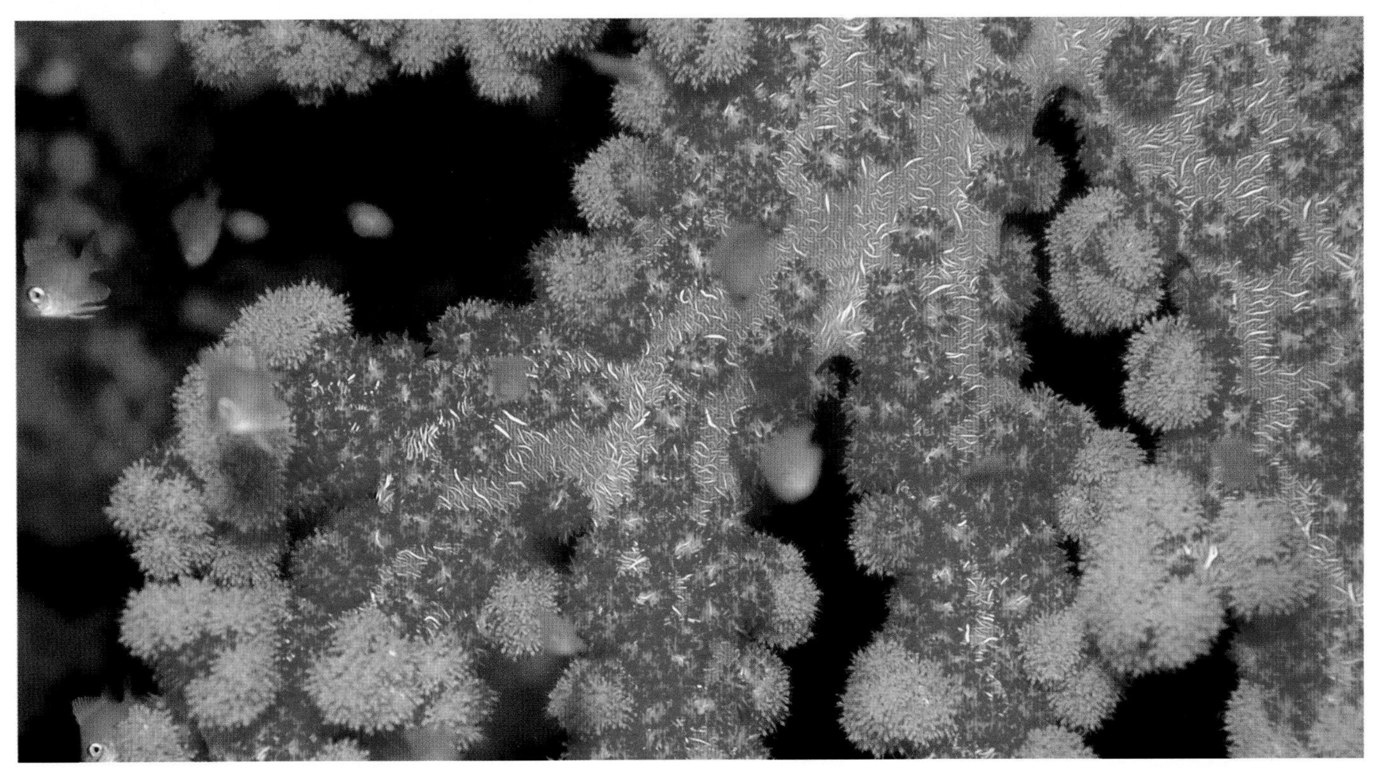

A very colourful *Dendronephthya* (*Spongodes*) sp., Solomon Islands.

Dendronephthya (*Roxasia*) sp., Solomon Islands.

Chironephthya

Pronunciation: KY-ro-NEPH-thee-uh

Common Name: *Dendronephthya*

Region: East Africa to the Western Pacific (Gosliner, *et al.*, 1996).

Description: Non-photosynthetic branchy soft corals with appearance somewhere between gorgonians and *Dendronephthya*, with brightly colored spicules and polyps. In some species drooping branches arise from an upright stalk, in others the entire colony is upright (Gosliner, *et al.*, 1996). The branches are stout and end abruptly without tapering off. Polyps are most concentrated at the ends of the branches, located in spiny calyces, with thick and large sclerites. Able to expand with water or deflate into a small tangle of stiff branches.

Similar Corals: *Nephthyigorgia* and *Siphonogorgia*.

Lighting Needs	0
Water Flow	5 - 9
Agressiveness	1
Hardiness	3

Placement

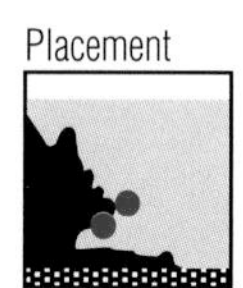

Food:

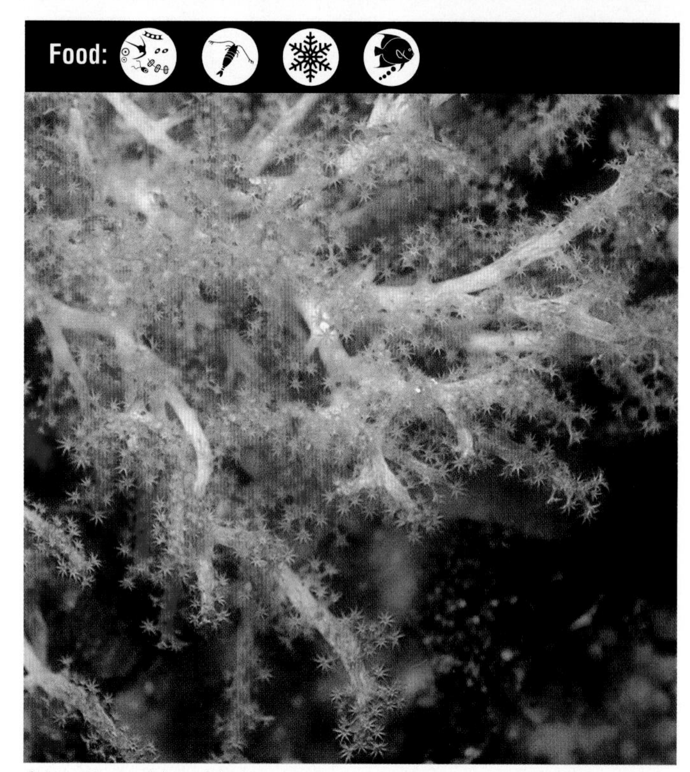

Chironephthya sp. Solomon Islands.

Chironephthya sp. growing from the underside of an overhang on current-swept reef wall. Solomon Islands.

Chironephthya sp.

The distinction between *Chironephthya* spp. and *Siphonogorgia* is not always clear.

Siphonogorgia

Pronunciation: SY-fo-no-GORG-ee-uh

Common Name: (among aquarists) *Dendronephthya*

Region: Western Pacific, Melanesia, Philippines

Description: Colorful arborescent soft corals. Rigid, but able to expand with water or deflate somewhat. No central axis. Branches formed from packed spindles. These sclerites afford a rough texture, though expanded colonies are somewhat slippery. Polyps completely retractile into the branches. Non-photosynthetic.

Similar Corals: *Nephthyigorgia* and *Chironephthya*.

Lighting Needs	0
Water Flow	5 - 9
Agressiveness	2
Hardiness	3

Placement

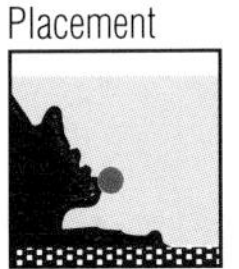

Siphonogorgia sp. Solomon Islands.

Siphonogorgia godeffroyi, one of the most exquisite soft corals.

Siphonogorgia godeffroyi with a resident goby. Solomon Islands.

Nephthyigorgia

Pronunciation: NEPH-thee-eh-GORG-ee-uh

Common Name: Chili Sponge, Red Finger (soft) Coral, Devil's Hand

Region: Indo-Pacific reef slopes with strong currents. Also in lagoon areas with strong tidal currents in shade attached to hard substrate.

Description: Tough thick tissue with some prominent sclerites. Small colony size, normally not much more than 6 in (15 cm) tall, with finger-like lobes or branches. There may be other species with taller colonies and finer branches. Colour is red, orange, or purple.

Similar Corals: Most similar to *Siphonogorgia* and *Chironephthya*. Small colonies may also be confused with *Eleutherobia*, *Minabea* or *Scleronephthya*, which occur in the same habitat and have orange forms.

Lighting Needs	0
Water Flow	3 - 10
Agressiveness	1
Hardiness	7

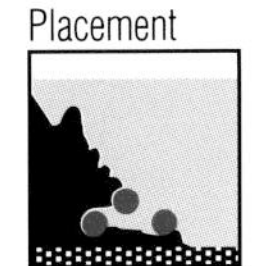

Nephthyigorgia sp. at the Löbbecke Museum in Düsseldorf, Germany.

Anthelia

Pronunciation: an-THEE-lee-uh

Common Name: *Anthelia*, waving hand polyp

Region: Red Sea to Hawaii

Description: *Anthelia* species have *Xenia*-like polyps, with long pinnules that afford a snowflake or tufty appearance. Colour is white, gray, brown, or pale blue. They grow by means of a creeping mat that may form stolon-like fingers. *Anthelia* polyps are not retractable and are monomorphic. There is probably more than one genus presently grouped under the single genus *Anthelia*, (Phil Alderslade, pers. comm.).

Similar Corals: *Xenia* and *Cespitularia* spp. form stalks, while *Anthelia* forms a creeping mat. *Clavularia* has similar polyps, but these are retractable into the club-like anthostele.

Lighting Needs	3 - 10
Water Flow	2 - 8
Agressiveness	4
Hardiness	7

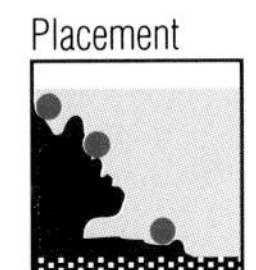

Anthelia cf. *philippinensis*. Solomon Islands.

Giant-polyped "*Anthelia*" in Daniel Knop's Aquarium, Sinsheim, Germany.

Giant-polyped "*Anthelia*" from Indonesia has very large polyps, Tentacle span up to 8 cm!

Another species of *Anthelia* from Indonesia.

Blue "*Anthelia*" from Indonesia can have extremely elongate polyp columns, up to at least 20 cm.

Blue "*Anthelia*" from Indonesia. The correct Identity of this coral is *Sansibia* (Alderslade, 2000).

Cespitularia

Pronunciation: sess-PITCH-yu-LAIR-ee-uh

Common Name: *Cespitularia*, Blue *Xenia*

Region: East Africa to Indonesia

Description: *Cespitularia* has an appearance somewhere between *Xenia* and *Alcyonium.* Colonies up to several inches tall and arborescent like *Alcyonium.* The polyps may pulse like *Xenia.* Colour is bright blue-white, green or reddish. Polyps are non-retractile.

Similar Corals: *Xenia, Anthelia, Efflatournaria, Alcyonium.*

Lighting Needs	5 - 10
Water Flow	4 - 9
Agressiveness	4
Hardiness	6

Placement

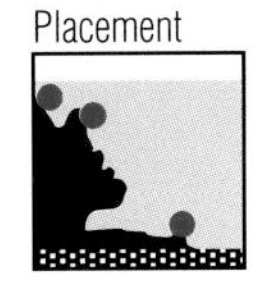

Food:

Tank-raised spectacularly colored *Cespitularia* in the Elos company display aquarium, Zoomark Milan.

Tank-raised *Cespitularia* sp., polyps open.

Heteroxenia

Pronunciation: HEH-teh-ro-ZEE-nee-uh

Common Name: Pulse corals, Pumping *Xenia*, Pump-end *Xenia*, Waving hand Polyps

Region: Red Sea and Indo-Pacific.

Description: Like *Xenia* but dimorphic, possessing two types of polyps: autozooids and siphonozooids. However, the siphonozooids develop as the colony grows, and may be absent in small specimens.

Similar Corals: *Xenia*, see next description.

Lighting Needs	4 - 10
Water Flow	4 - 9
Agressiveness	3
Hardiness	5

Placement

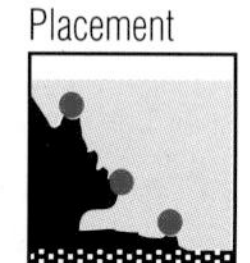

Heteroxenia sp. Note siphonozooids like pores on the surface of the capitulum. Solomon Islands.

Heteroxenia sp. Solomon Islands.

Xenia

Pronunciation: ZEE-nee-uh

Common Name: Pulse corals, Pumping Xenia, Pump-end Xenia, Waving hand Polyps

Region: Red Sea and Indo-Pacific.

Description: Encrusting or stalked, with non-retractile monomorphic polyps. Colonies usually quite soft, but larger, stalked varieties may be tougher. Some species are very slimy because of copiuous mucus they produce. The color and form of *Xenia* species is highly dependent on environmental conditions. Sclerites are minute platelets (Bayer, 1973).

Similar Corals: *Heteroxenia* is distinguished by its dimorphic polyps. *Anthelia* forms creeping mats while *Xenia* generally forms stalks. However in some *Anthelia* the mats divide into distinct clumps, and there are encrusting *Xenia* spp. without an obvious stalk. *Anthelia* polyps generally open flat in still water, whereas *Xenia* polyps have tentacles that curve inward toward the center of the polyp, with finer pinnules.

Lighting Needs	4 - 10
Water Flow	3 - 9
Agressiveness	4
Hardiness	7

Placement

Xenia sp. Red Sea. Eilat Israel.

The same *Xenia* sp. growing on the glass in an aquarium.

Cavernularia

Pronunciation: ka-ver-nyu-LAIR-ee-uh

Common Name: Sea Pen

Region: Mediterranean, Red Sea, Indo-Pacific to Eastern Pacific.

Description: Soft clavate (club shaped) colony. Primary polyp forms a muscular peduncle, like the column and foot of a sea anemone, which burrows and anchors the coral in the substrate. Secondary polyps are arranged around the entire length of the primary polyp. Some species are photosynthetic (Gosliner, *et al.*, 1996).

Similar Corals: *Veretillium* and *Lituaria* spp. are most similar to *Cavernularia*.

Lighting Needs	0 - 8
Water Flow	4 - 8
Agressiveness	1
Hardiness	5

Placement

Cavernularia cf. *obesa* lives with its base anchored in the sand.

Virgularia
Pronunciation: VER-gyu-LAIR-ee-uh

Common Name: Sea Pen

Region: Mediterranean, Red Sea, Indo-Pacific to Eastern Pacific.

Description: Flexible feather-like soft corals that live in sandy areas adjacent to reefs. Polyps located in rows of "leaves." Most are encountered at night when they expand from their burrow in the sand to feed on plankton. At least one species has symbiotic zooxanthellae and therefore remains expanded during the daytime to gather light. (Gosliner, *et al.*, 1996).

Similar Corals: *Virgularia* is one of a few genera of feather-like sea pens. Others include *Scytalium* and *Pteroeides.*

Lighting Needs	0 - 8
Water Flow	4 - 9
Agressiveness	1
Hardiness	2

Placement

Virgularia sp. Solomon Islands.

Erythropodium
Pronunciation: eh-RITH-ro-PO-dee-um

Common Name: Encrusting Gorgonian, Briareum

Region: *Erythropodium caribaeorum* is a Caribbean species. Other *Erythropodium* species are known from Indonesia, and one occurs in temperate waters, in Australia.

Description: Encrusting sheets with star-like polyps or polyps with tentacles that are long and stringy, like filamentous algae. An Indo-Pacific species has perforations in the encrusting sheet, which is composed of fused stolons. Usually encrusting sheets are light tan and the polyps are darker brown, but reddish tissue and sclerites on the underside may impart a purplish hue to the colony.

Similar Corals: *Erythropodium* is very similar in appearance to *Briareum* (and *Pachyclavularia*), and they are often confused. Although superficially they look extremely similar, *Briareum* and *Erythropodium* are not closely related. They have a different internal structure and quite different sclerites.

Lighting Needs	3 - 9
Water Flow	4 - 10
Agressiveness	8
Hardiness	10

Placement

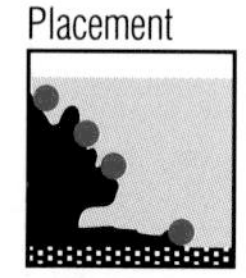

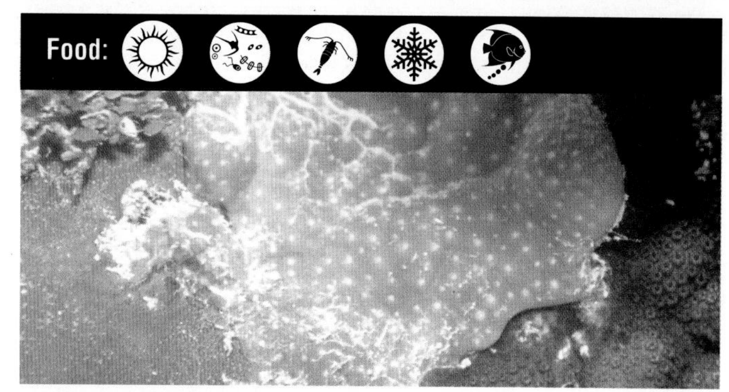

Erythropodium caribaeorum with polyps contracted, Key Largo, Florida.

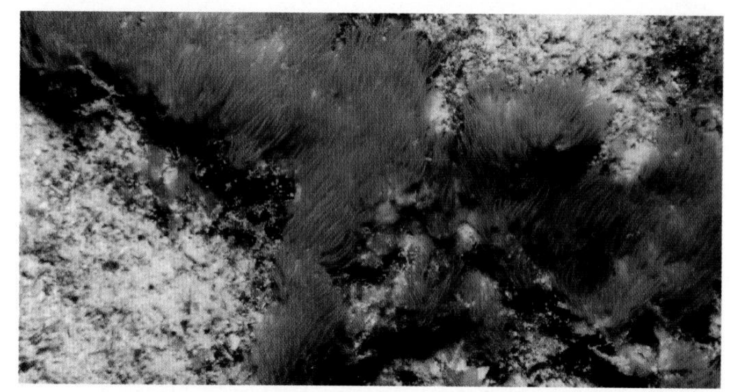

Erythropodium caribaeorum with polyps expanded in strong current, Key Largo, Florida.

This Indonesian *Erythropodium* forms creeping stolons which fuse into encrusting sheets.

Closeup of Indonesian *Erythropodium* showing the creeping stolons.

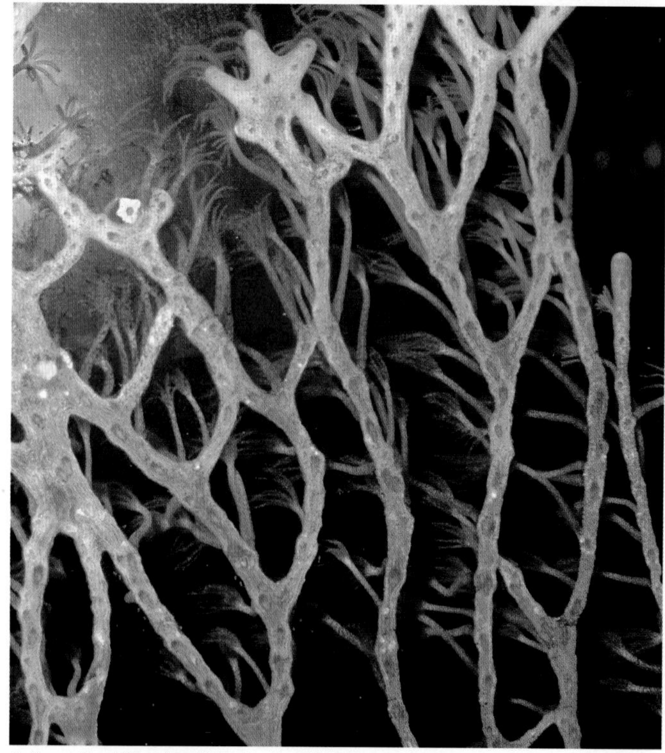

Erythropodium stolons viewed from the other side, here seen growing on the glass in an aquarium.

Chapter Two

Diodogorgia

Pronunciation: dee-oh-do-GORG-ee-uh

Common Name: Finger Sea Fan. Yellow Finger, Red Finger

Region: Atlantic and Caribbean.

Description: Brittle, breaks easily. Does not grow very large, usually about 10 cm (4 in) tall, up to 25 cm (10 in), and generally not more than 25 cm (10 in) across. The sclerites on the interior are reddish. Not photosynthetic. Two colour morphs. One is bright orange-yellow with red calyces and white polyps. The other is deep red with red calyces and white polyps.

Similar Corals: There are some gorgonians in the Indo-Pacific with the same colour combination, but no other gorgonians in the Caribbean would be mistaken for *Diodogorgia.*

Lighting Needs	0
Water Flow	4 - 10
Agressiveness	1
Hardiness	6

Placement

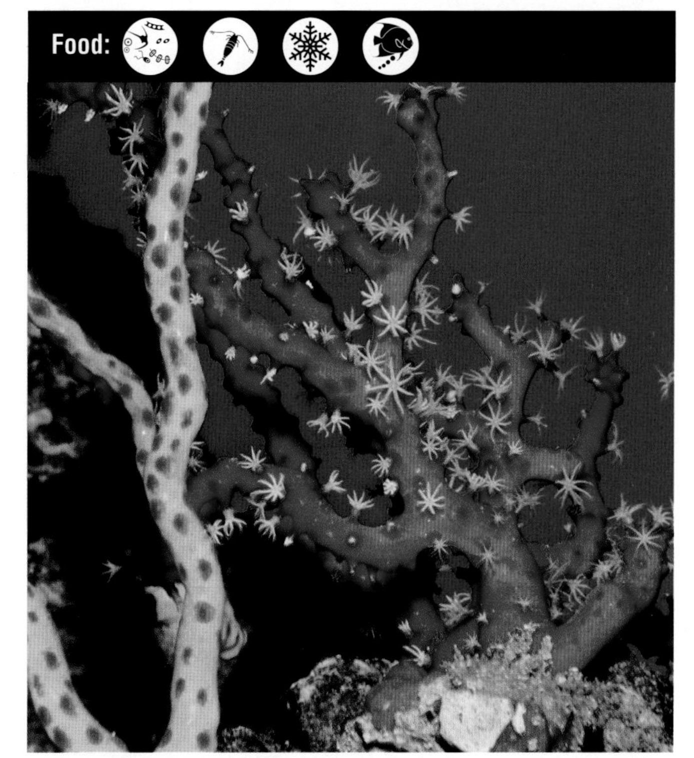

The two color morphs of *Diodogorgia nodulifera* from Florida.

Iciligorgia

Pronunciation: I-sill-ee-GORG-ee-uh

Common Name: Sea Fan, Semperina

Region: Atlantic and Caribbean, Indo-Pacific.

Description: Fan shaped gorgonians with sinuous banches. Non-photosynthetic, with polyps located mostly on the sides of the branches. Indo-Pacific forms may have a groove on the branches where the tissue has fused, and open tips where the tissue has not yet fused. See Grasshoff, (1999) for description of the Indo-Pacific species as *Iciligorgia.*

Similar Corals: The Caribbean species could be confused with *Pterogorgia*, but *Pterogorgia* has straight branches and is photosynthetic. The open grooves on the branch tips of the Indo Pacific forms also occurs in *Solenocaulon*, which forms much smaller colonies.

Lighting Needs	0
Water Flow	4 - 9
Agressiveness	1
Hardiness	4

Placement

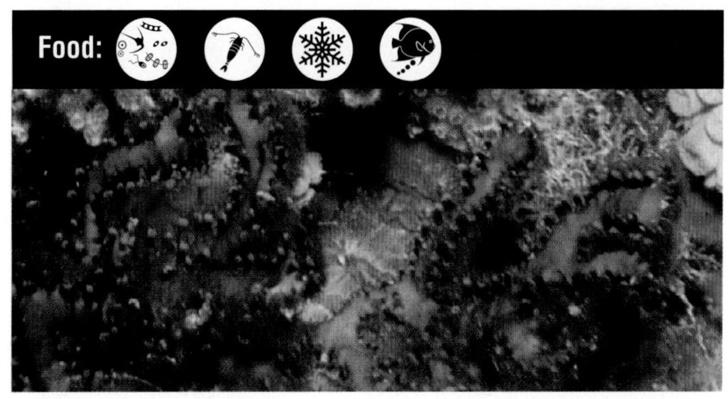

Iciligorgia schrammi. Key Largo, Florida.

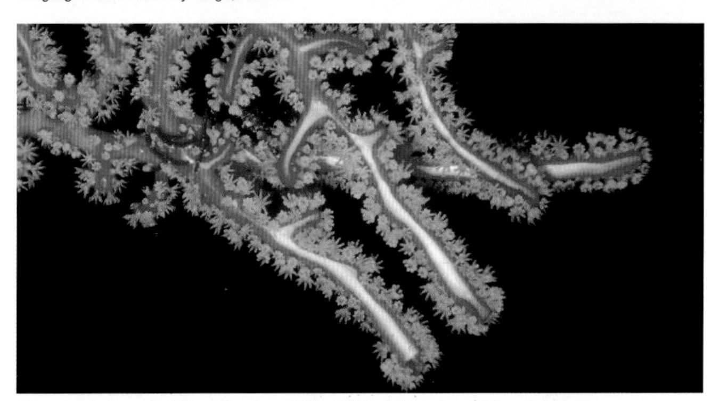

Close-up photograph of the unique branch tips of this *Iciligorgia* sp. Solomon Islands.

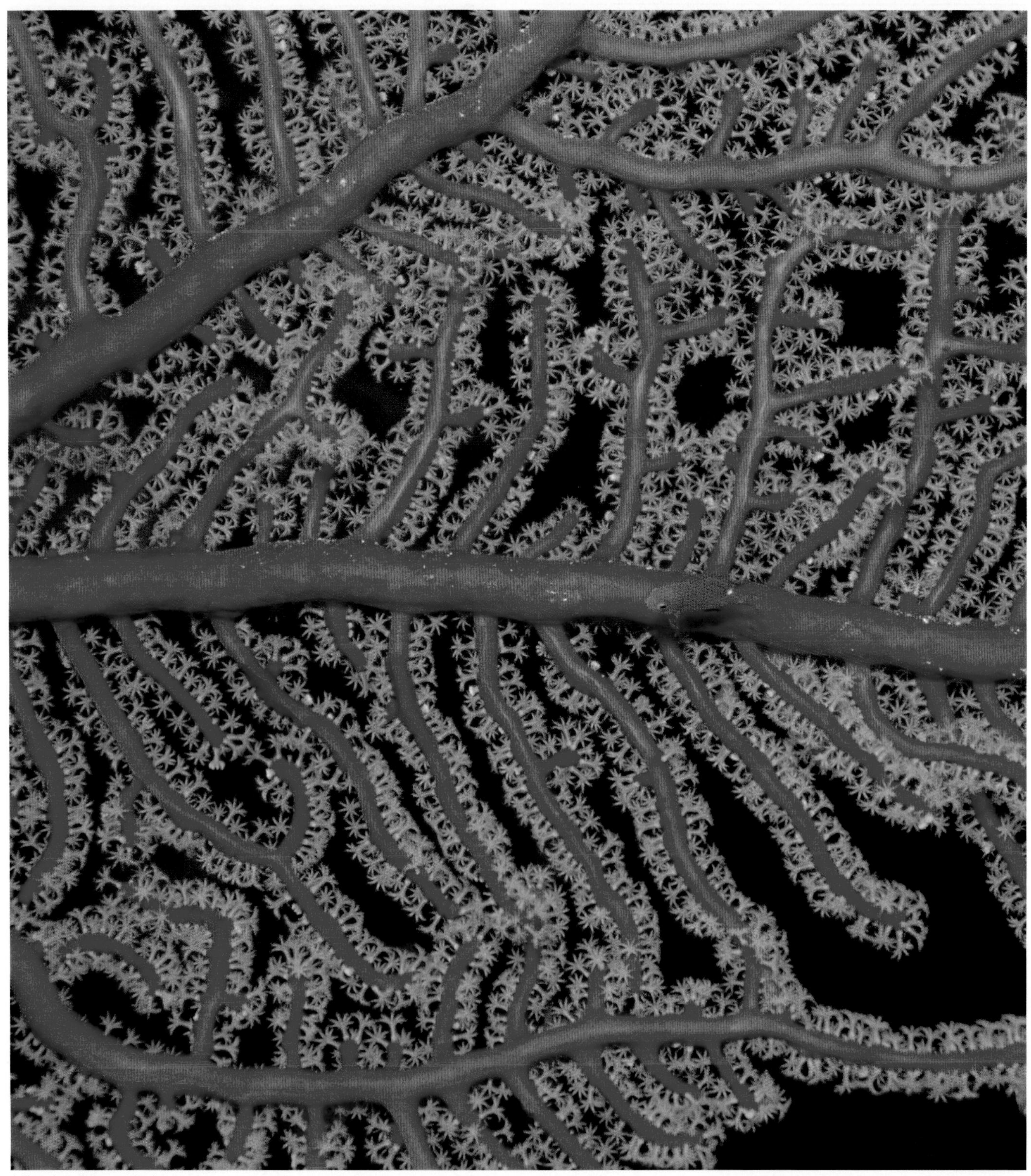

Iciligorgia sp. Solomon Islands.

Subergorgia

Pronunciation: SOO-bur-GORG-ee-uh

Common Name: Sea Fan

Region: Red Sea, Okinawa, Indonesia, Philippines, New Guinea, Solomon Islands.

Description: Extremely large planar intricately branched sea fans. Branches form net-like mesh. Some species with dichotomous branching (see Gosliner, et al. 1996).

Similar Corals: None

Placement

Lighting Needs	0
Water Flow	5 - 10
Agressiveness	1
Hardiness	2

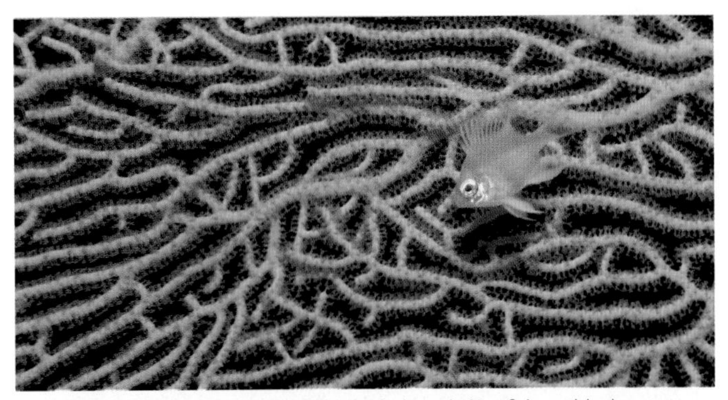

Subergorgia mollis offers shelter to a damselfish that feeds on plankton. Solomon Islands.

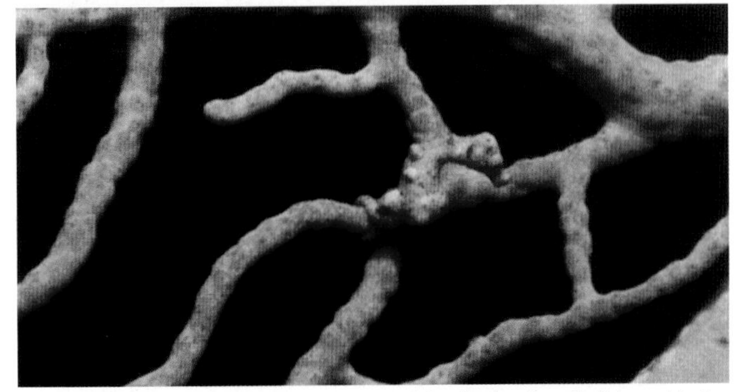

Amazing camouflage: a minute seahorse, *Hippocampus* cf. *bargibanti*, on *S. mollis*. Solomon Islands.

Subergorgia mollis with a small resident goby. Solomon Islands.

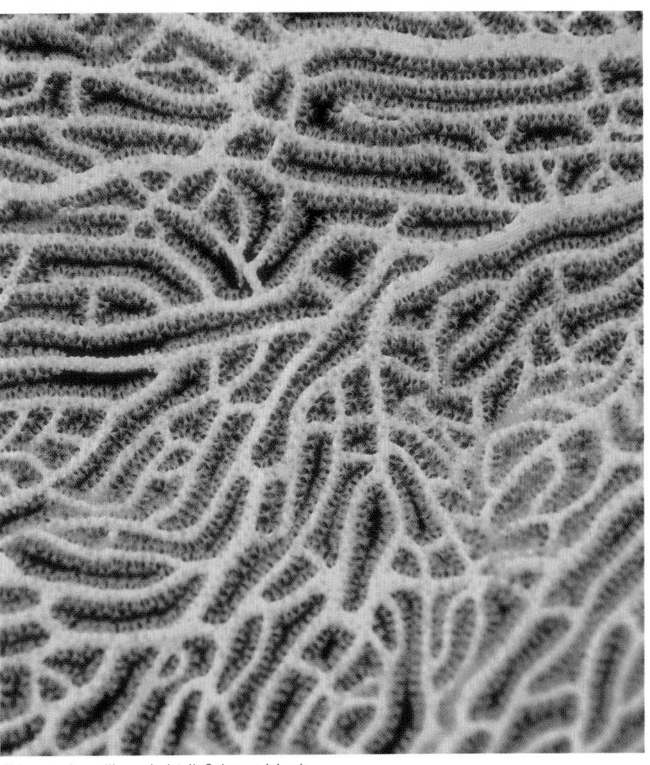

Subergorgia mollis mesh detail. Solomon Islands.

Melithaea

Pronunciation: MELL-lith-EE-uh (muh-LITH-ee-uh)

Common Name: Sea Fan

Region: East Africa to Indo-West Pacific, including Japan.

Description: Robust large planar intricately branched sea fans. Branches composed of links made from calcareous internodes and swollen nodes of horn-like material.

Similar Corals: *Acabaria*, which has much thinner branches and forms much smaller fans.

Lighting Needs	0
Water Flow	5 - 10
Agressiveness	1
Hardiness	2

Placement

Food:

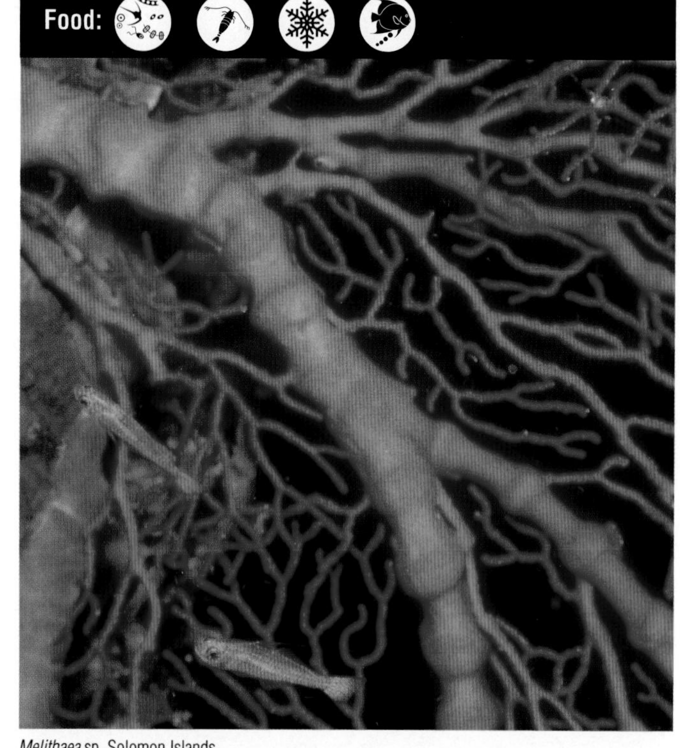

Melithaea sp. Solomon Islands.

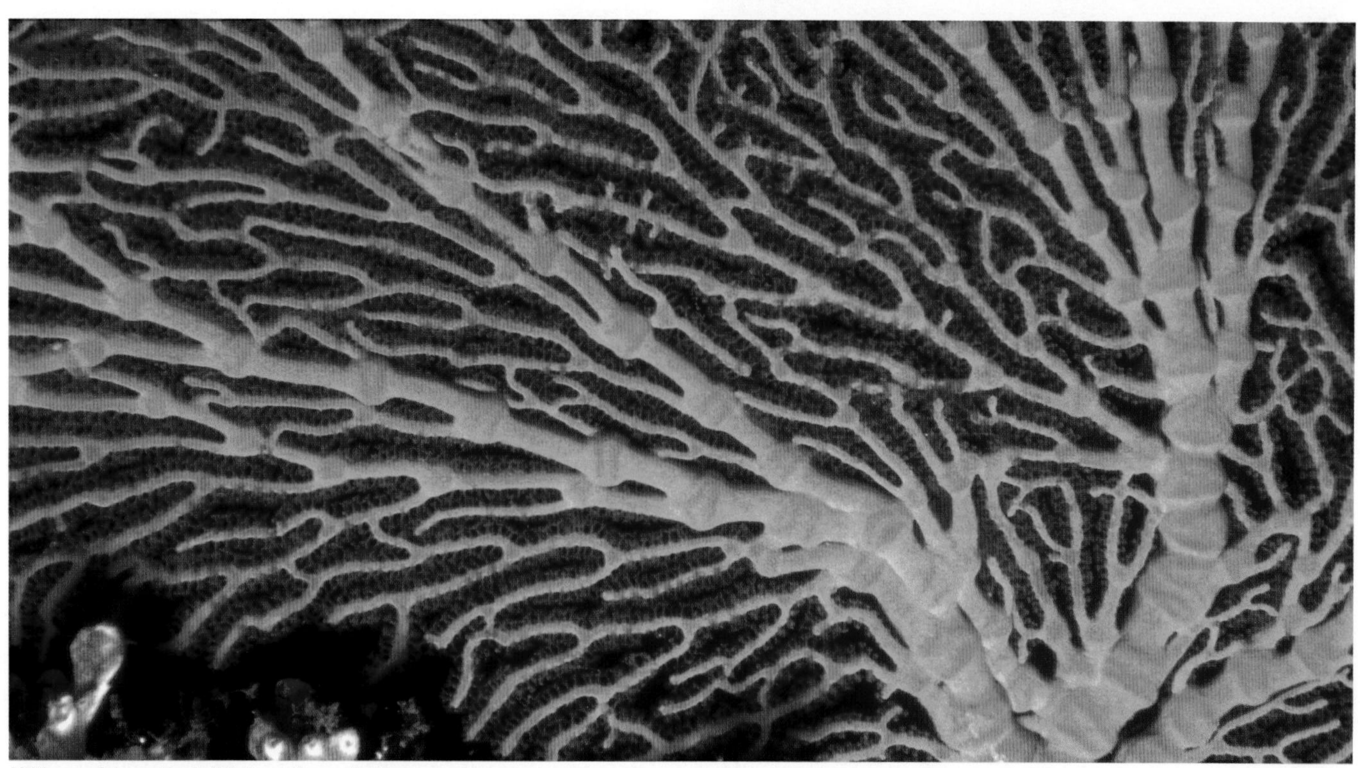

Melithaea sp. Solomon Islands. Note the swellings on the stems.

Acabaria

Pronunciation: AKH-uh-BAIR-ee-uh

Common Name: Sea Fan

Region: East Africa to Hawaii.

Description: Fine-branched delicate sea fans, sometimes bushy, sometimes fan-shaped. Branches composed of links made from calcareous internodes and swollen nodes of horn-like material.

Similar Corals: *Melithaea,* which has much thicker branches and forms much larger fans.

	Placement
Lighting Needs	0
Water Flow	4 - 10
Agressiveness	1
Hardiness	3

Food:

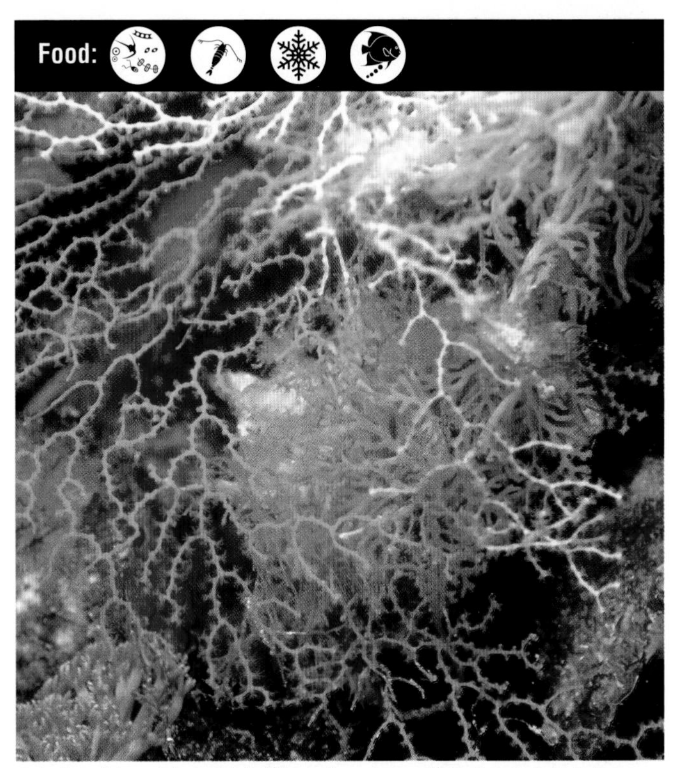

Acabaria sp. Solomon Islands. Note 3 different colors, a common feature in such *Acabaria* clumps.

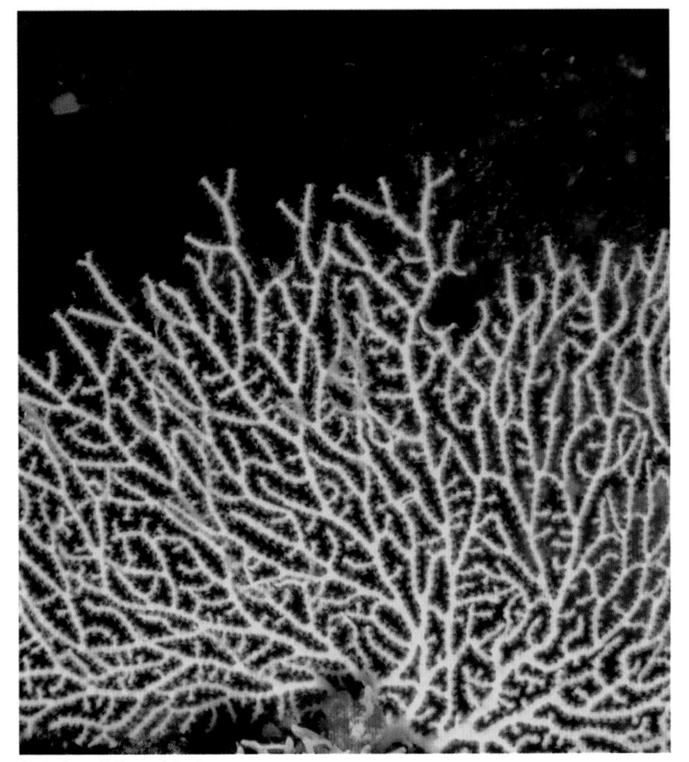

Acabaria sp. Solomon Islands.

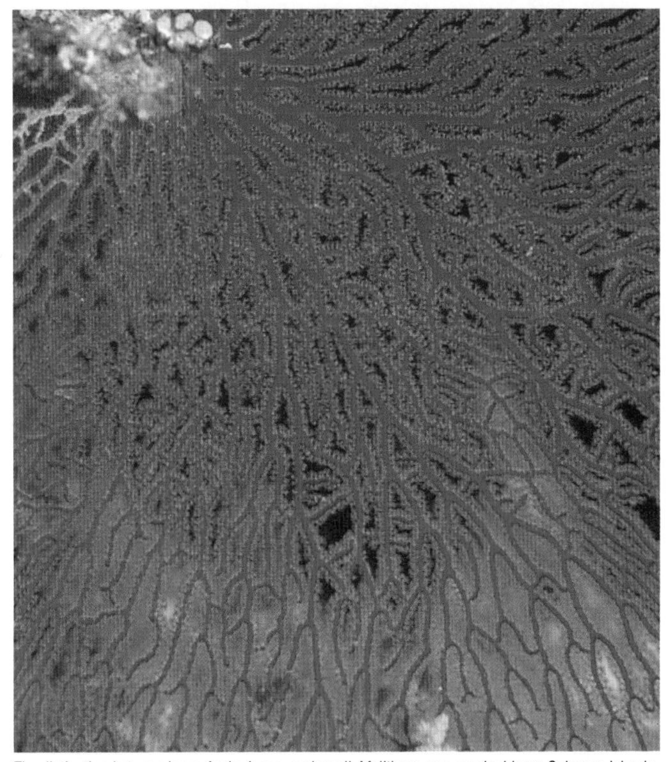

The distinction between large *Acabaria* spp. and small *Melithaea* spp. can be blurry. Solomon Islands.

Acalycigorgia

Pronunciation: A-kah-LISS-ee-GOR-gee-uh

Common Name: Sea Fan

Region: East Africa, Melanesia, Australia, Indonesia, Philippines, New Guinea, Solomon Islands.

Description: Tree-like or fan-like gorgonians with non-retractile polyps. Calyces are long and tubular, branches usually sinuous. Very colorful.

Similar Corals: *Muricella*

Placement

Lighting Needs	0
Water Flow	5 - 10
Agressiveness	1
Hardiness	4

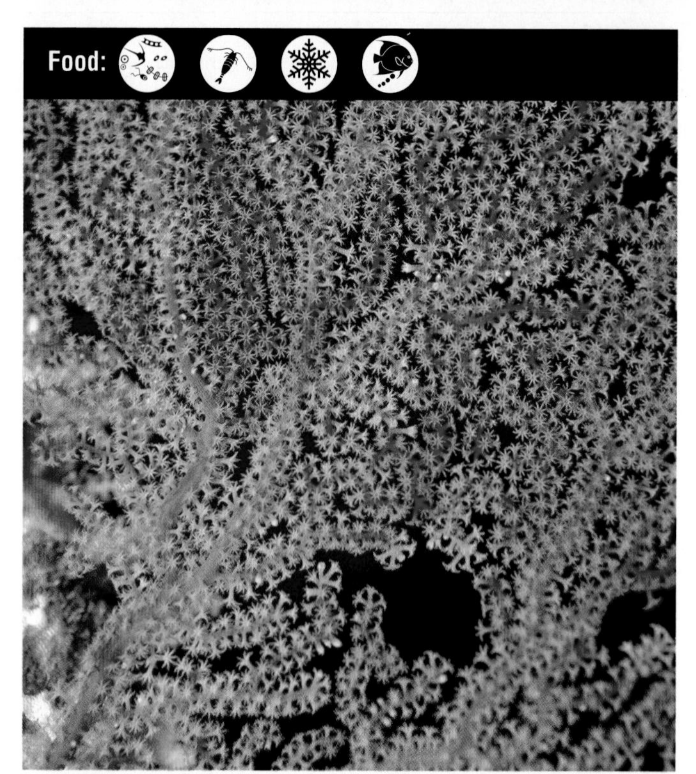

Acalycigorgia sp. Solomon Islands.

Muricella

Pronunciation: MYU-ree-SELL-uh

Common Name: Sea Fan

Region: Indonesia, Philippines, New Guinea, Solomon Islands.

Description: Large sea fans with intricate branches. Typically the rind color is pale grey while the calyces are a strongly contrasting red. Other color combinations exist. In some areas this fan harbours the uniquely camouflaged dwarf seahorse, *Hippocampus bargibanti.*

Similar Corals: *Acalycigorgia*

Placement

Lighting Needs	0
Water Flow	5 - 10
Agressiveness	2
Hardiness	3

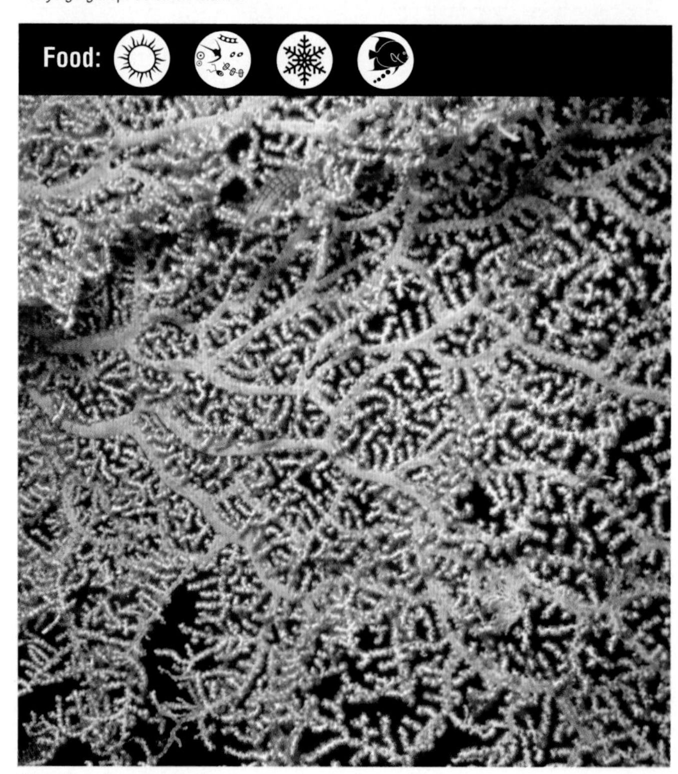

Muricella sp. Solomon Islands.

Muricea

Pronunciation: myu-RISS-ee-uh (myur-iss-EE-uh)

Common Name: Spiny Sea Fan, Spiny Gorgonian, Spiny Sea Rod, Silver Bush.

Region: Caribbean

Description: The several common *Muricea* species all have spiny projecting calyces that afford a rough texture when handled. Colonies may grow in one plane or may be bushy.

Similar Corals: May be confused with *Eunicea* species, which also have a spiny appearance, but *Muricea* never has purple sclerites in the axial sheath.

Lighting Needs	4 - 9
Water Flow	5 - 10
Agressiveness	4
Hardiness	8

Placement

Food:

Muricea sp. Hollywood, Florida.

Muriceopsis

Pronunciation: myu-RISS-ee-OPS-iss

Common Name: Feather gorgonian, Rough Sea Plume, Purple Bush

Region: Caribbean

Description: There are two common species and two or more uncommon ones. *Muriceopsis sulphurea* forms low bushes of short branches that are usually lemon yellow in the Southern Caribbean and Brazil. *Muriceopsis flavida* forms pinnately branched bushes.

Similar Corals: *Muriceopsis flavida* appears at first like a type of *Pseudopterogorgia* because its form is also pinnate (feather-like). Upon closer inspection one can see that the branches are thicker, rounder, and more robust than most *Pseudopterogorgia* species.

Lighting Needs	4 - 9
Water Flow	5 - 10
Agressiveness	4
Hardiness	8

Placement

Food:

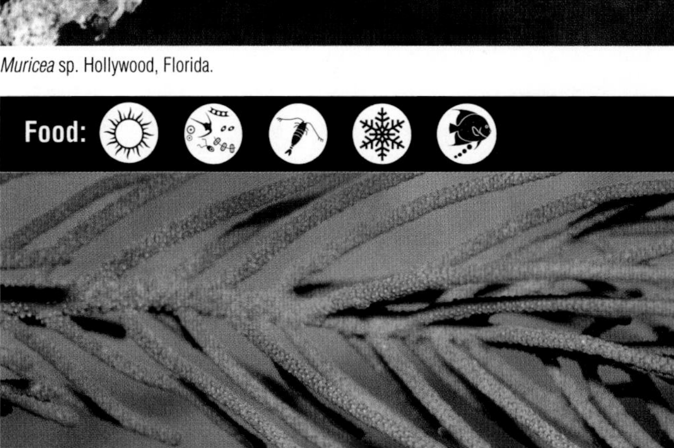

Muriceopsis flavida has round bumpy branches.

Muriceopsis sulphurea.

Eunicea
Pronunciation: yu-NISS-ee-uh (yu-nee-SEE-uh)

Common Name: Knobby candelabrum

Region: Caribbean

Description: Sclerites often purple, sometimes violet or nearly colourless. *Eunicea* species usually have characteristic knobby projections for calyces that afford an *Acropora*-like appearance when the polyps are closed. Colonies are often candelabrum shaped. There are many species, some with strongly projecting calyces, such as *E. laxispica*, and some with relatively smooth branches, such as *E. knighti.*

Similar Corals: Smooth forms resemble *Pseudoplexaura* or *Plexaurella. Eunicea* is more rigid than the former and the latter genus never has purple sclerites. *Muricea* species are similarly spiny, but have projecting spicules that give them a distinctively prickly texture. They do not have purple sclerites.

Lighting Needs	4 - 9
Water Flow	4 - 10
Agressiveness	2
Hardiness	7

Placement

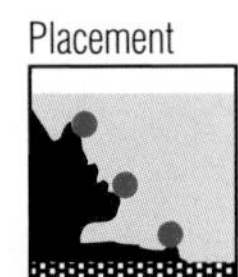

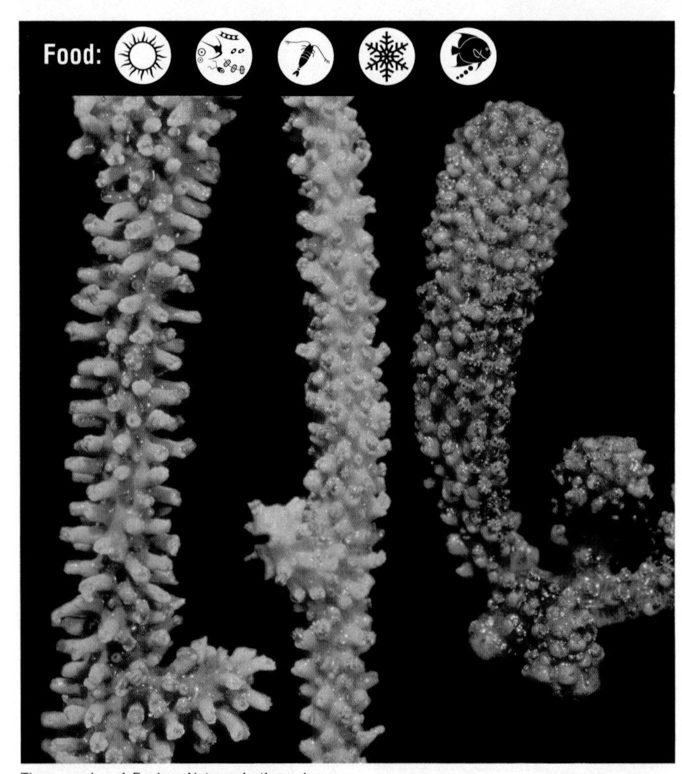

Three species of *Eunicea.* Note projecting calyces.

Thick-branched *Eunicea* sp. Key Largo, Florida.

A rare purple *Eunicea* sp. Florida Keys.

Plexaura
Pronunciation: plex-AW-ruh

Common Name: Sea Rod, Candelabrum

Region: Caribbean, Brazil

Description: *Plexaura homomalla* has branches about 1 cm thick that are chocolate brown with contrasting light brown polyps. *Plexaura flexuosa* may be a variety of colours, but the most striking one is bright purple with almost white polyps. Colonies often branch in one plane when small, becoming bushy when large. They grow to at least four feet tall.

Similar Corals: Similar to *Rumphella* of the Indo-West Pacific.

Lighting Needs	3 - 10
Water Flow	3 - 10
Agressiveness	1
Hardiness	7

Placement

The Purple Sea Rod, *Plexaura flexuosa* from Florida. Aquarium photo.

Plexaurella
Pronunciation: plex-aw-RELL-uh

Common Name: Corky Sea Fingers, Slit-pore Sea Rod

Region: Caribbean

Description: *Plexaurella* species have a corky appearance when the polyps are retracted. They are Light brown, almost yellow, with darker brown polyps. Small colonies are often shaped like a "Y", while large colonies are often bushy. Most *Plexaurella* spp. have crescent shaped pores when the polyps are closed, though some have round pores like the similar-looking *Pseudoplexaura* spp.

Similar Corals: *Pseudoplexaura* has more slippery texture and round pores when the polyps are closed. It also typically has a purple cortex while *Plexaurella* is uniformly yellowish brown throughout. Some smooth pale brown varieties of *Eunicea* may be confused with *Plexaurella*. *Eunicea* usually have dark or purplish sclerites in the cortex.

Lighting Needs	3 - 9
Water Flow	3 - 10
Agressiveness	1
Hardiness	9

Placement

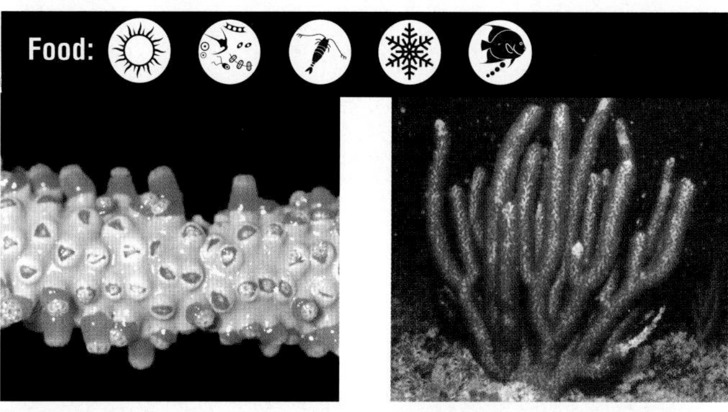

Closeup of the slit-shaped pores.

Plexaurella colony with expanded polyps.

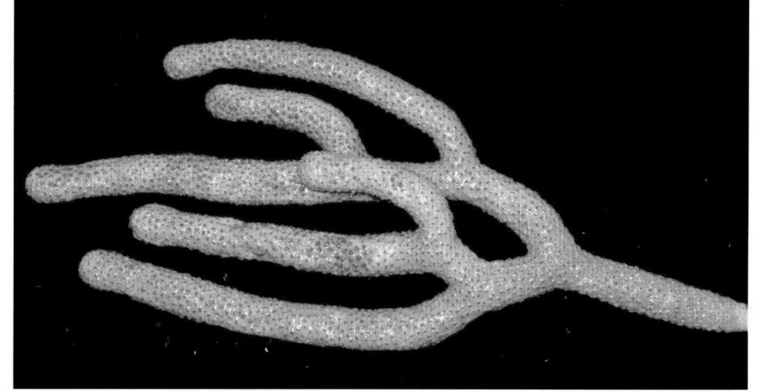
Typical colony shape of *Plexaurella*.

Pseudoplexaura
Pronunciation: SOO-doh-plex-AW-ruh

Common Name: Porous Sea Rod

Region: Caribbean

Description: Colonies are composed of long branches. Mature colonies are bushy and grow absolutely huge, to at least eight feet tall and several feet across. Slimy to the touch, with large, very beautiful polyps. Color usually purplish grey with brown polyps, sometimes yellow or green.

Similar Corals: Resemble *Plexaurella* spp., but *Pseudoplexaura* spp. are usually purplish gray instead of pale brown, and *Plexaurella* never has purple sclerites in the axial sheath.

Lighting Needs	3 - 8
Water Flow	4 - 9
Agressiveness	3
Hardiness	7

Placement
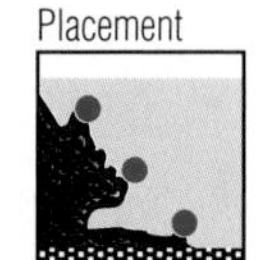

Food:

Portion of a large *Pseudoplexaura* "tree."

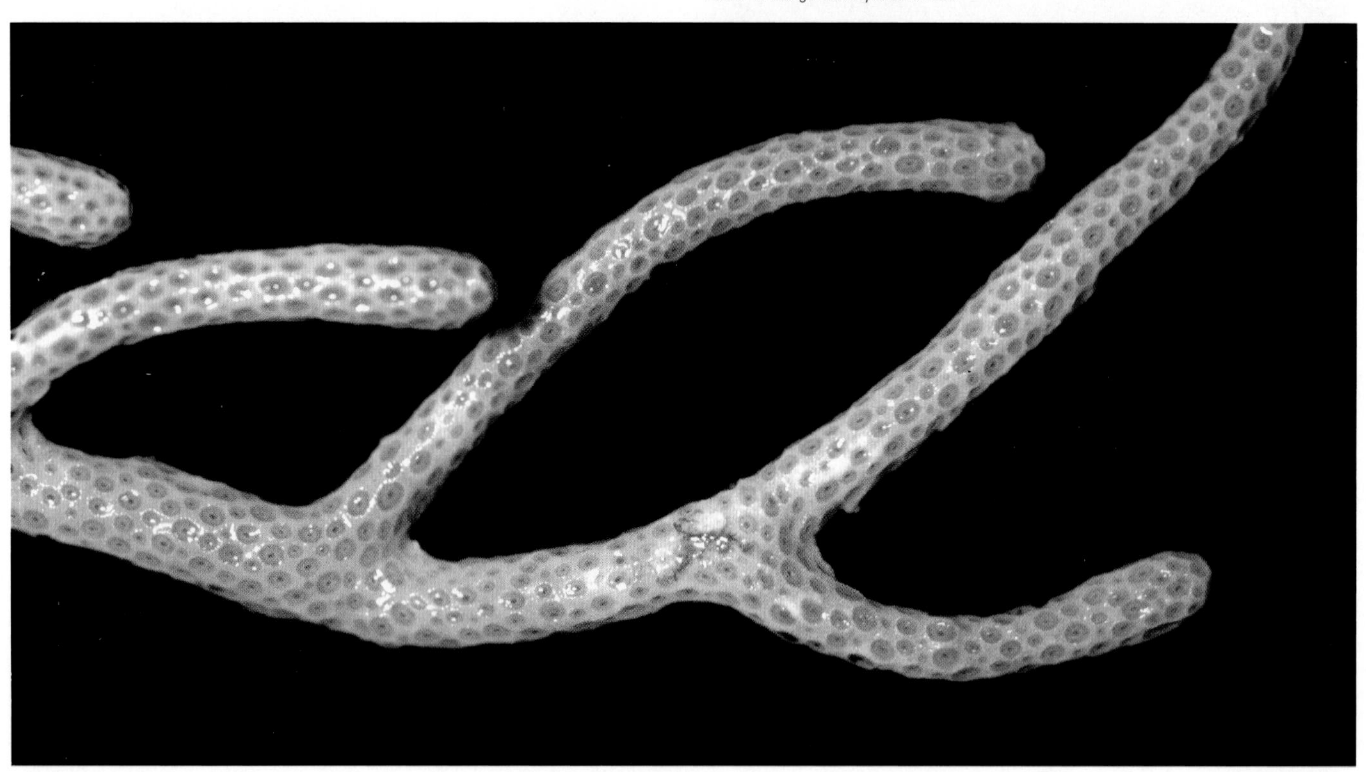

Pseudoplexaura looks similar to *Plexaurella*, but has round pore-like calyces and purple sclerites in the cortex.

Swiftia
Pronunciation: SWIF-tee-uh

Region: Caribbean.

Common Name: Orange Sea Fan, Soft Red Sea Fan, Orange Tree

Description: Bushy orange gorgonian, sometimes fan shaped but with loose branches. Large red polyps are distinctive.

Similar Corals: None

Lighting Needs	0
Water Flow	4 - 9
Agressiveness	1
Hardiness	4

Placement

Swiftia exserta.

Echinomuricea
Pronunciation: ee-KI-no-MYU-ree-SEE-uh

Common Name: Sea Fan

Region: Indonesia, Philippines, New Guinea, Solomon Islands.

Description: Small colorful gorgonians with open branches, often but not always fan-shaped.

Similar Corals: *Menella* (note: purple specimen in photo is probably *Menella. Acalycigorgia* is also similar. *Heterogorgia uatumani* (see Humann, 1993) from the Caribbean is very similar to the *Echinomuricea* pictured here.

Lighting Needs	0
Water Flow	4 - 9
Agressiveness	1
Hardiness	4

Placement

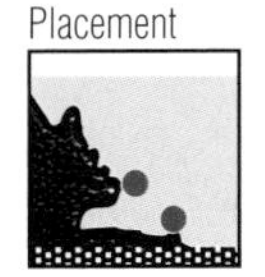

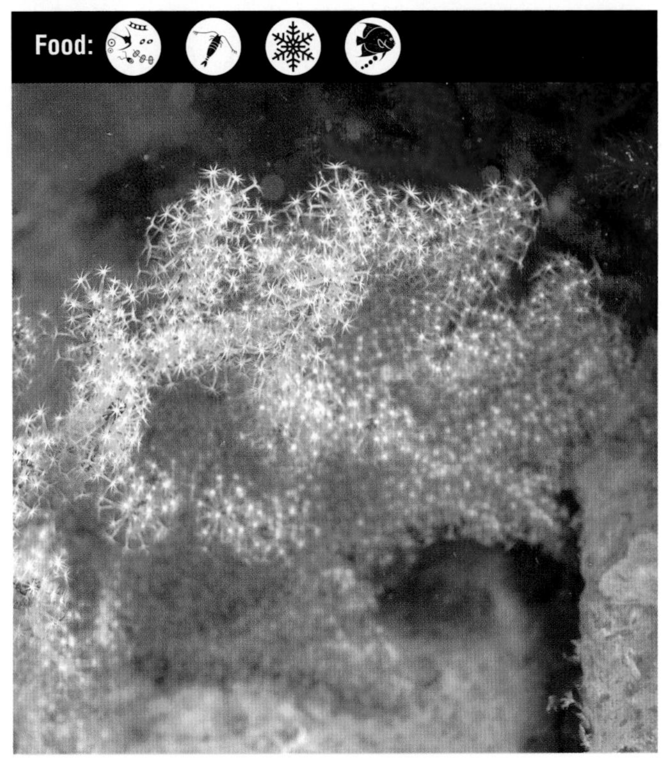

Echinomuricea sp. and *Menella* sp. on "The Wreck of the Anne." Solomon Islands.

Menella

Pronunciation: muh-NELL-uh

Common Name: Sea Fan

Region: East Africa, Indo-West Pacific.

Description: Colorful gorgonians with open branches, often but not always fan-shaped.

Similar Corals: *Leptogorgia* from the Caribbean. Also similar to *Guaiagorgia.*

Lighting Needs		0
Water Flow		4 - 9
Agressiveness		1
Hardiness		4

Placement

Menella sp. Aquarium photo.

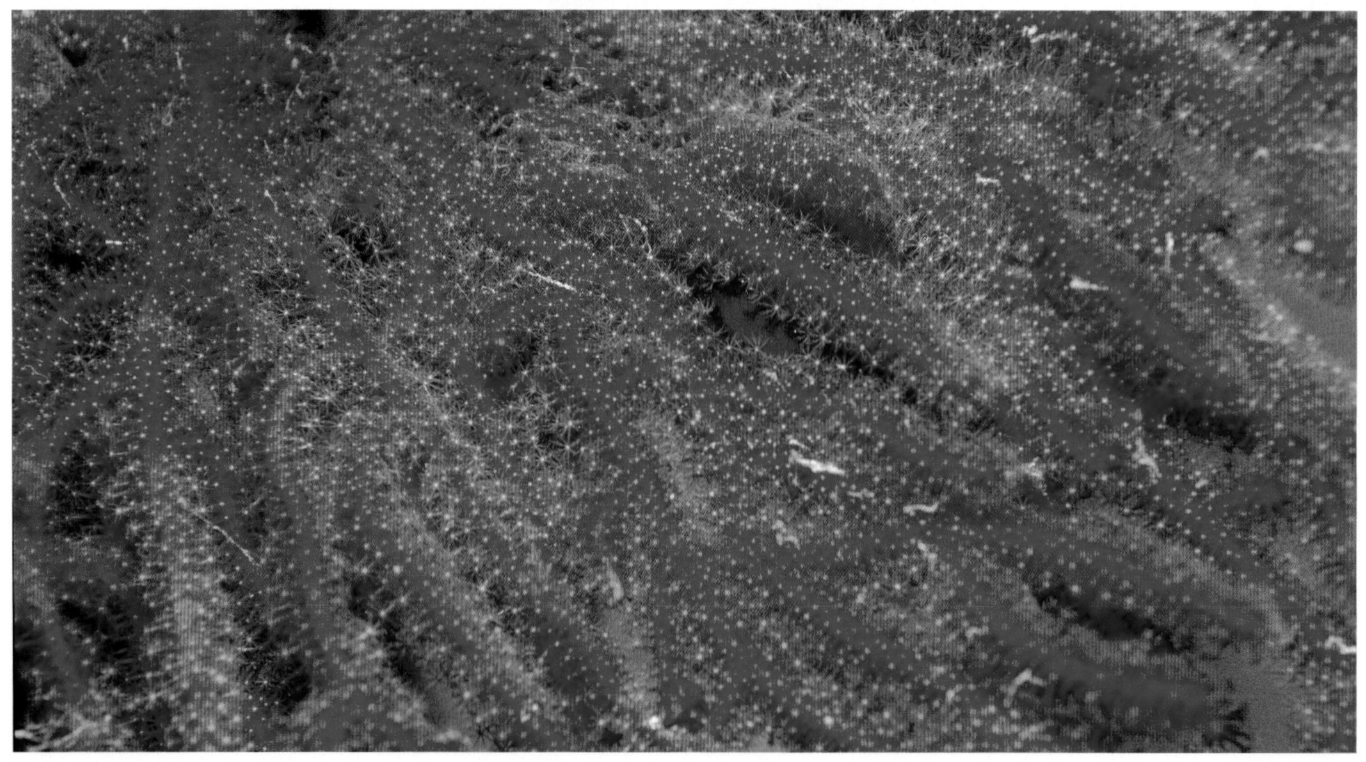

Menella sp. Solomon Islands.

Pacifigorgia

Pronunciation: pa-SIFF-ih-GORG-ee-uh

Common Name: Red Sea Fan, Panamic Sea Fan

Region: Eastern Pacific, Sea of Cortez down to Peru.

Description: Growth in one plane. Reddish colour, stiff horny skeleton, white or pale clear polyps. Described species include *P. adamsii* and *P. irene.*

Similar Corals: There are numerous other bright red sea fans in the Indo-Pacific with whitish polyps.

Lighting Needs	0
Water Flow	5 - 10
Agressiveness	1
Hardiness	2

Placement

Food:

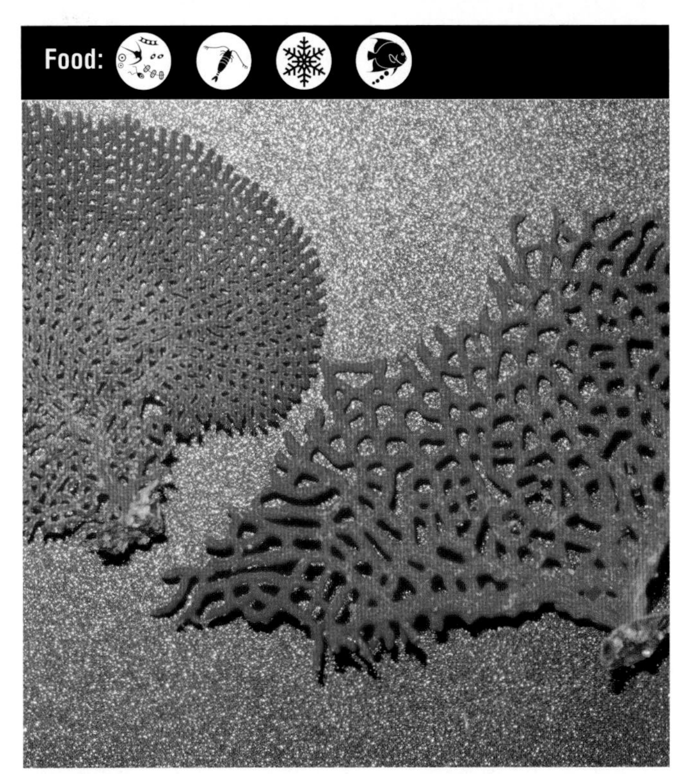

Pacifigorgia spp. from Puerto Vallarta, Mexico.

Guaiagorgia

Pronunciation: gwah-EE-uh-GORG-ee-uh

Common Name: Blue Gorgonian. Sea whip.

Region: Indonesia

Description: Sparsely branched colonies, branches approximately 4 to 6 mm in diameter, with small bright blue polyps. See Grasshoff and Alderslade, (1997) for description.

Similar Corals: Similar to *Menella* from the Pacific and Indian Oceans, and to *Leptogorgia* from Florida.

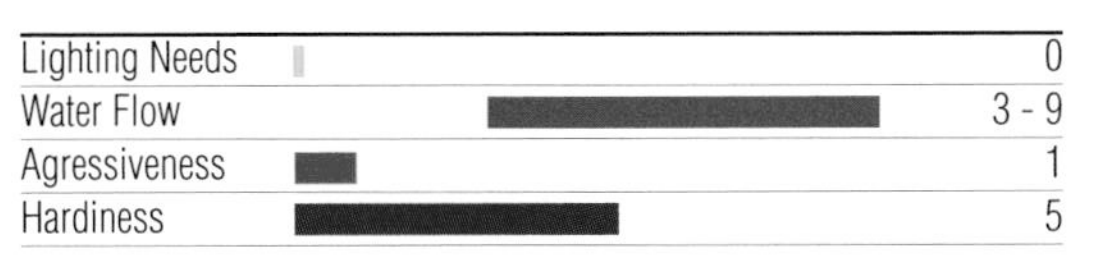

Placement

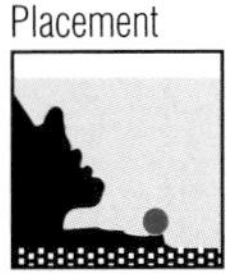

Food:

Guaiagorgia cf. *anas.* Aquarium photo, Toronto, Canada.

Gorgonia
Pronunciation: gor-GO-nee-uh

Common Name: Sea Fan

Region: Caribbean

Description: *Gorgonia ventalina* is the common variety of sea fan, with the branching flattened in the same plane as the fan. It is typically purple, but can also be pale gray or yellow. *G. flabellum* is distinguished by branches flattened perpendicular to the plane of the fan, and it is more rigid. It may be any of the aforementioned colors, but yellow is most typical. A third species, *Gorgonia mariae*, has branches that are rounded instead of flattened, and the branches are widely meshed and pinnate.

Lighting Needs	4 - 10
Water Flow	5 - 10
Agressiveness	1
Hardiness	7

Placement

Important note: Because of the curio trade in dead corals, the three Caribbean sea fan species are prohibited to collect in Florida, and many Caribbean localities. Where legal to collect, there is no harm done by harvesting small, four inch colonies since these are only about one year old or less, and clearly renewable. When they are collected, the small fragments of the base or holdfast that remain on the reef grow into new fans. Similarly, small fragments cut off of Sea Fans can be attached to stones and thus propagated for the aquarium trade. It is the author's intention to promote coral farming so that otherwise prohibited Caribbean hard corals and Sea Fans can be made available to the aquarium trade as small farm-raised colonies.

Food:

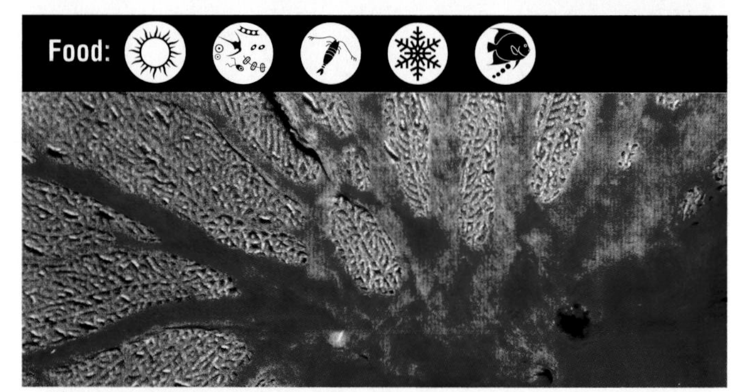

The base of a large *Gorgonia ventalina*, Key Largo, Florida

A small *Gorgonia ventalina*, Miami, Florida

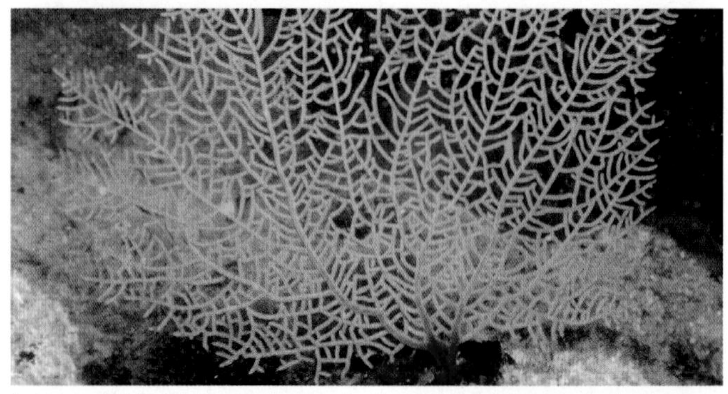

A widely meshed *G. ventalina*, looks like *G. mariae*. The latter has straighter secondary branches.

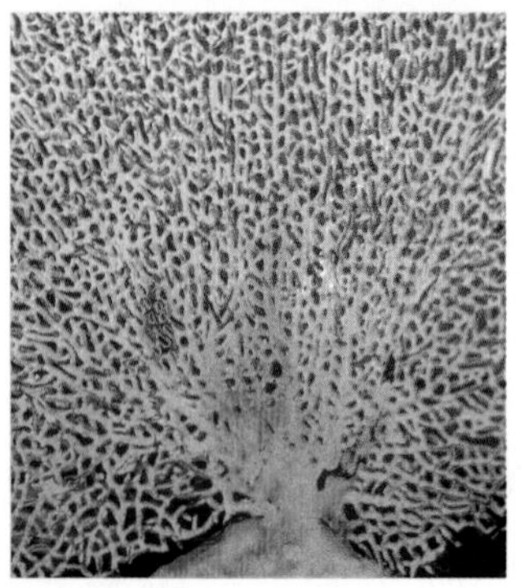

Gorgonia flabellum.

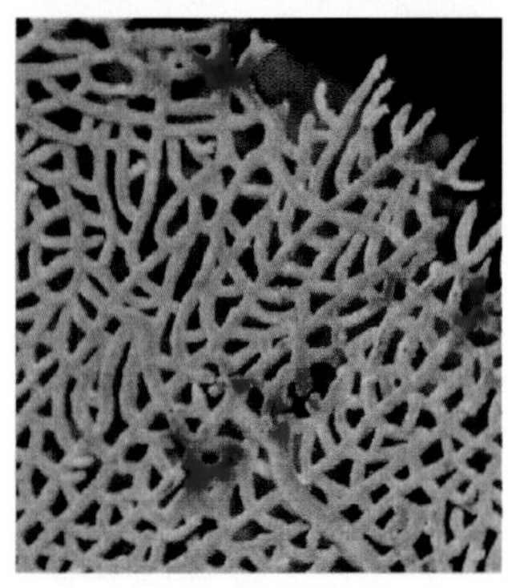

Branch detail of *Gorgonia flabellum.*

Phyllogorgia

Pronunciation: FY-lo-GORG-ee-uh

Common Name: Sea Fan, Brazilian Blade Sea Fan, Elephant's Ear Coral, Palma (in Brazil)

Region: Brazil, from the Rocas atoll, Fernando de Noronha, the Isle of Trindade, and along the Brazilian coast from Cera to Rio de Janeiro.

Description: *Phyllogorgia dilatata* is a special variety of sea fan from Brazil. The branching is flattened in one plane, and there are two colony forms, depending on water motion. In heavy pounding surf the colony develops thin rounded branches. In more quiet waters the colonies form leaf-like fans. The color is typically brown or gray, but it can also be yellow, and may have violet highlights when strongly illuminated. Polyps brown.

Similar Corals: There are no similar gorgonians in the Atlantic, but there are several similar looking genera in the Indo-Pacific.

Placement

Lighting Needs	4 - 9
Water Flow	4 - 9
Agressiveness	2
Hardiness	7

Phyllogorgia dilatata at the Löbbecke Museum in Düsseldorf, Germany.

Pseudopterogorgia

Pronunciation: SOO-doh-TAIR-oh-GORG-ee-uh

Common Name: Sea plume, Feather Gorgonian, Purple Frilly

Region: Caribbean primarily, but there may be some species in the Indo-Pacific.

Description: Sea plumes are most often shaped like feathers, but there are a few species that do not have this shape. Some species attain over eight feet (2.6 m) in height and even greater span side to side.

Similar Corals: *Muriceopsis flavida* has pinnate shape but the branches are rounded in section and have rough texture.

Placement

Lighting Needs	3 - 9
Water Flow	4 - 10
Agressiveness	4
Hardiness	8

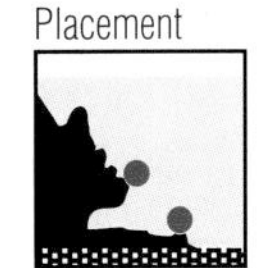

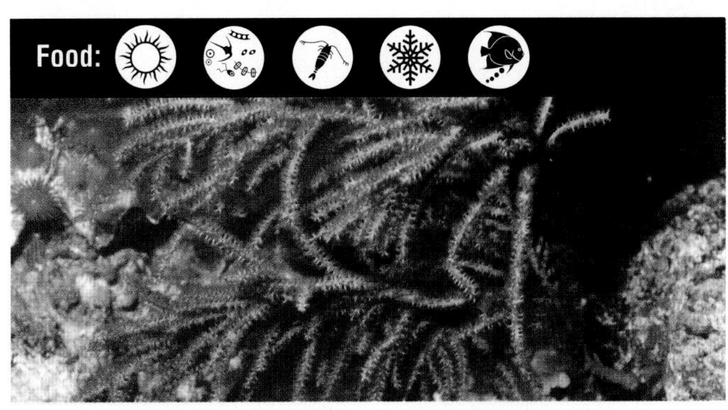

Pseudopterogorgia sp. Aquarium photo, Barrier Reef, Boca Raton, Florida.

Pseudopterogorgia sp. Hollywood, Florida.

Pseudopterogorgia americana. Florida.

Pterogorgia

Pronunciation: TAIR-oh-GORG-ee-uh

Common Names: Sea Blades, Angular Sea Whip, Cactus Gorgonian, Purple Ribbon, Yellow Ribbon.

Region: Caribbean

Description: flattened straight branches with polyps extending only from the edges.

Similar Corals: None.

Lighting Needs	4 - 10
Water Flow	3 - 10
Agressiveness	1
Hardiness	9

Placement

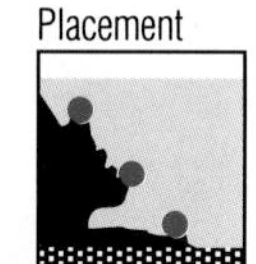

Pterogorgia guadalupensis, Florida Keys.

Pterogorgia anceps, Palm Beach, Florida.

Pterogorgia citrina, Key Largo, Florida.

Pinnigorgia

Pronunciation: PIN-ee-GORG-ee-uh

Common Name: Gorgonian

Region: Phillipines, Indonesia

Description: Pinnately branched to bushy creamy tan colonies. Branches approximately 4 mm in diameter, with small polyps colored the same as branches. See Grasshoff and Alderslade, (1997) for description.

Similar Corals: Similar to *Pseudopterogorgia* and *Muriceopsis* from the Caribbean.

Lighting Needs	3 - 10
Water Flow	3 - 10
Agressiveness	2
Hardiness	10

Placement

Pinnigorgia cf. *perroteti* from the Phillipines. Aquarium photo.

Rumphella

Pronunciation: rum-FELL-uh

Common Name: Sea Rod, Sea Whip

Region: Widespread through the western Indo-Pacific region.

Description: Light tan, pale yellow, brown, gray bushy gorgonian with continuous gorgonin axis. Sclerites are symmetrical clubs and spindles. One of the few photosynthetic Indo-Pacific gorgonians.

Similar Corals: This gorgonian is similar to Caribbean *Plexaurella* and *Plexaura* species. It also resembles *Pinnigorgia*, but has thicker branches.

Lighting Needs	4 - 9
Water Flow	4 - 9
Agressiveness	2
Hardiness	7

Placement

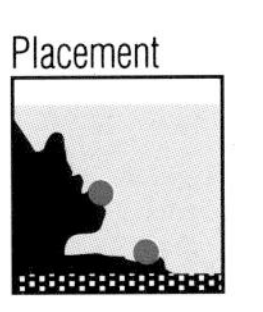

Rumphella sp. photographed at the Berlin Aquarium.

Junceella
Pronunciation: JUN-see-EL-luh

Common Name: Sea Whip

Region: East Africa, Melanesia, Australia, Indonesia, Philippines, New Guinea, Solomon Islands.

Description: Unbranched or sparsely branched long bow-shaped sea-whips often forming dense stands due to reproduction by breaking off of the branch tips.

Similar Corals: The author believes the two forms shown here may belong to separate genera. The grayish one is photosynthetic, with spiny calyces superficially similar to those of *Muricea*. The other species is not photosynthetic and has a smoother rind.

Lighting Needs	0 - 8
Water Flow	4 - 9
Agressiveness	1
Hardiness	5

Placement

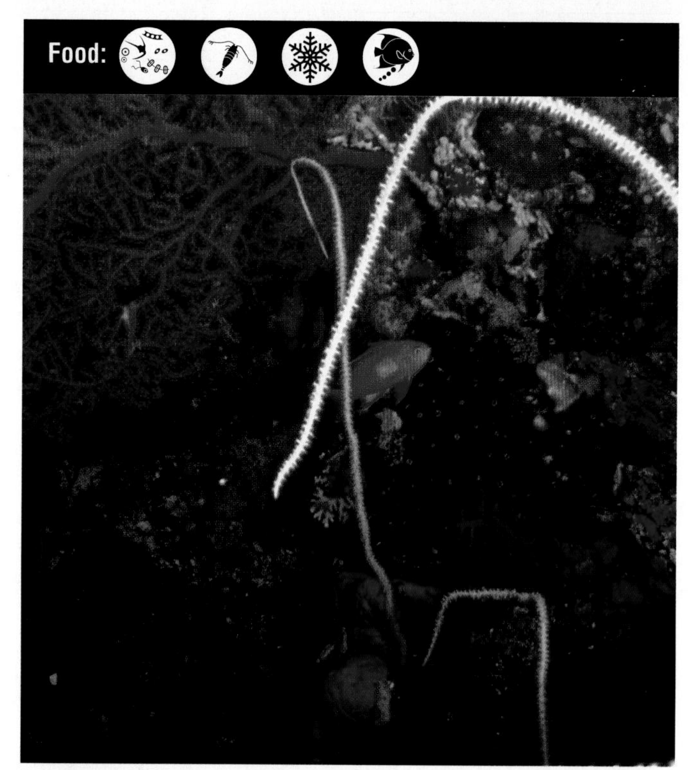

Non-photosynthetic *Junceela* forms long bow-like whips on a reef slope in the Solomon Islands.

This *Junceela* sp. appeared to have symbiotic zooxanthellae. Solomon Islands.

Isis

Pronunciation: ICE-iss

Common Name: Sea Fan

Region: Western Pacific

Distinguishing Characteristics: Axis composed of alternating node-like segments of gorgonin and calcium carbonate. The growth form is highly variable, depending on illumination and water flow. Has fan-like and leaf-like forms, in one plane or in a tangled bush.

Similar Corals: Superficially resembles *Plexaura* species from the Caribbean, but the skeleton (axis) is entirely different. Leafy colonies are similar in appearance to *Phyllogorgia*.

Lighting Needs	4 - 10
Water Flow	5 - 10
Agressiveness	2
Hardiness	7

Placement

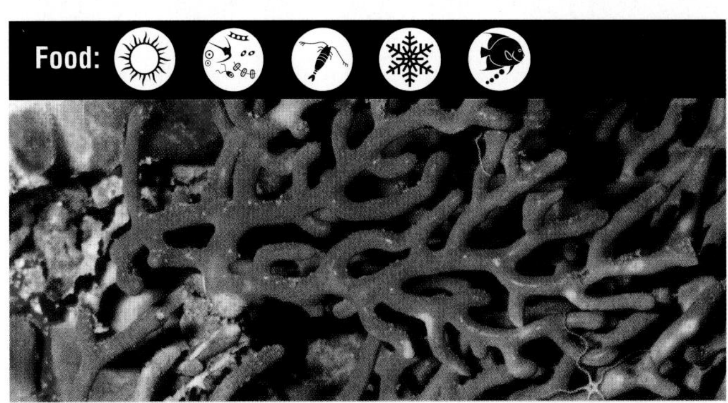

Isis hippuris, St. George's Aquarium, Sydney, Australia.

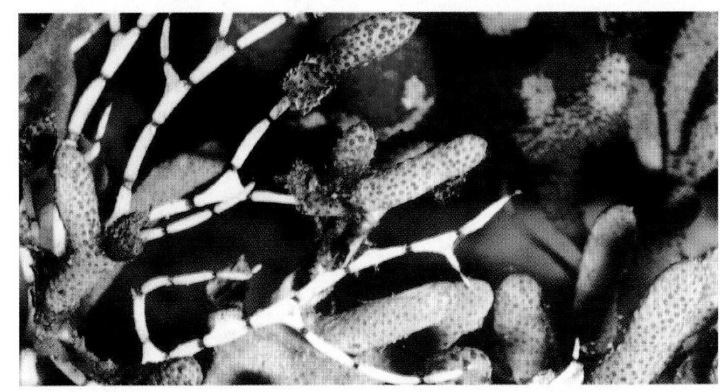

The jointed skeleton of *Isis hippuris* is composed of alternating nodes of $CaCO_3$ and gorgonin.

Clathraria

Pronunciation: klath-RAIR-ee-uh

Common Name: Sea Fan

Region: Red Sea, Western Pacific

Distinguishing Characteristics: Colonies are cream colored or yellowish tangled masses of thin, brittle branches. Branches clearly appear to be jointed and the axis is composed of alternating node-like segments of gorgonin and calcium carbonate. Really looks like a clump of algae.

Similar Corals: Bushy colonies of *Isis hippuris* can be similar-looking. The jointed appearance is sort of like *Acabaria*, but *Clathraria* has zooxanthellae.

Lighting Needs	3 - 8
Water Flow	3 - 8
Agressiveness	1
Hardiness	7

Placement

Clathraria rubrinodis, Red Sea.

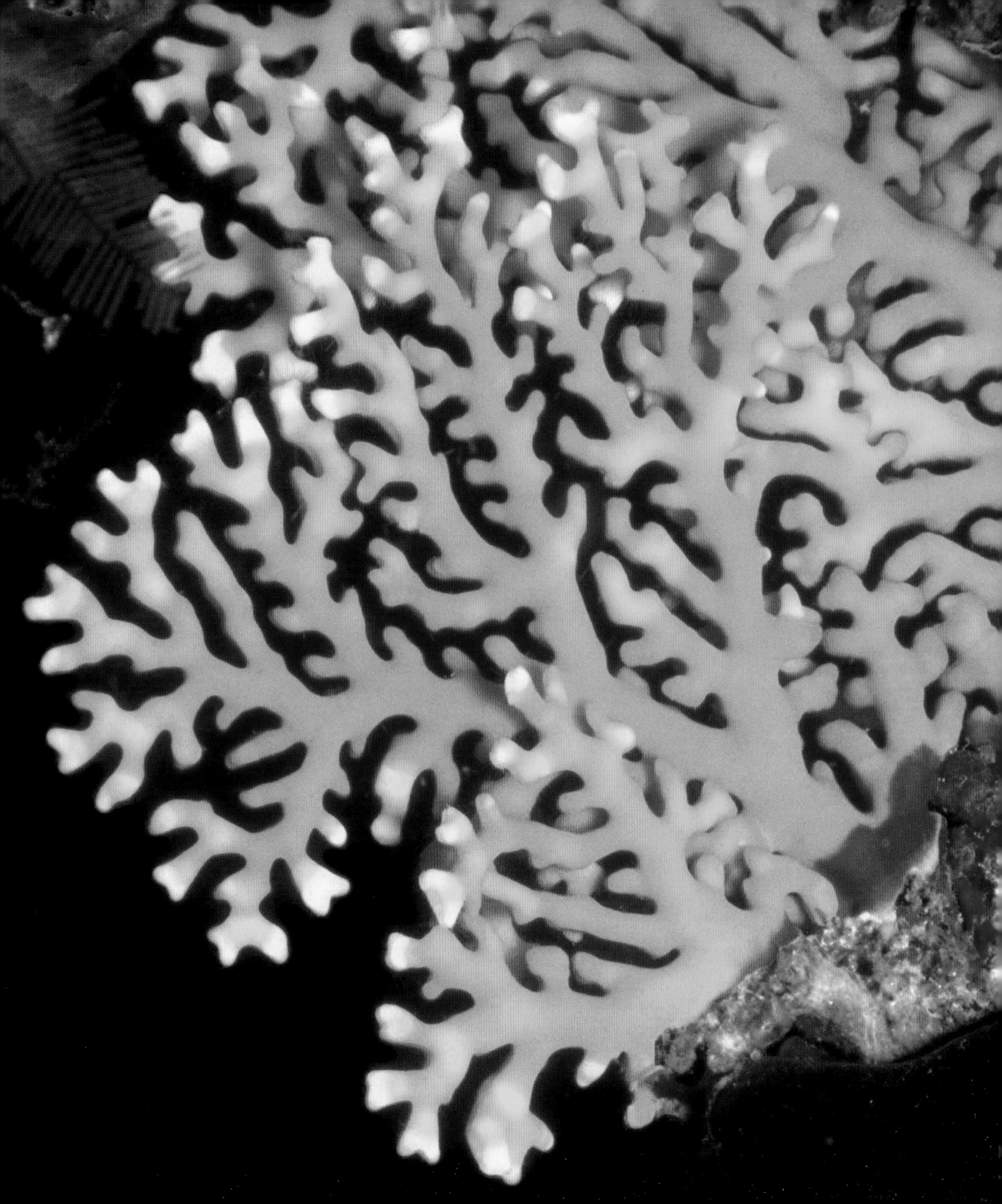

Fire Corals

Fire corals make a quick impression in the minds of divers who encounter them sooner or later: the first contact with *Millepora* spp. is always memorable. Divers typically think of them as special kinds of stony corals. While it is true that they form a calcium carbonate skeleton and they look like corals, fire corals are only distantly related to true stony corals.

The fire corals are "Hydrocorals," belonging to the Class Hydrozoa. Most hydrocorals form brittle calcium carbonate skeletons with very small pores from which two types of polyps emerge: Dactylozooids, which are defensive polyps that pack a powerful sting; and Gastrozooids, which are the polyps used for food capture and consumption. While most hydrocorals are brittle, some *Millepora* spp. form thick robust skeletons. Others are among the fasted-growing calcifying organisms. If one breaks a branch tip off of some of the fine-branched shallow water *Millepora* spp. from the Indo-Pacific, a stream of bubbles usually emanates. It is not known (by the author at least) whether these bubbles are oxygen produced by the photosynthetic zooxanthellae that live symbiotically in the tissues, or carbon dioxide produced by the rapid deposition of calcium carbonate. See a photo of this phenomenon with the description for *Millepora.*

The other "fire corals" covered here, *Stylaster* and *Distichopora,* do not usually sting as powerfully, are not photosynthetic, grow more slowly, and to a smaller size. They are inhabitants of the undersides of overhangs, and the entrances of caves. Their delicate lacy structure helps them trap plankton and particulate foods carried by the strong currents where these hydrocorals proliferate.

Stylaster and *Distichopora* are extremely colorful creatures, and their beauty is more than skin deep. The bright red, yellow, and purple pigments are imbedded in the skeleton, probably as various mineral salts deposited with the calcium carbonate.

The species of *Millepora, Stylaster* and *Distichopora* are not well described.

Stylaster

Pronunciation: sty-LASS-ter

Common Name: Lace Coral

Region: Caribbean, Brazil, Red Sea, Indo Pacific to Eastern Pacific

Description: Brightly colored usually fan-shaped branchy colonies with branches that taper to points, and polyps contained in small pores on the branches. Fine colorless tentacles extend from these pores. The calcium carbonate skeleton is pigmented. Some species may sting.

Similar Corals: *Distichopora* is similar but has blunt-tipped, usually thicker branches with polyps contained in a groove on the edges of the branch.

Placement

Lighting Needs		0
Water Flow		5 - 9
Agressiveness		1
Hardiness		1

Stylaster sp. Note the tapering branches and pores from which the dactylozooids emerge.

Distichopora

Pronunciation: dis-TICK-o-POR-uh (DISS-tee-COP-o-ruh)

Common Name: Lace Coral

Region: Indo Pacific, Central Pacific

Description: Brightly colored usually fan-shaped branchy colonies with blunt, usually paler branch tips. The calcium carbonate skeleton is pigmented. Polyps occur within a groove along the edges of branches. Fine colorless tentacles extend from this grove.

Similar Corals: *Stylaster* has finer branches that taper to points, and polyps contained in small pores on the branches. *Millepora* has fan shaped branchy species that are photosynthetic, with tentacles extending from pores over the entire branch surfaces.

Lighting Needs		0
Water Flow		5 - 9
Agressiveness		1
Hardiness		1

Placement

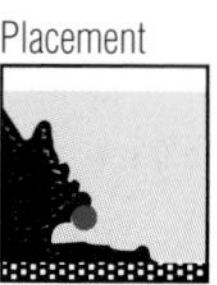

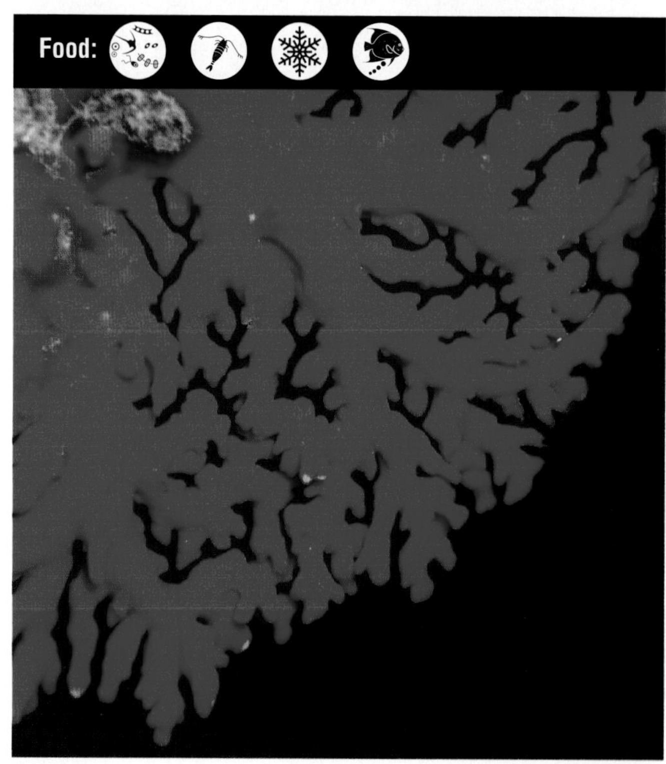

Distichopora sp.

Distichopora spp. are common even in sunlit crevices on steep reef walls in the Solomon Islands.

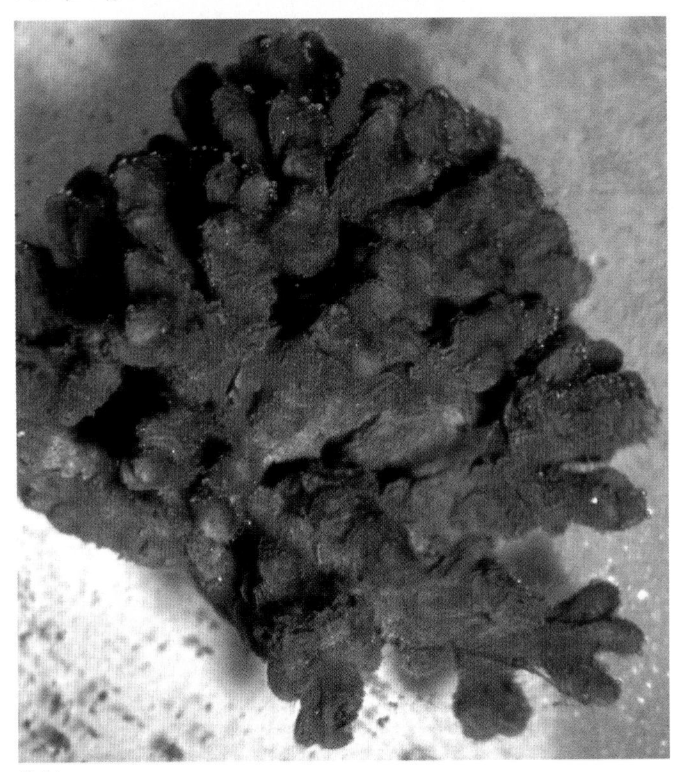

Distichopora sp.

Distichopora sp. Solomon Islands.

Millepora

Pronunciation: MILL-ee-POR-uh (MILL-uh-POR-uh)

Common Name: Fire coral

Region: Red Sea, Indo Pacific to Eastern Pacific, Caribbean to Brazil

Description: Encrusting, laminar, foliaceous, branchy, columnar colonies usually golden brown (because of symbiotic zooxanthellae) sometimes greenish, with small pores over the surface. Tentacles produce powerful sting.

Similar Corals: *Heliopora* (Blue coral) looks like *Millepora* but has eight-tentacled polyps.

Lighting Needs		4 - 10
Water Flow		2 - 10
Agressiveness		7
Hardiness		9

Placement

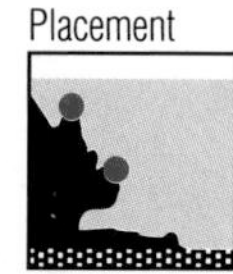

Millepora alcicornis. Key Largo, Florida. Note the visible hair-like dactylozoids that sting bare skin.

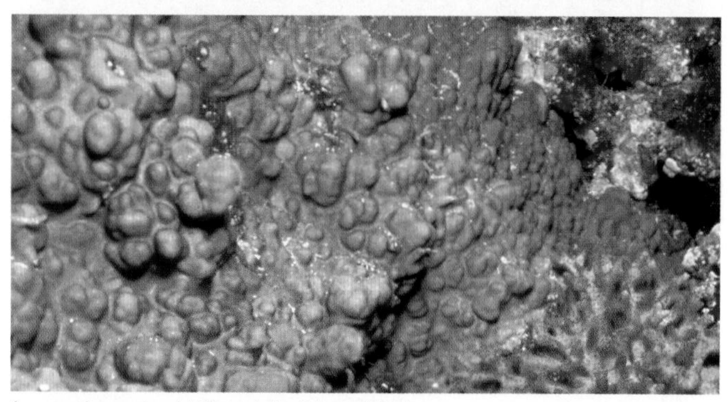

An encrusting species of *Millepora* in the Solomon Islands.

Millepora complanata. Key Largo, Florida.

Millepora sp. releasing a "fizz" of bubbles when a branch is broken. Solomon Islands.

Chapter Three

Millepora sp. forming "coraliths," free-living coral tumbleweeds. Anuha Is., Solomon Islands.

Lacy *Millepora* sp., Eilat, Israel.

Sprawling brittle *Millepora* sp. with a hovering clingfish, Solomon Islands.

New Discoveries

Anyone who explores the reef with an eye for small details is sure to encounter the uncommon on every dive, particularly in the western Pacific. However, one does not need to travel far to find something new. Even in my own back yard in south Florida I have noticed some new and unusual corals, some of which are shown in this book.

In the course of preparing the book I discovered several special corals that I could not identify. There were also some that I could identify, though their appearance was extremely deceptive! While I have already included some new discoveries and unidentified corals within the first two chapters, I decided to include others in this chapter, along with some anomalies that offer insight into the difficulty of classifying corals. The anomalies are of species already featured in chapter one, so there is no husbandry information associated with them here.

As a diver I have brief opportunities to observe the reef and record what I see with underwater cameras. By now the reader is probably aware that I also have ample opportunity to "explore the reefs" at home in my aquaria and in the many beautiful reef aquariums I have seen when I visit other aquarists and scientists who grow corals. There is much to learn from exploring the reefs both ways.

As one can see in this chapter, I encountered some apparently new stony corals in aquariums, one while visiting a pet store just weeks before completing this book, the other at a pet trade exhibition in Italy. I was fortunate to have my camera with me on both occasions.

Family pectiniidae

Common Name: Brain coral, *Pectinia.*

Region: Bali Indonesia

Description: Hemispherical thick submeandroid colonies with wide valleys and high walls with septa occasionally forming hydnophores.

Similar Corals: The specimen with long straight valleys and walls strongly resembled *Pectinia lactuca.* This resemblance may be responsible for this coral being overlooked in the field. The other specimen superficially resembled *Oulophyllia.* Veron (pers. comm.) will describe in *Corals of The World* (in press) a new species of *Pectinia* from the Indian Ocean that appears to be this coral. A *Pectinia* sp. that "mimics" *Oulophyllia,* found by the author in the Solomon Islands, may be the same coral.

Lighting Needs	3 - 8
Water Flow	2 - 9
Agressiveness	2
Hardiness	9

Placement

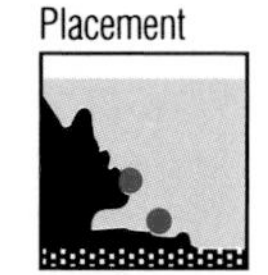

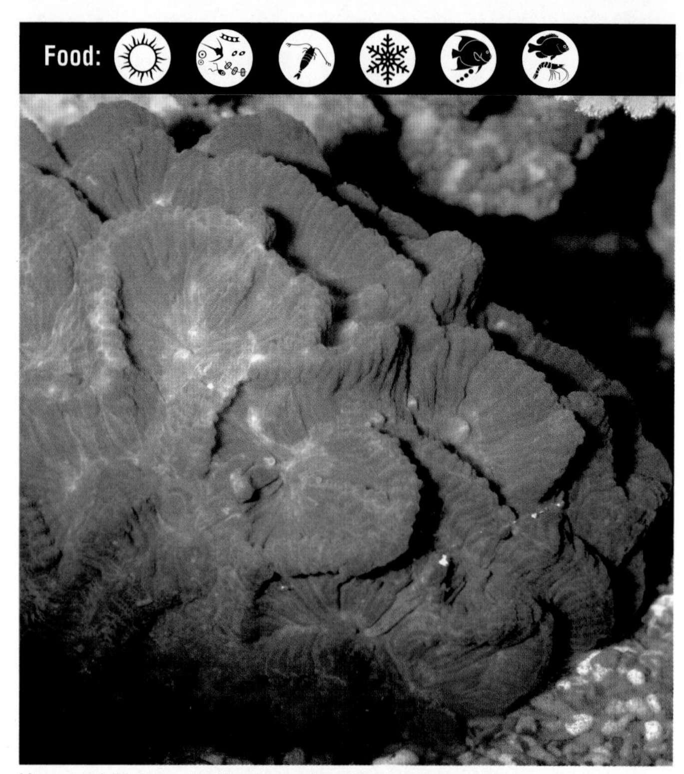

Mystery pectiniid photographed in a the aquarium of Gianluca Ventura, Milan Italy.

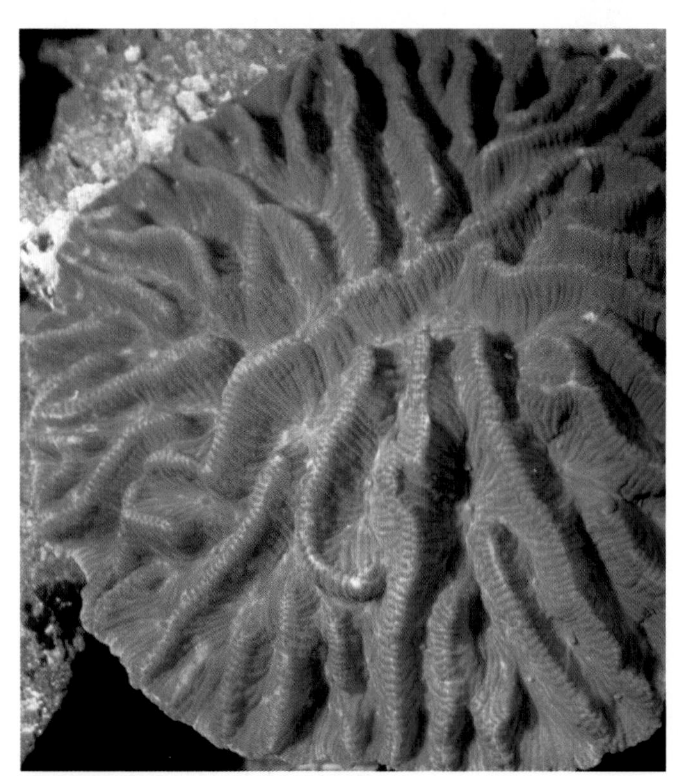

Mystery pectiniid photographed at Zoomark 99 in Milan Italy.

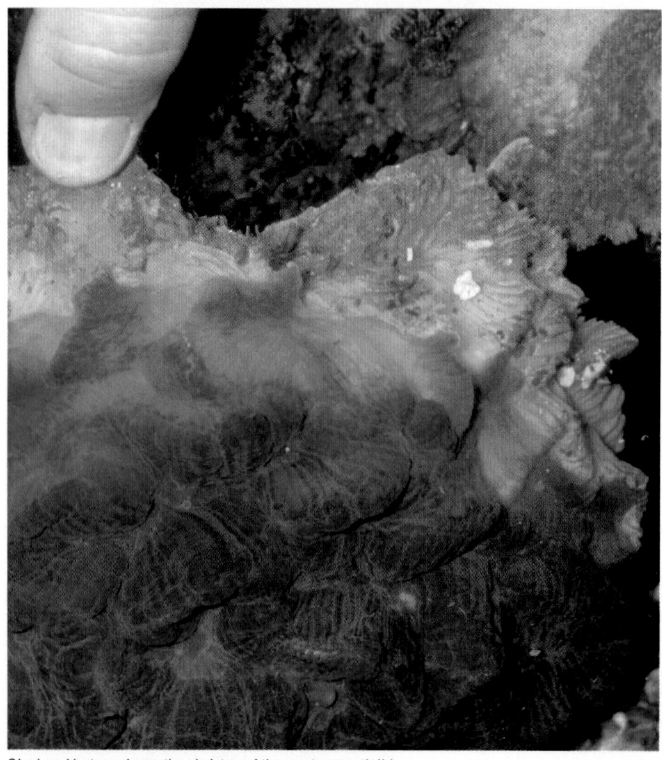

Gianluca Ventura shows the skeleton of the mystery pectiniid.

Family pectiniidae

Common Name: Open Brain coral, *Pectinia.*

Region: Indonesia

Description: Small laminar colony somewhat like *Echinophyllia echinata,* with a few upwardly projecting spires as in *Pectinia.* Thick fleshy polyps like a mussid.

Similar Corals: The author "discovered" this coral in the display aquarium at a shop in South Miami. It at first appeared to be *Australomussa rowleyensis,* but upon closer inspection it clearly was something quite special. The skeleton is thin and like that of a *Pectinia* spp., but the tissue was very thick, fleshy and inflated. This strange coral may belong to a new genus, or it may be a chimera- a rare hybrid cross between corals from different families.

Lighting Needs	3 -7
Water Flow	0 - 6
Agressiveness	4
Hardiness	10

Placement

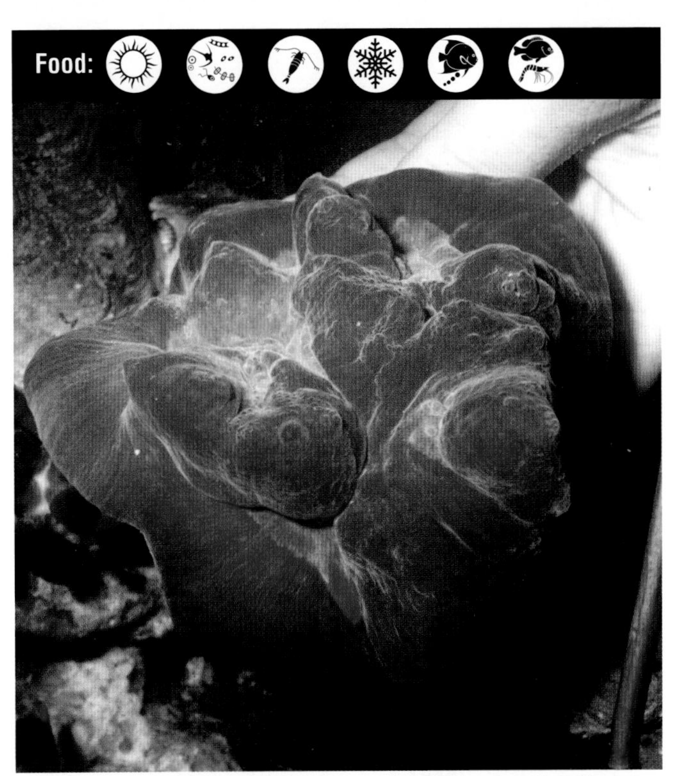

A strange and beautiful pectiniid coral living in an aquarium at Gables Aquariums, South Miami, FL.

The back side of this coral reveals a thin *Pectinia*-like skeleton.

Diploria Anomalies

Region: Caribbean, Atlantic

Description: Shown here are two variations of the normally meandroid genus *Diploria. Diploria clivosa* sometimes forms ceriod polyps on portions of a colony. Occasionally whole colonies are ceriod, and they look like *Goniastrea* transplanted to the Caribbean. *Diploria labrynthiformis* has an uncommon and beautiful form with wide open structure.

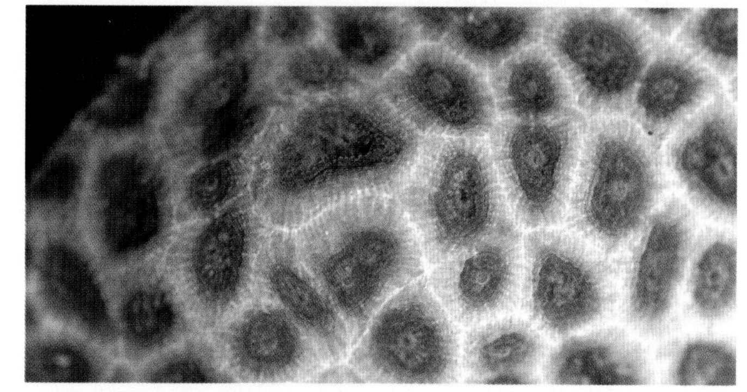

Diploria clivosa with cerioid polyps looks like a *Goniastrea* sp. Hollywood Beach, Florida.

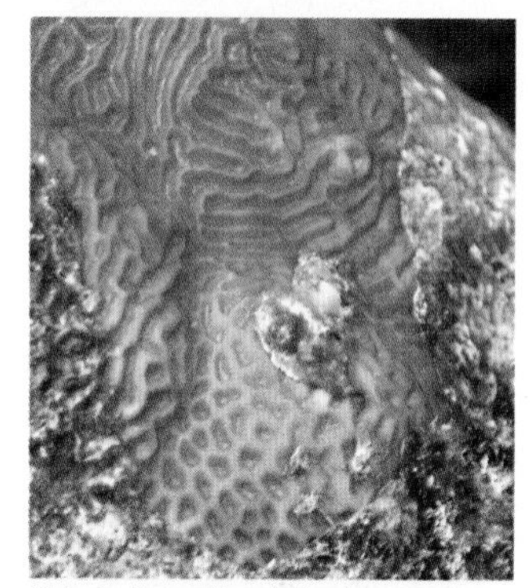

Diploria clivosa with cerioid polyps.

Diploria labrynthiformis with wide grooves.

Favia fragum Anomalies

Region: Caribbean, Atlantic

Description: The common "Golfball coral," *Favia fragum* has an amazing variety of forms. It may look like *Dichocoenia, Cladocora, Montastrea,* or even *Diploria.* Some have separate species names, such as *F. conferta* for meandroid forms and *F. gravida* for plocoid ones. All are probably variations of a single species. The phacelloid form appears to be associated with a red alga in the skeleton.

Compare this *F. fragum* to *Dichocoenia.*

Plocoid *Favia fragum.* Note red pigment, right.

Favia fragum form known as *F. conferta.*

Large *Favia fragum* . Boca Chica Key, Florida.

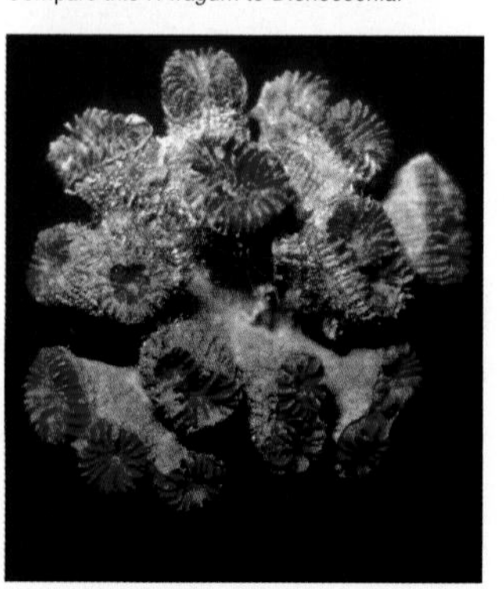

Favia fragum with skeleton like *Cladocora.*

Phacelloid *F. fragum* Tavernier, Florida.

Mystery soft coral

Region: Solomon Islands

Description: Tiny (3mm) orange and yellow polyps on thin but quite visible orange stolons. Underwater photographers using a macro lens will notice many similar types of undescribed soft corals on western Pacific reefs. Photosynthetic ones grow amongst clumps of algae and sponges. Non-photosynthetic ones like this orange stoloniferan line the undersides of ledges.

Unknown soft coral that grows on the undersides of ledges along steep reef walls. Solomon Islands.

Mystery soft coral

Region: Indonesia

Description: The soft coral shown here was featured in Sprung and Delbeek (1997), as a possible species of *Cervera,* based on a specimen examined by P. Alderslade. It resembles that genus and *Cornularia*, but has not been positively identified (P. Alderslade, pers. comm.). It produces 3mm diameter polyps from a mesh of proliferating stolons. The author has seen two other tiny species from Indonesia that seem to belong to the same genus.

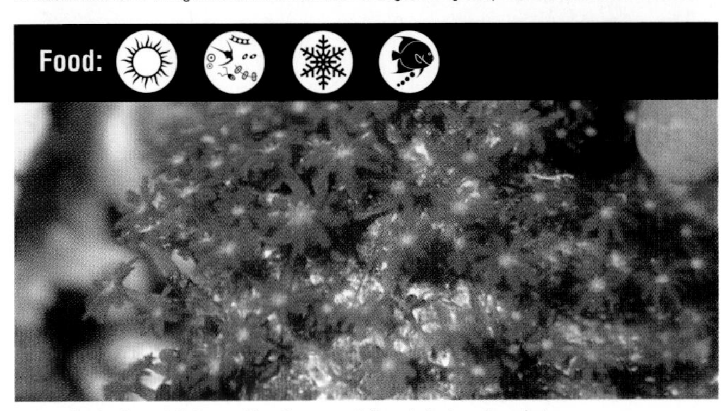

Undescribed soft coral that resembles *Cervera* and *Cornularia.* Aquarium photo.

Mystery soft coral

Region: Solomon Islands

Description: This beautiful soft coral is featured in Colin and Arneson (1995) as a species of *Pachyclavularia.* The author collected a specimen of what appeared to be the same coral and sent it to be examined by Phil Alderslade. It appears to be a primitive xeniid (P. Alderslade, pers. comm.). Note that the pinnules appear to be fused.

This beautiful blue soft coral has very small polyps with fused pinnules.

Mystery Sea Whip

Region: Solomon Islands.

Description: This distinctive sea whip that mimics the corkscrew shaped antipatharians has probably been described, but the author did not find a name for it. It seems to be an ellisellid.

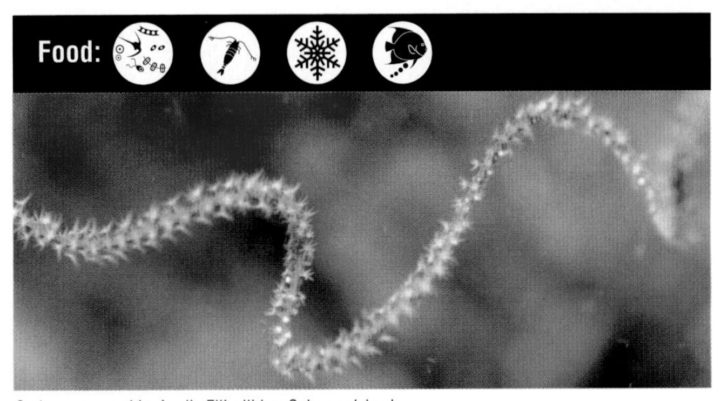

Corkscrew sea whip, family Ellisellidae. Solomon Islands.

acrosphere - Swelling at the tip of a tentacle, full of nematocysts.

ahermatypic - Literally non-reef building. Common use: corals that do not have zooxanthellae.

alcyonacean - octocorals including stolonifera, soft corals, and gorgonians, but not including sea pens.

anastomosis - Fusion of lateral branchlets forming bridges between adjacent branches.

anthocauli - tiny polyp buds that develop asexually on the skeletons of for example *Fungia*, *Herpolitha, Polyphyllia*, *Cynarina*. They may eventually break-off and become free-living polyps.

anthocodia (pl. anthocodiae) - The distal portion of a polyp, including the mouth and the eight tentacles. The anthocodia may be retracted into a calyx, the polyparium, cortex, or rachis.

anthostele - the thick, often sclerite stiffened lower part of the polyp into which the anthocodia may be withdrawn; calyx.

arborescent - tree-like octocorals that have a definite stalk (Nephthea) or stem (gorgonians).

autozooid - a polyp with eight well-developed tentacles that functions in feeding and defense. In monomorphic species it is the only type of polyp, in dimorphic species it is the larger, more conspicuous type of polyp.

axis - the internal skeletal support structure found in gorgonians and sea pens, composed of gorgonin, calcium carbonate, or both.

calyx (pl. calyces) - a hard or stiff protuberance forming a tube or cup into which the soft distal part of the polyp retracts in some soft coral species. The calyx does not contract into the coenenchyme or stolon, though it may press flat when the colony is disturbed and fully contacted. A wart-like projecting anthostele.

capitate - unbranched colonies having a head or broad upper portion situated on a basal stalk.

capitulum - the broad rounded polyp-bearing "head" arising from the basal stalk. Also polyparium.

catkin - a cluster of polyps forming a branch tip that, when contracted, has the appearance of the catkin of a willow tree. Characteristic of many members of the family Nephtheidae.

cf. - an abbreviation of "conferre," the Latin word meaning to compare. This is used with tentative species identifications, suggesting they should be compared with the formal description of the named species.

clavate - shaped like a club.

cnidaria - phylum that contains hydras, hydroids, jellyfish, sea anemones, and corals.

coenenchyme - the tissue of an octocoral that surrounds the polyps and consists of mesogloea with sclerites imbedded in it.

columella - central axis structure formed from inner ends of septa.

corallimorpharia - order of zoantharia closely related to corals, commonly called "mushroom anemones" or "false corals."

corallite - the coral structure or cup formed by an individual polyp in a colony.

corallum - the entire coral formed by a colony of polyps.

contractile - the polyps are capable of shrinking in size and folding the tentacles over the mouth, but unable to pull into the calyx or polyparium. Compare to retractile.

cortex - coenenchyme surrounding the medulla and containing the polyps in some gorgonian species.

costae - continuations of the septa beyond the wall or theca.

dichotomous - as in the letter y, the point of division produces two branches.

digitate - having finger-like lobes.

digitiform - a colony that is unbranched but finger-like in shape.

dimorphic - having two different kinds of polyps, autozooids and siphonozooids.

divaricate - branching.

distal - the outermost part

ecosystem - all the organisms in a biotic community and the abiotic environmental factors they interact with.

epitheca - the vertical coral wall rising from the basal plate.

fecal pellet - the feces of many marine organisms, particularly of herbivores, are formed into lightweight pellets by their digestive systems.

genus - a grouping of related species with common characteristics.

glomerate - sphere-shaped.

gorgonian - an octocoral that attaches to the substrate by means of a basal holdfast, and having an internal axis or medulla. Usually having a branchy plant-like or fan-like growth form, and a skeleton made of a horny organic material e.g. Sea Fan.

gorgonin - the internal axis of many gorgonians is composed of a black or brown tough fibrous horn-like protein. Also secreted as part of the gorgonian's holdfast.

hard or stony coral - Scleractinia. The true reef-building corals and solitary, fleshy, non-reef-building species. They have tentacles that number in multiples of six. Some species have no tentacles at all.

holdfast - the basal portion of a soft coral or gorgonian that attaches it to a hard substrate. May contain consolidated sclerites or, as in most gorgonians, be a sheet of gorgonin.

hydrostatic skeleton - a structural support against which the muscular system can act, provided by control of water pressure.

lobate - consisting of several stout lobes.

marine snow - Particulate colloidal organic matter drifting in the water column, formed by the release of dissolved organic substances in the water and subsequent chemical physical and biological reactions with them. Also includes the discarded "skins" of planktonic creatures and detritus. A very important food source for filter feeding invertebrates, including corals.

medulla - in some gorgonians, the inner support structure composed of consolidated sclerites; as opposed to an axis of gorgonin or solid calcium carbonate not from spicules. May occur as a layer around a central axis of gorgonin.

medusa - a bell-shaped swimming stage of some types of cnidaria, i.e. jellyfish and hydrozoans. Anemones and corals do not have a medusa stage.

monomorphic - soft coral colonies possessing just one type of polyp. The polyps are called autozooids.

monotypic - a genus containing only one species.

needles - a type of needle-shaped sclerite.

nematocyst - microscopic stinging body composed of a capsule containing an ejectable harpoon. Used for prey capture, attachment to substrate, and defense.

non-retractile - opposite of retractile.

octocoral - a member of the phylum Coelenterata (Cnidaria), class Anthozoa characterized by normally having eight tentacles on each polyp.

octocorallia - see soft coral.

paliform lobes - large, vertical teeth projecting upward from the inner margins of the septa.

photosynthesis - the process by which plants use light energy to make food.

photosynthetic - able to make food by photosynthesis.Corals have tiny plants called zooxanthellae living within their tissues, and so together they are called photosynthetic.

phytoplankton - microscopic algae suspended in the part of the water column that is penetrated by light.

pinnules - lateral branches on the tentacles of a soft coral polyp that give it a feather-like appearance.

polyp - basic living unit of a coral.

polyparium - see capitulum.

rachis - the upper polyp-bearing region of a pennatulacean (sea pen).

retractile - the state in which a polyp can be withdrawn into a calyx, the polyparium, the cortex or the rachis.

Scleractinia - stony or hard corals.

sclerite - spicule made of calcium carbonate imbedded in the tissue of most soft corals (octocorallia). Part of the skeletal/structural support element in soft corals.

septa - radiating vertical plates, lying inside the corallite wall.

septa-costae - radial elements of the corallite, form the septa and the costae.

septal teeth - lobes or spines along the margins of septa.

soft coral - Octocorallia. Those corals that have eight tentacles on each polyp. Many different forms exist. They may be soft, leathery, or may even produce a hard skeleton.

spicule - Sclerite. A skeletal element in soft corals composed of calcium carbonate. In sponges similar skeletal elements may be composed of silicon dioxide.

stolon - ribbon or root-like growth extensions that adhere to the substrate and link the polyps in Stoloniferan soft corals such as *Clavularia* spp.

stoloniferan - octocorals that have the polyps linked on root-like growth extensions that adhere to the substrate.

supporting bundle - what appears to be a shield, cup or sheath below an individual anthocodia, composed of one or a few large sclerites. Typical of nephtheidae and also of some gorgonians.

sweeper polyp - elongated polyps that serve an aggressive function, stinging neighboring corals and other sessile invertebrates.

sweeper tentacle - elongated tentacles of polyps that have increased numbers of nematocysts and can be used in aggressive encounters with neighbors.

tentacles - finger-like (feather-like in soft corals) structures that encircle mouth of a polyp. Used for prey capture, defense, gas exchange, reproduction and light absorption.

terpene - Organic compound having a strong odor, manufactured by soft corals to discourage predation.

tubercles - wart-like projections on sclerites.

turbidity - reduced clarity in water. Usually caused by suspended organic or inorganic particles.

umbellate - shaped like an umbrella.

zoanthids - small anemone-like anthozoans with no skeleton; solitary or colonial e.g. *Palythoa, Parazoanthus* and *Zoanthus.*

zooplankton - animals that drift in the water column. Most are microscopic. Some are larval forms of larger organisms.

zooxanthellae - these are the tiny dinoflagellates that live symbiotically with corals, tridacnid clams, and some sponges, providing food to their host and in return getting the nitrogen, phosphorous and carbon dioxide they need for growth. *Symbiodinium* spp.

Aceret, T.L., Sammarco, P.W. and J.C. Coll. (1995a). Toxic effects of alcyonacean diterpenes on scleractinian corals. *J. Exp. Mar. Biol. Ecol. 188:63-78.*

Aceret, T.L., Sammarco, P.W. and J.C. Coll. (1995b). Effects of diterpenes derived from the soft corals *Sinularia flexibilis* on the eggs, sperm and embryos of the scleractinian corals *Montipora digitata* and *Acropora tenuis. Mar. Biol. 122:317-323.*

Achituv, Y. and Y. Benayahu. (1990). Polyp dimorphism and functional, sequential hermaphroditism in the soft coral *Heteroxenia fuscescens* (Octocorallia). *Mar. Ecol. Progr. Ser. 64:263-269.*

Alcock, A. (1893). On some newly-recorded corals from the Indian Seas. J. *Asiat. Soc. Bengal (Nat. Hist.),* 62(2):138-49.

Alderslade, P. (1983). *Dampia pocilloporaeformis,* a new genus and species of Octocorallia (Coelenterata) from Australia. *The Beagle. Occasional Papers of the Northern Territory Museum of Arts and Sciences.* 1(4): 33-40.

Alderslade, P. 2000. Four new genera of soft corals (Coelenterata: Octocorallia), with notes on the classification of some established taxa. *Zoologische Mededlingen, Leiden* 74: 237-249

Alino, P.M. and J.C. Coll. (1989). Observations of the synchronized mass spawning and post-settlement activity of octocorals on the Great Barrier Reef, Australia: Biological aspects. *Bull. Mar. Sci. 45:697-707.*

Allee, W. C. (1923) Studies in marine ecology: IV. The effect of temperature in limiting the geographical range of invertebrates of the Woods Hole littoral. *Ecology,* 4, 341-354.

Atrigenio, M.P. and P.M. Alino. (1996). Effects of the soft coral *Xenia puertogalerae* on the recruitment of scleractinian corals. *J. Exp. Ecol. Biol. 203:179-189.*

Baba, K. (1954). Coral Reef animals, in Tsutsui, Y. (ed.) Tokara Island (in Japanese). *Asa1a Syasin,* 2: 44-55.

Babcock, R. (1990). Reproduction and development of the blue coral *Heliopora coerulea* (Alcyonaria: Coenothocalia). *Mar. Biol. 104:475-481.*

Bassett-Smith, P.W. (1890). Report on the corals from the Lizard and Macclesfield Banks, China Sea. *Ann. Mag. Nat. Hist.,* 6: 353-374.

Bayer, F. 1973. Colonial Organization in Octocorals. *In:* Boardman R. S., Cheetham, A. H. and W. A. Oliver (eds.): *Animal Colonies: Development and Function Through Time* (pp 69-93). Dowden, Hutchinson & Ross, Inc. Stroudsburg, Pa., USA

Bayer, F. (1981). Key to the genera of Octocorallia exclusive of Pennatulacea (Coelenterata: Anthozoa) with diagnoses of new taxa. *Proc. Biol. Soc. Wash. 94:902-947.*

Bayer, F., Grasshoff, M. and J. Verseveldt (eds.). (1983). Illustrated trilingual glossary of morphological terms applied to Octocorallia. E.J. Brill and W. Blackhuys, Leiden, The Netherlands.

Bedot, M., (1907). Madreporaires d'Amboine. Rev. Suisse Zool., 15,143-292, 46 pls.

Belbin, L. (1987). *PATN Pattern analysis package reference manual.* CSIRO Division of Wildlife and Rangelands Research.

Benayahu, Y. and Y. Loya. (1983). Surface brooding in the Red Sea soft coral *Parerythropodium fulvum fulvum* (Forksål, 1775). *Biol. Bull. 165:353-369.*

Benayahu, Y. and Y. Loya. (1984a). Life history studies on the Red Sea soft coral *Xenia macrospiculata* Gohar, 1940. I. Annual dynamics of gonadal development. *Bio. Bull. 166:32-43.*

Benayahu, Y. and Y. Loya. (1984b). Life history studies on the Red Sea soft coral *Xenia macrospiculata* Gohar, 1940. II. Planulae shedding and post larval development. *Bio. Bull. 166:44-53.*

Benayahu, Y. and Y. Loya. (1986). Sexual reproduction of a soft coral: synchronous and brief annual spawning of *Sarcophyton glaucum* (Quoy and Gaimard, 1833). *Biol. Bull. 170:32-42.*

Benayahu, Y. (1995). Species composition of soft corals (Octocorallia, Alcyonacea) on the coral reefs of Sesoko Island, Ryukyu archipelago, Japan. *Galaxea 12:103-124.*

Benayahu, Y., van Ofwegen, L.P., and P. Alderslade. (1998). A case study of Variation in two nominal species of *Sinularia* (Coelenterata: Octocorallia), *S. brassica* May, 1898, and *S. dura* (Pratt, 1903), with a proposal for their synonymy. *Zool. Verh. Leiden* 323 (1998).

Beress, L. (1982) Biologically active compounds from coelenterates. *Pure Appl. Chem.,* 54, 1981-1994.

Bernard, H.M. (1896). The genus *Turbinaria.* The Genus *Astraeopora. Cat. Madreporarian Corals Br. Mus. (Nat. Hist.),* 2:1-166.

Bernard, H.M. (1897). The Genus *Montipora.* The Genus *Anacropora. Cat. Madreporarian Corals Br. Mus. (Nat. Hist.),* 3:1-192.

Bernard, H.M. (1903). The family Poritidae: I. The Genus *Goniopora. Cat. Madreporarian Corals Br. Mus. (Nat. Hist.),* 4:1-206.

Bernard, H.M. (1905). The family Poritidae: II. The genus *Porites.* Pt. I. *Porites* of the Indo-Pacific region. *Cat. Madreporarian Corals Br. Mus. (Nat. Hist.),* 5:1-303.

Bernard, H.M. (1906). The family Poritidae: II. The genus *Porites. Pt. II. Porites* of the Atlantic and West Indies with the European fossil forms. The genus Goniopora. A supplement to Vol. 4. *Cat. Madreporarian Corals Br. Mus. (Nat. Hist.),* 6: 1-173.

Best, B.A. (1988). Passive suspension feeding in a sea pen: effects of ambient flow on volume flow rate and filtering efficiency. *Biol. Bull. 175:332-342.*

Bigger, C. H. and Hildemann, W. H. (1982) Cellular defense systems of the Coelenterata. In N. Cohen and M. M. Sigel (eds.), *The Reticuloendothelial System,* Vol. 3, Plenum, New York, pp. 59-87.

Bingman, C. (1995). The Effect of Activated Carbon Treatment on the Transmission of Visible and UV Light Through Aquarium Water. Part 1: Time-course of Activated Carbon Treatment and Biological Effects. *Aquarium Frontiers.*2:3. p 4.

Bingxian, G. (1986). A sketch of the current structures and eddy characteristics in the East China Sea, (in Chinese). *Studia Marina Sinica,* 27: 2-21.

Borel Best, M. & Hoeksema, B. (1987). New observation on scleractinian corals from Indonesia: 1. Free-living species belonging to the Faviina. *Zoologische Mededelingen,* 61 (27): 387-403.

Borneman, Eric. H. and Jonathan Lowrie. 1999. Advances in captive husbandry and propagation: an easily utilized reef replenishment means from the private sector? manuscript from presentation at the International Conference on the Scientific Aspects of Coral Reef Assessment, Monitoring, and Restoration, National Coral Reef Institute, Ft. Lauderdale, FL.

Blainville, H. M. de, (1823). Meandrine *in:* Dictionnaire des Sciences naturelles, Paris, 29, 374377.

Blainville, H.M. de (1830). Zoophytes, in *Dict. des Sci. Nat.,* Paris, 60: 295-364.

Blainville, H. M. de, (1834). Manuel dActinologie ou de Zoophytologie. Paris, 2, 694 pp. 101 pls.

Blank, R. J. and Trench, R. K. (1985) Speciation and symbiotic dinoflagellates. *Science,* 229, 656-658.

Bodansky, M. (1923) Comparative studies of digestion III. Further observations on digestion in coelenterates. *Amer. J. Physiol.,* 67, 547-550.

Boschma, H. (1923). Knospung und Verwandte Erscheinungen bei *Fungia fungites und Fungia actinifonnis. Treubia,* 3:149-79.

Boschma, H., (1925). Madreporaria 1. Fungiidae. Vidensk. Meddr Dansk naturh. Foren., 79, 185-259, pls. 5-I I.

Boschma, H., (1948). The species problem in *Millepora. Zool.* Verh., 1,1-111,15 pls.

Boschma, H., (1959). Revision of the Indo-Pacific species of *Distichopora.* Bijdr. Dierk., 29,122-171.

Brazeau, D.A. and H.R. Lasker. (1989). The reproductive cycle and spawning in a Caribbean gorgonian. *Biol. Bull.* 176:1-7.

Brazeau, D.A. and Harvell, C. D. (1994). Genetic structure of local populations and divergence between growth forms in a clonal invertebrate, the Caribbean octocoral *Briareum asbestinum. Mar. Biol.* (Berlin) 119 (1): 53-60.

Brook, G. (1891). Descriptions of new species of Madrepora in the collections of the British Museum. Ann. Mag. Nat. Hist., 8(6): 458-71.

Brook, G. (1892). Preliminary descriptions of new species of *Madrepora in* the collections of the British Museum. Pt. II. *Ann. Mag. Nat. Hist.,* 10(6): 451-65.

Brook, G. (1893). The genus *Madrepora. Cat. Madreporarian Corals Br. Mus. (Nat. Hist.), 1:* 1-212.

Bruggemann, F. (1877a). Neue Korallen-Arten aus dem Rotten Meer und von Mauritius. *Abh. Naturwiss. Ver. Bre~nen,* 5: 395 400.

Bruggemann, F. (1877b). Notes on stony corals in the British Museum. Pt. m. A revision of recent solitary Mussaceae. *Ann. Mag. Nat. Hist., ser. 4, 20:* 300-12.

Bruggemann, F., (1878). Ueber einige Steinkorallen von Singapore. Jahresber. naturwiss. Verein. Bremen, 5, 534594.

Bruggemann, F., (1879a). Corals *in.* Zoology of Rodriguez. Phil. Trans. R. Soc. Lond., B. Biol. Sci., 168, 569-579.

Bruggemann, F., 1879b. Ueber die Korallen der Insel Ponape. J. Mus. Godeffroy, Hamburg, 5, 201-212.

Buss, L. W., McFadden, C. S. and Keene, D. R. (1984) Biology of hydractiniid hydroids. 2. Histocompatibility effector system/competitive mechanism mediated by nematocyst discharge. *Biol. Bull.,* 167, 139-158.

Cairns, S., Hartog, J. D. den and Arneson, C. (1986) Class Anthozoa (Corals, anemones). In W. Sterrer (ed.), Marine *Fauna and Flora of Bermuda. A Systematic Guide to the Identification of Marine Organisms,* John Wiley & Sons, New York, pp. 159-194.

Carpent, K.E., V.H. Niem (eds). (1998). FAO species identification guide for fishery purposes. The living marine resources of the Western Central Pacific. Vol. 1. Seaweeds, corals, bivalves and gastropods. FAO, Rome pp. 1-686.

Chamisso, A. de & Eysenhardt, C.G. (1821). De animalibus quibusdam e classe Vermium linneana, in circumnavigatione terrae, auspicante Comite N. Romanzoff, duce Ottone de Kotzebue, annuis 1815-1818. *Nova Acta Leopold., 10(2):* 343-74.

Chang, S. S., Prezelin, B. B. and Trench, R. K. (1983) Mechanisms of photoadaptation in three strains of the symbiotic dinoflagellate *Symbiodinium microadriaticum. Mar. Biol.,* 76, 219-229.

Chevalier, J.P. (1971). Les scleractiniaires de la melanesie Franc,aise (NouvelleCaledonie, Iles Chesteffield, Iles Loyaute, Nouvelles- Hebrides). lere Partie. *Expd. R~fs Coralliens Nouvelle- Caledonie,* Fond. Singer-Polignac, Paris, 5: 5-307.

Chevalier, J.P. (1975). Les scleractiniaires de la melanesie Francaise (Nouvelle Caledonie, Iles Chesteffield, Iles Loyaute, Nouvelles- Hebrides). 2eme Partie. *Exped. Recifs Coralliens Nouvelle- Caledonie,* Fond. Singer-Polignac, Paris, 7: 5-07

Colin, P.L. and C. Arneson. (1995). *Tropical Marine Invertebrates. A Field Guide to the Marine Invertebrates Occurring on Tropical Pacific Coral Reefs, Seagrass Beds and Mangroves.* Coral Reef Press, Beverly Hills, CA.

Coll, J.C. and P.W. Sammarco. (1986). Soft corals: chemistry and ecology. *Oceanus 29:33-37.*

Coll, J.C., Bowden, B.F., Tapiolas, D.M. and W.C. Dunlap. (1982). In situ isolation of allelochemicals released from soft corals (Coelenterata: Octocorallia): a totally submersible sampling apparatus. *J. Exp. Mar. Biol. Ecol. 60:293-299.*

Connel, J. H., (1973). Population ecology of reef building corals. *In.* Jones, O. A. and R. Endan, (eds.) Biol. Ecol. of Coral Reefs, 2, 205-295.

Conover, R. J. (1978) Transformation of organic matter. In O. Kinne (ed.), *Marine Ecology, Vol. 4, Dynamics,* John Wiley & Sons, New York, pp. 221-499.

Chou, L.M. & Yamazato, K. (1990). Community structure of coral reefs within the vicinity of Motobu and Sesoko, Okinawa, and the effects of human and natural influences. *Galaxea, 9:* 9-75.

Claereboudt, M. & Hoeksema, B.W. (1987). *Fungia (Verrillofungial spinifer* spec. nov., a new scleractinian coral (Fungiidae) from the Indo-Malayan region. *Zool. Meded. (Leiden),* 61: 303-309.

Crossland, C. (1952). Madreporaria, Hydrocorallinae, *Helicpora and Tubipora. Sci. Rep. Great Barrier Reef Exped.* 1928-29. *Br. Mus. (Nat. Hist.), 6(3):* 85-257.

Dai, C.D and M.C. Lin. 1993. The effects of flow on feeding of three gorgonians from southern Taiwan. *J. Exp. Mar. Biol. Ecol. 173:57-69.*

Dana, J.D. (1846-1849). United States Exploring Expedition during the years 18381842. *Zoophytes,* 7:1-740. Lea & Blanchard, Philadelphia.

Dana, J.D. (1872). *Coral and coral islands.* List of species of corals by Verrill, A.E.

DElia, C. F. and Cook, C. B. (1988) Methylamine uptake by zooxanthellae/ invertebrate symbioses: insights into host ammonium environment and nutrition. *Limnol. Oceanogr.,* 33, 1153-1165.

Delbeek, J. C. (1989). Soft corals spawn in the aquarium. *Freshwater and Marine Aquarium Magazine 12(3):128-129.*

Delbeek, J.C. & Sprung, J. (1994) *The Reef Aquarium* Vol 1. Ricordea Publishing, Coconut Grove, Florida.

Denny, M. W., Daniel, T. L. and Koehl, M. A. R. (1985) Mechanical limits to size in wave-swept organisms. *Ecol. Monogr.,* 55, 69-102.

Dinesen, Z. (1980). A revision of the coral genus *Leptoseris* (Scleractinia: Fungina: Agriciidae). Mem. Qld. Mus., 20(1):181-235.

Ditlev, H. (1980) *A Field-guide to the Reef-building Corals of the Indo-Pacific.* Dr. W. Backhuys, Publisher. Rotterdam.

Doderlein, L. (1901). Die Korallengattung *Fungia. Zool. Anz., 24:* 351-60.

Doederlein, L., (1902). Die Korallengattung *Fungia.* Schenkenberg. naturf. Gesell; Abh., 27, 162 pp., 25 pls.

Dudler, N., Yellowlees, D. and Miller, D. J. (1987) Localization of two L-glutamate dehydrogenases in the coral *Acropora latistella. Arch. Biochem. Biophys.,* 254, 368-371.

Dunlap, W. C. and Chalker, B. E. (1986) Identification and quantitation of near-UV absorbing compounds (S-320) in a hermatypic scleractinian. *Coral Reefs,* 5, 155-159.

Dunlap, W.C., Chalker, B.E. and J.K. Oliver. (1986). Bathymetric adaptations of reef-building corals at Davies Reef, Great Barrier Reef, Australia. 3: UV-B absorbing compounds. *J. Expo. Mar. Biol. Ecol. 104:239-248.*

Dunlap, W.C. and Y. Yamamoto. (1995). Small-molecule antioxidants in marine organisms: antioxidant activity of mycosporine-glycine. *Comp. Biochem. Physiol. B 112(1):105-114.*

Duncan, M.P. (1884). A Revision of the Families and Genera of the Sclerodermic Zoantharia, ED. & H., or Madreoporaria. *Linn. Soc. J. Zool.,* 18:118.

Dykens, J. A. (1984) Enzymic defenses against oxygen toxicity in marine cnidarians containing endosymbiotic algae. *Mar. Biol. Lett.,* 5, 291-301.

Dykens, J. A. and Shick, J. M. (1982) Oxygen production by endosymbiotic algae controls superoxide dismutase activity in their animal host. *Nature,* 297, 579-580.

Edmunds, P. J. and Davies, P. S. (1986) An energy budget for *Porites porites* (Scleractinia). *Mar. Biol.,* 92, 339-347.

Edwards, H., Milne & Haime, J. (1848a). Recherches sur les polypiers. Mem. 1 Observations sur la structure et le developpement des polypiers en general. *Ann. Sci. Nat. Zool., 3e ser., 9:* 37-89.

Edwards, H., Milne & Haime, J. (1848b). Recherches sur les polypiers. Mem. 3 Monographie des Eupsammides. *Ann. Sci. Nat. Zool., 3e. ser., 10:* 65-114.

Edwards, H., Milne & Haime, J. (1848c). Recherches sur les polypiers. Mem. 4 Monographie des Astreides. *Ann. Sci. Nat. Zool., 3e. ser., 10:* 209-320.

Edwards, H., Milne & Haime, J. (1848d). Note sur la classification de la deuxieme tribu de la famille des Astreides. C.R. *Hebd. Seances Acad. Sci.,* 27(20): 490-7.

Edwards, H., Milne & Haime, J. (1849a). Memoire sur les polypiers appartenant a la famille des Oculinides, au groupe intermediaire des Oculinides, au groupe intermediaire des Pseudastreides et a la famille des Fongides. *C.R. Hebd. Seances Acad. Sci.,* 29: 67-73.

Edwards, H., Milne & Haime, J. (1849b). Recherches sur les polypiers. Mem. 4 Monographie des Astreides. *Ann. Sa. Nat. Zool.,* 3e. *ser., 11:* 233-312.

Edwards, H., Milne & Haime, J. (1850). Recherches sur les polypiers. Monographie des Astreides. *Ann. SCI. Nat. Zool.,* 3e *ser., 12:* 95-107.

Edwards, H., Milne & Haime, J. (1851a). Recherches sur les polypiers. Mem. 6 Monographie des Fongides. *Ann. Sci. Nat. Zool.,* 3e. *ser., 15:* 73-144.

Edwards, H., Milne & Haime, J. (1851b). Recherches sur les polypiers. Mem. 7 Monographie des Poritides. *Ann. Sci. Nat. Zool.,* 3e. ser., 16: 21-70.

Edwards, H., Milne & Haime, J. (1851c). Monographie des polypiers fossiles des terrains paleozoiques precedee dun tableau general de la classifications des polypes. *Arch. Mus. Nat. Hist. Nat. (Paris),* 5:1-505.

Edwards, H., Milne & Haime, J. (1857-1860). *Histoire naturelle des Coralliaires.* Paris, 1, 2 ~ 3:1-326,1-632,1-560.

Eguchi, M. (1935a). Stony corals of Tokyo Bay (in Japanese). *Plant and Animal,* 4(2): 66-74. EGUCHI, M. (1935b). On the Madreporanan corals from the Sagaimi Bay and Tokyo Bay (in Japanese). Zool. Mag., 47.

Eguchi, M. (1968). II. The scleractinian corals of Sagami Bay, in Biological Laboratory, Imperial Household (ed.) *The hydrocorals and scleractinian corals of Sagami Bay collected by H.M. The Emperor of Japan,* Maruzen Co. Ltd., Tokyo, ClC74, pl. C1-33.

Eguchi, M. (1970a). On geology and corals of marine park area of Saga Prefecture (in Japanese). *Rep. Mar. Park Cent., Saga Prefect.:* 25-34.

Eguchi, M. (1970b). On geology and corals of marine park site of Tottori Prefecture (in Japanese). Rep. *Mar. Park Cent., Tottori Prefect:.* 11-16.

Eguchi, M. (1971). Scleractinia of Goto Island (in Japanese). Rep. *Mar. Park Cent., Nagasaki Prefect.:* 19-31.

Eguchi, M. (1972a). Corals of the coast of south Izu, Shizuoka Prefecture (in Japanese). Rep. *Mar. Park Cent., Shi~uoka Prefect.:* 19-25.

Eguchi, M. (1972b). On coral fauna of Kushimoto and nearby (in Japanese). *Mar. Parks. J.,* 21: 7-9.

Eguchi, M. (1973). Coral fauna of the Tsushima Islands, Nagasaki Prefecture (in Japanese). Rep. *Mar. Park Cent., Nagasaki Prefect.:* 45-56.

Eguchi, M. (1974). Scleractinian corals from sites proposed for the Marine Park at Kerama and Yaujama Islands (in Japanese). Mar. Parks Cent. (ed.). Mar. Park Survey, Okinawa Reef: 37-48.

Eguchi, M. (1975a). Notes on coral genera of the Yaeyama Islands Group, with description of a new species, *Cladocora kabiraensis* n.sp. *Proc. Jpn. Soc. Syst. Zool., 11:* 1-4.

Eguchi, M. (1975b). Coral fauna of Nagasaki Prefecture (in Japanese). Rep. *Mar. Park Cent., Nagasaki Prefect.,* 56: 39-46.

Eguchi, M. & Fukuda, T. (1972). 1nvertebrata (chiefly coral fauna) of Marine Park of Iki Island, Nagasaki Prefecture (in Japanese). Rep. *Mar. Park Cent., Nagasaki Prefect.: 45-48.*

Eguchi, M. & Miyawaki, T. (1975). Systematic study of the scleractinian corals of Kushimoto and its vicinity. *Bull.* Mar. *Park. Res. Stns.,* 1: 47-62.

Eguchi, M. & Mori, R. (1973). A study of fossil corals from Tateyarna city and its environs and recent coral fauna of Chiba Prefecture, Central Japan (in Japanese). *Bull. Tokyo Coll. Domest. Sci.,* 13: 41-57.

Eguchi, M. & Shirai, 5. (1977). In SHIRAI, 5. (1980) *Ecological encyclopedia of the marine animals of the Ryukyu Islands* (in Japanese), Okinawa Kyoiku Shuppan, Japan.

Ehrenberg, C.G. (1834). Beitrage zur physiologischen Kenntniss der Corallenthiere im Allgemeinen und besonders des Rothen Meeres. *Abh. Akad. Wiss. D.D.R.:* 25-380.

Ellis, J. & Solander, D. (1786). *The natural history of many curious and uncommon zoophytes,* London, 1: 1-208.

Fabricius, K.E. 1995. Slow population turnover in the soft coral genera *Sinularia* and *Sarcophyton* on mid- and outer-shelf reefs of the Great Barrier Reef. *Mar. Ecol. Progr. Ser. 126:145-152.*

Fabricius, K.E. and D.W. Klumpp. 1995. Wide-spread mixotrophy in reef-inhabiting soft corals: The influence of depth, and colony expansion and contraction on photosynthesis. *Mar. Ecol. Progr. Ser. 126:145-152.*

Fabricius, K.E., Benayahu, Y. and A. Genin. (1995a). Herbivory in asymbiotic soft corals. *Science 268:90-92.*

Fabricius, K.E., Genin, A. and Y. Benayahu. (1995b). Flow-dependent herbivory and growth in zooxanthellae- free soft corals. *Limnol. Oceanogr. 40:1290-1301.*

Fabricius, K. E., and Alderslade, P. 2001. *Soft Corals and Sea Fans. A comprehensive guide to the tropical shallow-water genera of the Central-West Pacific, the Indian Ocean and the Red Sea.* AIMS. Townsville. Australia.

Farrant, P.A. (1985). Reproduction in the temperate Australian soft coral *Capnella gaboensis. Proc. 5th Int. Coral Reef Congr. Tahiti, French Polynesia* 4:319-324.

Faulkner, D.J. (1992). Biomedical uses for natural marine chemicals. *Oceanus 35(1):29-35.*

Faustino, L. A., (1927). Recent Madreporaria of the Philippine Islands. *Bur. Sci. Manila,* Monogr.22,310pp., 100pls.

Fischer de Waldheim (1807). *Description du Museum Demidoff,* Moscow, 3: 295-6.

ForskÅl, P. (1775). Descriptiones Animalium, Avium, Amphibiorum, Piscium, Insectorum, Vermium que in intinere orientali observavit Petrus Forskal. IV. Corallia. *Hauniae:* 131-9.

Fosså, S., and A. J. Nilsen. (1992). *Korallenriff-Aquarium Band 1.* Birgit Schmettkamp Verlag, Bornheim, Germany, 158 pp.

Fosså, S., and A. J. Nilsen. (1992). *Korallenriff-Aquarium Band 2.* Birgit Schmettkamp Verlag, Bornheim, Germany, 203 pp.

Fosså, S., and A. J. Nilsen. (1993). *Korallenriff-Aquarium Band 3.* Birgit Schmettkamp Verlag, Bornheim, Germany, 333 pp.

Fosså, S., and A. J. Nilsen. (1995). *Korallenriff-Aquarium Band 4.* Birgit Schmettkamp Verlag, Bornheim, Germany, 447 pp.

Fosså, S., and A. J. Nilsen. (1996). *Korallenriff-Aquarium Band 5.* Birgit Schmettkamp Verlag, Bornheim, Germany, 352 pp.

Fosså, S., and A. J. Nilsen. (1996). *The Modern Coral Reef Aquarium Vol 1.* Birgit Schmettkamp Verlag, Bornheim, Germany, 447 pp.

Fosså, S., and A. J. Nilsen. (1998). *The Modern Coral Reef Aquarium Vol 2.* Birgit Schmettkamp Verlag, Bornheim, Germany, 447 pp.

Fujiwara, 5. (1979). Distribution of reef-building corals in Japanese waters (in Japanese). Undergraduate thesis, Univ. Ryukyus.

Fujiwara, 5. (1985). Marine Park in Ogasawara Islands. Mar. Parks J., 68: 11-14. Fukuda, T. & IWASE, F. (1984). Hermatypic corals in Danjo Islands (in Japanese). *Mar. Parks J.,* 61: 3-6.

Gardiner, J.S. (1898a). On the fungid corals collected by the author in the South Pacific. *Proc. Zool. Soc. Lond.:* 525-539.

Gardiner, J. S., (1898b). On the perforate corals collected by the author in the South Pacific. Zool. Soc. Lond. Proc., 257-276, 2 pls.

Gardiner, J.S. (1899). On the astraeid corals collected by the author in the south Pacific. *Proc. Zool. Soc. Lond.:* 734-764.

Gardiner, J.S. (1905). Madreporaria. III. Fungida. IV. Turbinolidae. *Fauna Geog. Maldive Laccadive Arch.,* 2: 933-957.

Gardiner, J.S. (1909). The Madreporarian corals. I. The family Fungiidae, with a revision of its genera and species and an account of their geographical distribution. *Trans. Linn. Soc. Lond.,* 12(2): 257-290.

Gerth, H. (1921). Coelenterata. Anthozoa. In: K. Martin (ed.), Die Fossilien von Java auf Grund einer Sammlung von Dr. R. D. M. Verbeek und von Anderen. *Samml. Geol. Reichs-Mus. Leiden* 1 (2): 387-445.

Gomme, J. (1982) Epidermal nutrient absorption in marine invertebrates: a comparative analysis. *Amer. Zool.*, 22, 691-708.

Goreau, T. F. (1959) The physiology of skeleton formation in corals: I. A method for measuring the rate of calcium deposition by corals under different conditions. *Biol. Bull.*, 116, 59-75.

Gosliner, T., Williams, G.C. and D. Behrens (1996). *Coral Reef Animals of the Indo-Pacific*. Sea Challengers, Monterey, CA, USA, 314 pp.

Grasshoff, M. (1984) Cnidarian phylogeny-a biomechanical approach. In *Recent Advances in the Paleobiology and Geology of the Cnidaria, Paleontographica Americana*, No. 54, Paleontological Research Institution, Ithaca, New York, pp. 127-135.

Grasshoff, Manfred. (1999). The shallow water gorgonians of New Caledonia and adjacent islands. *Senkenbergiana Biologica* 78 (1/2):1-245

Grasshoff and Alderslade (1997), *Senkenbergiana Biologica* 77(1): 23-35.

Gray, J.E. (1842). Pocilloporidae *in Synopsis British Museum,* 44th edn.

Gray, J.E. (1847). An outline of an arrangement of stony corals. *Ann. Mag. Nat. Hist., 19:* 120-8.

Gregory, J.W. (1900). The fossil Corals of Christmas Island, in ANDREWS (ed.) British Museum (Natural History) *A Monograph of Christmas Island:* 206-225.

Habe, T. (1989). Corals of Amitori Bay and Sakiyama Bay. *Studies on the protection and growth of coral reefs and removal of the Crown- of-Thorns starfish*. Dept. Education, Japan, (3):1-266.

Haime, J. (1852). In Bellardi, L. (ed.) Catalogue raisonne des fossiles nummulitiques du comte de Nice. *Bull. Soc. Geol. Fr., ser. 2, 7:* 249.

Hamada, T. (1963b). Some problems on the Numa Coral Bed in Chiba Prefecture (in Japanese with English Abstract). *Geol. Soc. Jpn. (Special Bull.):* 94-119.

Hand, C. (1959) On the origin and phylogeny of the coelenterates. *Syst. Zool.*, 8, 191-202.

Hand, C. (1966) On the evolution of the Actiniaria. In W. J. Rees (ed.), *The Cnidaria and Their Evolution*, Academic Press, London, pp. 135-146.

Harvell, C.D., Fenical, W. and C.H. Greene. (1988). Chemical and structural defenses of Caribbean gorgonians (*Pseudopterogorgia* spp.) I: Development of an *in situ* feeding assay. *Mar. Ecol. Progr. Ser. 49:287-294.*

Harvell, C.D., Fenical, W., Roussis, V., Ruesink, J.L., Griggs, C.C. and C.H. Greene. (1993). Local and geographic variation in the defensive chemistry of a West Indian gorgonian coral (*Briareum asbestinum*). *Mar. Ecol. Progr. Ser. 93:165-173.*

Herndl, G. J. and Velimirov, B. (1985) Bacteria in the coelenteron of Anthozoa: control of coelenteric bacterial density by the coelenteric fluid. *J. Exp. Mar. Biol. Ecol.*, 93, 115-130.

Herndl, G. J., Velimirov, B. and Krauss, R. E. (1985) Heterotrophic nutrition and control of bacterial density in the coelenteron of the giant sea anemone *Stoichactis giganteum. Mar. Ecol. Prog. Ser.*, 22, 101-105.

Hildemann, W. H., Bigger, C. H. and Johnston, I. S. (1979) Histoincompatibility reactions and allogeneic polymorphism among invertebrates. *Transplant. Proc.*, 11, 1136-1141.

Hill, D. (1956) Rugosa. In R. C. Moore (ed.), *Treatise on Invertebrate Paleontology. Part F, Coelenterata*, University of Kansas, Lawrence, pp. F233-F324.

Hirata, K. & Oosako, N. (1968a). Corals of northern Amarni-oshima (in Japanese). *Rep. Underwater Mar. Parks Cent.:* 209-215.

Hirata, K. & Oosako, N. (1968b). Corals of onshore bays in Yamato-mura (in Japanese). *Rep. Undenwater Mar. Parks Cent.:* 223-224.

Hirata, K., Zaisho, T. & Oosako, N. (1969). *Possible locations of Kagoshima Marine Park and lists of marine invertebrates*. Kagoshima Prefect. (Publ.)

Hodgson, G. (1985). A new species of *Montastrea* (Cnidaria, Scleractinia) from the Philippines. *Pac. Sci.,* 39(3): 283-290.

Hodgson, G. & ROSS, M.A. (1982). Unreported scleractinian corals from the Philippines. *Proc. Fourth Int. Coral Reef Symp.,* 2:171-175.

Hoeksema, B.W. (1989). Taxonomy, phylogeny and biogeography of mushroom corals (Scleractinia: Fungiidae). *Zool. Verh. (Leiden),* 254:1- 678.

Hoffmeister, J.E. (1925). Some corals from American Somoa and the Fiji Islands. *Pap. Dep. Mar. Biol. Carnegie Inst. Wash.,* (Publ. 343), 22:1-90.

Hori, N. (1977). A morphometrical study on the geographical distribution of coral reef. *Geogr. Rep. Tokyo Metropl. Univ.,* 5:1-75

Horikoshi, M. (1979). Regional ecosystems in the tropical coastal region - Kabira Cove, Ishigaki Island as a model of the physiographic unit of regional ecosystems (in Japanese), in HORIBE, Y. (ed.) *Environ. Mar. Sa.,* 3:145-170. Tokyo Press.

Horikoshi, K., Kitano, Y., Yamazato, K. & Nishihira, M. (1975). Ecosystems of the coral sea in Okinawa - Preliminary survey of Kabira Bay in Ishigaki Island (in Japanese). *Environ. and Hum. Survival:* 230-247.

Horst, C. J. (1919). A new species of *Fungia. Zool. Meded. (Leiden),* 5: 65-6.

Horst, C. J. Van Der (1921). *The Madreporaria of the Siboga Expedition,* Pt. II. *Madreporaria Fungida.* Siboga Exped. 16b, 1-46.

Horst, C. J. Van Der (1922). Percy Sladen Trust Expedition: 9. Madreporaria Agariciidae. Trans. Linn. Soc. Lond. (2) Zool. 18, 417-429, pls. 31-32.

Hyman, L.H. 1940. *The Invertebrates: Protozoa through Ctenophora.* McGraw-Hill Book Co. Inc., New York, London, 726 pp.

Hyman, L. H. (1940) Chapter VII. Metazoa of the tissue grade of construction- the radiate phyla-Phylum Cnidaria. In *The Invertebrates: Protozoa through Ctenophora,* McGraw-Hill, New York, pp. 365-661.

Imajima, M. (1969). Report on the natural view of the Bonin Islands (in Japanese), *Marine fauna of the Bonin Islands* ser. 2,: 145-177. Tokyo Metropolitan Government.

Imajima, M. (1970a). Report on the natural view of the Bonin Islands (in Japanese), *Marinefauna of the Bonin Islands* Tokyo Metropolitan Government, ser. 2,: 225-251.

Imajima, M. (1970b). *Nature in the Bonin Islands,* TUYAMA, T. & ASAMI, S. (eds.) (in Japanese) Chapter 6 Marine fauna: 179-186.

Ishino, M. & Otsuka, K. (1970). On the coastal "Kyucho", a catastrophic influx of offshore water from the Kuroshio, in MARR, J.C., (ed.) *The Kuroshio.* EastWest Center Press: 61-67.

Iwase, H. & Nomura, K. (1988). Distribution of stony and soft corals and crownof-thorns starfish in Sekisei Lagoon (in Japanese). *Mar. Parks J.,* 80: 8-12.

Jackson, J. B. C. (1977) Competition on marine hard substrata: the adaptive significance of solitary and colonial strategies. *Amer. Nat.,* 111, 743-767.

Jackson, J. B. C. (1979) Morphological strategies of sessile animals. In G. Larwood and B. R. Rosen (eds.), *Biology and Systematics of Colonial Organisms. Systematics Association Special* Vol. No. 11, Academic Press, London, pp. 499-555.

Jackson, J. B. C. (1985) Distribution and ecology of clonal and aclonal benthic invertebrates. In J. B. C. Jackson, L. W. Buss and R. E. Cook (eds.), *Population Biology and Evolution of Clonal Organisms,* Yale University Press, New Haven, pp. 297-355.

Kamezaki, N., Nomura, K. & Ui, S. (1987). Population dynamics of stony corals and *Acanthaster planci* in Sekisei lagoon, Okiniawa (1983-1986) (in Japanese). *Mar. Parks J.,* 74:12-19.

Kawabe, M. (1980). Sea level variaffons around the Nansei Islands and the large meander in the Kuroshio south of central Japan. J. *Oceanogr. Soc. Jpn.,* 36: 227-235.

Kawabe, M. (1985). El Nino effects in the Kuroshio and western north Pacific, in Wooster, W.S. & Fluhardy, D.L. (eds.) *El Nino North: Nino effects in the eastern subartic Pacific Ocean.,* Washington: 31- 43.

Kawabe, M. (1986). Transition process between the three typical paths of the Kuroshio. J. *Oceanogr. Soc. Jpn.,* 42(3):174191.

Kawabe, M. & Yoneno, M. (1987). Water and flow variations in Sagami Bay under the influence of the Kuroshio Path. J. *Oceanogr. Soc. Jpn.,* 43(5): 283-294.

Kawaguti, S. (1983). Stony corals of Kabira Bay Ishigaki Is. *Rep. Okinawa Prefect. Fish. Exp. Stn., Yaeyama Branch:* 9-16.

Kikuchi, T. (1968). *Fauna and flora of the seas around the Amakusa Marine Biological Laboratory* (in Japanese). Pt. VII. Amakusa Marine Laboratory, Kyushu Univ.

Kikuchi, T. (1985). *Checklist of the shore fauna in Tsuji-shima islet, Amakusa,* West Kyushu. Publ. Amakusa Mar. Biol. Lab., 8(1): 65-88.

Kikuchi, T. & Araga T. (1980). Underwater views in offshore of Arnakusa Islands (in Japanese). *Rep. Mar. Park Cent., Kumamoto Prefect.:* 43-47.

Kinzie, R. A., III (1974) Experimental infection of aposymbiotic gorgonian polyps with zooxanthellae. *J. Exp. Mar. Biol. Ecol.,* 15, 335-345.

Kinzie, R. A., III and Chee, G. S. (1979) The effect of different zooxanthellae on the growth of experimentally reinfected hosts. *Biol. Bull.,* 156, 315-327.

Klunzinger, C.B. (1879). *Die Korallentheire des Rothern Meeres. n. Die Madreporaceen und Oculinaceen. Ill. Die Astraceen und Fungiaceen.* Berlin, Verlag der Gutmannschen Buchandlung. II: 85 pp., III: 100 pp.

Konaga, S., Nishiyama, K., Ishizaki, H. and Hanzawa, Y. (1980). Geostrophic current south-east of Yakushima Island. *La Mer* 18:1-16.

Kurata, Y., Mimura, T., Takahashi, K. Shioya, T. & Hirose, I. (1969). *Report on the basic research for development of fisheries in the Bonin Islands* (in Japanese), Tokyo Fisheries Experimental Station Chapter 5 A general view of the coral reefs of the Bonin Islands: 130-160.

LaBarre, S.C. and J.C. Coll. (1986). Movement in soft corals: An interaction between *Nephthea brassica* (Coelenerata: Octocorallia) and *Acropora hyaccinthus* (Coelenerata: Scleractinia). *Mar. Biol. 72:119-124.*

LaBarre, S.C., Coll, J.C. and P.W. Sammarco. (1986). Defensive strategies of soft corals (Coelenterata: Octocorallia) of the Great Barrier Reef. II. The relationship between toxicity and feeding deterrence. *Biol. Bull. 171-565-576.*

Laborel, 1., (1970). Madreporaries et Hydrocoralliens recifaux des cotes bresiliennes. Systematique, ecologie, repartition verticale et geografique. Result. Campagne Calypso. Ann. Inst. Oceanogr. (9) 47,171-229.

Lamarck, J.B.P. de (1801). *Systeme des animaux sans vertebres*. Paris: 1-432.

Lamarck, J.B.P. de (1816). *Histoire naturelle des animaux sans vertebres*. Paris, 2: 1-568.

Lamberts, A. E. (1984). The Reef Corals *Lithactinia* and *Polyphyllia* (Anthozoa, Scleractinia, Fungiidae): A Study of Morphological, Geographical, and Statistical Differences. *Pac. Sci.* (38) 1: 12 - 27.

Lasker, H.R. (1990). Clonal propagation and population dynamics of a gorgonian coral. *Ecology* 71:1578-1589.

Lasker, H.R. and K. Kim. (1996). Larval development and settlement behaviour of the gorgonian coral *Plexaura kuna* (Lasker, Kim and Coffroth). *J. Exp. Mar. Biol. Ecol.* 207:161-175.

Lee, R. F., Hirota, J. and Barnett, A. M. (1971) Distribution and importance of wax esters in marine copepods and other zooplankton. *Deep-Sea Res.*, 18, 1147-1165.

Leone, P.A., Bowden, B.F., Caroll, A.R. and J.C. Coll. (1995). Chemical consequences of relocation of the soft coral *Lobophytum compactum* and its placement in contact with the red alga *Plocamium hamatum. Mar. Biol. 122:675-679.*

Lenhoff, H. M., Heagy, W. and Danner, J. (1976) A view of the evolution of chemoreceptors based on research with cnidarians. In G. O. Mackie (ed.), *Coelenterate Ecology and Behavior*, Plenum, New York, pp. 571-579.

Lesser, M. P., Stochaj, W. R., Tapley, D. W. and Shick, J. M. (1990) Physiological mechanisms of bleaching in coral reef anthozoans: effects of irradiance, ultraviolet radiation, and temperature on the activities of protective enzymes against active oxygen. *Coral Reefs,* 8, 225-232.

Lewis, J.B. (1982). Feeding behaviour and feeding ecology of Octocorallia (Coelenterata: Anthozoa). *J. Zool. Lond. 196:371-384.*

Lindstedt, K. J. (1971b) Chemical control of feeding behavior. *Comp. Biochem. Physiol.*, 39A, 553-581.

Link, H.T. (1807). *Beischreibung der Naturalien-Sammlungen der universitat zu Rostock.,* 3: 161-65.

Linnaeus, C. (1758). *Systema naturae. I Regnum animale. Ed. X.*

Linnaeus, C. (1767). *Systema naturae. I Regnum animale. Ed. XII.*

Loyal B., (1972). Community structure and species diversity of hermatypic corals at Eilat, Red Sea. Mar. Biol., 13,10()123.

Ma, T. Y. H., (1959). Effect of water temperature on growth rate of reef corals. Oceanogr. Sinica 2nd series of private research publication. Special volume, no. 1, 1 16 pp., 320 pls.

Maida, M, Sammarco, P.W. and J.C. Coll. (1995). Effects of soft corals on scleractinian coral recruitment. I: Directional allelopathy and inhibition of settlement. *Mar. Ecol. Progr. Ser. 121:191-202.*

Marenzeller, E. von, (1901). Ostafrikanische Steinkorallen. Naturwiss. Ver. Hamburg. Verh. (3 ser.) 18,117-134,1 pl.

Marenzeller, E. von, (1907). Expedition S. M. Schiff Pola in das Rote Meer. Zool. Ergeb. 26-Riffkorallen. Denkschr. Akad. Wiss. Wien, 80, 27-97, pls. 1-29.

Masuda, k. & Hayashi, K. (1989). *Marine Invertebrates* (in Japanese). Tokai Univ.: 1-255.

Masuda K. (1986). Reef-building corals, seaweeds and sediments of the reef flat and moat off Shiraho (in Japanese). *Sci. Rep. Shiraho Coral Reef,* Ishijaki Island World Wildlife Fund.

Matthai, G. (1914). Revision of the recent colonial asrraeidae possessing distinct corallites. *Trans. Linn. Soc. Lond. Zool., ser.* 2,17:1-140.

Matthai, G. (1924). Report on the madreporarian corals in the collection of the Indian Museum, Calcutta. Mem. Indian Mus., X, 1-59.

Matthai, G. (1928). *Cat. Madreporarian Corals Brit. Mus. (Nat. Hist.).* Pt. VII. A monograph of the recent meandroid Astraeidae. London, Trustees of the British Museum (Natural History): 288.

Matthai, G. (1948). On the mode of growth of the skeleton in the fungid corals. Phil. Trans. R. Soc. Lond., B, 233, 177-196, pls. 3-14.

Michelin, H. (1843). Description dune nouvelle espece du genre fongie. *Mag. de Zool.,* Paris, 5

Milne-Edwards, H. & J. Haime, (1848). Monographie des Turbinolides. (Recherces des Polypiers, Mem. 2). - Ann. Sci. Natur. Paris (3. ser. Zool.), 9, 211-344.

Milne-Edwards, H. & J. Haime, (1848, 1849, 1850). Monographie des Astreides. (Recherces sur les Polypiers, Mem. 4). Ibid. 10, 209-320,1848.11, 235-312,1849.12, 95-197,1850.

Milne-Edwards, H. & J. Haime, (1851). Monographie des Poritides. (Recherces sur les Polypiers, Mem. 7). Ibid., 16, 21-70.

Milne-Edwards, H. & J. Haime, (1860). Histoire naturelle des coralliaires, 2, 633 pp.

Miyamoto, T., Tamada, K., Ikeda, N., Komori, T. and R. Higuchi. (1994) Bioactive diterpenoids from Octocorallia: 1. Bioactive diterpenoids: *Litophynols* A and B from the mucus of the soft coral *Litophyton* sp. *J. Nat. Prod. 57:1212-1219.*

Miyamoto, T., Takenaka, Y., Yamada, K. and R. Higuchi. (1995) Bioactive diterpenoids from Octocorallia: 2. Deoxyxeniolde B, a novel ichthyotoxic diterpenoid from the soft coral *Xenia elongata. J. Nat. Prod. 58:924-928.*

Miyawaki, T. (1978). The additional scleractinian corals of Kushimoto. *Bull. Mar. Park Res. Stn., 2:* 99-104.

Moll, H. & Best, M.B. (1984). New Scleractinian from the Spermonde Archipelago, South Sulawesi, Indonesia. *Zoologische Mededelingen,* 58(4): 47-58.

Moriyasu, 5. (1972). The Tsushima Current, in Stommel, H. & Yoshida, K. (eds.) *Kuroshio, Physical aspects of the Japan Current:* 353-369.

Muzik, K. (1984a). *Ishigah Iagoon coral sur~ey. 1. Research on Environmental disruption. Towards Interdisciplinary Cooperation,* 13(4): 68-70.

Muzik, K. (1984b). *Ishigah Iagoon coral survey. 11. Research on Environmental disruption. Towards Interdisciplinary Cooperation,* 14(1): 70-72.

Nakamori, T. (1986). Cornmunity structures of Recent and Pleistocene hermatypic corals in the Ryukyu Islands, Japan. *SCI. Rep. Tohoku Univ. ser. 2, (Geol.),* 56(o: 71-133.

Nakasone, Y., Yamazato, K., Nishihira, M., Kamura, S. & Aramoto, Y. (1974). Preliminary report on the ecological distribution of benthic animals on the coral reefs of Sesoko Island, Okinawa (in Japanese with English surnmary). *Ecol. Stud. Nat. Con. Ryukyu Is., 1:* 213-236.

Nemenzo, F. (1955). Systematic study on Philippine shallow water Scleractinians: I. Suborder Fungiida. *Nat. App. Sci. Bull. Philipp.,* 15(1): 3-83

Nemenzo, F. (1959). Systematic study on Philippine shallow water Scleractinians: II. Suborder Faviida. *Nat. App. Sci. Bull. Philipp.,* 16(1-4): 73-135.

Nemenzo, F. (1960). Systematic studies on Philippine shallow water Scleractinians: m. Suborder Caryophillida. *Nat. App. Sci. Bull. Philipp.,* 17(3, 4): 207-213.

Nemenzo, F. (1964). Systematic studies on Philippine shallow water Scleractinians: V. Suborder Astrocoenida. *Nat. App. Sci. Bull. Philipp.,* 18(3, 4):193-223.

Nemenzo, F. (1967). Systematic studies on Philippine shallow water Scleractinians: VI. Suborder Astrocoeniida (Montipora and Acropora). *Nat. Appl. Sci. Bull. Philipp.,* 20(1): 1-141.

Nemenzo, F. (1967). Systematic studies on Philippine shallow-water Scleractinians: VI. Suborder Astrocoeniida (Montipora and Acropora). *Nat. Appl. Sci. Bull. Philipp.,* 20(2):1-224.

Nemenzo, F. (1971). Systematic studies on Philippine shallow water Scleractinians: VII. Additional forms. *Nat. App. Sci. Bull. Philipp.,* 23(3):142-185.

Nemenzo, F. (1976). New species and new records of corals from the Philippines. *Nat. App. Sci. Bull. Philipp.,* 28: Z9-276.

Nemenzo, F. (1979). New species and new records of stony corals from west central Philippines. *Philipp. J. Sci.,* 108(1-2):1-25.

Nemenzo, , F. (1980). Fungiid corals from central Philippines. *Kalikasan, Philipp. J. Biol.,* 9 (2-3): 283-302.

Nemenzo, F. & Monecillo, E. (1981). Four new scleractinian species from Arangasa Inlet (Surigao del sur Province, Philippines). *Philip. J. Sci.,* 18:120-128.

Nishihira, M. (1988). *Field guide to hertnatypic corals of Japan.* Tokai Univ. Press: 241 pp.

Nishihira, M., Yamazato, K., Nakazone, Y., Kamura, S. & Aramoto, Y. (1974). Notes on the *Acanthaster* infestation on the coral reefs around Sesoko Island, Okinawa (in Japanese with English summary). *Ecol. Stud. Nat. Cons. Ryukyu Is., 1:* 237-254.

Nishihira, M., Yanagiya, K. & Sakai, K. (1987). A preliminary list of hermatypic corals collected around Kudaka Island, Okinawa. *Galaxea,* 6: 5-60.

Nishihira, M. & Yokochi, H. (1990). A tenative list of hermatypic corals of Sakiyama Bay Nature Conservation Area, Iriomate Island, Okinawa (in Japanese). *Nature Conservation Bureau Environment Agency:* 95-105.

Nitani, H. (1972). Beginning of the Kuroshio, in Stommel, H. & Yoshida, K. (eds.). *Kuroshio, Physical aspects of the Japan Current:* 129-163.

Nomura, K. & Kamezaki, N. (1987). The present condition of crown-of-thorns starfish and corals of Haterama Island, Yaegama Group (in Japanese). *Mar. Parks J.,* 73: 16-19.

Oken, L. (1815a). Lehrbuch der Naturgeschichte. III. Zoologie. *Schmid, Leipzig, Jena.,* 1: 59-74.

Oken, L., (1815b). 1. Zunft. Erdkorallen, Steinkorallen. Lehrbuch der Naturgeschichte, Dritter Theil, Zoologie, Erste Abteilung, Fleischlose Thiere, pp. 59-74.

Oliver, W. A., Jr. (1980) The relationship of the scleractinian corals to the rugose corals. *Paleobiology,* 6, 146-160.

Ooishi, 5. (1970). Marine invertebrate fauna of the Ogasawara and Volcano Islands, collected by Ooishi, S., Tomida, Y., Izawa, K. & Manabe, S. (eds) in *Report of the marine biological expedition to the Ogasawara (Bonin) Islands.* Toba Aquarium and theAsahi Shimbun Publ. Co., Nagoya, 1968, 75-104.

Ooishi, S. & Yagi, S. (1964). Invertebrate fauna of Amarni-osima (in Japanese). *Rep. Mar. Biol. Exp. Amami-osima,* Asahi Shinbun Publ. Co., Tokyo: 43-46.

Ortmann, A., (1888). Studien uber Systematik und geographische Verbreitung der Steinkorallen**.** Zool Jahrb. Abt. Syst. Geogr. Biol. Tiere, 3,143-788.

Ortmann, A. (1889). Beobachtungen an Steinkorallen von der Sudk~iste Ceylons. Zool. Jahrb. Abt. Syst. Oekol. Geogr. Biol. Tiere, 4: 493-590.

Ortmann, A. (1890). Die Morphologie des Skeletts der Steinkorallen in Beziehung zur Koloniebildung. Z. Wiss. *Zool.,* 50: 278-316.

Otsuka, K. (1985). Characteristics of the Kuroshio in the vicinity of the Izu Ridge. J. *Oceanogr. Soc. Japan* 41(6): 441-451.

Otsuka. K. & Ishino, M. (1988). Investigation of current systems with drift-bottle in the subtropical region of the northwestern Pacific Ocean. J. *Tokyo Univ. Fisheries,* 75(2): 275-294.

Pallas, P.S. (1766). *Elenchus Zoophytorum.* Den Haag: 1-451.

Patterson, M. R. (1984) Patterns of whole colony prey capture in the octocoral, *Alcyonium siderium. Biol. Bull.,* 167, 613-629.

Patterson, M. R. (1985) *The Effects of Flow on the Biology of Passive Suspension Feeders: Prey Capture, Feeding Rate, and Gas Exchange in Selected Cnidarians.* Ph.D. dissertation, Harvard University, Cambridge, Massachusetts, 342 pp.

Patterson, M. R. and Sebens, K. P. (1989) Forced convection modulates gas exchange in cnidarians. *Proc. Nat. Acad. Sci.* USA, 86, 8833-8836.

Patterson, M.R. 1991. The effects of flow on polyp-level prey capture in an octocoral, *Alcyonium siderium. Biol. Bull. 180:93-102.*

Penry, D. L. and Jumars, P. A. (1987) Modeling animal guts as chemical reactors. *Amer. Nat.*, 129, 69-96.

Percival, E. (1968) Marine algal carbohydrates. Oceanogr. *Mar. Biol. Ann. Rev.*, 6, 137-161.

Percival, E. and McDowell, R. H. (1967) *Chemistry and Enzymology of Marine Algal Polysaccharides,* Academic Press, New York, 219 pp.

Pillai, C.S. (1973). A review of the genus *Anacropora* Ridely (Scleractinia, Acroporidae) with the description of a new species. J. *Mar. Biol. Assoc. India,* 15(1): 296-301.

Pillai, C.S.G. & Scheer, G. (1974). On a collection of Scleractinia from the Strait of Malacca. *Proc. 2nd Int. Coral Reef Sy~np., 1:* 445-464.

Pillai, C.S.G. & Scheer, G. (1976). Report on the stony corals from the Maldive Archipelago. *Zoologica,* 126: 1-83.

Putterbaugh, E. and Borneman, E. (1996). A Practical Guide To Corals For The Reef Aquarium. Crystal Graphics. Lexington Kentucky.

Quelch, J.J. (1884). Preliminary notice of new genera and species of Challenger reef-corals. *Ann. Mag. Hist. Zool. Bot. Geol. Ser.,* 5(13): 292-7.

Quelch, J.J. (1886). Report on the reef-corals collected by H.M.S. Challenger during the years 1873-76. *Rep. Sa. Results Voyage H.M.S. Challenger Zool.,* 16(3): 1-203.

Quoy, J.R.C. & Gaimard, J.P. (1833). Zoophytes, in Dumont dUrville, J.S.C. (ed.) Voyage de decouvertes de lAstrolabe, execute parordre du Roi, pendant les annees 1826-29, sous le commandement de M.J. Dumont dUrville. *Zoologie, 4:* 175-254.

Rahav, O., Dubinsky, Z., Achituv, Y. and Falkowski, P. G. (1989) Ammonium metabolism in the zooxanthellate coral, *Stylophora pistillata. Proc. R. Soc. Lond.*, B, 236, 325-337.

Rehberg, H. (1892). Neue und wenig bekannte Korallen. *Abh. Naturwiss. Ver. Hambg., 12(1):* 1-50.

Ridley, S.O. (1884). On the classificatory value of growth and budding in the Madreporaria and on a new genus illustrating this point. *Ann. Mag. Nat. Hist.,* 13: 284291.

Robson, E. A. (1985) Speculations on coelenterates. In S. C. Morris, J. D. George, R. Gibson and H. M. Platt (eds.), *The Origins and Relationships of Lower Invertebrates, Systematics Association Special Vol. No. 28,* Clarendon Press, Oxford, UK, pp. 60-77.

Rodriguez, A.D. (1995). The natural products chemistry of West Indian Gorgonian octocorals. *Tetrahedron 51:4571-4618.*

Rodriguez, A.D., Cobar, O.M. and N. Martinez. 1994. Isolation and structures of sixteen new asbestinin diterpenes from the Caribbean gorgonian *Briareum asbestinum. J. Nat. Prod. 57:1638-1655.*

Ross, M.A. & Hodgson, G. (1982). A quantitative study of hermatypic coral diversity and zonation of Apo Reef, Mindoro, Philippines. *Proc. Fourth Int. Coral Reef Sy?np., 2:* 281-291.

Roughgarden, J. (1975) Evolution of marine symbiosis-a simple cost-benefit model. *Ecology,* 56, 1201-1208.

Rubenstein, D. I. and Koehl, M. A. R. (1977) The mechanisms of filter feeding: some theoretical considerations. *Amer. Nat.*, 111, 981-994.

Rudi, A., Ketzinel, S., Goldberg, I., Stein, Z., Kashman, Y., Benayahu, Y. and M. Schleyer. (1995). Antheliatin and zahavins A and B, three new cytotoxic xenicane diterpenes from two soft corals. *J. Nat. Prod. 58:1581-1586.*

Sakaguchi, Y. (1954). On some Anthozoa from Kii, Japan. J. *Zool. Bot. Soc. Kishu Biol., 1:* 123-124.

Sakai, K. & Yamazato, K. (1987). Preliminary list of hermatypic corals around Sesoko Island, Okinawa with a note on the decrease of the species richness from 1980 to 1986. *Galaxea,* 6: 43-51.

Sammarco, P.W. Coll, J.C., La Barre, S. and B. Willis. (1983). Competitive strategies of soft corals (Coelenterata: Octocorallia): allelopathic effects on selected scleractinian corals. *Coral Reefs 2:173-178.*

Sammarco, P.W. (1996). Comments on coral reef regeneration, bioerosion, biogeography, and chemical ecology: future directions. *J. Exp. Mar. Biol. Ecol. 200:135-168.*

Sammarco, P.W. and J.C. Coll. (1988). The chemical ecology of alcyonarian corals (Coelenterata: Octocorallia). In: Scheuer, P.J. (ed) *Bio-organic marine chemistry.* Vol. 2. Springer-Verlag, Berin, Heidelberg, pp. 87-116.

Sammarco, P.W., Coll, J.C., La Barre, S. and B. Willis. 1983. Competitive strategies of soft corals (Coelenterata: Octocorallia): allelopathic effects on selected scleractinian corals. *Coral Reefs 2:173-178.*

Saville-Kent, W. (1871). New madrepores. *Proc. Zool. Soc. Lond.,* 1871.

Saville-Kent, W. (1891). Notes on new and little known Australian Madreporaceae. *Rec. Aust. Mus.,* 1:123~.

Saville-Kent, W. (1893). *The Great Barrier Reef of Australia. Its products and potentialities.* W.H. Allen and Co., London, 1-387.

Scelfo, G. M. (1986) Relationship between solar radiation and pigmentation of the coral *Montipora verrucosa* and its zooxanthellae. In P. L. Jokiel, R. H. Richmond and R.A. Rogers (eds.), *Coral Reef Population Biology, Hawaii Inst. Mar. Biol. Tech. Rept. No. 37,* pp. 440-451.

Scheer, G. & C. S. G. Pillai, (1974). Report on the Scleractinia from the Nicobar Islands. Zoologica (Stuttg.), 42, heft 122, 1-75, 33 pls.

Schlichter, D. (1982). Nutritional strategies of cnidarians: the absorption, translocation and utilization of dissolved nutrients by *Heteroxenia fuscescens*. *Amer. Zool.* 22: 659-669.

Schlichter, D. (1982b). Epidermal nutrition of the alcyonarian *Heteroxenia fuscescens* (Ehrb.): Absorption of dissolved organic material and lost endogenous photosynthates. *Oecologia 53:40-49.*

Schlichter, D. and G. Liebezeit. (1991). The natural release of amino acids from the symbiotic coral *Heteroxenia fuscescens* (Ehrb.) as a function of photosynthesis. *J. Exp. Mar. Biol. Ecol. 150:83-90.*

Schmidt, H. (1974). On evolution in the Anthozoa. In: *Proc. 2nd Int. Coral Reef Symp.*, Vol. 1, Great Barrier Reef Committee, Brisbane, Pp. 533-560.

Schoenberg, D. A. and Trench, R. K. (1980a) Genetic variation in *Symbiodinium (=Gymnodinium) microadriaticum* Freudenthal, and specificity in its symbiosis with marine invertebrates. I. Isoenzyme and soluble protein patterns of axenic cultures of *Symbiodinium microadriaticum. Proc. R. Soc. Lond.*, B, 207, 405-427.

Schoenberg, D. A. and Trench, R. K. (1980b) Genetic variation in *Symbiodinium (=Gymnodinium) microadriaticum* Freudenthal, and specificity in its symbiosis with marine invertebrates. II. Morphological variation in *Symbiodinium microadriaticum. Proc. R. Soc. Lond.*, B, 207, 429-444.

Schoenberg, D. A. and Trench, R. K. (1980c) Genetic variation in *Symbiodinium (=Gymnodinium) microadriaticum* Freudenthal, and specificity in its symbiosis with marine invertebrates. III. Specificity and infectivity of *Symbiodinium microadriaticum. Proc. R. Soc. Lond.*, B, 207, 445-460.

Schweigger, A.F. (1819). *Beobachtungen auf naturhistorischen Reisen- Anat. physiol. Untersuchungen ueber Corallen.* Berlin.

Scrutton, C. T. (1979) Early fossil cnidarians. In M. R. House (ed.), *The Origin of Major Invertebrate Groups. Systematics Association Special Vol. No. 12*, Academic Press, London, pp. 161-207.

Searle, A. G., (1956). An illustrated key to the Malayan hard corals. Malay. Nat. J., 11 (I & 2), 1-28.

Sebens, K.P. (1977). Autotrophic and heterotrophic nutrition of coral reef zoanthids. In: *Proc. 3rd Int. Coral Reef Symp. 397-404.*

Sebens, K. P. (1982) The limits to indeterminate growth: an optimal size model applied to passive suspension feeders. *Ecology*, 63, 209-222.

Sebens, K. P. and M.A.R. Koehl. (1984). Predation on zooplankton by the benthic anthozoans *Alcyonium siderium* (Alcyonacea) and *Metridium senile* (Actinaria) in the New England subtidal. *Mar. Biol. 81:255-271.*

Sebens, K. P. (1984). Water flow and coral colony size: interhabitat comparisons of the octocoral *Alcyonium siderium. Proc. Nat. Acad. Sci. USA*, 81, 5473-5477.

Sebens, K. P. and J.S. Miles. (1988). Sweeper tentacles in a gorgonian octocoral: morphological modifications for interference competition. *Biol. Bull. 175:378-387.*

Sebens, K. P. and DeRiemer, K. (1977) Diel cycles of expansion and contraction in coral reef anthozoans. *Mar. Biol.*, 43, 247-256.

Sebens, K. P. and Koehl, M. A. R. (1984) Predation on zooplankton by two benthic anthozoans, *Alcyonium siderium* (Alcyonacea) and *Metridium senile* (Actiniaria), in the New England subtidal. *Mar. Biol.*, 81, 255-271.

Shelton, G. A. B. (1982) Anthozoa. In G. A. B. Shelton (ed.), *Electrical Conduction and Behaviour in Simple Invertebrates,* Oxford University Press, New York, pp. 203-242.

Shelton, G. A. B. and Holley, M. C. (1984) The role of a local electrical conduction system during feeding in the Devonshire cup coral *Caryophyllia smithii* Stokes and Broderip. *Proc. R. Soc. Lond.*, B, 220, 489-500.

Sheppard, C.R.C. (1979). Interspecific aggression between reef corals with reference to their distribution. *Mar. Ecol. Prog. Ser. 1:237-247.*

Shick, J. M., Lesser, M. P. and Stochaj, W. R. (1990) Ultraviolet radiation and photooxidative stress in zooxanthellate Anthozoa: the sea anemone *Phyllodiscus semoni* and the octocoral *Clavularia* sp. Symbiosis, 8

Shin, Y. (1979). Stony corals of Nikijima (in Japanese). *Mar. Parks Cent. Rep., 68.*

Shirai, S. (1963). Report of the Investigation for Marine Resources in NigistimaBay (in Japanese). *The Pacific:* 1-71.

Shirai, S. (1980). *Ecological encyclopedia of the marine animals of the Ryukyu Islands* (in Japanese). Okinawa Kyoiku Shuppan: Japan 636 pp.

Shirai, S. (1986). Scleractinia of Mie Prefecture, in *Mie Ken, Nature and its Animals* (in Japanese). Mie-ryosho-shippamkai:572-593.

Shirai, S., Sasaki, A. & Katayama, Y. (1965). Report of the Investigations for Kumano-nada Marine Park, Suzushima Area in Mie Prefecture (in Japanese). *The Pacific:* 1-50.

Shirai, S & Sano, Y. (1985). *The Report of the coral reefs around the sea of Ishigaki Island, Okinawa, Japan.* Inst. Development Pacific Nat. Res.

Sleigh, M.A. (1989) Adaptations of ciliary systems for the propulsion of water and mucus. *Comp. Biochem. Physiol.*, 94A, 359-364.

Smith, H. G. (1939) The significance of the relationship between actinians and zooxanthellae. *J. Exp. Biol.*, 16, 334-345.

Song, J.T. (1982). *A study on the classification of the Korean Anthozoa 7. Scleractinia (Hexacorallia).* Natural History Museum, Ewha Womont University, 25(3):131-140.

Spengler, L. (1781). Beskrivelse over et ganske besonderliat Corall prodeskt. *K. Dan. Vidensk.* Selsk. Biol. Skr., 1: 240.

Sponaugle, S. (1991). Flow patterns and velocities around a suspension-feeding gorgonian polyp: Evidence from physical models. *J. Exp. Mar. Biol. Ecol. 148:135-145.*

Sponaugle, S. and M. LaBarbera. (1991). Drag-induced deformation: a functional feeding strategy in two species of gorgonians. *J. Exp. Mar. Biol. Ecol. 148:121-134.*Sprung, J. (1989) Reef Notes. *Freshwater and Marine Aquarium Magazine* 12:11

Sprung, J. & Delbeek, J.C. (1997). *The Reef Aquarium* Vol Two. Ricordea Publishing, Coconut Grove. Florida.

Stochaj, W. R. (1988) The effects of ultraviolet and visible radiation on UV absorbing compounds in cnidarians. *Amer. Zool.*, 28, 192A (abstract).

Stochaj, W. R. (1989) *Photoprotective Mechanisms in Cnidarians: UV-Absorbing Compounds and Behavior.* M. Sc. thesis, University of Maine, Orono, Maine. 67 pp.

Stoddart, J. A. (1983) *A genotypic diversity measure.* J. Hered., 74, 489.

Stoddart, J. A., Ayre, D. J., Willis, B. and Heyward, A. J. (1985) Self-recognition in sponges and corals? *Evolution,* 39, 461-463.

Studer, T. (1878). Ubersicht der steinkorallen aus der Familie der Madreporaria aporosa *Eupsammia* und *Turbinaria,* welche auf der Reise S.M.S. *Gazelle* um die Erde gesammelt wurden. *K. Akad. Wissen,* Berlin Monatsber, 42: 625-655.

Studer, T., (1881). Beitrage zur Fauna der Steinkorallen von Singapore. Mitt. naturforsch . Ges. Bern (1880), 979, 15 53 .

Studer, T., (1901). Madreporarien von Samoa, den Sandwich Inseln und Laysan. Zool. Jahrb. Abt. Syst. Geogr. Biol. Tiere, 14 (5), 3X8 428, pls. 23-31.

Stutchbury, S. (1833). An account of the mode of growth of young corals of the genus *Fungia. Trans. Linn. Soc. Lond., 16:* 493-7.

Sugiyama, T. (1937). On the recent reef-building corals found in the Japanese seas (in Japanese). *Contrib. Inst. Geol. and Paleontol. Tohoku Univ.,* 22: 1-60.

Suzuki, K. (1972). A study of the coral fauna of Irimote Island, in *Rep. Investigation of Irimote Islands* (in Japanese). Tokai Univ.: 92-99.

Szmant-Froelich, A. (1981) Coral nutrition: comparison of the fate of 14C from ingested labelled brine shrimp and from the uptake of $NaH_{14}CO_3$ by its zooxanthellae. *J. Exp. Mar. Biol. Ecol.*, 55, 133-144.

Tachikawa, H. (1990). Study of the corals of the Ogasawara Is., (in Japanese). *Rep. Ogasawara Mar. Res. Cent.,* 89(8).

Takahashi, K. (1983). Shallow water scleractinian corals around Hachizyo Is. *Mar. Parks J.,* 60: 7-10.

Takahashi, K. & Koba, M. (1978). A preliminary investigation of the coral reef at the southern coast of Ishigaki Island, Ryukyus (in Japanese). *Sa. Rep. Tohoku Uniu, Ser. 7 (Geog.),* 28(1): 49-60.

Tepoot, P. and Teepoot, I. (1996). *Marine Aquarium Companion: Southeast Asia.* New Life Publications. Homestead, Florida.

Thiel, M. E., (1932). Madreporaria. Zugleich ein Versuch einer vergleichende Ökologie der gefundene Formen. Mem. Mus. R. Hist. nat. Belg., Hors Ser., 2 (12), 1-177, pls. 1-21.

Tixier-Durivault, A. (1964). Stolonifera et Alcyonacea. *Galathea Reports* 7:43-58.

Tokioka, T. (1953). 1nvertebrate fauna of the intertidal zone and the Tokara Islands, I. Introductory notes, with the outline of the shore and the fauna. *Publ. Seto. Mar. Biol. Lab.,* 3(2).

Tokioka, T. (1968). Preliminary observations made by Mr S. Harnahir on the growth of the giant colony of the madreporarian coral *Pavona frondifera* Lamarck, found in a core on the southwestern coast of Sikoku Island. *Publ. Seto Mar. Biol. Lab.,* XVI(I): 55-59.

Trench, R. K. and Blank, R. J. (1987) *Symbiodinium microadriaticum* Freudenthal, *S. goreauii* sp. nov., *S. kawagutii* sp. nov. and *S. pilosum* sp. nov.: gymnodinioid dinoflagellate symbionts of marine invertebrates. *J. Phycol.,* 23, 469-481.

Tribble, g.W. & Randall, R.H. (1986). A description of the high-latitude shallow water coral comrnunities of Miyake-jima, Japan. *Coral Reefs,* 4:151-159.

Uchida, H. & Fukuda, T. (1988a). *Coral guide. 1* (in Japanese). Southern Press Pty. Ltd.: 240 pp.

Uchida, H. & Fukuda, T. (1988b). *Coralguide. 2* (in Japanese). Southern Press Pty. Ltd.: 246 pp.

Uda, M. (1953). The Kuroshio and its branch currents in the seas adjacent to Itachijo Island in relation to fisheries (Report 1). *Rec. Oceanog. Works Jpn., new ser.,* 1(1):1-10.

Uda, M. (1953). On the storrny current ("Kyucho") and its prediction in the Sagami Bay (in Japanese). J. *Oceanogr. Soc. Jpn.,* 9:15-22.

UI, S. (1985). Past and current distribution of crown-of-thorns starfish and hermatypic corals in Sekisei lagoon, Yaeyama Is., Okinawa (in Japanese). *Mar. Parks* J., 64:13-17.

Umbgrove, J.H.F. (1939). Madrepora from the Bay of Batavia. *Zool. Meded., 22(12)*: 1-64.

Umbgrove, J.H.F. (1940). Madreporaria from the Togian reefs (Gulf of Tomini, North Celebes). Rijksmuseum natuurlijke Historie Leiden *Zool. Meded., 22:* 265-310.

Utinomi, H. (1956). Invertebrate fauna of the intertidal zone of the Tokara Islands. XVI. Stony corals and hydrocorals. *Publ. Seto Mar. Biol. Lab. 5(3):* 339-346.

Utinomi, H. (1965a). *Preliminary list of the corals of south-west Shikoku* (in Japanese). Zool. Taxonomy Assoc. (Publ.): 1-6.

Utinomi, H. (1965b). *Revised catalogue of scleractinian corals from the southwest coast of Sikoku in the collections of the Ehime University and the Ehime Prefectural Museum, Matsuyama.* Publ. Seto Mar. Biol. Lab., 13(3): 245-61.

Utinomi, H. (1966). Outline of shallow-water coral fauna on the coasts of Kii Peninsula (in Japanese). Surv. *Rep. on Jap. Assoc. Nature Prot.,* 27: 97-102.

Utinomi, H. (1970). *Corals of Ehime Prefecture* (in Japanese). Nat. Mus. Ehime Prefect. Yagi, S. (Publ.): 61 pp.Utinomi, H. (1971). *Scleractinian corals from Kamae Bay, Oita Prefecture, north-east of Kyushu, Japan.* Publ. Seto Mar. Biol. Lab., 19(4): 203-29.

Utinomi, H. (1972). On coral fauna of Kushimoto and nearby (in Japanese). *Mar. Parks J.,* 21: 6-7.

Vacelet, E. and B.A. Thomassin. (1991). Microbial utilization of coral mucus in long term in situ incubation over a coral reef. *Hydrobiologia 211:19-32.*

Van Alstyne, K.L. and V.J. Paul. (1992). Chemical and structural defenses in the sea fan *Gorgonia ventalina*: effects against generalist and specialist predators. *Coral Reefs 11:155-159.*

Van Alstyne, K.L., Wylie, C.R., Paul, V.J. and K. Meyer. (1992). Antipredator defenses in tropical Pacific soft corals (Coelenterata: Alcyonacea). I. Sclerites as defenses against generalist carnivorous fishes. *Biol. Bull. 182:231-240.*

Vaughan, T.W. (1907). Recent Madreporaria of the Hawaiian Islands and Laysan. *U.S. Natl. Mus. Bull.,* 59(9):1-427.

Vaughan, T.W. (1918). Some shoal-water corals from Murray Islands, Cocos Keeling Islands and Fanning Island. *Pap. Dep. Mar. Biol. Carnegie Insf. Wash.,* 9 (Publ. 213): 51-234.

Vaughan, T.W. (1932). A new coral generic name. J. *Washington Acad. Sci.,* 22(1819): 506.

Vaughan, T.W. & Wells, J.W. (1943). Revision of the suborders, families and genera of the Scleractinia. *Geol. Soc. Am. Spec. Pap., 44:1- 363*

Veron, J. E. N. & M. Pichon, (1976). Scleractinia of Eastern Australia. Part 1, Families Thamnasteriidae, Astrocoeniidae, Pocilloporidae. Austral. Inst. Mar. Sci. Monogr. Ser., 1,1-86.

Veron, J. E. N., M. Pichon & M. Wijsman-Best, (1977). Scleractinia of Eastern Australia. Part 2, Families Faviidae, Trachyphyllidae. Ibid. 3,1-233.

Veron, J.E.N. (1980). Hermatypic Scleractinia of Hong-Kong - an annotated list of species, in *Proc. First Intern. Mar. Biol. Workshop: The Marine Flora and Fauna of Hong Kong and Southern China,* Morton, B.S. & Tseng, C.K. (eds). Hong Kong Univ. Press 111- 125.

Veron, J.E.N. (1986a). New Scleractinia from Australian coral reefs. *Rec. West. Aust. Mus.,* 12(1): 147-183.

Veron, J.E.N. (1986b). *Corals of Australia and the Indo-Pacific.* Angus & Robertson: 644 pp.

Veron, J.E.N. (1988). Comparisons between the herrnatypic corals of the southern Ryukyu Islands of Japan and the Great Barrier Reef of Australia. *Galaxea, 7:* 211-231.

Veron, J.E.N. (199Oa). Re-examination of the reef corals of Cocos (Keeling) Atoll. *Rec. West. Austr. Mus.,* 14(4): 553-581.

Veron, J.E.N. (199Ob). New Scleractinia from Japan and other Indo-west Pacific countries. *Galaxea, 9:* 95-173.

Veron, J.E.N. 2000. Corals of the World. AIMS. Townsville, Australia.

Veron, J.E.N. (1993). *A Biogeographic Database of Hermatypic Corals. Species of the Central Indo-Pacific Genera of the World.* Australian Inst. of Mar. Sci. Monograph Ser. vol 10.

Veron, J.E.N. (1995). *Corals In Space and Time. The Biogeography & Evolution of The Scleractinia.* Cornell University Press. Ithaca, New York.

Veron, J.E.N. & Hodgson, G.A. (1989). Annotated checklist of the hermatypic corals of the Philippines. *Pac. Sci.,* 43(3): 234-287.

Veron, J.E.N. & Minchin, P.R (in press) Correlations between sea surface temperature and the distribution of hermatypic corals of Japan *Continental Shelf Res.*

Veron, J.E.N. & Pichon, M. (1980). Scleractinia of Eastern Australia. III. Families Agariciidae, Siderastreidae, Fungiidae, Oculinidae, Merulinidae, Mussidae, Pectiniidae, Caryophylliidae, Dendrophylliidae. *Aust. Inst. Mar. Sci. Monogr., vol.* 4: 422 pp.

Veron, J.E.N. & Pichon, M. (1982). Scleractinia of Eastern Australia. rv. Family Poritidae. *Aust. Inst. Mar. Sci. Monogr., vol.* 5:159 pp.

Veron, J.E.N. Pichon, M. & Wijsman-Best, M. (1977). Scleractinia of Eastern Australia. II. Families Faviidae, Trachyphylliidae. *Aust. Inst. Mar. Sci. Monogr., vol. 3: 233 pp.*

Veron, J.E.N. & Wallace, C. (1984). Scleractinia of eastern Australia. V. Family Acroporidae. *Aust. Inst. Mar. Sci. Monogr., vol.* 6: 485 pp.

Verrill, A.E. (1864). List of the polyps and corals sent by the Museum of Comparative Zoology to other institutions in exchange, with annotations. *Bull. Mus. Comp. Zool. (Harv. Univ.), 1:* 29-60.

Verrill, A.E. (1866). Synopsis of the polyps and corals of the North Pacific Exploring Expedition: 1853-1856, with descriptions of some additional species from the West Coast of North America. m. Madreporaria. *Comm. Essex Inst. Salem., 5: 6.*

Verrill, A.E. (1901). Variations and nomenclature of Bermudian, West Indian and Brazilian reef corals, with notes on various Indo-Pacific corals. *Trans. Connecticut Acad. Arts Sci., 11:163-68.*

Verrill, A.E. (1902). Notes on corals of the genus *Acropora* (Madrepora Lam.) with new descriptions and figures of types, and of several new species. *Trans. Connecticut Acad. Arts Sci., 11:* 207-66.

Verseveldt, J. 1977. Australian octcorallia (Coelenterata). *Aust. J. Mar. Freshwater Res.* 28:171-240.

Verseveldt, J. 1980. A revision of the genus *Sinularia* May (Octocorallia, Alcyonacea). *Zoologische Verhandelingen 179:1-128.*

Verseveldt, J. 1977. Octocorallia from various localities in the Pacific Ocean. *Zoologische Verhandelingen* 150: 1-42

Verseveldt, J. (1983) The Octocorallian Genera *Spongodes* Lesson, *Neospongodes* Kükenthal and *Stereonephthya* Kükenthal. *Beaufortia,* 33:1. 1-13.

Wallace, C. C., (1978). The coral genus *Acropora* in the central and southern Great Barrier Reef province. Mem. Qd. Mus., 18, 273-319, pls. 43-103.

Weinberg, S. 1986. Mediterranean Octocorallia: description of *Clavularia carpediem* n. sp. and synonymy of *Clavularia crassa* and *C. ochracea* on etho-ecological grounds. *Bijdragen tot de Dierkunde* 56(2): 232-246.

Weis, V. M. (1989) Induction of carbonic anhydrase activity in symbiotic cnidarians. In R. B. Williams (ed.), *5th International Conference on Coelenterate Biology.* Programme and Abstracts, University of Southampton, Southampton, UK, p. 97.

Weis, V. M., Smith, G. J. and Muscatine, L. (1989) A CO_2 supply mechanism in zooxanthellate cnidarians: role of carbonic anhydrase. *Mar. Biol.,* 100, 195-202.

Wells, J.W. (1934). Some fossil corals from the West Indies. Proc. U.S. Natl. Mus., 83: 7]-110.

Wells, J. W., (1935). The genotype of Physophyllia and a living species of Astrocoenia. Ann. Mag. Nat. Hist. (ser. 10),15, 339-344.

Wells, J.W. (1937). Coral studies. Part 2: Five new genera of the Madreporaria. Bull Am. Paleontol., 23, 238-250.

Wells, J.W. (1954). Recent corals of the Marshall Islands. *Prof. Pap. U.S. Geol. Surv., 260-I:* 385-486.

Wells, J.W. (1955). Recent and subfossil corals of Moreton Bay, Queensland. *Univ. Qd. Pap. Dept. Geol. n.s.,* 4:1-18.

Wells, J. W. (1956) Scleractinia. In R. C. Moore (ed.), *Treatise on Invertebrate Paleontology. Part F, Coelenterata,* University of Kansas, Lawrence, pp. F328-F444.

Wells, J.W. (1959). Notes on Indo-Pacific Scleractinian Corals. Parts I & 2. Pac. Sci., 19, 286-90.

Wells, J.W. (1961). Notes on Indo-Pacific scleractinian corals. III. A new reef coral from New Caledonia. *Pac. Sci.,* 15(2):189-91.

Wells, J.W. (1964). The Recent Solitary Mussid Scleractinian Corals. *Zool. Meded.,* 39, 375-384.

Wells, J.W. (1966a). Notes on Indo-Pacific scleractinian corals. IV. A second species of *Stylocoeniella. Pac. Sci., 20(2):* 203-205.

Wells, J.W. (1966b). Evolutionary development in the scleractinian family Fungiidae. *Symp. Zool. Soc. Lon, 16:* 223-46.

Wells, J.W. (1968). Notes on Indo-Pacific scleractinian corals. V. A new speaes of *Alveopora* from New Caledonia. VI. Further notes on *Bantamia merletti* Wells. Pac. Sci., 22(2):274-6.

Wells, J.W. (1971a). Notes on Indo-Pacific Scleractinian corals. VII *Catalaphyllia,* a new genus of reef corals. *Pac. Sci.,* 25(3): 368- 71.

Wells, J.W. (1972). Notes on Indo-Pacific Scleractinian Corals. Pan 8. Scleractinian corals from Easter Island. Ibid., 26,183-190.

West, J. M., Harvell, C. D., and A.-M. Walls (1993) Morphological plasticity in a gorgonian coral (*Briareum asbestinum*) over a depth cline. *Mar. Ecol. Prog. Ser.* 94, 61-69.

West, J. M., Harvell C. D. and Walls A. M., (1993). Morphological plasticity in a gorgonian (*Briareum asbestinum*) over a depth cline. *Mar. Ecol. Prog. Ser.* 94: 61-69.

Wijsman-Best, M. (1972). Systematics and ecology of New Caledonian Faviinae (Coelenterata, Scleractinia). *Bijdr. Dierkd.,* 42(1):1- 76.

Wijsman-Best, M. (1973). A new species of the Pacific coral genus *Blastomussa* from New Caledonia. *Pac. Sci.,* 27(2):15455.

Wijsman-Best, M. (1976). Biological results of the Snellius Expedition. XXVII. Faviidae collected by the Snellius Expedition. II. The genera *Favites, Goniastrea, Platygyra, Ouphyllia, Leptoria, Hydnophora* and *Caulastrea. Zool. Med.,* 50(4): 45-63.

Wilkens, P. 1990. *Invertebrates: Stone and False Corals, Colonial Anemones.* Engelbert Pfriem Verlag, Wuppertal, germany, 134 pp.

Wilkerson, F. P. and Trench, R. K. (1985) Nitrate assimilation by zooxanthellae maintained in laboratory culture. *Mar. Chem.,* 16, 385-393.

Williams, G. C. (1975) *Sex and Evolution,* Princeton University Press, Princeton, New Jersey, 200 pp.

Williams, G.C. (1992). The Alcyonacea of southern Africa. Stoloniferous octocorals and soft corals (Coelenterata, Anthozoa). *Annals of the South African Museum* 100(3): 249-358.

Williams, Gary C. (1993) *Coral Reef Octocorals. An Illustrated Guide to the Soft Corals, Sea Fans and Sea Pens inhabiting the Coral Reefs of Northern Natal.* Durban Natural Science Museum, Durban, South Africa, 64 Pp.

Wood, E. (1983) *Corals of the World.* TFH Publications, Neptune City, N.J. 256 pp.

Wylie, C.R. and V.J. Paul. (1989). Chemical defenses on three species of *Sinularia* (Coelenterata: Alcyonacea): effects against generalist predators and the butterflyfish *Chaetodon unimaculatus* Bloch. *J. Exp. Mar. Biol. Ecol. 129:141-160.*

Yabe, H. & Eguchi, M. (1935b). Revision of the reef coral genera *Echinopora, Oxyphyuia, Mycedium, Oxypora* and *Physophyllia. Proc. Imp. Aald. Jpn., 11(10):* 429-31.

Yabe, H. & Sugiyama, T. (1931). A study of recent and semi-fossil corals of Japan. *Sci. Rep. Tohoku Imperial Univ. (Geol.), ser.* 2,14:119-133.

Yabe, h. & Sugiyama, T. (1932a). Reef corals found in Japanese seas. Sci. *Rep. Tohoku Imp. Univ., Ser.* 2, *(Geol.),* 15(2):143-168.

Yabe, H. & Sugiyama, T. (1932b). A living species of *Stylocoenia* recently found in Japan. *Jpn. J. Geol. Geogr., IX* (3-4).

Yabe, H. & Sugiyama, T. (1932c). Notes on three new corals from Japan. *Jpn. J. Geol. Geogr. IX* (1-2).

Yabe, H. & Sugiyama, T. (1933a). Geographical distribution of reef corals in Japan, Past and Present (in Japanese). *Proc. Jpn. Assoc. Advan. Sci.,* 8(3): 335-341.

Yabe, H. & Sugiyama, T. (1935a). Revised lists of the reef corals from the Japanese seas and of the fossil reef corals of the raised reefs and the Ryukyu Limestone of Japan. J. *Geol. Soc. Jpn.,* 42(502): 279-403.

Yabe, H. & Sugiyama, T. (1935b). *Stylocoeniella,* a new coral genus allied to *Stylocoenia* and *Astrocoenia*. *Jpn. J. Geol. Geogr.,* 12(3- 4):103-105.

Yabe, H. & Sugiyama, T. (1935c). Geological and geographical distribution of Reef Corals in Japan. J. *Paleontol,* 9(3):183-217.

Yabe, H. & Sugiyama, T. (1935d). A new living coral, *Pseudosiderastrea tayamai,* from Dobo in Wamar, Aru Island. *Proc. Jpn. Acad., 11(9):* 373-378.

Yabe, H. & Sugiyama, T. (1936). Some deep-water corals from the Palau Islands. *Proc. Imp. Academic Tokyo, 12.*

Yabe, H. & Sugiyama, T. (1937). Two new species of reef-building corals from Yoron-zima and Amami-O-sima. *Proc. Imp. Acad. Tokyo,* 13(10): 425-429.

Yabe, H. & Sugiyama, T. (1941). Recent reef building corals from Japan and the south sea islands under the Japanese mandate. II. Sci. *Rep. Tohoku Univ. Geol., ser. 2, spec. vol.* 2: 67-91.

Yabe, H. & Sugiyama, T. & Eguchi, M. (1936). Recent reef-building corals from Japan and the south sea islands under the Japanese mandate. r Sci. *Rep. Tohoku Uniu Geol., ser. 2, spec. vol.* 1:1-66.

Yagi, S. (ed.) (1970). *Illustrated catalogue of scleractinian corals etc. stored in the Ehime Prefectural Museum.* (Scleractinia identified by Utinomi, H.). Prefectural Museum, Matsuyama. (Publ.): 61 pp.

Yamaguchi, M. (1986). *Acanthaster planci* infestations or reefs and coral assemblages in Japan: a retrospective analysis of control efforts. *Coral Reefs,* 5: 23 30.

Yamazato, K. (1971). Benthic organisms of the Ryukyu Islands, in *Problems of marine geology of the area around Kyushu* by Geological Society of Japan and 4 other societies (in Japanese) 111-119.

Yamazato, K. (1978). Tentative list of corals found at a reef near the Sesoko Marine Science Laboratory, in *Studies on fauna, flora and main organisms for experiments around marine and inland water biological stations in Japan.*

Yamazato, K., Sato, M. and H. Yamashiro. (1981). Reproductive biology of an alcyonacean coral, *Lobophytum crassum* Marenzeller. *Proc. 4th Int. Coral Reef Symp., Manila, vol2.*

Yamazato, K. (1985). In Kokushi, H. (ed.) *Coastal oceanography of Japanese Islands.* Tokai Univ. Press: 1078-1090.

Yamazato, K., Kamura, S. & Hidaka, M. (1980). The sheltered coral reef cornmunities of Kume Island (in Japanese). *Rep. Sesoko Sci. Cent.,* 49:133-144.

Yamazato, K., Kamura, S., Nakasone, Y., Aramoto, Y& Nishihira, M. (1976). Ecological distribution of the reef associated organisms in the Bise Shinzato coast of Okinawa. *Ecol. Stud. Nat. Cons. Ryukyu Is.,* 2:1-30.

Yamazato, K, Nishihira, M., Nlshijima, S., Kamura, S., Nakasone, S., Shokita, S. & Yoshino, T. (1978). Studies on the biota and on the ecology of some important experimental organisms around Sesoko Island, Okinawa, in *Studies on the biota and on the ecology of some important experimental organisms around the marine and freshwater laboratories of the Japanese nationaI universities* (in Japanese). Assoc. Directors Mar. Freshwater Lab. Jpn. Natioral. Univ. (eds): 223 233.

Yamazato, K., Nishihira, M., Nakasone, Y., Kamura, S. & Aramoto, Y. (1974). Biogeomorphical notes on the Sesoko Island reefs, Okinawa (in Japanese with English summary). *Ecol. Stud. Nat. Cons. Ryukyu Is., l:* 201-212.

Yamazato, K., Shimabukro, S. & Sakai, K. (1982). Corals of Uotsuri- shima (in Japanese). *Publ. Tropical Mar. Sci. Cent.,* Ryukyu Islands: 36-55.

Yasumoto, M. (1986). Coral community of Shirako coral reef areas correlating ecological problems with geographic advantage (in Japanese). *Sci. Rep. Shiraho Coral Reef,* Ishijaki Island World Wildlife Fund.

Yajima, T., Osamu, S., Okamoto, T., Shirai, Y., Shinya, T. & Matada, M. (1986). Ecological distribution of the reef coral, *Oulastrea crispata* (Lamarck) at the shore region in the vicinity of Tsukumo Bay (in Japanese with English abstract). *Bull. Jpn. Sea Res., 18:* 21-26.

Yoon, j. & Yasuda, I. (1987). Dynamics of the Kuroshio large meander: two-layer model. J. *Phys. Oceanogr.,* 17(1): 66-81.

Yoshioka, P.M. and B. Buchanan-Yoshioka. (1991). A comparison of the survivorship and growth of shallow-water gorgonian species of Puerto Rico (West Indies). *Mar. Ecol. Progr. Ser. 69:253-260.*

Zou, R. (1980). Studies on the corals of the Xisha Islands. IV. Two new hermatypic scleractinian corals (in Chinese). *Nanhai Studia Marina Sinica,* 1:117-118.

Index

You should be able to find this book in your local library, book store, dive shop, aquarium shop, pet store, or public aquarium. If you cannot find it locally, please contact:

Published by
Ricordea Publishing
Miami, Florida, USA
Tel 305.662.1236 Fax 305.662.1802

Distributed by
Two Little Fishies, Inc.
4016 El Prado Blvd.,
Coconut Grove, Florida, 33133 USA
Tel 305.661.7742 Fax 305.661.0611
eMail: twolilfishes @ Compuserve.com
Website: www.twolilfishies.com